Haunted Miniatures

Terrifyingly Tiny Projects for
the Spooky Crafter

Ashley Voortman
Author of *Creepy Crafts*

PAGE STREET
PUBLISHING CO.

PAGE STREET
PUBLISHING CO.

First published in 2026 by
Page Street Publishing Co.
27 Congress Street, Suite 1511
Salem, MA 01970
www.pagestreetpublishing.com

Distributed by Macmillan, sales in Canada by The Canadian Manda Group.

30 29 28 27 26 1 2 3 4 5

ISBN-13: 979-8-89003-456-4

Library of Congress Control Number: 2025949556

Edited by Marissa Giambelluca
Cover and book design by Molly Kate Young for Page Street Publishing Co.
Photography by Ashley Voortman

Printed and bound in China

Dedicated to
anyone who has never skipped
to the end of one of my videos
especially my husband and
daughter . . .*

**PS: I know you skipped*

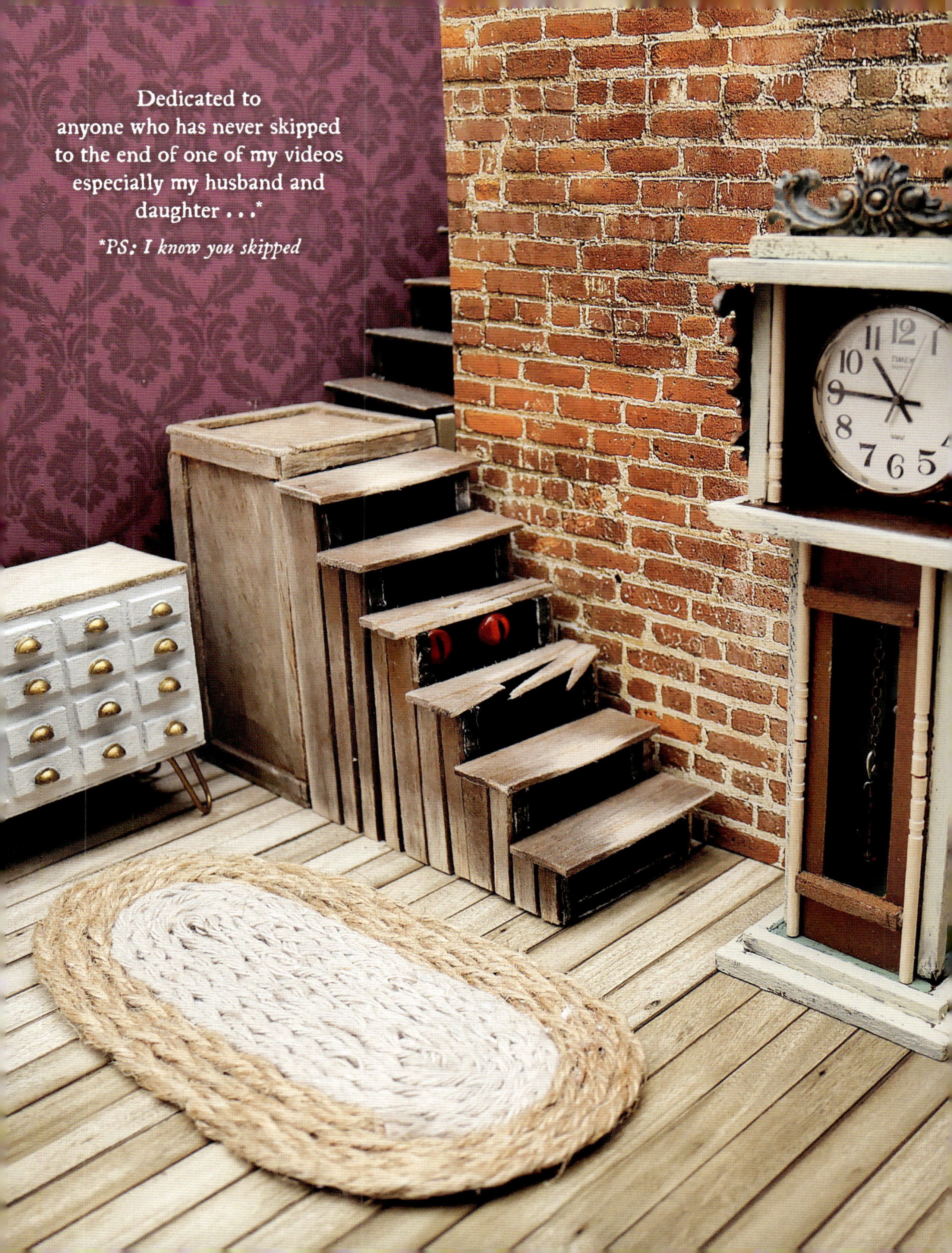

Contents

Introduction

Welcome, fellow miniature lovers! With this book as your guide, we'll be diving into the magical and haunted world of miniature making! Your best weapon? The glue gun!

I wrote this book after a disappointing trip to the library where I couldn't find a single book on the shelf about miniatures. Maybe someone checked them all out, but who would be *that* obsessed with miniatures . . . Oh wait . . . me! Anyways, I decided to just write my own. You know, the book I wish I could have checked out!

So here's what I hope you get from this book: First, I want to give you the confidence to wield that glue gun and exacto knife to craft any of the projects in this book. Then I want you to take that confidence and use it to create your very own custom haunted miniatures (the way you want them).

Second, I want to encourage you to use recycled materials whenever you can! You'd be surprised how spooky your everyday junk can be! *WARNING: This book could cause hoarding.*

And last but not least, I want to remind you that making miniatures should be fun, messy, and a *little* weird. Never stressful! It's not about being "perfect" (haunted stuff never is). It's about being creative.

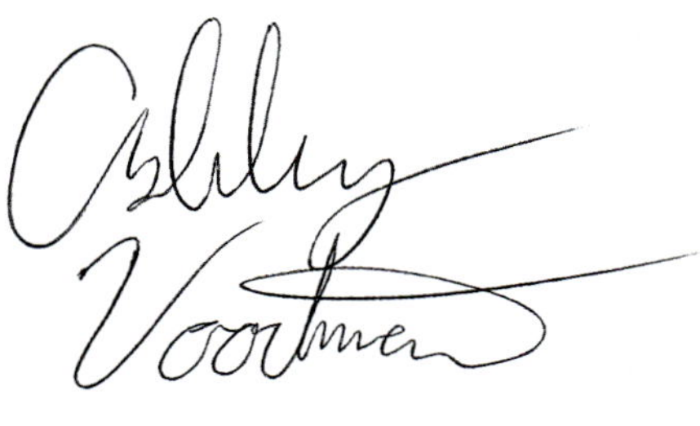

Using Recycled Materials

Don't buy new when used will do! Being resourceful is part of the fun! Here are some examples.

Chipboard

Thick, sturdy paper that looks like cardboard only without the squiggly stuff in the middle. You can find it lots of places, like cereal boxes, flat mailers, product packaging, sheets used to separate items like prints . . . lots of places!

Clear Plastics

Thin clear plastic can come from take-out containers, produce boxes, or even those frustrating contraptions they put some products in that you can't open without cutting yourself. The smoother and flatter, the better.

Shrink plastic works great too. Did you know you can use #6 plastics as shrink plastic? Yup!

"Wooden" Circles

Any small circular object works. Buttons, coins, jar lids . . . They usually don't need to be wood. Wood is just what I use.

Square Wooden Dowels or Sticks

Balsa wood sticks are convenient, but chopsticks often work too. They come in both square and round shapes. In a pinch, you can cut strips of balsa wood and glue them together. It can be messy, but it works.

Fabrics

Reuse old clothes, produce bags, or fancy packaging you'd normally toss out.

Wire

Floral wire is cheap and abundant. Paper clips are also great short wires. The plastic coatings can be stripped off or melted if you're careful.

Pro Tips

1. Chipboard, balsa wood, and foam core can often be swapped. Just keep in mind: Chipboard bends easily. Balsa wood is stronger. Foam core is thick and light.
2. You can make things look like old metal without using old metal. I use Sculpt Nouveau Metal Coatings and Sculpt Nouveau Patina Stains a lot. You coat with the metal coating first, then you spray or splotch the patina on, and it "rusts" the paint to make it look old. You can also dry brush orange over this to give it more of a rust factor.

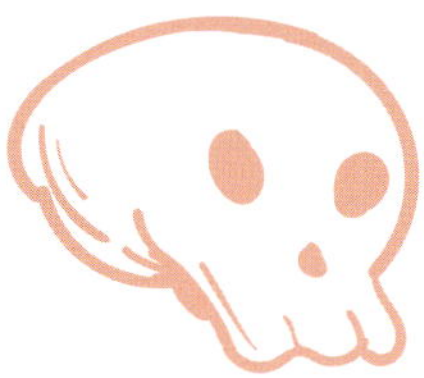

Measuring

"Just Eyeball It." I can feel my publisher cringe while I'm writing this, and I get it! Usually, things need to be a certain length and width, but for a lot of these projects, you just need to use your own judgment. Your junk may be a different size than my junk and that's okay. We don't junk shame here! But that does mean that some of your measurements might differ from mine.

Get a ½ x ½–inch (1.3 x 1.3–cm) grid cutting mat! It makes cutting and measuring pieces easy peasy and most of my projects will follow this grid.

Glue

Choosing the right glue is often more about preference than strict rules. I may suggest a glue but feel free to experiment. You might be using different materials (aka trash) than I used, so the best glue for the job will be different. As long as you have superglue, craft glue, and hot glue, you're good!

Superglue

Pros: Works on most nonporous items. Sets quickly. Great for smooth surfaces. Decently strong.

Cons: Doesn't work on paper or fabric. Melts plastic and foam. Gets hot when applied to foam. Will fog clear plastic. Feels terrible on your fingertips!

Tip: *Less is more. A tiny drop goes a long way!*

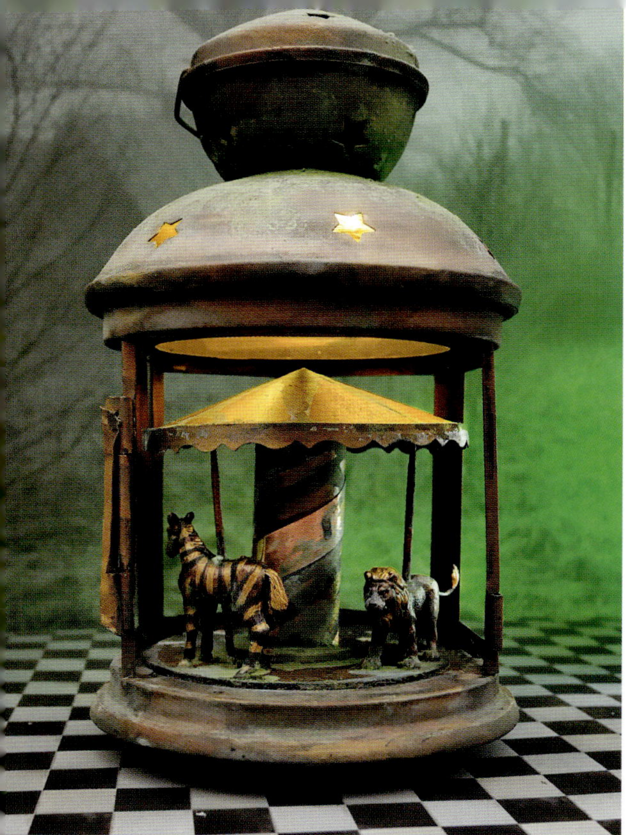

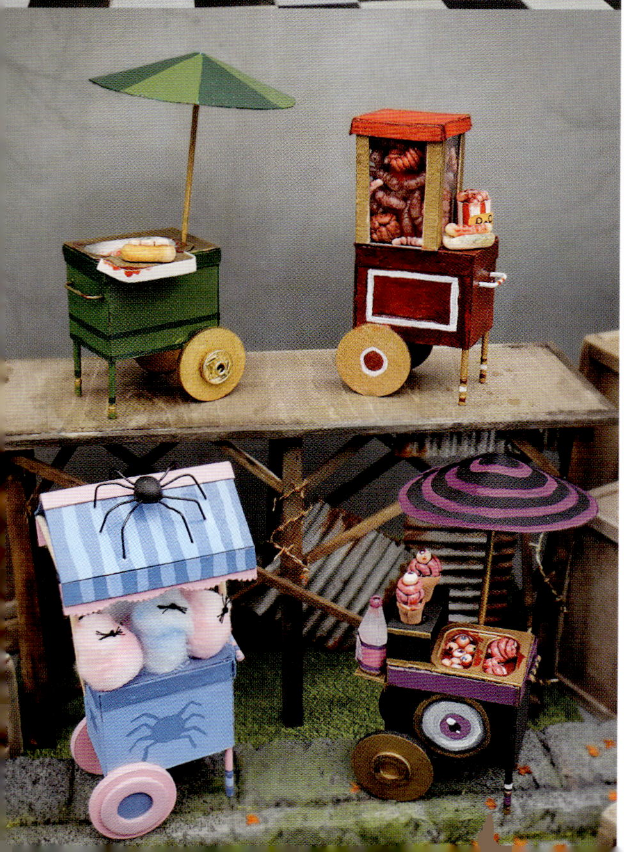

Craft Glue

Pros: Great for wood, paper, and foliage. Can be used as a clear coat. Longer dry time = longer work time. Feels great peeling off your fingertips!

Cons: Long dry time = waiting for glue to dry. Isn't super strong.

Tip: *Precision tip bottles are well worth the extra cost.*

Hot Glue

Pros: Quick. Ugly in a good way. Works great on most fabrics. You can sculpt with it. Usually peels off when you make a mistake.

Cons: Not very strong. Ugly in a bad way. Bulky. Will melt things. OUCHY on fingers!

Tip: *Utilize the temperature setting if you have it!*

Hotter temps = more work time.

Colder temps = quicker hold (better for heat-sensitive items).

Tips for Making Haunted Hidey Holes

In which we plan for all of your delightfully creepy creations . . .

Before you make your miniature (or many miniatures, depending on how ambitious you are), have you thought at all about what you'll do with it? Sure, you could put it on a shelf and forget about it. I do plenty of that! But wouldn't it be awesomerest if you could put your miniatures inside a . . . drumroll please . . . Haunted Hidey Hole*?!

**For sake of space and sanity, I will now be referring to my Haunted Hidey Hole as HHH.*

Materials for Your Hole

I'm not going to explicitly tell you how to build an HHH. Instead, I'm just going to give you a few tips for making your own HHHs. The easiest HHH building material is foam core. It glues together well with superglue and can be painted pretty easily!

Foam core is also great for adding texture like bricks. Cut your foam core into small brick-sized rectangles and peel the paper off one side. Pick at the edges with your nails. Glue in a brick pattern and paint. BAM! Super easy bricks!

Balsa wood is probably the best material for the shell of your HHH. Balsa wood comes in different densities. I use the low-density for most things because it's easy to cut, and a medium-to-high density for structure and strength.

Honestly, there are lots of things you can use to build HHHs from scratch; you may just need to look outside the box. (Ooo, a box is also a good material!)

Building a Good Hole

Okay, we have the materials, now how do we design it? I like to draw inspiration from doll-houses or look up stages from plays/theaters. You can see how these are laid out and pull ideas from there. Sketching out how you want your HHH to look and planning things out ahead of time is the difference between "Oh, cool HHH," and "WOAH, how'd you make that amazing HHH? You a witch or something?"

Finding a Hole in the Wild

Don't want to make a hole for your hauntings to hide in? I don't blame you . . . Actually, it can be more satisfying to hunt down the perfect hole in the wild! Just think of *"the wild"* as a flea market or the recycling bin in the break room. You have to pounce on it before it runs away! (Or before the recycling truck comes.)

Some HHH options

- **Jewelry boxes:** Take the drawers out.
- **Dollhouse:** It's basically ready to be moved into.
- **Birdcage or lantern:** Comes with a convenient hanging handle.
- **Old world globes:** Globes are hollow. Cut a hole and use the space inside.
- **Bell alarm clocks:** It's like a circle window with legs! Gut it and use its shell.
- **Empty containers:** Coffee tin, chip can, milk jug, kitty litter pail. Just cut a hole in the side.
- **Picture frames:** Take the back off and use foam core to make a deeper box behind it.
- **Halloween pumpkins:** Most of these are hollow, which makes for a great HHH. Just buy them after Halloween for a discount.

Use your imagination. Anything with a spot that stuff can sit in is a potential HHH. I even made a HHH in a gumball machine once.

Lighting up Your Hole

There are a few options for lighting your HHH.

LED DIY Lights

- Pre-wired LED lights (any color)
- A battery holder (I like the CR2032 ones with an on/off switch)
- Batteries (CR2032 if you got the one above)
- Wire stripper
- Electrical tape

Use your wire stripper to remove about ½ inch (1.3 cm) of the plastic coating from each end of the LEDs and battery holder, exposing the wires inside.

LEDs are directional, so they only work if the positive wires are connected to the positive side of the battery holder and negative to negative. Test it out. If your light doesn't light up, don't panic! Just flip the connections. Also, check that your lights are switched on. I can't tell you how many times I've done that!

Another thing to remember is you can't daisy chain them together. (I know! It would be so much easier if you could!) The battery just isn't strong enough and your lights won't work well. Instead, twist all the positive LED wires together and twist them to the battery positive wire, then tape and do the same with the negatives. Always test before you tape! I'm dyslexic, so I always have a flipped wire somewhere.

Once your wires are twisted firmly together, taped, and tested, hot glue them into your project. You can either drill holes or, if you're careful, use a wood burner to make a hole to stick your light in.

But WAIT, if this sounds like too much work, I totally get it! Here are some other options:

Fairy Lights

Much easier, though a less precise way to light up your HHH. Some of them even come with remotes so you can turn them on and off. Most fairy lights can be cut to whatever size you want. If you only want three lights, just cut the rest off. They're cheap and you can buy them in bulk.

Tea Candles

Another easy-to-install option, they're great for making creepy, ambient lighting. Sure, they're a pain in the tokus to turn on and off, but you can't argue because they do look nice.

LED Strip Lighting Kits

These can get kind of spendy, but if you're looking for an even, consistent light, these are better. I think they're usually used behind TVs or under kitchen cabinets. They come in a wide range of colors and options. Just note that you're constrained to a strip, so you won't be able to snake them into weird corners.

Coloring Your Lights

If all you have are white lights, but you want one to be red (for say, lighting up a demonic ticket booth), use colored cellophane. You can place red (or whatever color) cellophane in front of the light to change the color. You can also use a marker to change the color, but this is less precise.

Light-Up Signs and Stained-Glass Windows

The best sign/window material I've found is frosted shrink plastic. They are clear enough before you shrink them that you can easily trace something and opaque enough when you do shrink them that you won't see your naked light bulb behind it.

Shrink plastic shrinks about a third of its size, so you can add tons of detail in black pen, then after it dries, color it in with a translucent marker. Once you shrink it, it looks outstanding! Add a box around it with balsa wood or chipboard and place a light inside and BAM! Amazing little lit-up sign or stained-glass window!

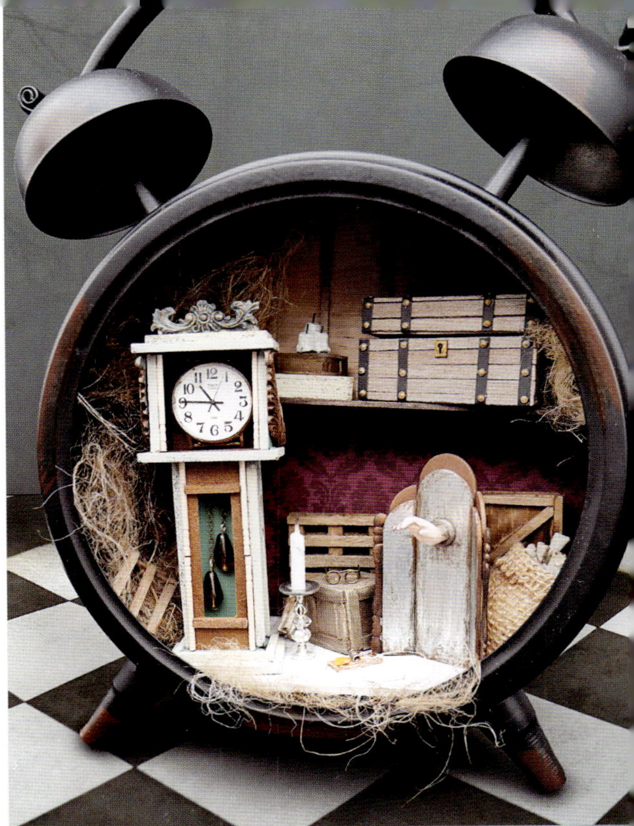

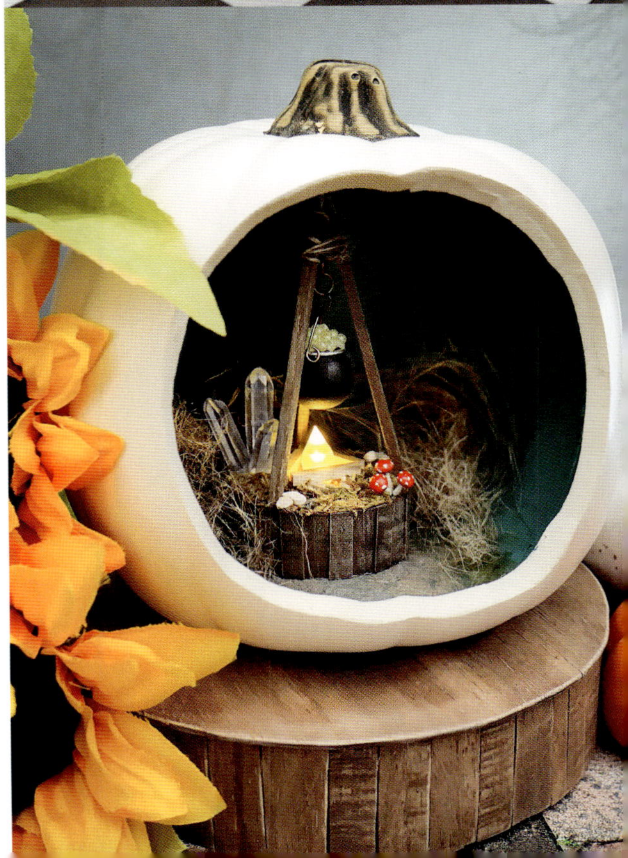

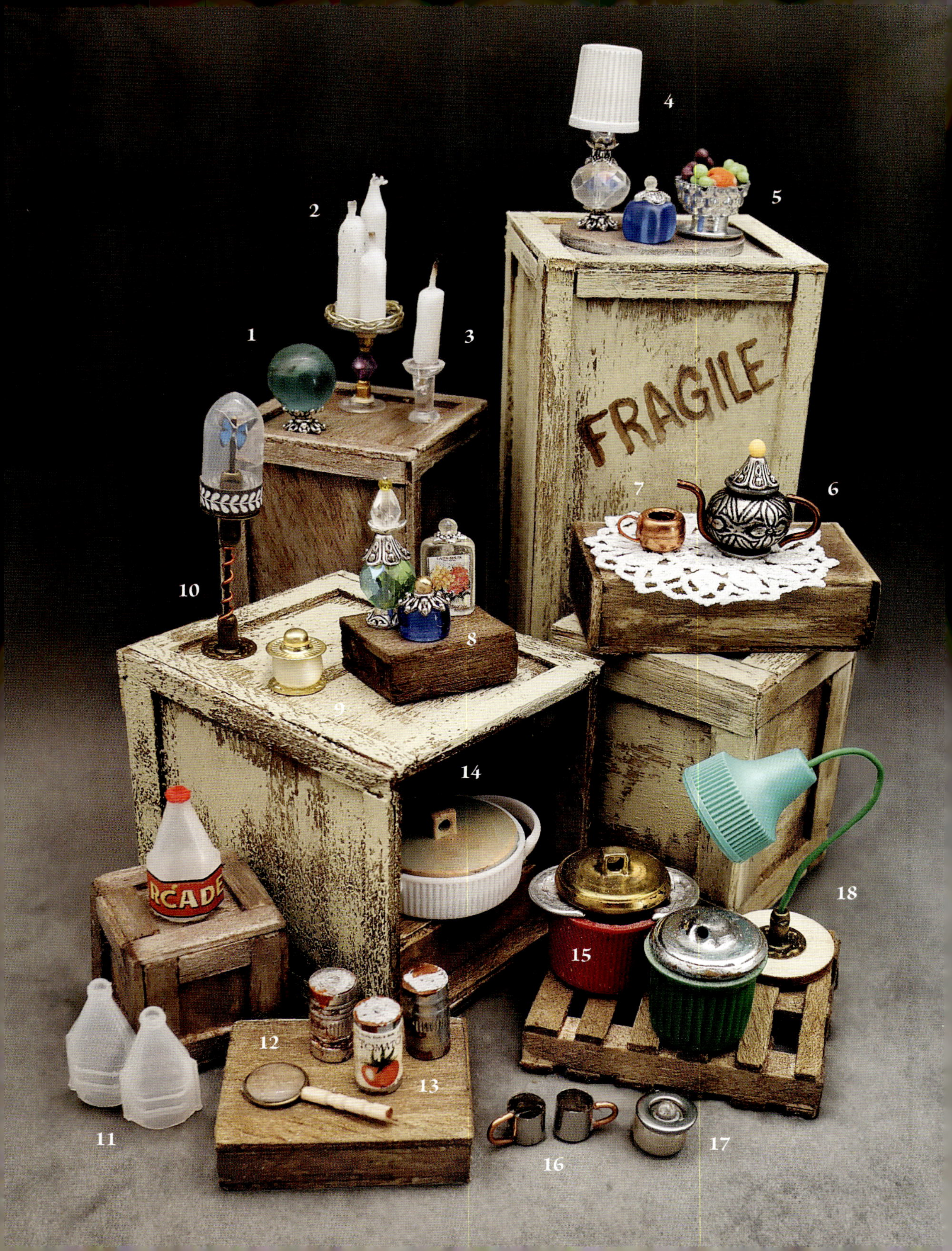

1
2
3
4
5
FRAGILE
6
7
8
9
10
RCADE
11
12
13
14
15
16
17
18

Miniature Items

1. Marble
   Bead Caps

2. Birthday Candles
   Earring Backs
   Bead
   Washer
   Wire

3. Birthday Candle
   Thumbtack

4. Plastic Cap
   Glass Bead
   Bead Caps

5. Polymer Clay
   Ornament Top
   Eyelet Washer

6. Silica Gel Ball
   Bead Cap
   Washer
   Metal Bead
   Wire

7. Pony Bead
   Wire

8. Beads
   Bead Caps
   Wire

9. Snap Fastener Studs
   Pony Bead

10. Clear Plastic Vial
    Thin Washi Tape
    Printed Bug
    Wire
    Snap Fastener Posts

11. Single-Dose Eye Drops

12. Jump Ring
    UV Resin
    Toothpick End

13. Pencil Tops

14. Shank Button
    Plastic Cap
    Creamer Pull Tab

15. Shank Button
    Pop Tabs
    Plastic Cap

16. Glass Fuse Caps
    Wire

17. Washers
    Small Bead
    Pony Bead

18. Eye Drops Cap
    Paper Clip
    Snap Fastener Post
    Wooden Disk

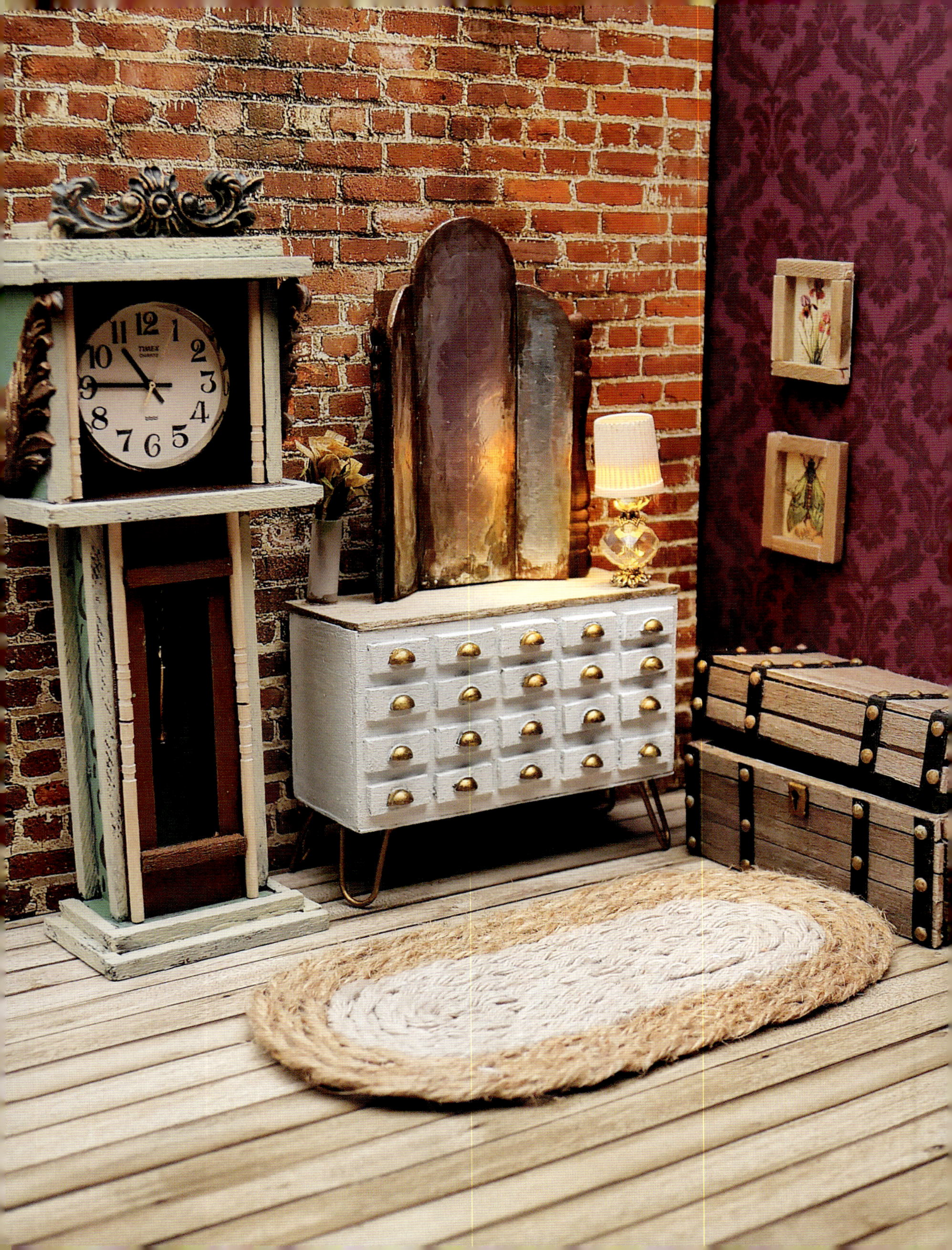
TIMEX

Haunted House

The house on Lonely Lane had been abandoned forever and everyone was scared of it. Legend says you should:

Never open any chests in the house. Never look into any mirror. Never get caught in the house at midnight.

But, let's be honest, haunted houses are like crack to teenagers!

Alice, *a teenager*, loved haunted things! She wanted to see this house for herself. Alice knew the legend and arrived with plenty of time before midnight. *Or so she thought* . . .

Going up the spooky stairs, she found a room with a single chest inside. Curiosity getting the best of her, she looked. She knew she shouldn't have, but it was calling to her! Inside was a doll she'd thrown out years ago. One that scared the bejesus out of her! Shocked, she backed up and bumped into a mirror she swore wasn't there when she entered.

Startled by her own reflection, she blinked and then . . . a dark figure in the mirror . . . was it moving toward her? Thinking it must be her eyes, she spun around. (Like they do in every horror movie instead of running.) Nothing. Turning back to the mirror the figure now had its hand on her shoulder!

Finally doing what she should have done in the first place, she ran! Tumbling down the stairs and hitting the floor hard, she looked back up to see eyes glowing red under the stairs. Frozen in fear the clock began to chime. Both hands pointed straight to 12 o'clock! MIDNIGHT?! It can't be! She looked at her watch, 11. Her heart sunk, daylight savings!

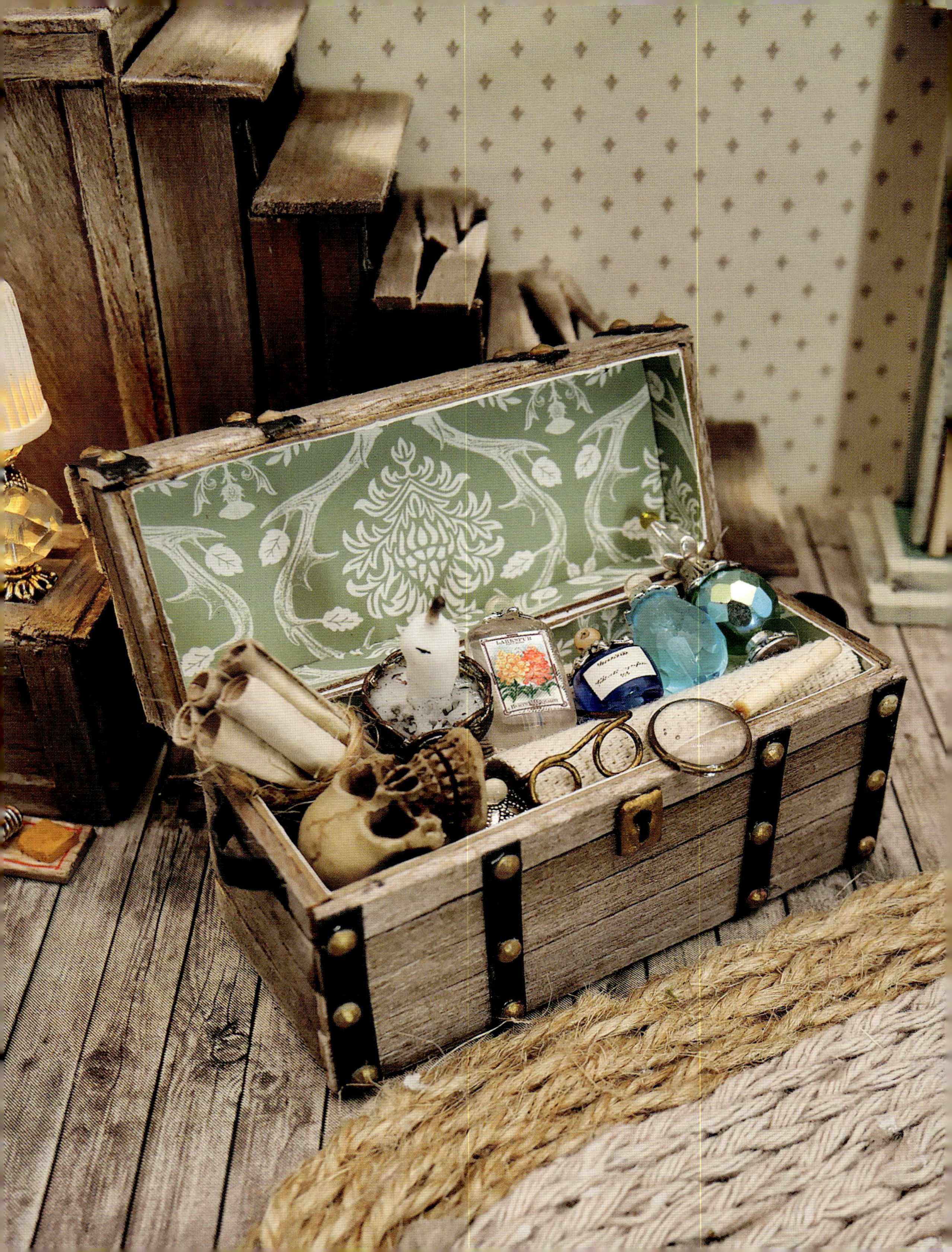
LARKSPUR

Chest of Secrets

Everything you have ever lost ends up in the chest of secrets. Even things you wish would stay lost! Do you dare open it?

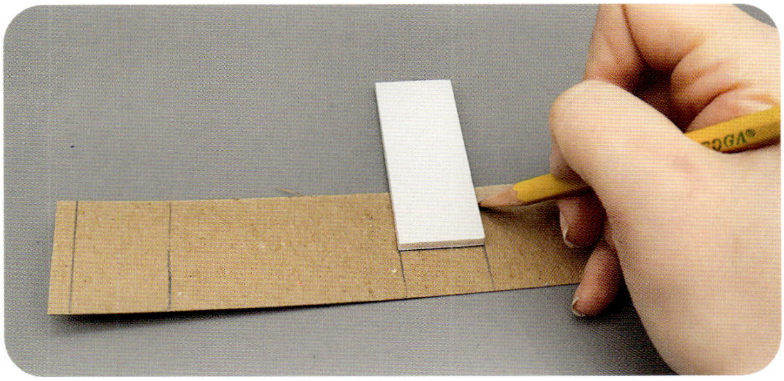

Cut the following:

- **Qty: 2**—1 x 2½ inches (2.5 x 6.4 cm) (foam core)
- **Qty: 1**—1½ x 7¼ inches (3.8 x 18.4 cm) (chipboard)

Using the pieces you just cut as templates, trace them onto your decorative paper and cut with an exacto knife (or scissors). Set aside.

Grasp a foam core rectangle and place it at the corner of the chipboard strip, then mark a line (template on page 213 for reference). Rotate 90° and reposition next to your mark and mark again. Continue until you have four lines along the length of your chipboard strip, giving you a cute little ¼-inch (6-mm) tab at the end. Don't even think about cutting it off!

Using a glue stick, slap your paper onto the back side of the chipboard. Let this dry or cure or whatever. Score (careful not to cut through) the lines on the chipboard with an exacto knife and ruler.

Trim ½ inch (1.3 cm) off the top of your chipboard, giving you one ½-inch (1.3-cm)-wide and 1-inch (2.5-cm)-wide strip.

Fold your scores to make two boxes. Remember that tab we kept? Glue that tab on the inside of the other end on both strips. This is the base of your chest.

Tools

- exacto knife, ruler, & cutting mat
- pencil
- glue stick
- glue
- paint
- toothpick

Materials

- foam core
- chipboard
- decorative paper
- plain paper
- balsa wood
- black paper
- plastic diamond drills (or puff paint)
- polymer clay

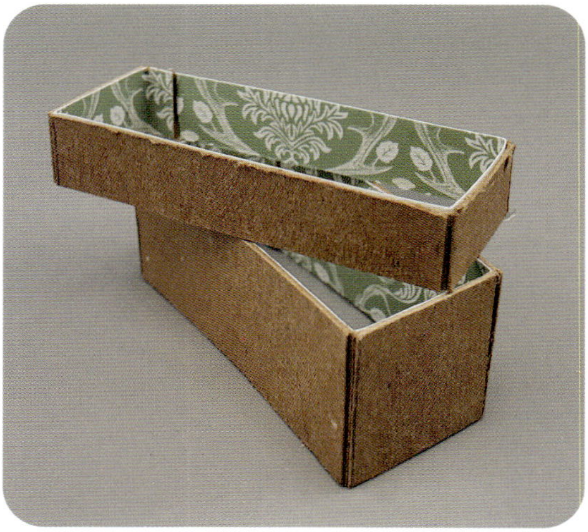

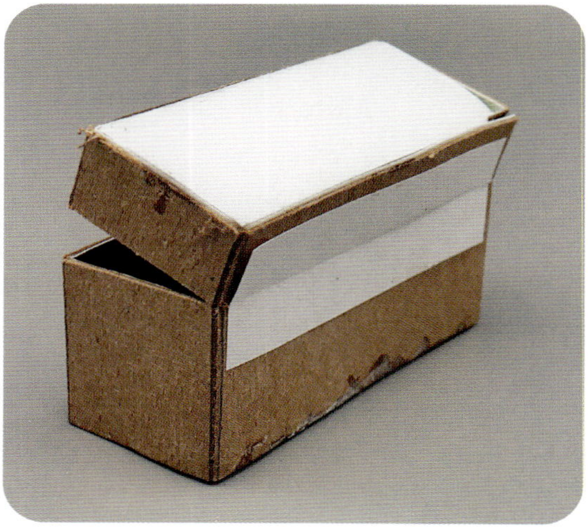

Glue the corresponding decorative paper to each foam core rectangle.

These should fit snugly into the chipboard boxes you just made. Go ahead, slide them in now if you don't believe me. *Told you!* Glue them in place. One at the bottom of the larger box. One at the top of the smaller box.

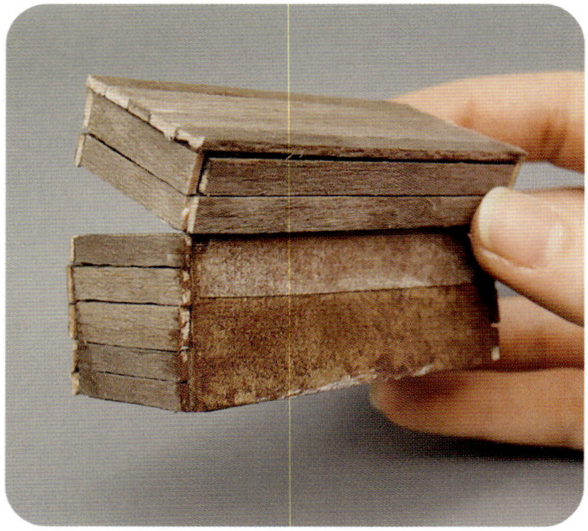

Let's make the chest more "chest shaped". Stack your boxes on top of each other and glue a strip of plain paper to the back like a hinge. Paint the outside of your classic chest brown.

Cut and stain brown the following balsa wood:

- **Qty: 12**—1 x ¼ inch (2.5 cm x 6 mm) ***side paneling***
- **Qty: 14**—2⅖ x ¼ inch (6 cm x 6 mm) ***front paneling***

Don't stress on the ¼-inch (6-mm) side. Slightly varied widths give it a rustic look.

Slap that wood on your chest! Glue strips along the sides first then the front and top. Lastly, glue two strips to the back of the lid. Leave the rest blank. *Nobody looks at the back of chests anyway, and it won't open right if you do.*

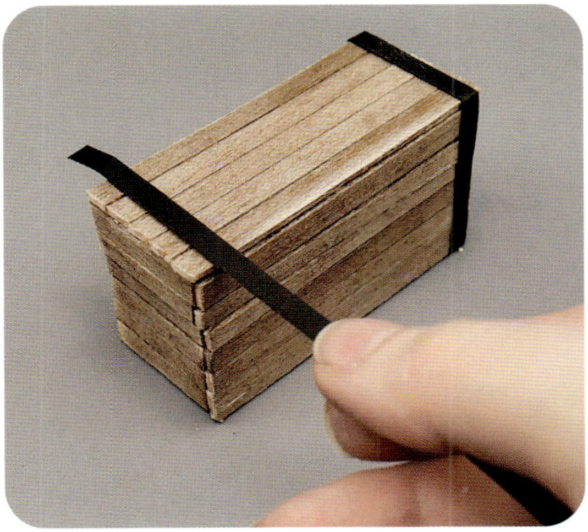

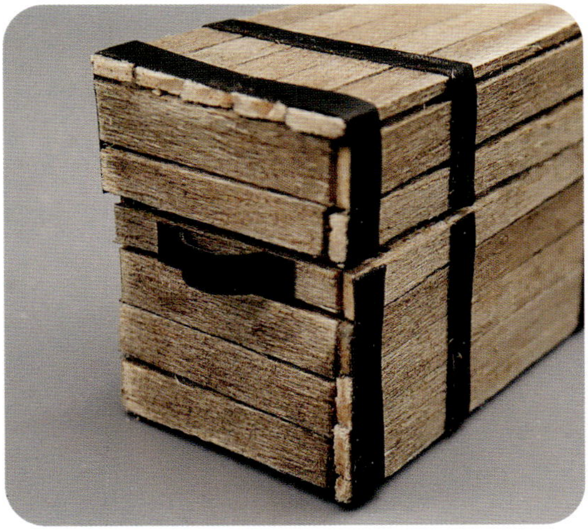

Let's make some chest straps! Cut four strips of black paper, each about ¼ x 4 inches (6 mm x 10.2 cm). *No black paper? No problem! Just paint some black!*

Glue two straps on either edge of the chest starting from the back of the lid, around the front, and under the bottom of the chest. *"How am I going to open it now?" Hold your biscuits! I'm getting to it!*

Glue two more straps in the center about 1 inch (2.5 cm) apart. Once the glue has dried, take an exacto knife and carefully slice open your lid so that it opens freely.

Your chest is heavy, so we're going to need some handles to handle it. Glue two 1-inch (2.5-cm) strips in C shapes on each end of your chest.

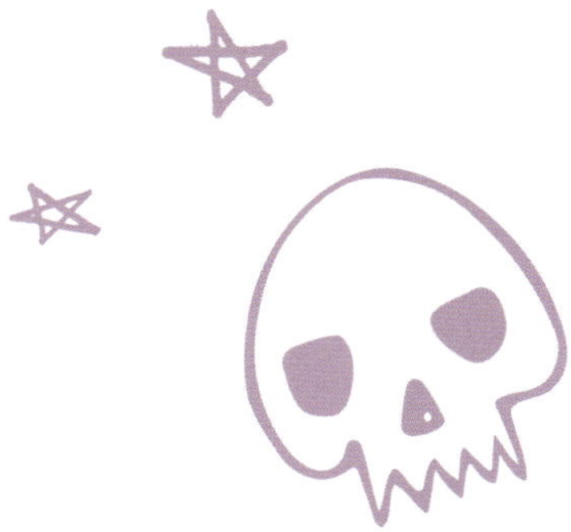

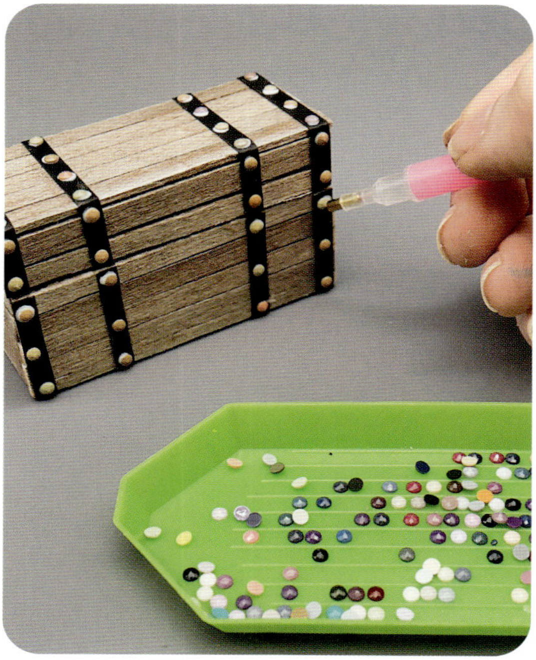

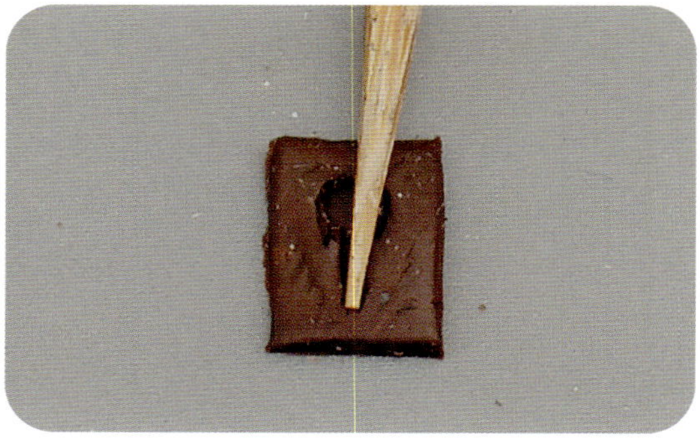

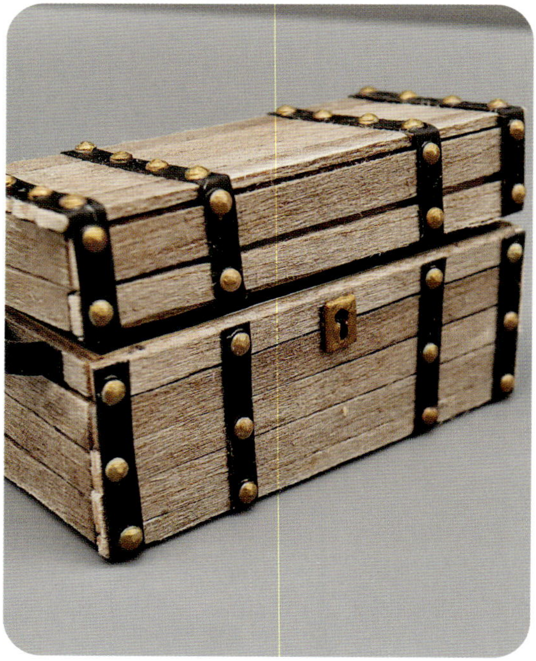

Clay Sizer
Lock

Note: *Having plastic diamond drills would be amazing! But honestly who has those? You can replace them with puff paint or drops of glue.*

Evenly space out your drills or drops along your black straps to look like metal rivets. (I did nine for each strip but you do you, boo.) If you use drips, wait for them to dry before you paint them gold.

Let's lock up our secrets! Grab some clay. (Polymer works great but any is fine.) Shape it into a flat rectangle. For crispy edges, trim with an exacto knife.

With a toothpick, press the blunt end into the top of your rectangle and lay the sharp end at the bottom to make a keyhole.

Harden your clay according to the package instructions, then paint it gold with a black hole.

Glue your lock onto the front of your chest.

Congratulations! Now go fill your chest with all your tiny secrets! (See page 12 for some miniature secrets you could store in your chest.)

The Midnight Clock

Legend has it that if you stand in an owl's shadow as the clock strikes midnight, during a full moon, on the first Wednesday of the month, you might see a ghost. Or at the very least, question your life choices.

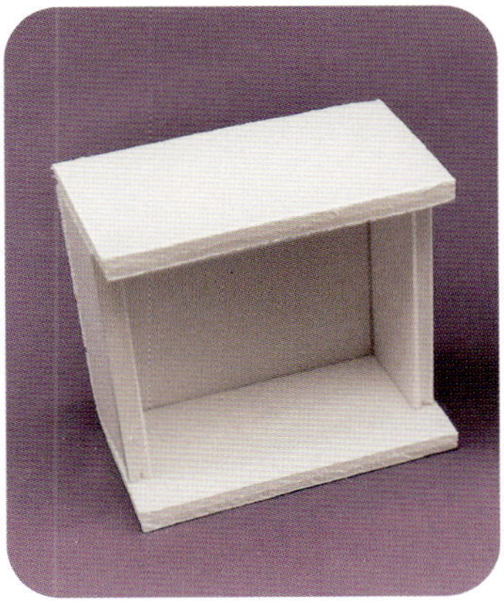

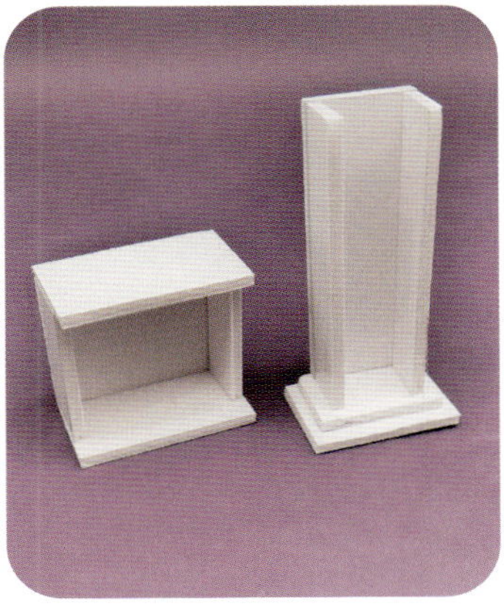

Tools

- exacto knife, ruler, & cutting mat
- glue
- paint
- superglue
- pliers/wire cutter

Materials

- foam core
- ⅛" (3-mm) square dowels
- head pins
- 2 beads
- chain
- chipboard
- old watch
- decorations (optional)

Cut the following out of foam core:

- **Qty: 1**—1½ x 1½ inches (3.8 x 3.8 cm) ***back***
- **Qty: 2**—1½ x ¾ inch (3.8 x 1.9 cm) ***sides***
- **Qty: 2**—1 x 1¾ inch (2.5 x 4.5 cm) ***top & bottom***

Lay the face ***back*** flat on the table. Glue the two face ***sides*** at a 90° angle along the edges of the ***back*** in a U shape.

Glue the face ***top and bottom*** across the remaining two sides to make a box.

Cut the following out of foam core using the templates on page 213:

- **Qty: 1**—¾ x 1¼ inches (1.9 x 3.2 cm) ***small foot***
- **Qty: 1**—1½ x 1 inch (3.8 x 2.5 cm) ***large foot***
- **Qty: 1**—3 x 1 inch (7.6 x 2.5 cm) ***back***
- **Qty: 2**—3 x ½ inch (7.6 x 1.3 cm) ***sides***

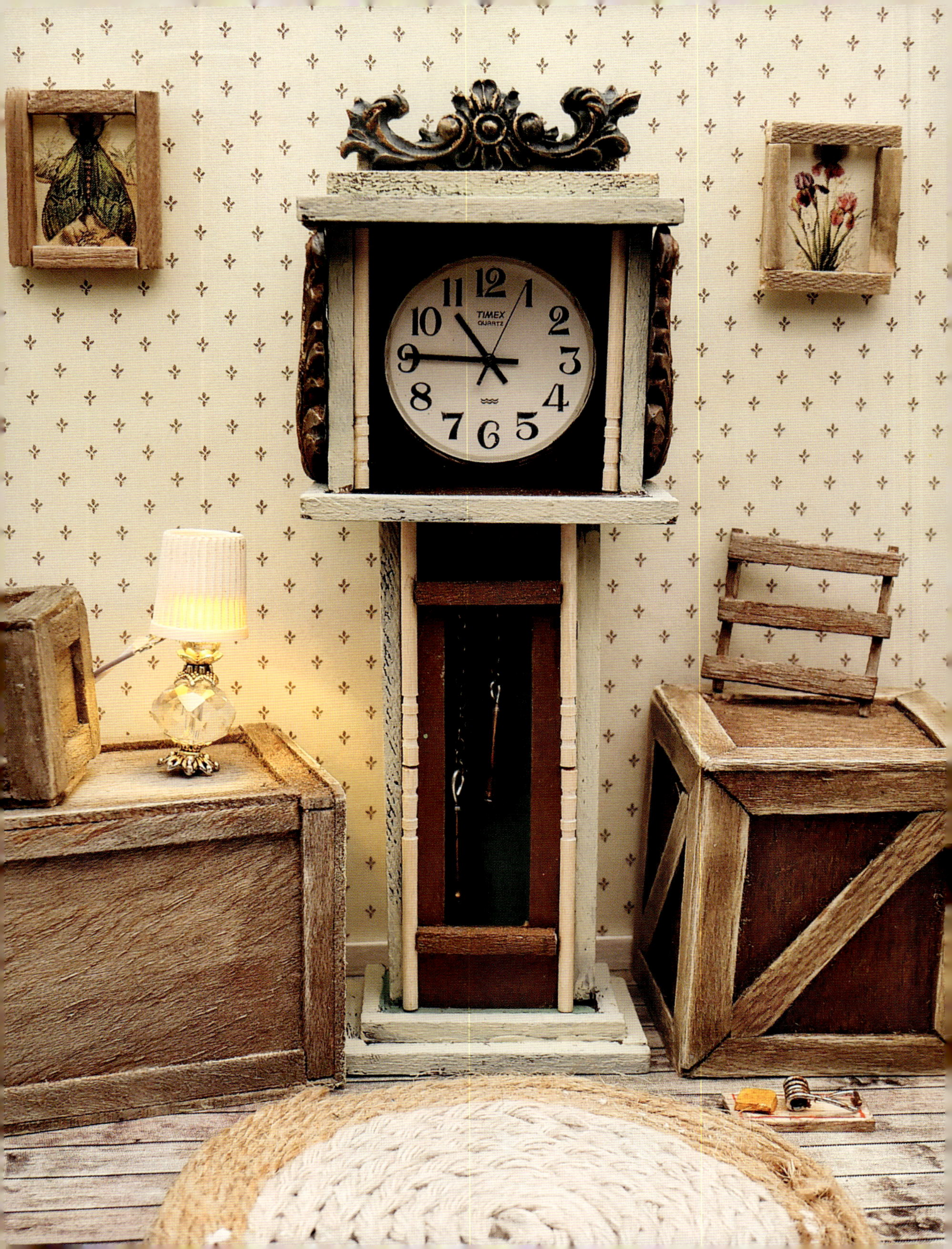
TIMEX
QUARTZ

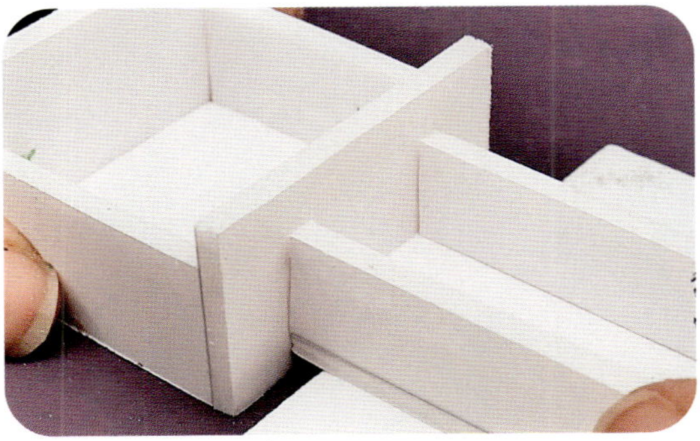

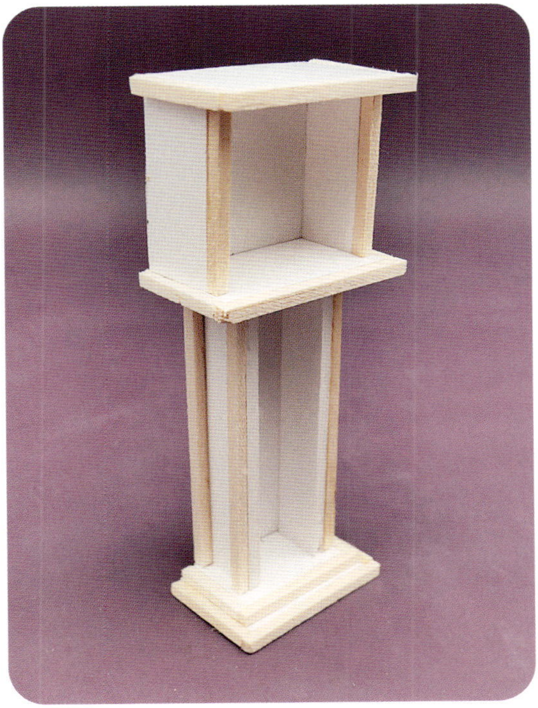

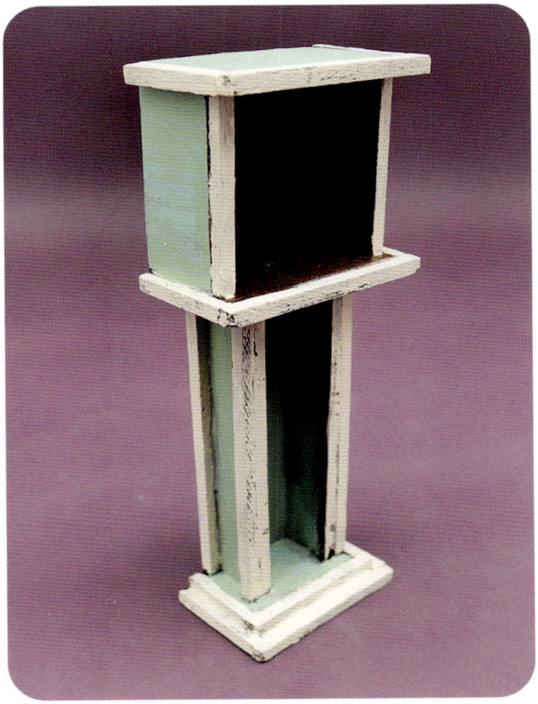

Center and glue the ***small foot*** on top of the ***large foot*** along one long edge to create a step. Set aside.

Lay the ***back*** flat on the table "portrait style."

Glue the two ***sides*** at a 90° angle on top of the ***back*** to form a U-shaped gutter.

Glue the foot to the bottom edge of your "gutter," flush with the back.

Lay the back of the trunk on a scrap of foam core so that it sits a little off the table. Apply glue to the bottom of the face and lay it on its back flush with the table and press the two pieces together.

Cover up all those ugly, gross raw edges with ⅛-inch (3-mm) square dowels.

What color are you going to paint your clock? Ghastly green? Bloody red? . . . Some other color I can't think of? Paint it and set it aside to dry.

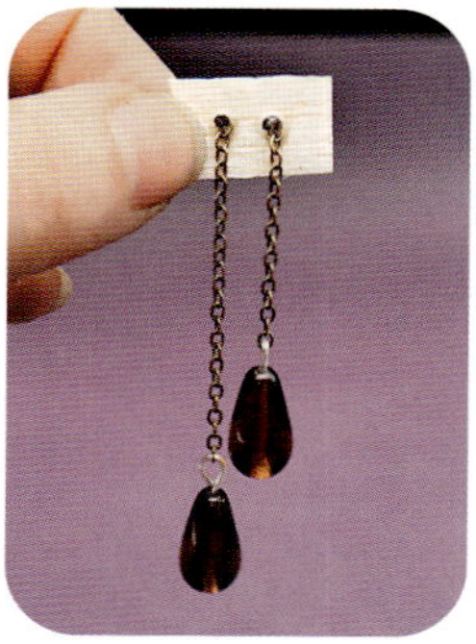

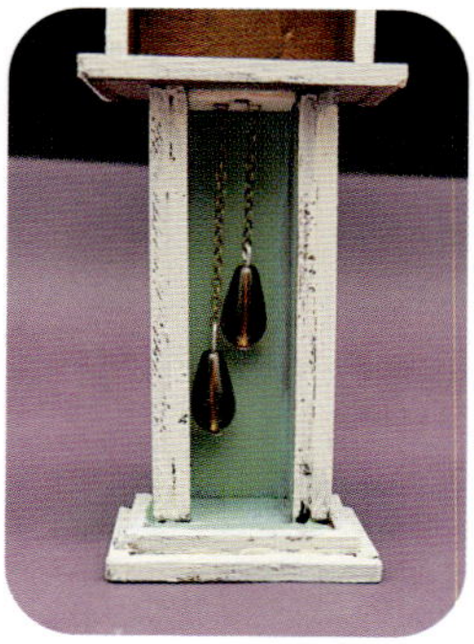

Clock dangly bits! Feed a head pin through your bead. Let your bead rest on the head and bend a hoop in your pin near the hole.

Thread a 1½-inch (3.8-cm)-long chain through the hoop. Repeat this so you have two dangly bits but thread the other with a 1-inch (2.5-cm)-long chain.

Take a scrap of chipboard roughly ¾ x ½ inch (1.9 x 1.3 cm) and use two head pins to pin your two chains through the scrap so that they are side by side. Superglue the pins and clip the excess off the back with pliers or a wire cutter.

Glue this scrap into the top crevice of your trunk so that your dangly bits freely dangle inside your trunk.

Cut a 1 x 3–inch (2.5 x 7.6–cm) rectangle out of chipboard. This will be the window to your clock.

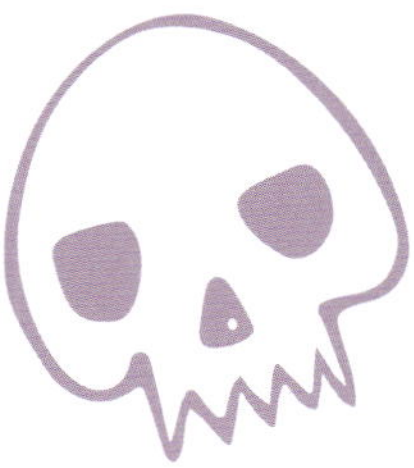

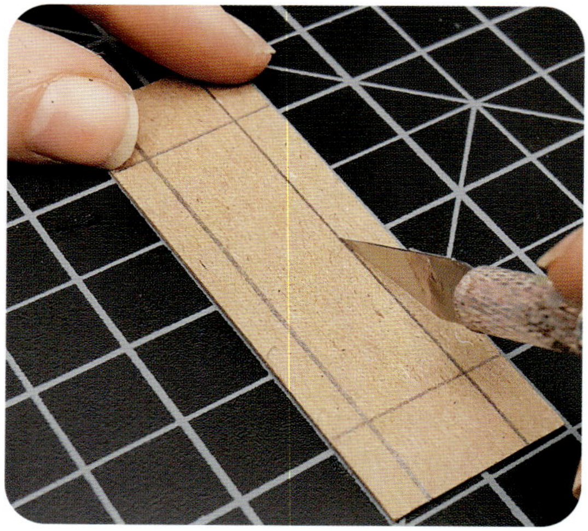

Cut a rectangle out of the middle, roughly 2 x ½ inch (5 x 1.3 cm). Paint and glue it to the front of your clock.

Pop in an old watch face if you have one.

No watch? No worries! *You can print one out and put it on a button, paint one on a wooden circle, or thrift a broken one from a thrift store. Thrift stores are my happy place.*

Decorate your haunted clock with whatever weird bits and pieces you might have lying around. Balsa wood scraps, toothpicks, broken jewelry, floral trinkets . . .

Challenge yourself by using stuff around the house! The weirder the better. It just adds to the magic and story of your clock!

Sinister Stairs

Did you hear that?! I think there's something under the "Stairs."
Is it sinister? Probably . . . Did you see those eyes?
Oh, also they're called "Sinister Stairs."

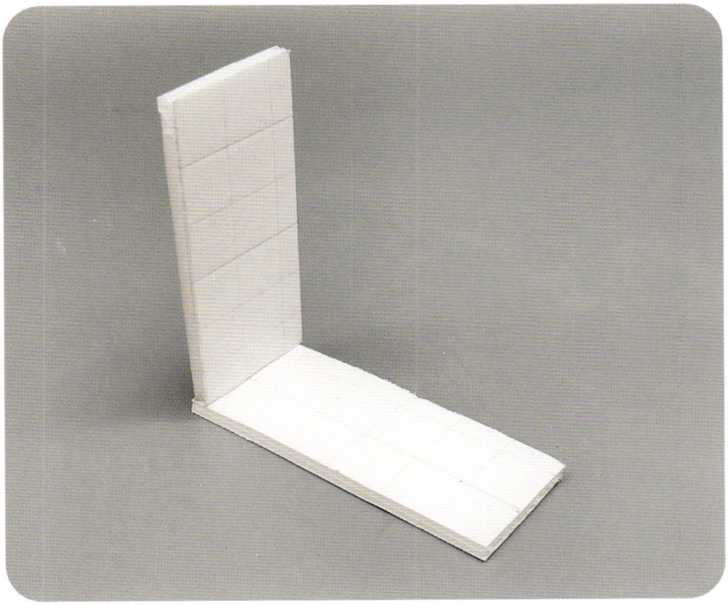

Tools

- exacto knife, ruler, & cutting mat
- glue
- paint
- pencil
- scissors
- silicone mat
- hot glue
- sandpaper

Materials

- foam core
- balsa wood
- 2 toothpicks

Cut the following out of foam core. A template is on page 214 for reference.

- **Qty: 2**—3 x 1¼ inches (7.6 x 3.2 cm) ***back & bottom***
- **Qty: 1**—3 x 3½ inches (7.6 x 8.9 cm) ***stair side***

Cut the following out of balsa wood. A template is on page 214 for reference.

- **Qty: 6**—½ x 1¾ inch (1.3 x 4.5 cm) ***steps***

Take a ***back & bottom*** piece and measure the thickness of your foam core. Trim that much off the short edge. Glue the short edges of your ***back & bottom*** pieces together in an L.

Paint the inside of the L black (like my SOUL . . . muahaha) and set it aside to dry.

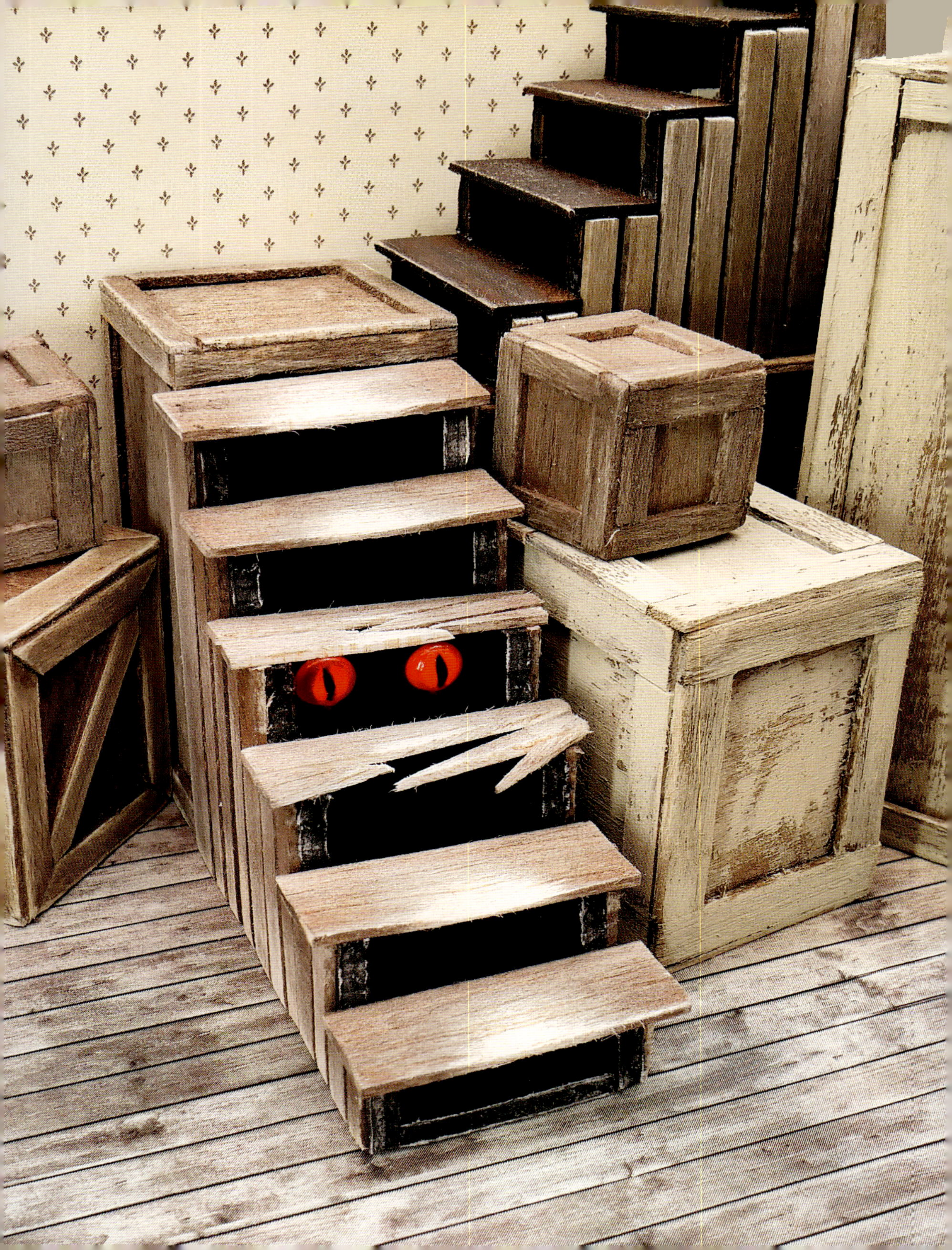

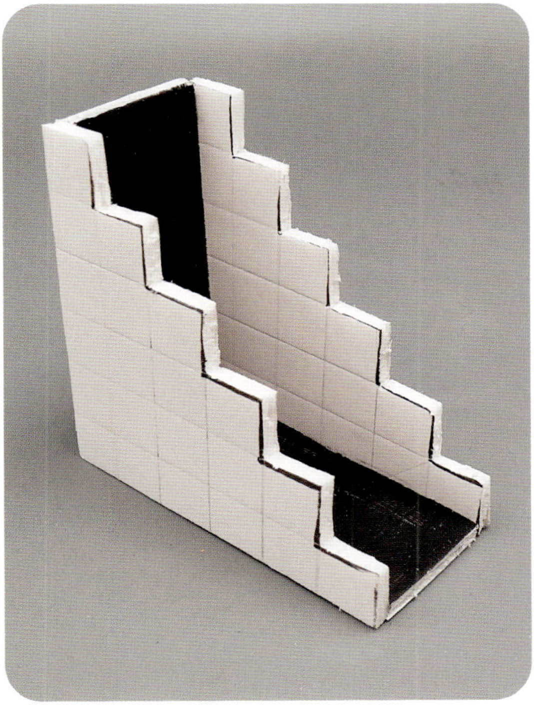

Take the ***stair side*** piece and draw a ½ x ½–inch (1.3 x 1.3–cm) grid on it.

Tip: *Using a cutting mat that has ½-inch (1.3-cm) squares makes this much easier! Just line up your ruler to the squares and draw lines.*

With this grid, making stairs will be a snap! Start one square in from the short edge and use your exacto knife to cut a zigzag from one edge to the other. Pull it apart and now you have two ***stair sides***!

Glue your ***stair sides*** to the outside of your L. Paint the inside black.

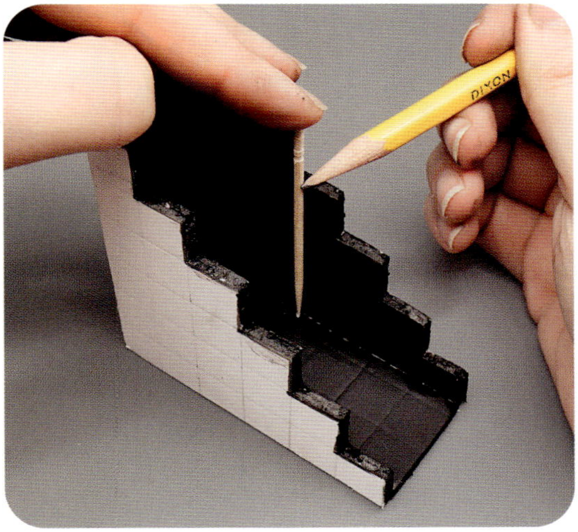

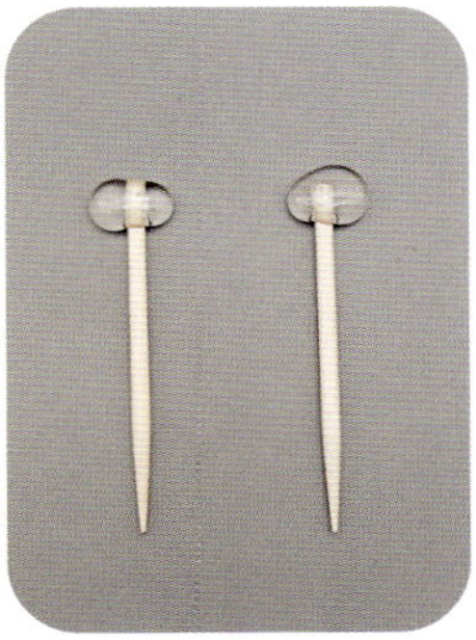

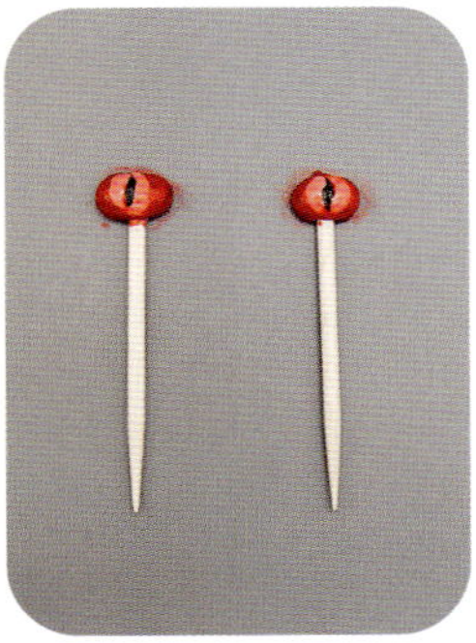

Let's get spooky! Cut two toothpicks so that they're just tall enough to reach the third step from the inside. Keep the pointy end intact.

Lay your toothpicks on your silicone mat and add a drop of hot glue to the cut end of each toothpick. The drops should cover but not go over the top. Let this cool, and no matter how tempting, do NOT peel it yet!

Paint the hot glue dots red with black cat-like pupils. *You can add glow-in-the-dark paint around the pupils if you're feeling extra.* Now you may peel!! YAY!

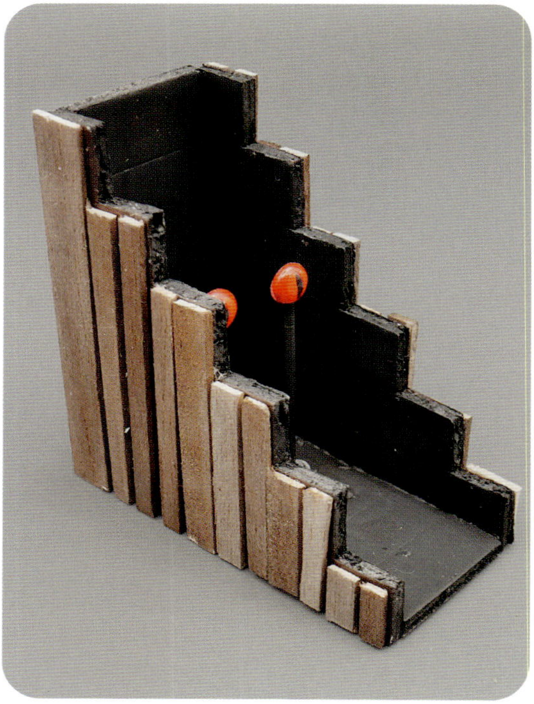

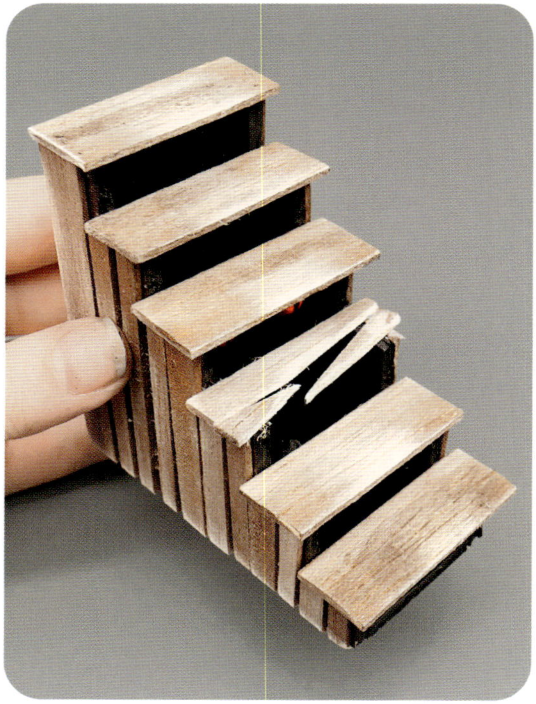

Paint the toothpick sticks black and poke them into the bottom of your staircase so that the eyes peek out under the third stair. Glue in place.

Paint the outside of your staircase brown.

Cover the outside surface of your staircase with strips of ¼-inch (6-mm) brown-painted balsa wood to make '80s style paneling. Retro's back, right?

Paint your six ½ x 1¾–inch (1.3 x 4.5–cm) steps brown. Glue them onto each zigzag step.

Optional: *You can crack one or two steps so that it looks like someone was stomping on them, maybe trying to crush the monster underneath?*

Add some realism by gently sanding a worn-down path in the center of each step.

SHWABAM! You just made some spooky sinister steps!

The Looking Glass

Humm, that's strange. When the clock struck midnight, the mirror started looking peculiar . . . I'd stay away from it if I were you.

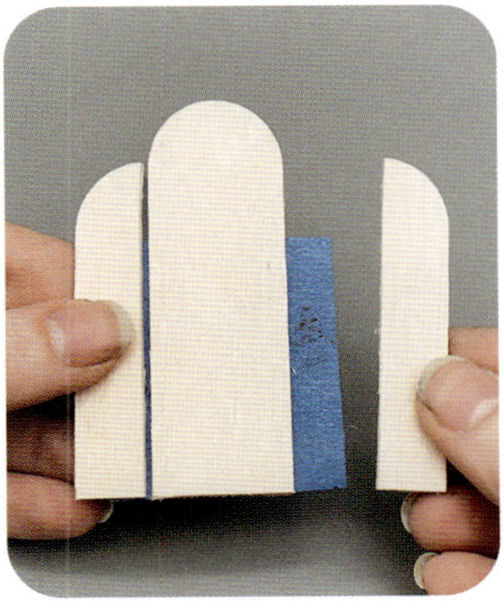

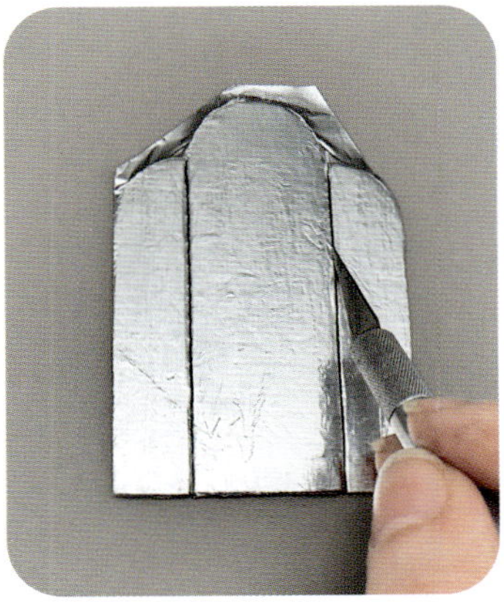

Tools

- exacto knife, ruler, & cutting mat
- tape
- craft glue
- superglue
- paint
- hot glue

Materials

- 1" (2.5-cm)-wide tongue depressor
- aluminum foil
- 2 disposable cocktail forks (or similar)
- severed doll hand (optional)

Cut 3 inches (7.6 cm) off one end of a tongue depressor and 2½ inches (6.4 cm) off the other end to create two arches. Slice the shorter of the two in half to make two half arches.

Tape the two half arches on either side of the taller arch with the bottoms lined up. Be sure to leave a small gap between the pieces so that they can bend inward later.

Flip it over so that the tape is at the bottom and spread a thin, even layer of craft glue over the surface.

Cut a square of aluminum foil (with minimal wrinkles if possible) to fit over the pieces of wood and smooth it out over the surface. Be careful to not rip the foil. Let this dry.

Place your mirror so the foil is face down on your cutting mat and trim the excess foil off with an exacto knife.

Flip it back over and carefully cut between the three arches. Avoid cutting the tape on the back! Each piece will be separate but still connected by tape.

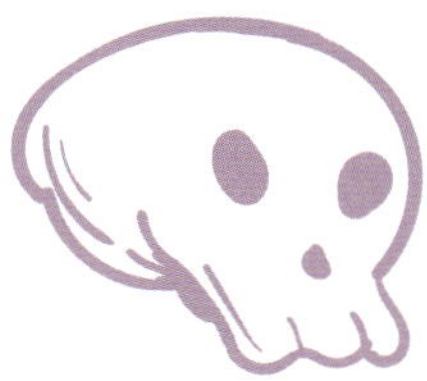

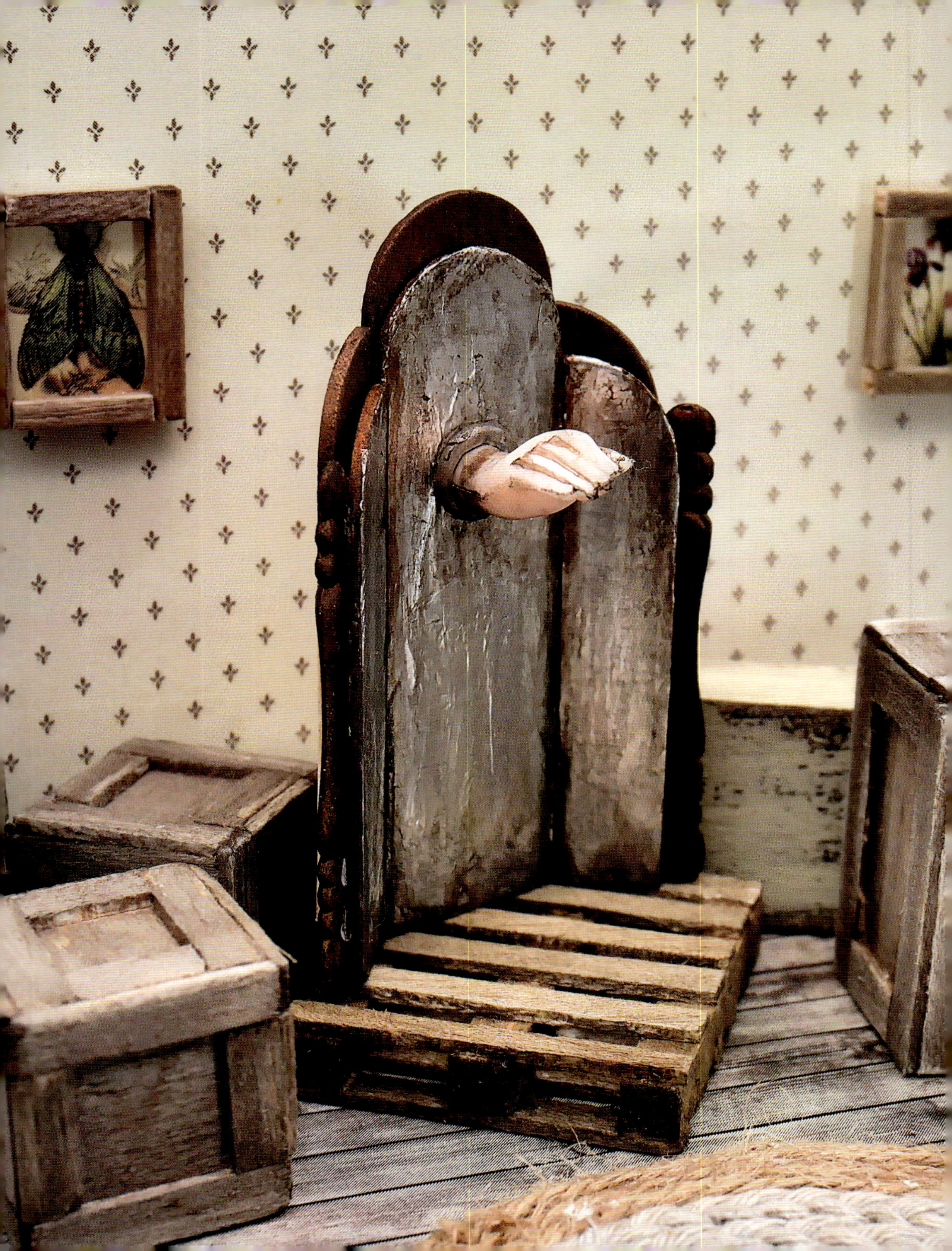

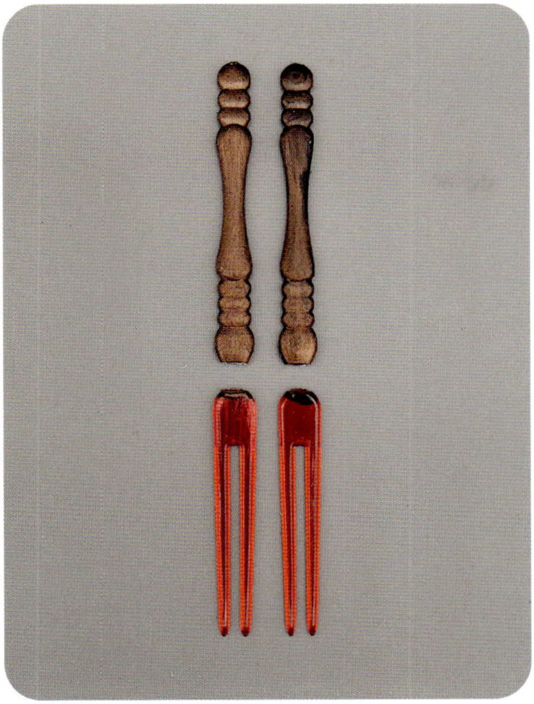

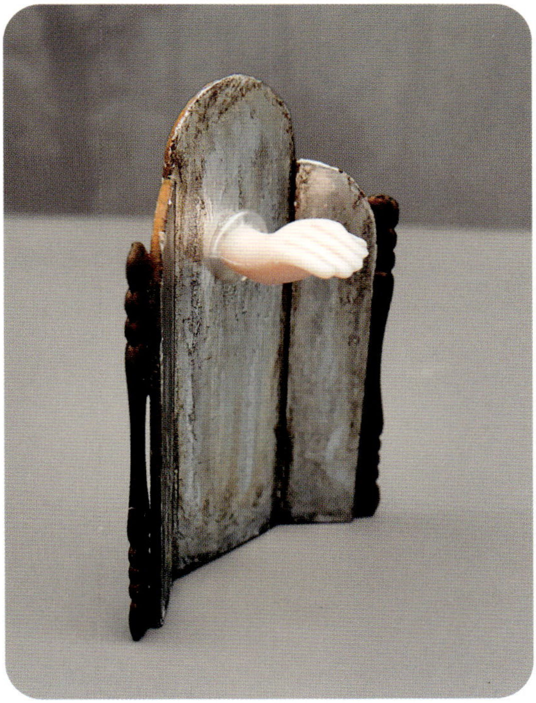

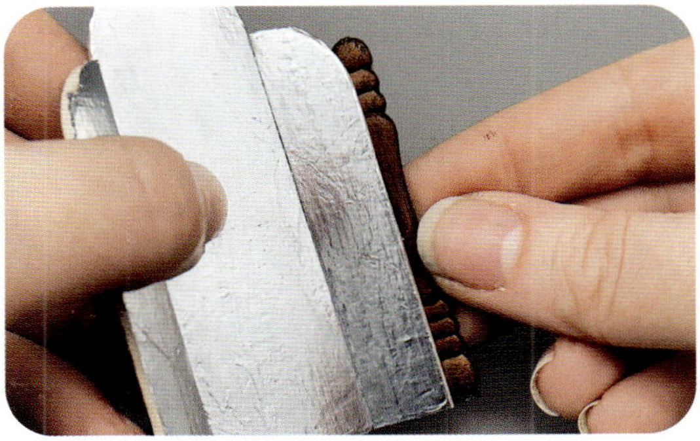

Bend the two side arches inward to create a curved shape. Use superglue to freeze it in place.

Take two disposable cocktail forks and paint them bronze or brown.

Hold them up to the sides of your mirror and trim as needed. Glue them onto each side as spooky trim.

If you're adding a hand, trim it below the wrist and hot glue it to the center of your mirror, like it's reaching out to pull you in!

Paint the hot glue silver to make it blend with your mirror. Add some "ghostly" dirt or just regular dirt-colored paint to the edges of your mirror.

For a more finished look, glue additional arches to the back painted the same color as the cocktail fork trim. Now you have a mirror worthy of sucking you into the fifth or possibly sixth dimension!

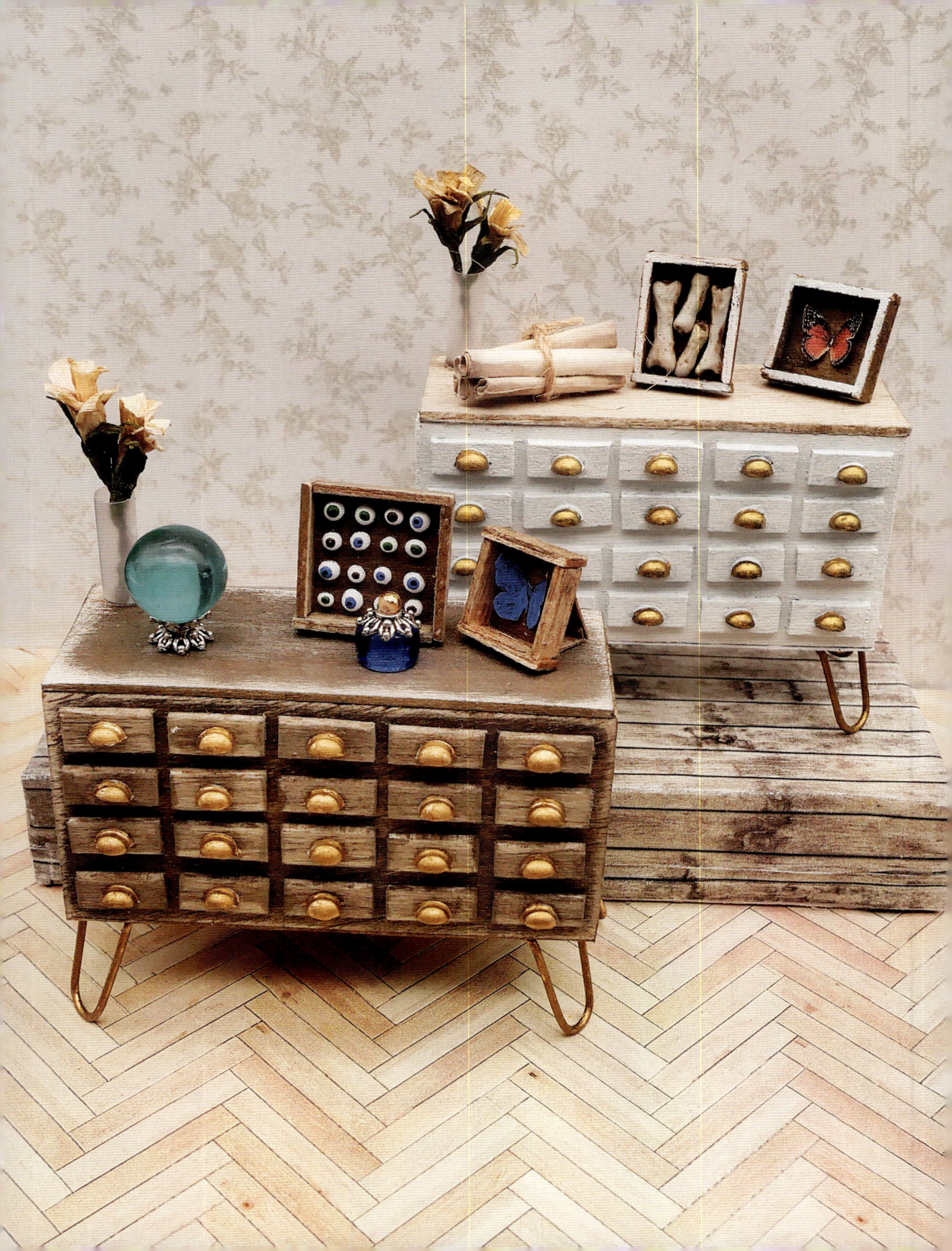

Apothecary Drawers

Think of all the wonderful little things that could be in these drawers. Mouse hearts, cat whiskers, deadly nightshade, that button I lost yesterday . . . If it's my button, do you think I could get that back? I kinda need it.

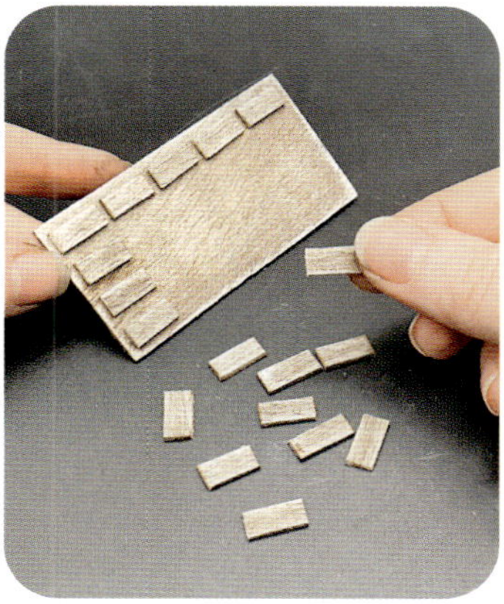

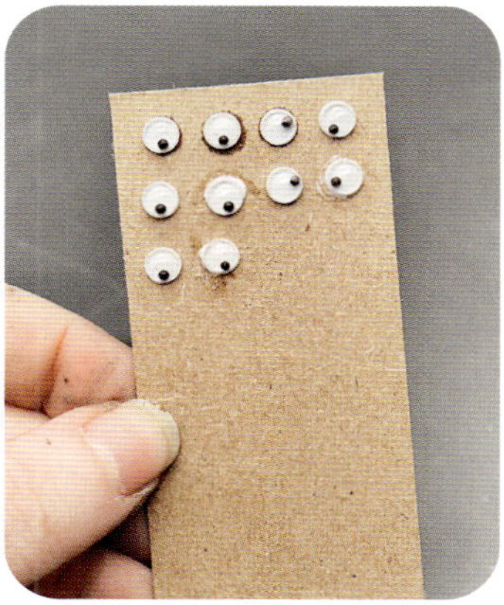

Table

Cut and paint the following balsa wood. A template is on page 215 for reference.

- **Qty: 20**—½ x ¼ inch (1.3 cm x 6 mm) ***drawers***
- **Qty: 2**—3 x 1½ inches (7.6 x 3.8 cm) ***front & back***
- **Qty: 1**—3 x 1¼ inches (7.6 x 3.2 cm) ***top***
- **Qty: 2**—1 x 1½ inches (2.5 x 3.8 cm) ***sides***

Glue your twenty ***drawers*** evenly spaced on the ***front*** (five across and four down). Set it aside.

Let's make some handles for all those drawers. Superglue ten small googly eyes onto a scrap piece of chipboard.

Stop them from looking at you (because it's rude to stare) by spray-painting the whole thing gold and letting it dry.

Tools

- exacto knife, ruler, & cutting mat
- paint
- glue
- superglue
- gold spray paint
- pliers/wire cutter
- scissors
- pencil

Table Materials

- balsa wood
- 10 small googly eyes
- chipboard
- 4 paper clips

Flowers Materials

- crepe paper (cream & green)
- floral wire (paper covered preferred)
- clear straw

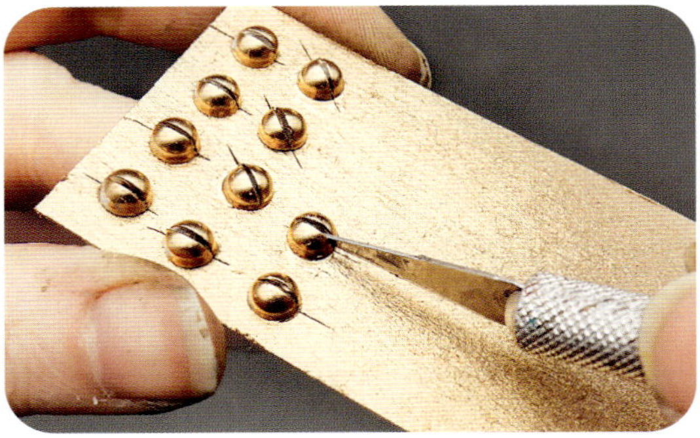

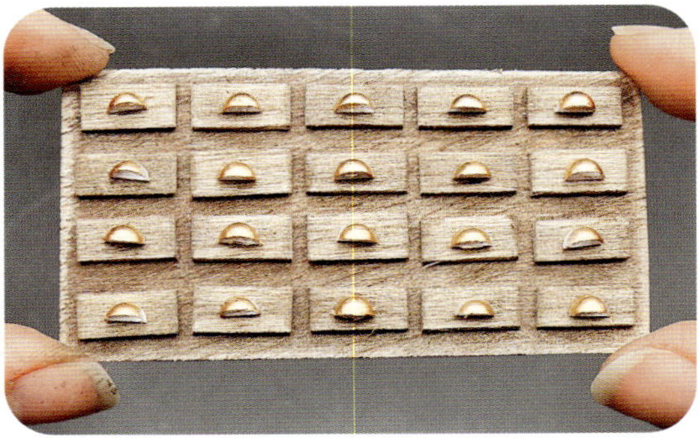

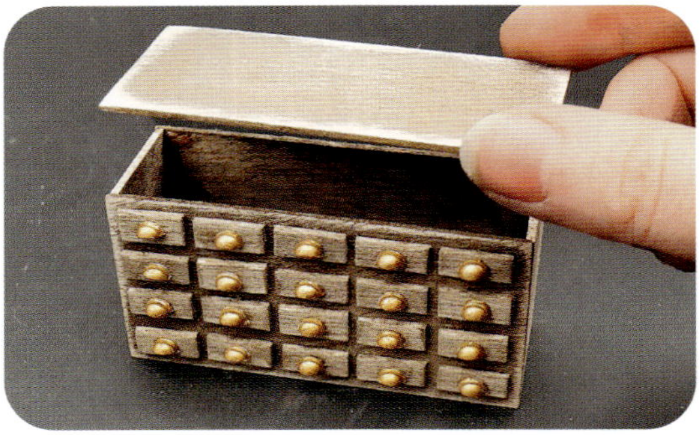

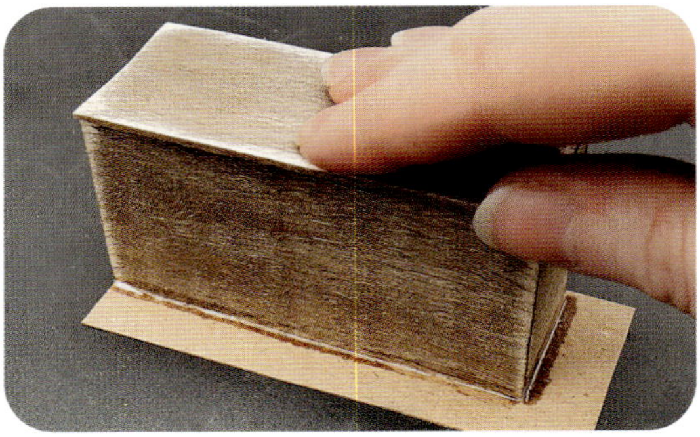

Once dry, split each eye in half with an exacto knife. *Ouch!*

Peel each half dome off, and glue one on the front of each ***drawer***.

Glue the ***sides*** at a 90° angle on the back of the ***drawer front*** to make a U shape. Then glue the ***back*** on to match the front. Glue the ***top*** piece on . . . well . . . the top. You should now have a rectangle cube . . . *a rec-cube?*

Out of chipboard, cut a rectangle that's slightly larger than the ***top***. Run a bead of glue around the bottom edge of your table and squish it onto the chipboard. Once dry, trim off the excess. *It's the bottom, no one cares about the bottom.*

Let's make some legs! Using pliers or a wire cutter, snip off the larger loop of 4 paper clips so you're left with four Us.

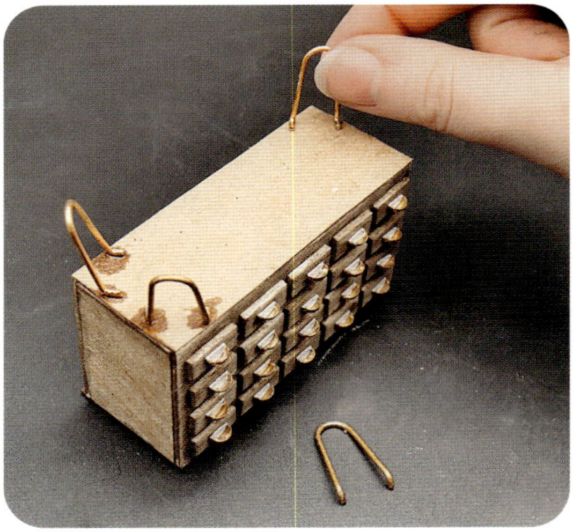

Bend the ends of your paper clips at 90° angles and gently spread them apart. Spray paint these gold to match your handles.

Superglue each leg to the bottom of your table.

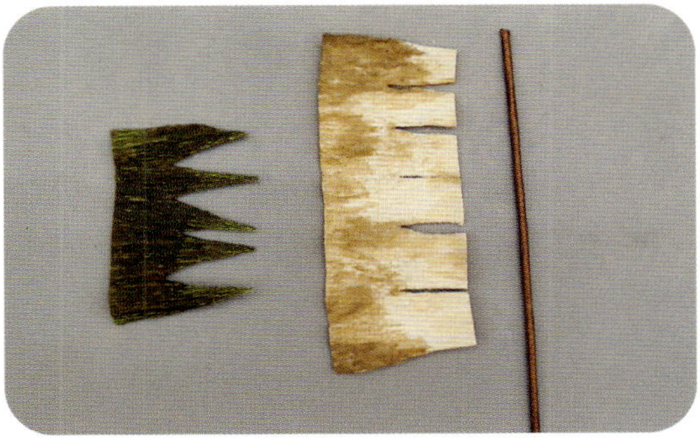

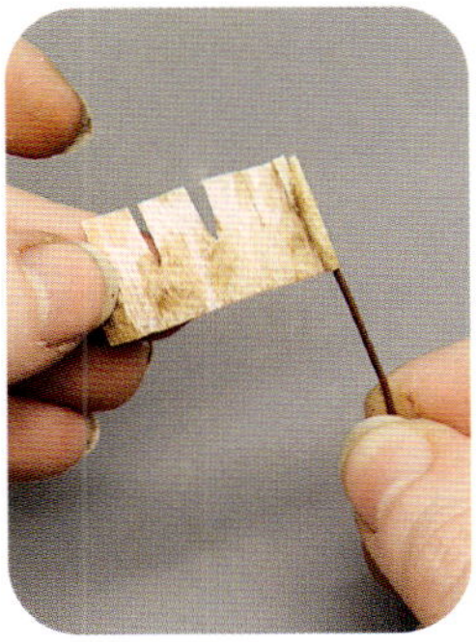

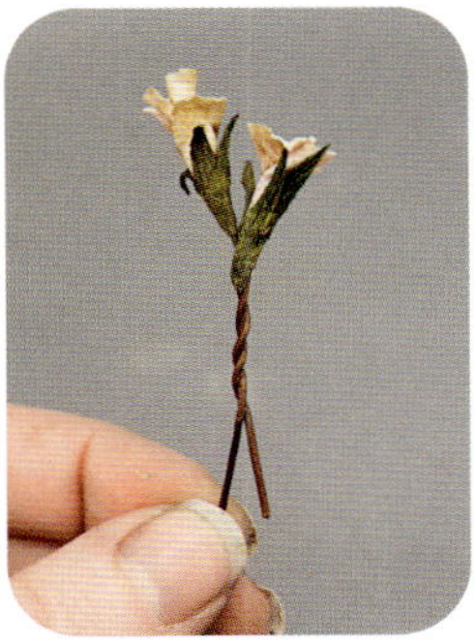

Flowers

Cut the following out of crepe paper:

- **Qty: 2**—~¾ x 2 inches (1.9 x 5 cm) (cream)
- **Qty: 2**—~¾ x 1 inch (1.9 x 2.5 cm) (green)

Take one cream piece and cut four to five vertical slits along the long edge and dab watered-down brown paint along the edge without slits.

Glue the short edge of this to the end of a 2-inch (5-cm) piece of floral wire. Keep the slits facing up. Wrap and glue the rest of the paper around the wire, creating a flower. Set it aside.

Take one green piece and cut triangles out of the long edge, making it zigzagged.

Wrap the zigzagged part around a pencil to curl the leaves.

Wrap and glue this below your flower.

Gently fluff the petals and leaves to give the flower a more floral shape.

Repeat the process to make two flowers, then twist the stems together.

Cut ½ inch (1.3 cm) off the end of a drinking straw for the vase.

Trim the stems so that the flowers are just outside the vase.

Glue your straw vase to the top corner of your table, then glue your flowers in it.

Decorate your apothecary cabinet with other creepy goodies, like the specimens from page 119 or the miniatures on page 12.

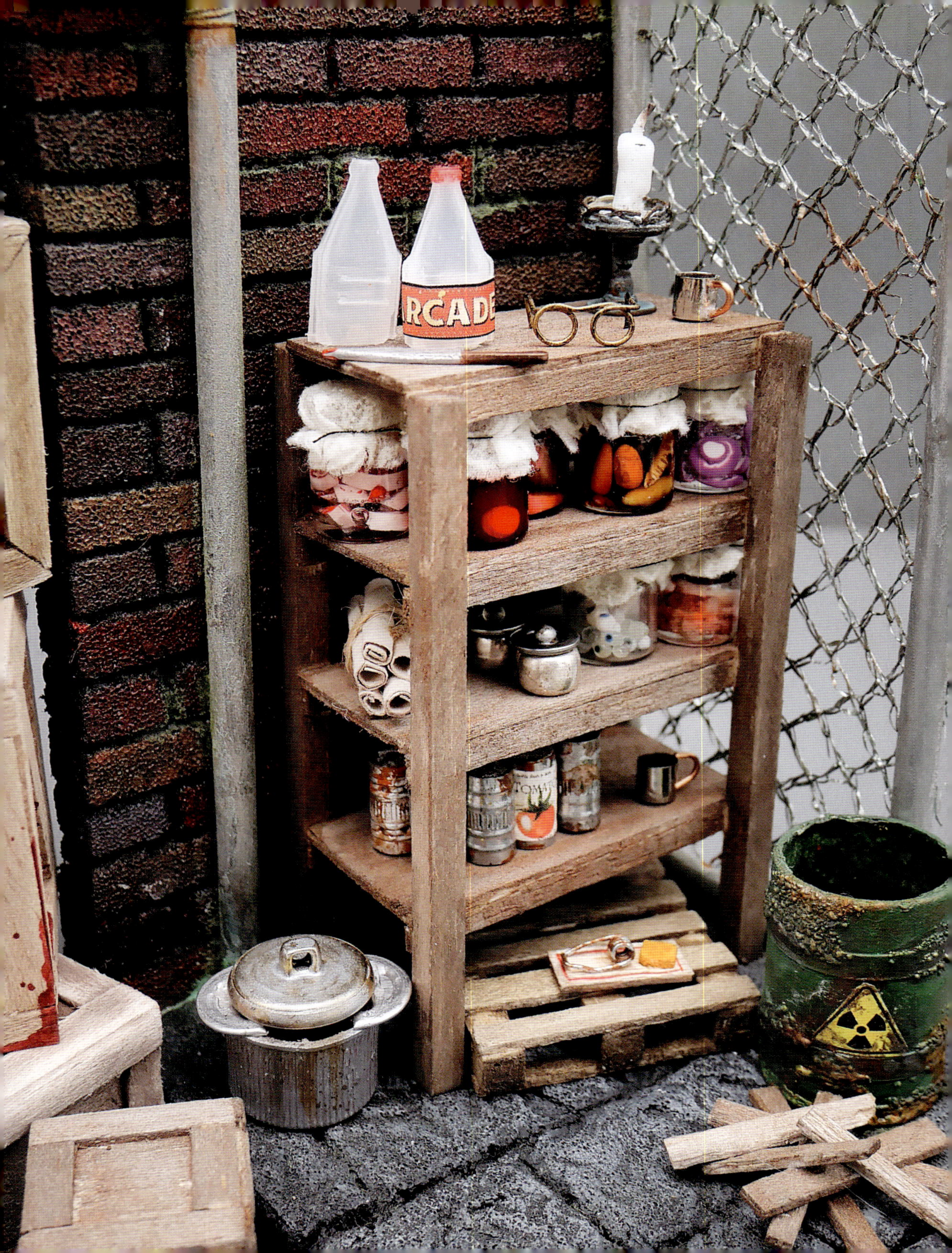

Apocalypse!!!

Get your bunker shelves stocked and your weapons organized because we're only one toxic waste barrel away from the apocalypse! Will you be lucky enough to become a zombie, or will you have to fight for the rest of your (probably short) life? Either way, be more prepared than Mary!

You see, Mary *thought* she had everything under control. Weapons? Sharp. Shelves? Stocked. Feast? . . . PICKLE-LESS! She FORGOT the dang pickles! You can't have a feast without pickles! Dang it, Mary!

So, Mary went on a supply run down Shank Alley. I mean, really, Mary? Who goes shopping somewhere literally called "Shank Alley"?

Well, surprise, surprise, Mary was shanked . . . by a zombie. I know, you're wondering, "Can a zombie shank someone?" and "WHY would Mary go down an alley named Shank Alley and expect not to be shanked?"

There are only two options I can think of.

They have absolutely amazing pickles down Shank Alley.

Mary's an idiot. I mean, she didn't even take a weapon. WTF, Mary?

Unfortunately, we'll never know what Mary was thinking because Mary is now living (or un-living rather) among the zombies. The tragic part (other than Mary being an idiot) is that her feast will go pickle-less and moldy. There's nothing sadder than a moldy, pickle-less feast!

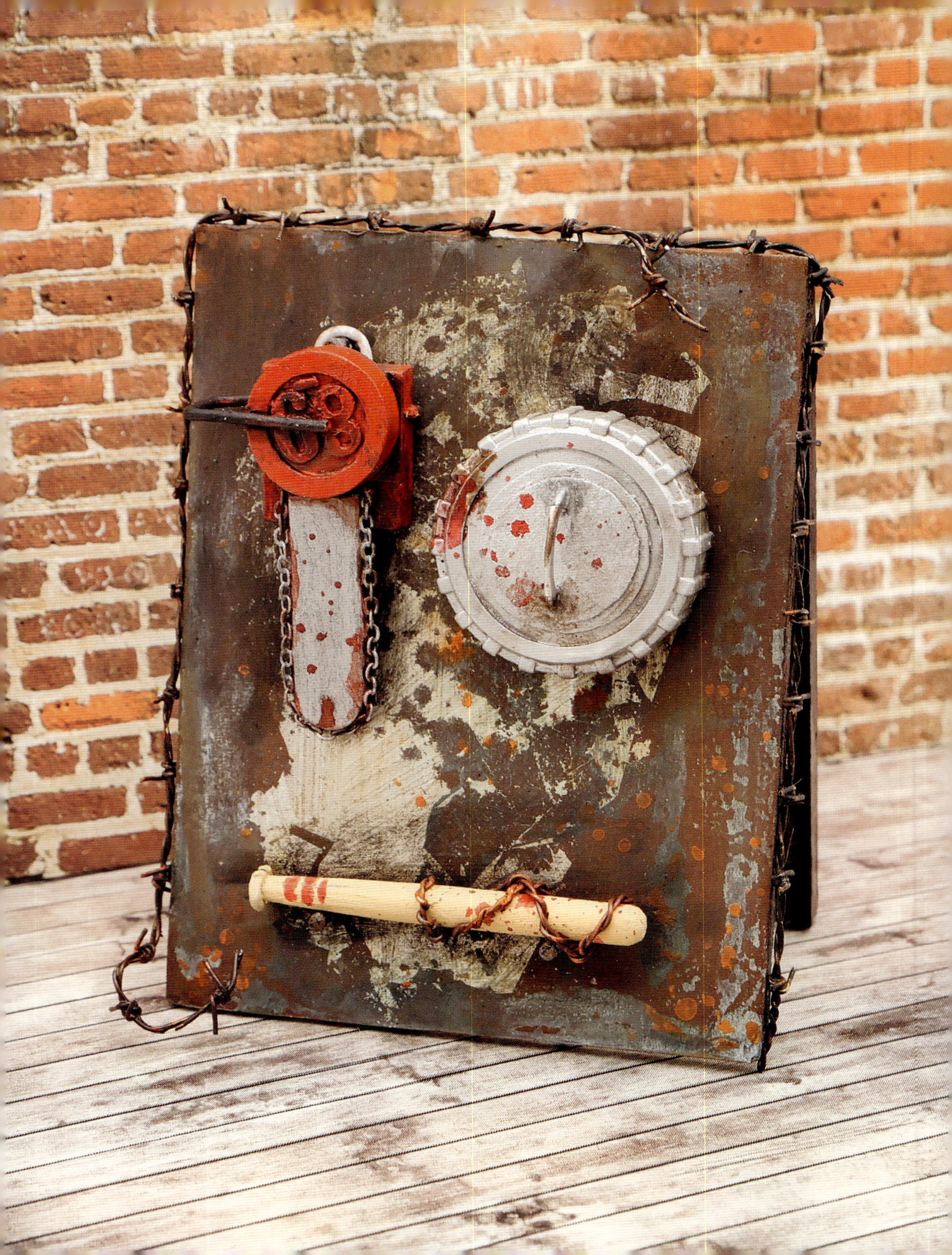

Weapons Rack

Weapons! You're gonna need a few in the apocalypse! Especially if you're traveling to Shank Alley! Be sure to keep them organized in a rack for quick retrieval!

Tools

- exacto knife, ruler, & cutting mat
- sandpaper
- wire cutter
- glue
- paint
- writing utensil
- thumbtack

Baseball Bat Materials

- disposable chopstick
- floral wire

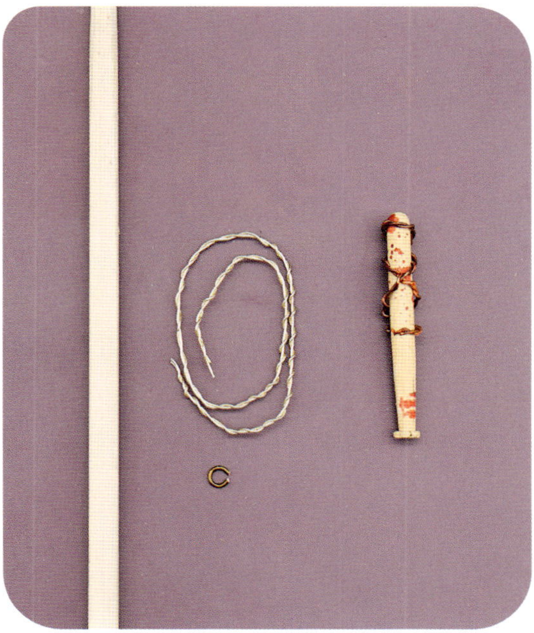

Chainsaw Materials

- Scrabble® tile (or similar square)
- round bingo number (or similar disk)
- popsicle stick
- small chain
- large paper clip

Shield Materials

- flat cap (example: contact lens cap)
- chipboard
- pop can pull tab

Rack Materials

- foam core
- chopstick (or square dowel)
- 4 toothpicks
- barbed wire (page 60)

Baseball Bat (aka The Bludgeoner 2000)

Cut about 2 inches (5 cm) off the pointy end of a chopstick and sand the thicker end to make it rounded like a bat.

Wrap wire once around the skinny end, trim with wire cutters, and glue it in place for a handle.

Paint your bat tan or yellow or whatever color a postapocalyptic zombie-killing bat would be.

Twist two 5-inch (12.7-cm)-ish long pieces of floral wire together.

Paint your twisted wire rusty orange and wrap it menacingly around your bat. Trim off any excess. Now your Bludgeoner 2000 is ready for bludgeoning!

Make it look like it already bludgeoned something, with splatters of blood (aka paint). Set it aside.

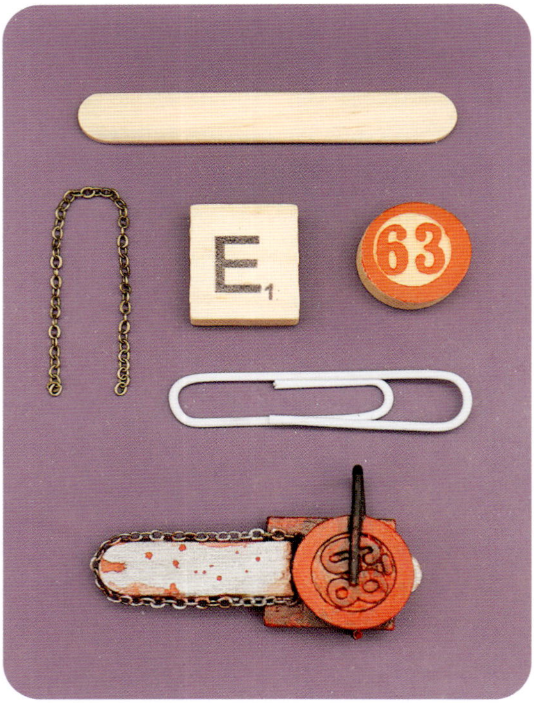

Chainsaw of Massacre

Paint your Scrabble tile and round bingo number "chainsaw red." Glue the bingo number off-center on top of the Scrabble tile. One side of the tile should have a little more space than the other, and the bingo number will hang off like ⅛ inch (3 mm) or so.

Cut a 1-inch (2.5-cm) piece off the end of a popsicle stick and glue the flat edge on the extra space on the Scrabble tile.

A chainsaw without a chain is just a saw. Glue a small chain around the edge of the popsicle stick.

Cut the big loop off a paper clip about ¾ inch (1.9 cm) down and glue it like it's hugging the Scrabble and bingo pieces. This is the chainsaw handle.

Cut the smaller loop of your paper clip about ¼-inch (6-mm) loop and glue it on the back end of your bingo piece. This is how we hang the chainsaw.

Paint the saw blade silver and go wild with the blood splatters. This is the apocalypse after all . . .

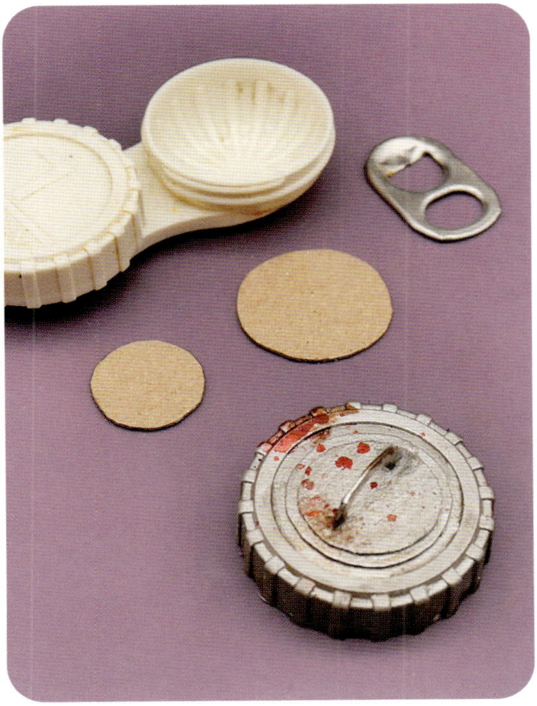

Trash Can Lid of Shielding

Take your contact lens cap (or similar item) and cut two progressively smaller circles out of chipboard to fit over your cap to cover up any writing. Glue them on your cap for a smooth surface.

Paint it silver with red and brown splatters. *Those are just apocalypse juices!*

Pop the tab off a pop can (or soda can, depending on where you live) and cut the smooth loop off the top using a wire cutter. Glue it onto the top of your cap as a handle.

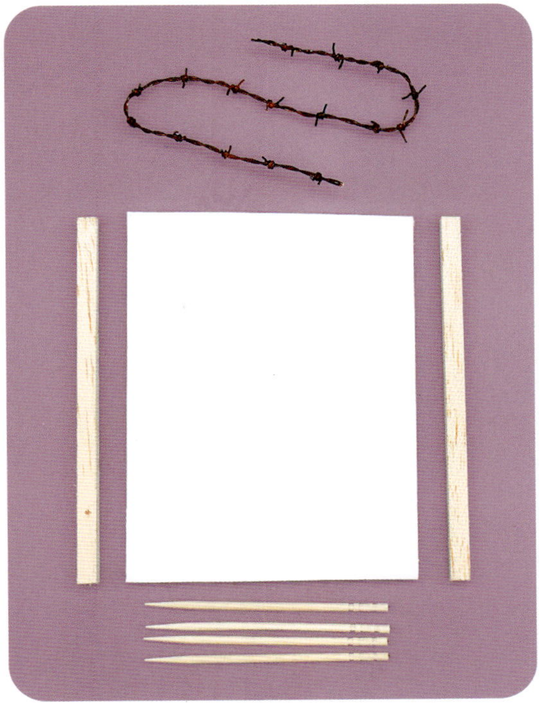

Weapons Rack

Cut the following out of foam core:

- **Qty: 1**—4 x 3 inches (10.2 x 7.6 cm)

Cut the following off a chopstick or square dowel:

- **Qty: 2**—4 inches (10.2 cm)

Trace your weapons on top of the foam rectangle to figure out how you want your rack laid out. Use a thumbtack to poke holes in the foam core at the hanging points of each weapon.

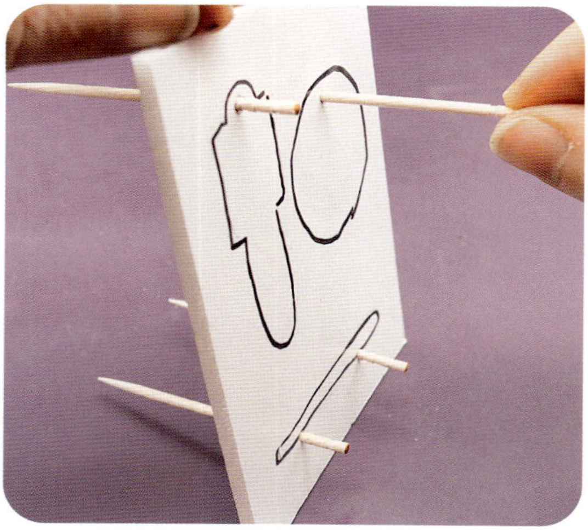

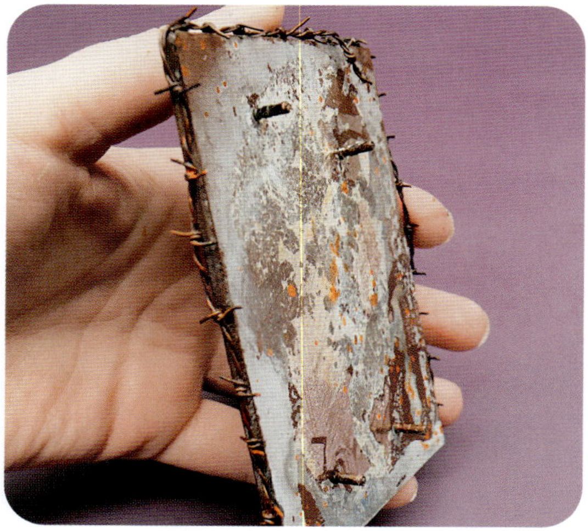

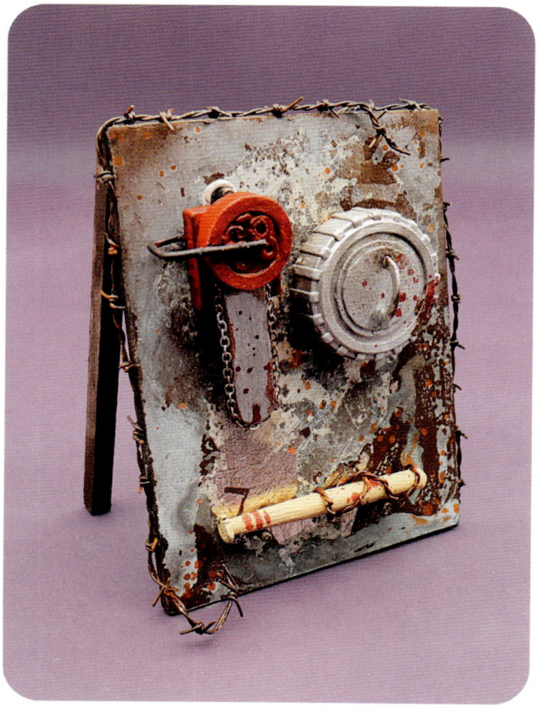

Push toothpicks into the holes you just made almost all the way through your foam core. Leave just enough sticking out for hanging your weapons.

Once it's perfect, glue these toothpicks in place. Using a wire cutter, trim the excess off the back.

Paint your rack silver and bronze with orange rust spots.

Make about 12 inches (30.5 cm) of barbed wire (see page 60) and wrap it around the edges of your rack, avoiding the bottom.

Cut the end of each 4-inch (10.2-cm) square dowel at a 60-ish° angle. Paint them brown and glue them on the back of your rack as legs.

Hang your weapons up and you're done! Just be sure to put your weapons back after use. Don't get caught in the apocalypse without them!

Bunker Shelf

It's best to be prepared for the worst. Make sure you have plenty of stock before the zombies come and knock. Wait, do zombies knock?

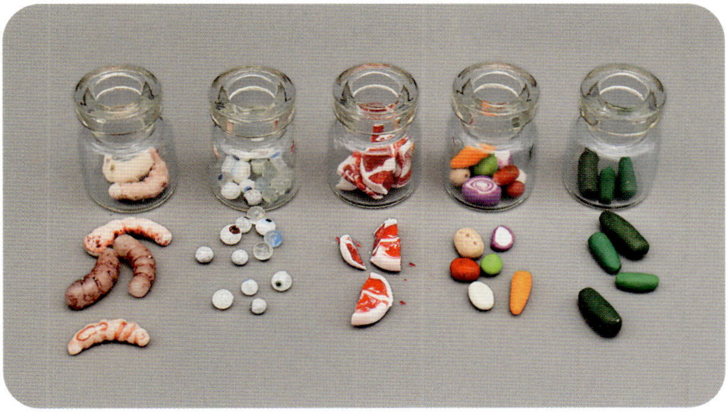

Preserves

Have delicious items on hand to fill your jars. Use polymer clay and sculpting tools to create them. Here are some examples to consider: maggots, eyeballs, sliced meat, vegetables.

Fill your jars a quarter with epoxy resin. Drop your ingredients in each jar. Use a toothpick to nudge the "food" around so everything looks oh so yummy!

Add extra spookiness by tinting your resin with reds or browns. It really gives you that "not so freshly" canned look!

As you fill your jars, think about the story behind them. Would your bunker dwellers make a complete meal in a jar, like an eyeball oregano soup, or will your postapocalyptic family separate their ingredients? You decide.

Tools

- sculpting tools
- toothpick
- scissors
- glue
- superglue
- exacto knife, ruler, & cutting mat
- pencil
- paint

Preserves Materials

- polymer clay
- maggots (page 181)
- eyeballs (page 194)
- meats (page 47)
- vegetables (page 48)
- 4–6 small glass jars (<1" [2.5 cm])
- epoxy resin (preferably UV)
- resin dye (optional)
- paper towel
- string

Shelf Materials

- ¼" (6-mm) or $\frac{3}{16}$" (5-mm) square dowels
- balsa wood

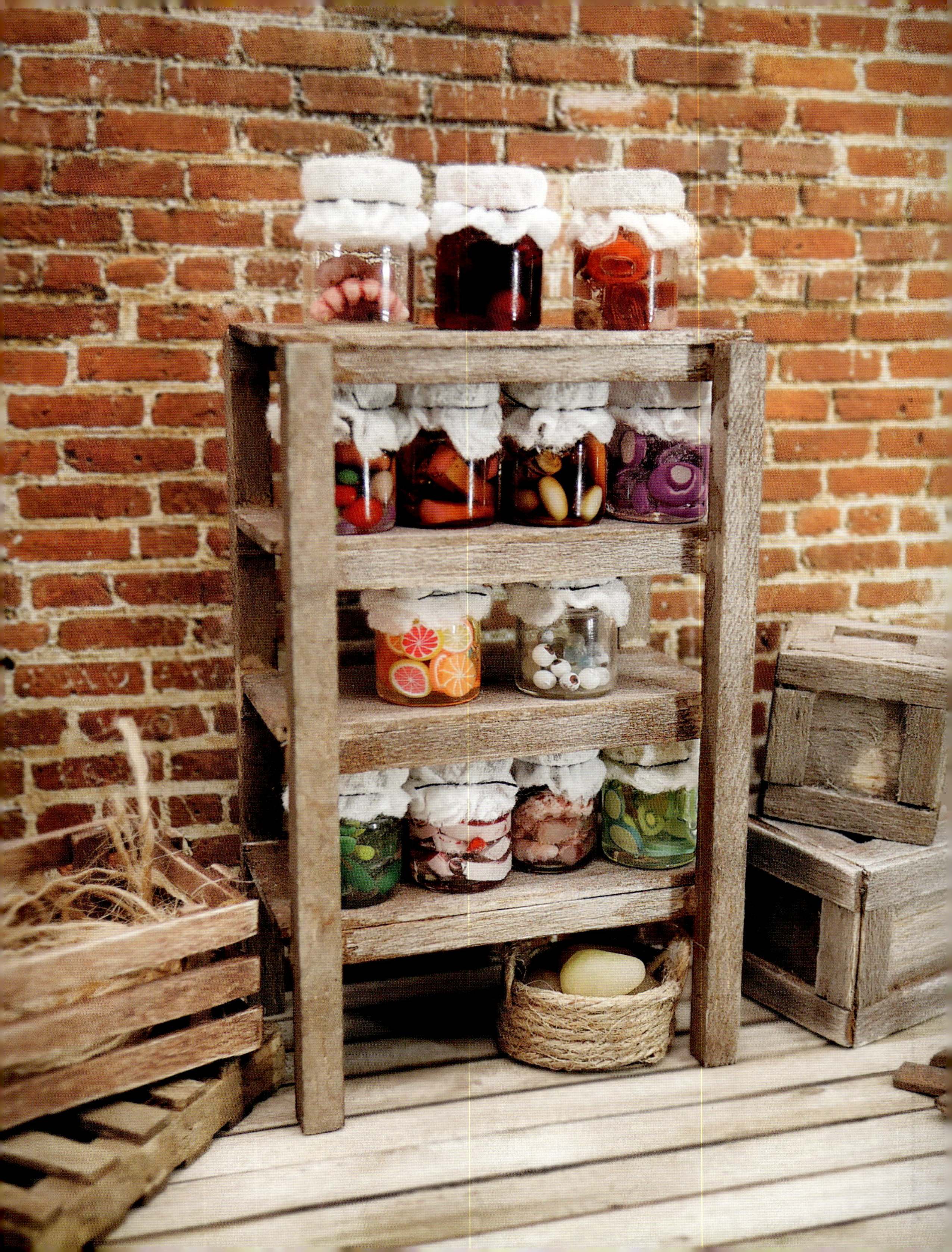

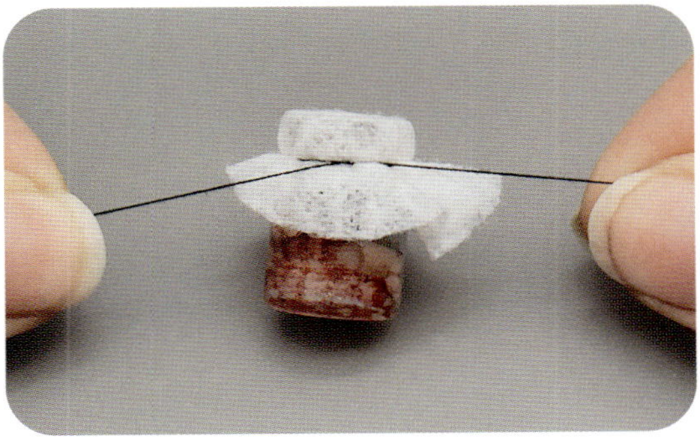

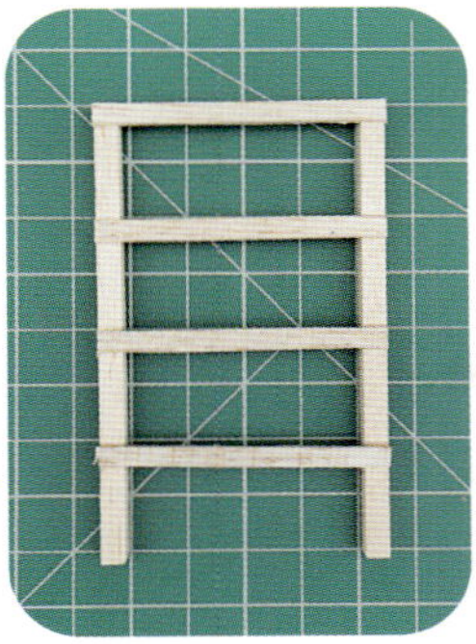

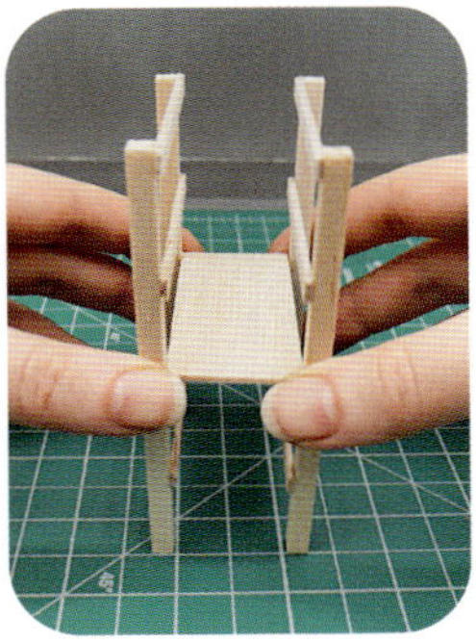

Top off your jars with additional resin until they are three-quarters full. Harden according to the package instructions.

Now to finish them off. Cut a roughly 1-inch (2.5-cm) circle out of a paper towel or cloth and superglue it to the top of each jar opening. Just make sure it's large enough to fold down around the rim of your jar.

Fold the cloth around the rim of your jar and hold it in place with a tied string. Snip off any excess fabric. Voilà! One perfectly preserved preservative.

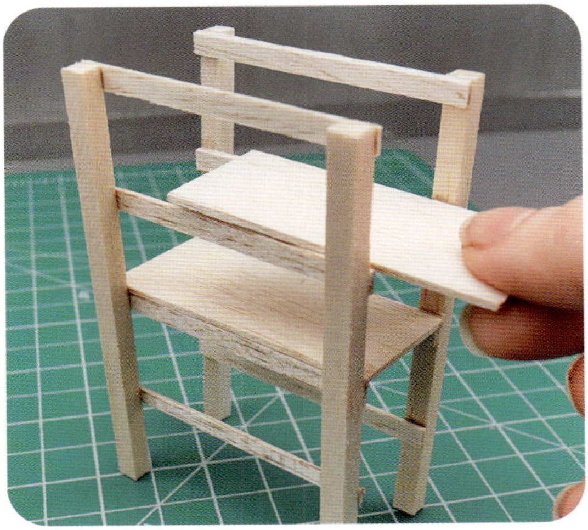

Shelf

Cut the following square dowels:

- **Qty:** 4—4 inches (10.2 cm) ***legs***

Cut the following out of balsa wood:

- **Qty: 8**—2½ x ¼ inch (6.4 cm x 6 mm) ***supports***

Mark your four ***legs*** in 1-inch (2.5-cm) intervals with a pencil. On a cutting mat, lay two ***legs*** down spaced 2 inches (5 cm) apart.

Glue a ***support*** across the top of your two legs then three more just below each 1-inch (2.5-cm) mark.

Repeat with the remaining pieces to create two sides.

Cut the following out of balsa wood:

- **Qty:** 4—1¼ x 2½ inches (3.2 x 6.4 cm) ***shelfy bits***

Stand up your two sides vertically, with the ***supports*** facing in. Glue one of your ***shelfy bits*** between them, resting it on the middle set of ***supports***. Now slide the rest of the ***shelfy bits*** across the remaining supports. Glue them in place.

Paint your shelf brown and add your preservative jars.

Tip for living through the apocalypse: Only share the questionable preserves.

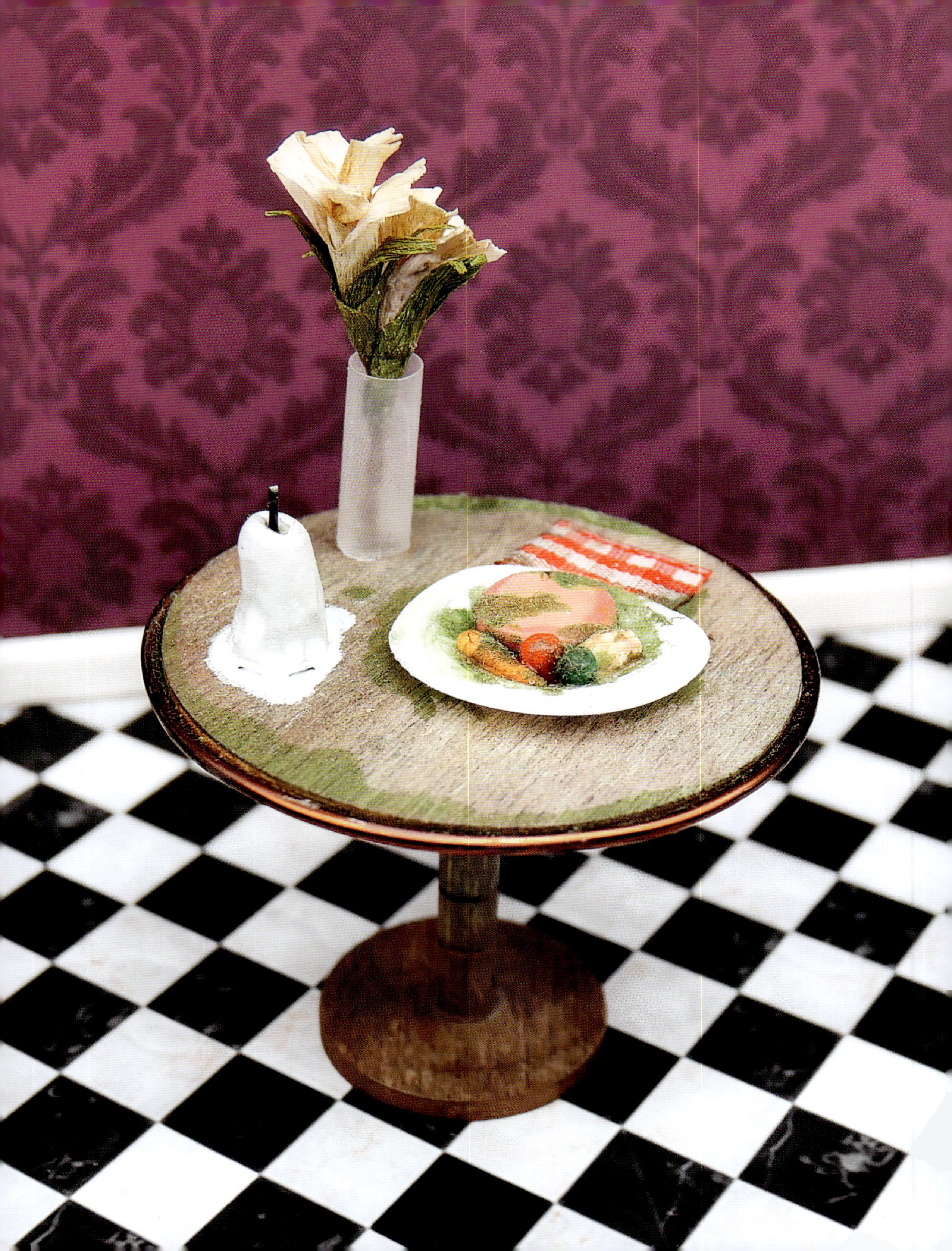

A Lonely Dinner

I assume the company at the end of the world is lacking in a bit of conversation.

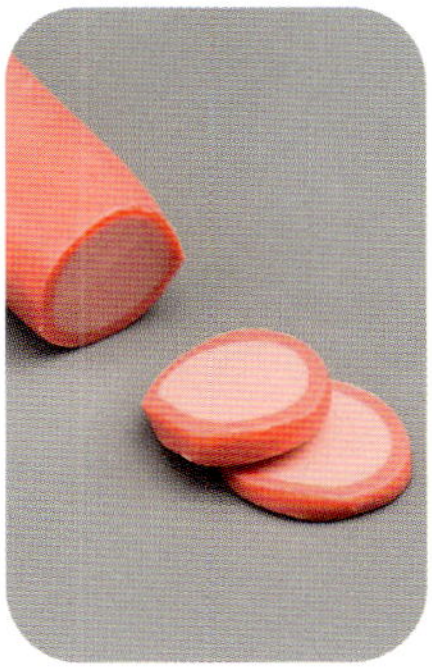

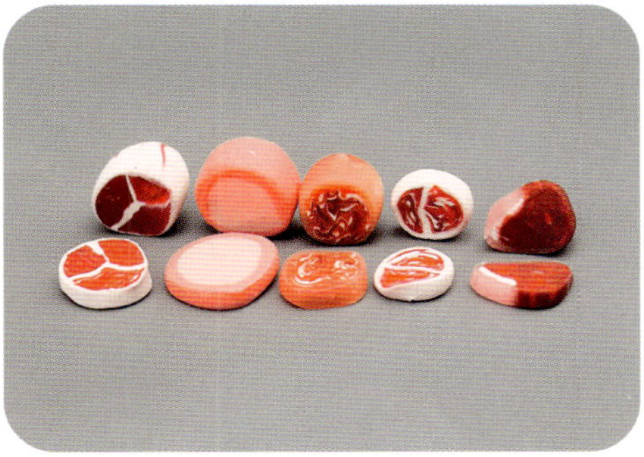

Tools

- rolling pin for clay
- exacto knife, ruler, & cutting mat
- scissors
- sandpaper
- paint
- glue

Meat, Vegetables, & Plate Materials

- polymer clay
- creamer pull tab
- green flocking (if you have it)
- plaid ribbon (optional)
- table (page 130)
- flowers (page 35)
- candle (page 101)

Meat

Roll a light pink log from polymer clay, about 2 x ¾ inch (5 x 1.9 cm).

Take about twice as much clay in a darker pink color, and flatten it with a rolling pin until it's as thick as 3½ business cards. Make this the same width as your pink log and just long enough to wrap around your log once. Trim off any excess.

Roll your log with open palms as evenly as possible until it's about ⅖ inch (1 cm) thick.

Place your log in the freezer for at least 30 minutes.

Take your log directly from the freezer to a cutting mat and slice it thinly with a sharp exacto knife. Bake according to the package instructions.

Play around with different meat variants using this same method. For example: Try combining two or even three logs but with red centers and a thin white rope in the middle for a bone. Try mixing red and white clay to get a marbled meat look.

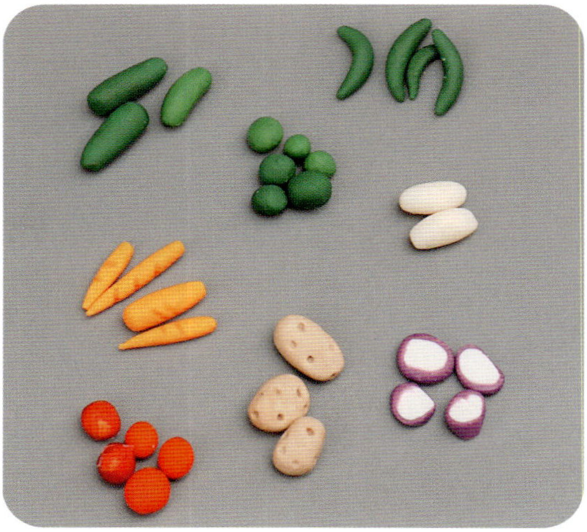

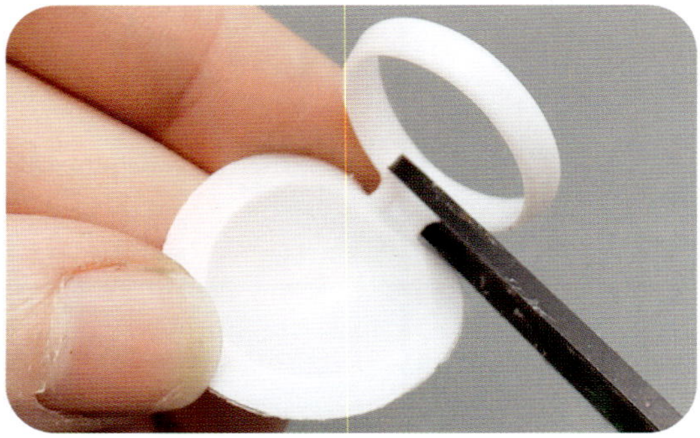

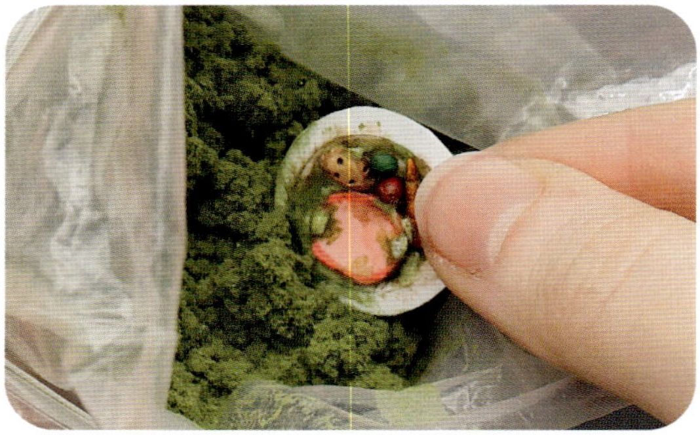

Vegetables

Roll tiny balls and logs of clay in various colors to make miniature veggies, like carrots, peas, green beans, potatoes, PICKLES, etc.

Shape as needed, slightly curved for green beans, skinny point for carrots . . . You get the idea. Bake according to the package instructions.

Plate

Take a creamer pull tab, cut the loop off, and sand the tab. This will be your plate.

Paint the bottom of your plate with watered-down green paint.

Glue a slice of meat on one side and a few tiny veggies on the other.

Paint watered-down brown over the top so that it only oozes in the nooks and crannies. This makes it look like your food has been sitting there for a while, as you would expect in the apocalypse.

Add a few spots of glue around your food and dip it in green flocking to create mold.

Optionally, you can make an adorable little napkin with a piece of plaid ribbon.

Make the table from page 130 and glue your plate down. Add the flowers from page 35 and candle from page 101 to finish off your table. The apocalypse can be rough, so gluing things down is essential!

Fallout Feast

A leftover remnant from the "before times," now it's just a science experiment on what food grows the most mold. My money's on the seven-layer salad!

Tools

- exacto knife, ruler, & cutting mat
- paint
- glue
- wire brush, toothbrush, or pipe cleaner
- sandpaper
- craft glue
- superglue
- pliers/wire cutter
- hammer

Table Materials

- balsa wood
- ¼" (6-mm) or 3⁄16" (5-mm) square dowels

Mugs Materials

- glass fuse
- floral wire
- small washer

Cookies Materials

- polymer clay
- button battery blister pack
- earring backs
- chipboard
- green flocking (optional)

Buns Materials

- polymer clay
- twine/hemp
- smooth cap
- green flocking or green paint

Salad Materials

- dosing syringe
- plastic ring from earring back
- green paper
- polymer clay
- green flocking or green paint

Candlestick Materials

- head pin
- 2 earring backs
- beads
- floral wire
- small washer
- candles (page 101)

Cooking Pot Materials

- 2 pop tabs
- small cap
- shank button
- 4 plates (page 48)
- 1 cutting board (page 160)
- 10 maggots (page 181)

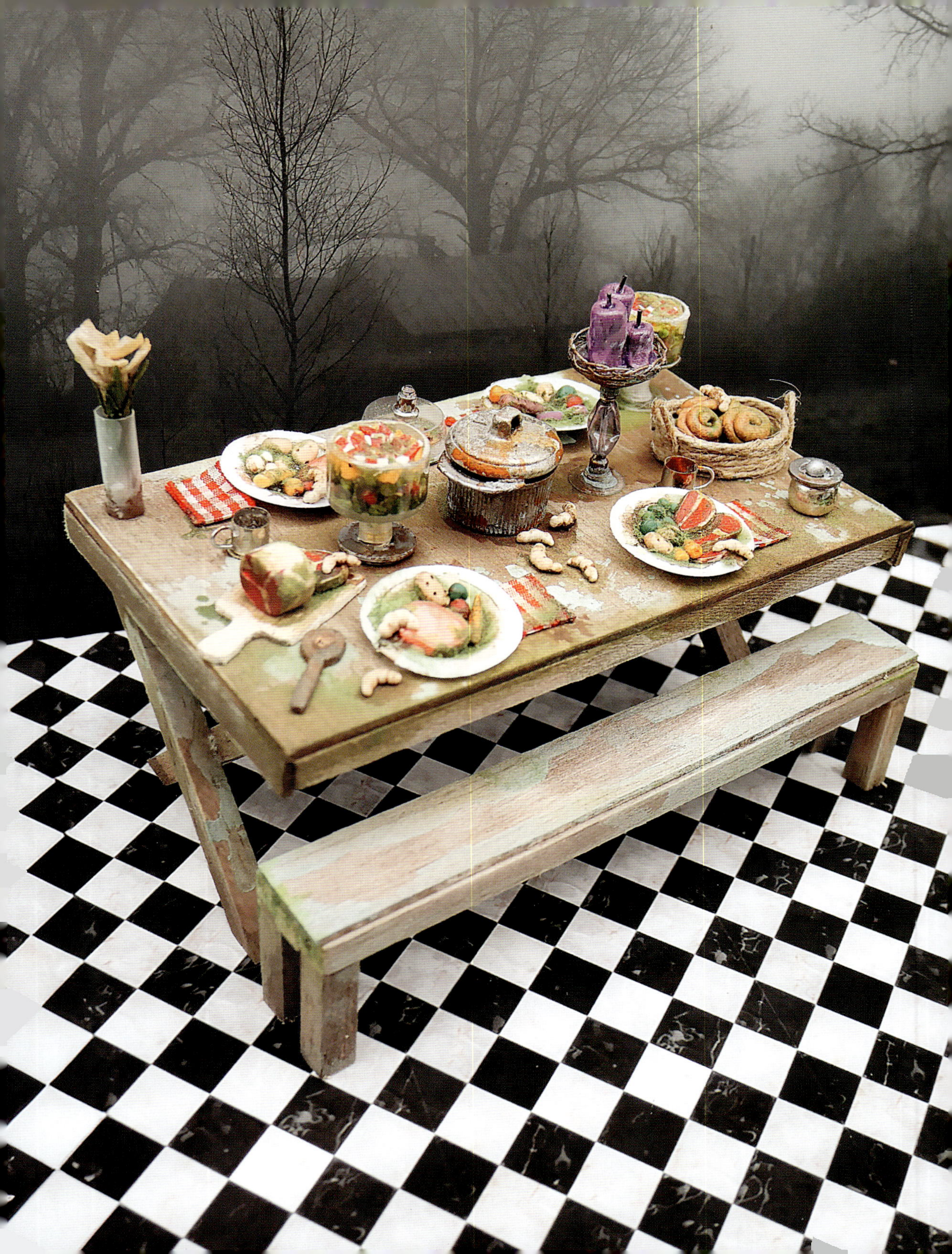

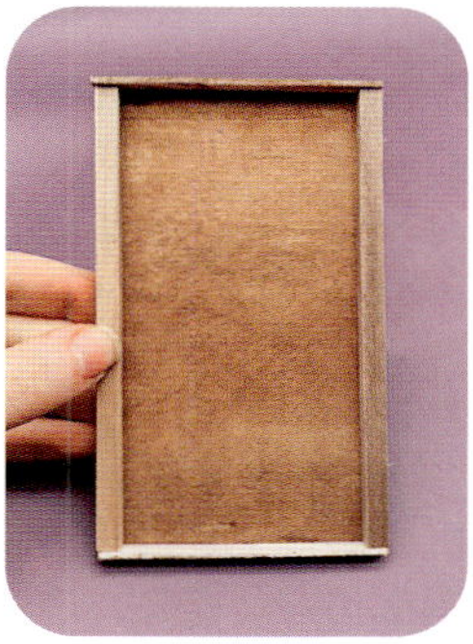

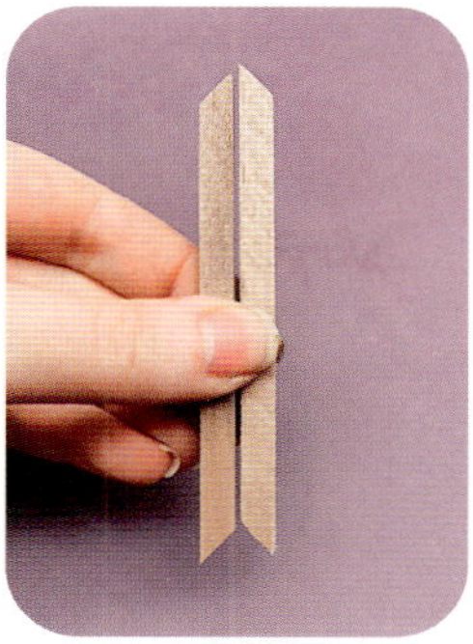

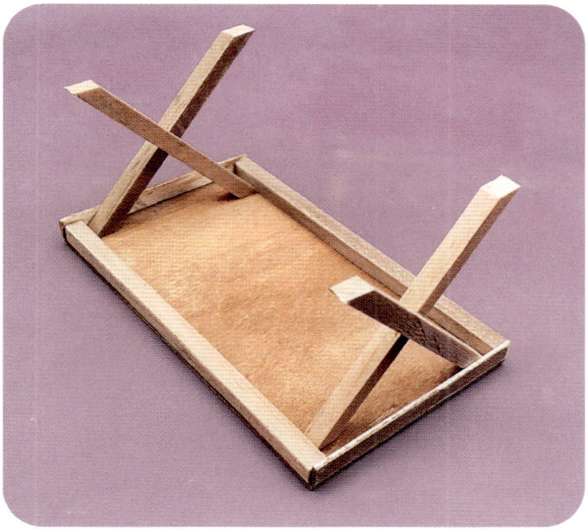

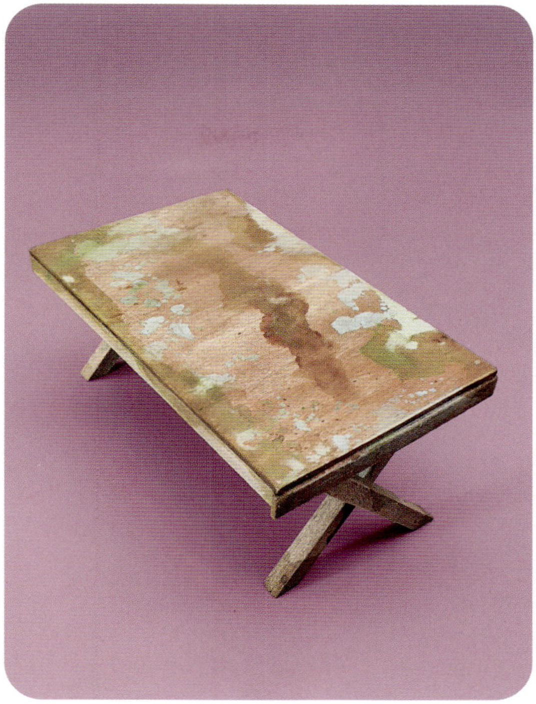

Table

Cut and paint brown the following balsa wood:

- **Qty: 1**—3 x 5 inches (7.6 x 12.7 cm) ***tabletop***
- **Qty: 2**—¼ x ³⁄₁₀ inch (6 x 8 mm) ***short side***

Cut and paint brown the following square dowels:

- **Qty: 2**—5 inches (12.7 cm) ***long side***
- **Qty: 4**—4 inches (10.2 cm) ***legs***

Glue the ***long side*** dowels along the 5-inch (12.7-cm) underside of your ***tabletop*** and the ***short side*** pieces on the 3-inch (7.6-cm) side of your ***tabletop***. Set it aside.

Cut each leg end at a 45° angle (slanting the same on both ends).

Glue the legs to the underside of your ***tabletop*** in the four corners in an X-marks-the-spot shape.

Paint lots of green and brown stains on the top of your table. Because the apocalypse isn't clean.

Let's add a feast to this fallout!

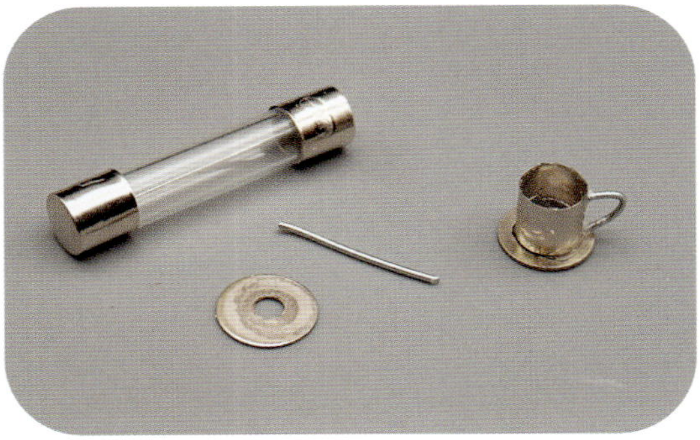

Clay Sizer
Cookies
x1 x3

Mugs

Remove the cap off a glass fuse and glue a wire to the side for a handle. You can even place a washer under it to make a little plate.

Cookies

Flatten your tan ball of clay and texture it with a wire brush, toothbrush, or pipe cleaner.

Roll out a thin piece of brown clay and cut tiny chunks off with an exacto knife for chocolate chips.

Bake according to the package.

Let's add a "cookie cloche." *Which is fun to say . . . try it!*

Cut the dome out of a button battery package (or similar type of package).

Glue an earring back to the top for a handle.

Cut a matching circle out of chipboard for the base.

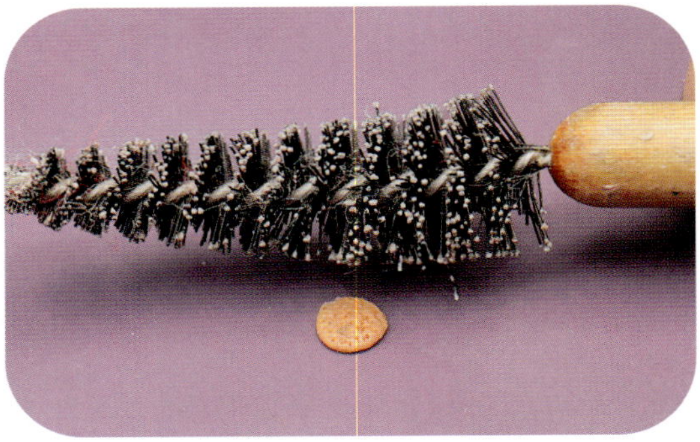

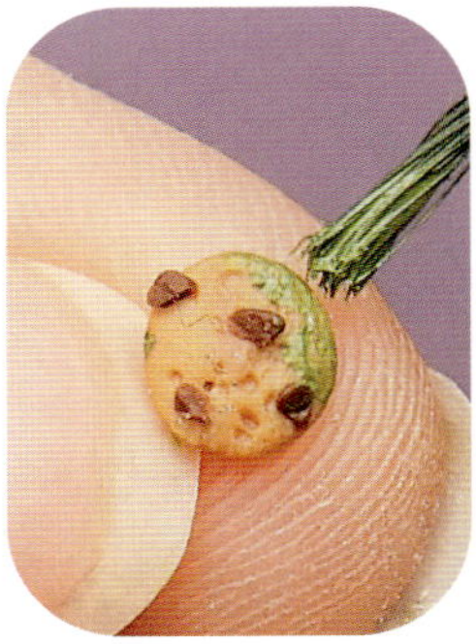

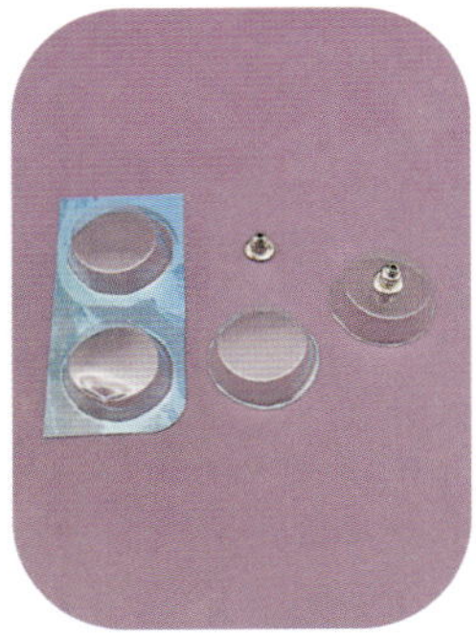

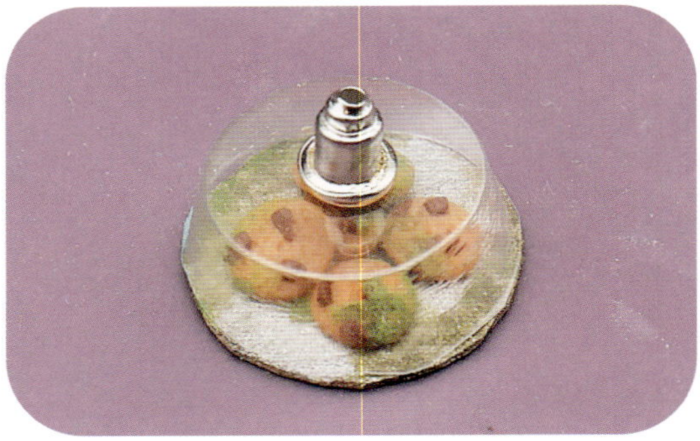

The cloche might keep your cookies from getting dusty in the apocalypse, but it won't keep mold away. Add green paint or flocking to make your cookies apocalypse-tastic!

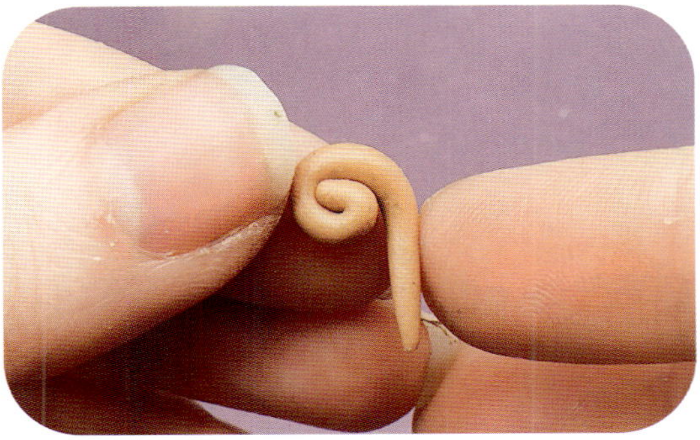

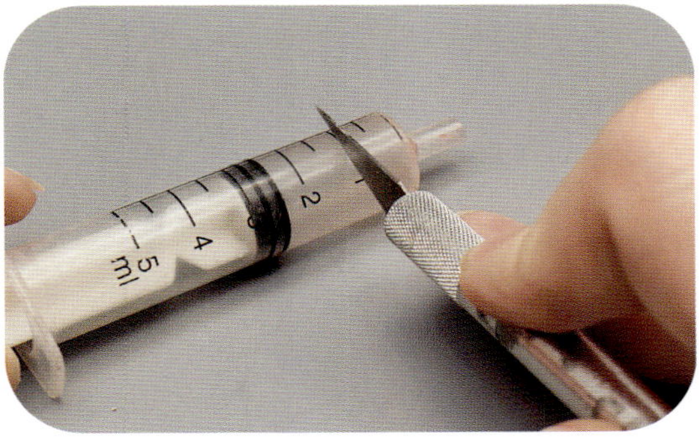

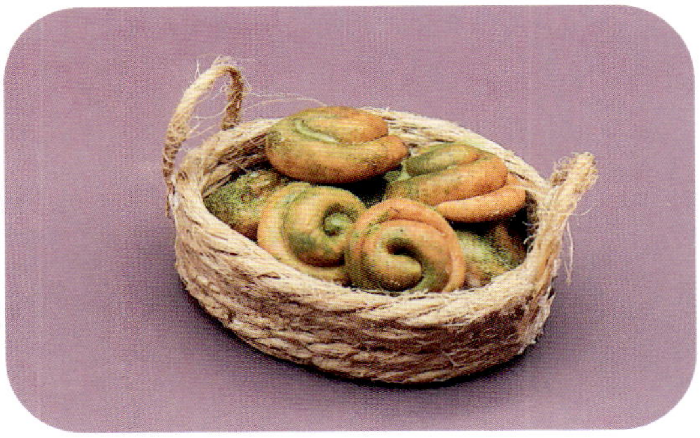

Clay Sizer
Buns
x6

Buns

Snake a pea-sized amount of tan clay and spiral it. Bake your buns . . .

On page 97, we make a similar basket, just make this one shorter and glue handles onto the sides. Like everything else, add green paint or flocking for mold.

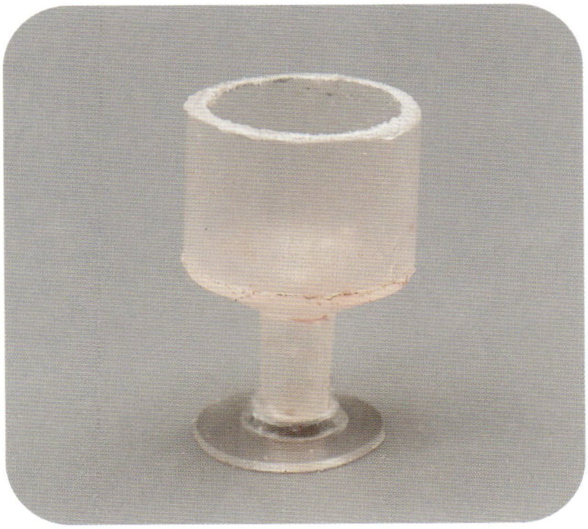

Layered Salad

It's not a true fallout feast without at least seven layers of salad!

Cut the top off a dosing syringe at about the 1-ounce (30-ml) mark. Sand the cut edge if needed and scrape off any markings with your fingernail.

Use the plastic ring from an earring back as a base by popping out the metal part. Glue it onto the nozzle tip.

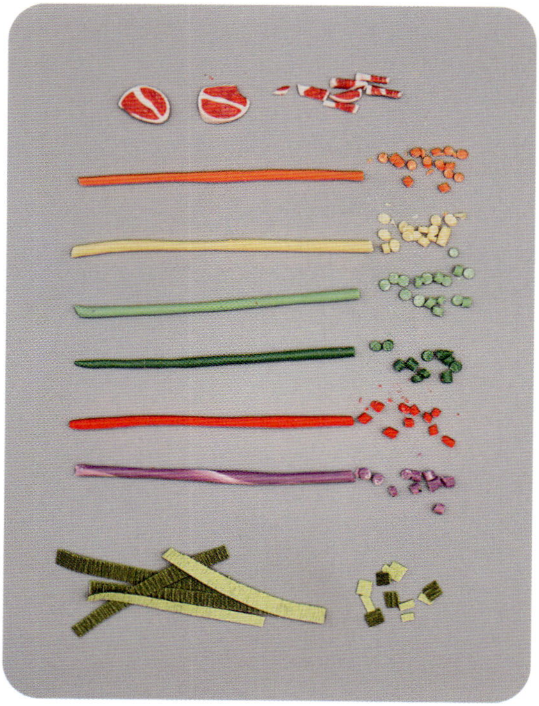

Next, we need to fill the salad bowl. Cover the bottom of your bowl with a layer of craft glue. Cut up some green paper into tiny squares and sprinkle inside.

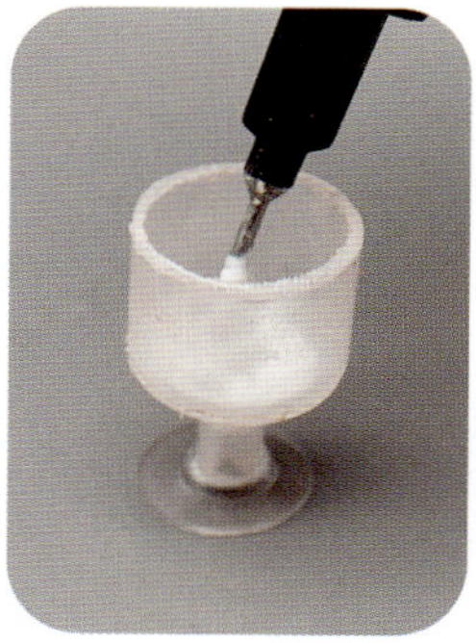

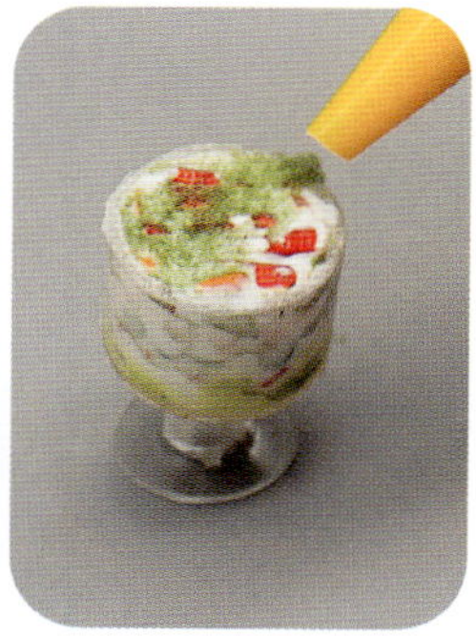

Bake thin strands of polymer clay in salad-y colors (orange, yellow, green, red, purple).

HI-YA them into bits (or use an exacto knife). Layer each color in your salad bowl with craft glue.

If you like bacon, top off your salad with cut up meat from page 47.

There's no way the salad will stay fresh through the apocalypse so spritz on green flocking for, you guessed it, more mold.

Note: *Your salad will take a long time to dry if done all at once. But once it dries, you'll see all of your colorful layers.*

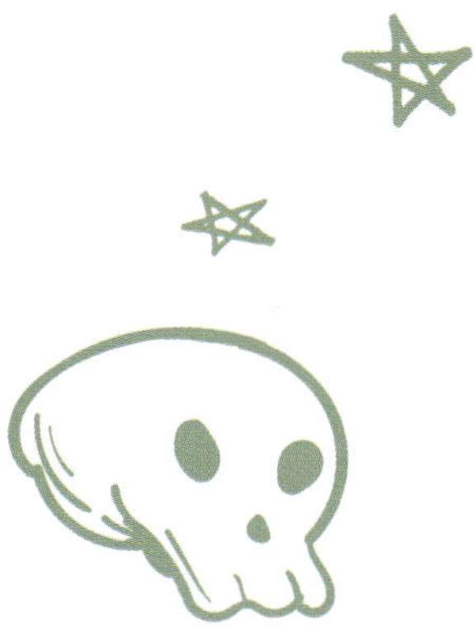

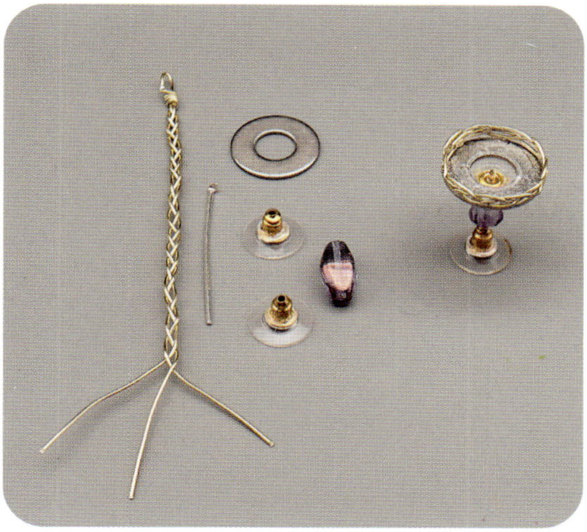

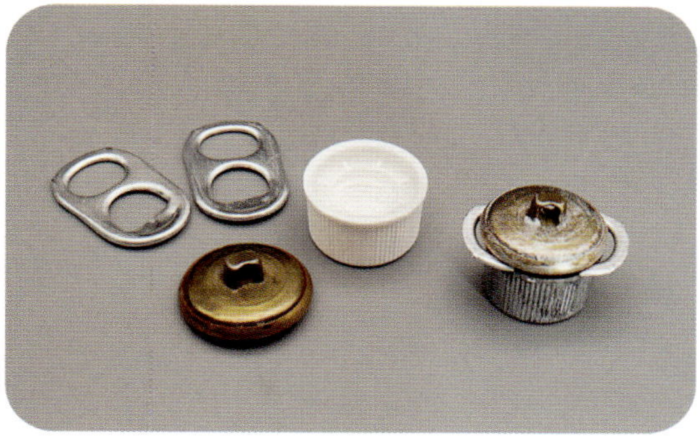

Candlestick

Push a head pin through an earring back (flat side down), a bead, then another earring back (flat side up). Superglue it in place and snip off the excess pin with pliers or a wire cutter. This is the stick part of your candlestick. Set it aside.

Loosely braid floral wire and flatten it with hammer. Glue this around your washer, then glue the washer on your candlestick.

Because there's probably no electricity in the apocalypse add your candle from page 101.

Cooking Pot

Cut the loops off of two pop tabs with a wire cutter for handles. Glue one on each side of a small cap and stick a slightly larger shank button on top for a lid.

Paint it silver with rusty patches, like it's been long forgotten.

Glue all of your items to the top of your table so they won't move. Add plates from page 48, a cutting board from page 160, and some maggots to top it off from page 181.

Now we're ready for a Fallout Feast! Just don't forget the pickles!

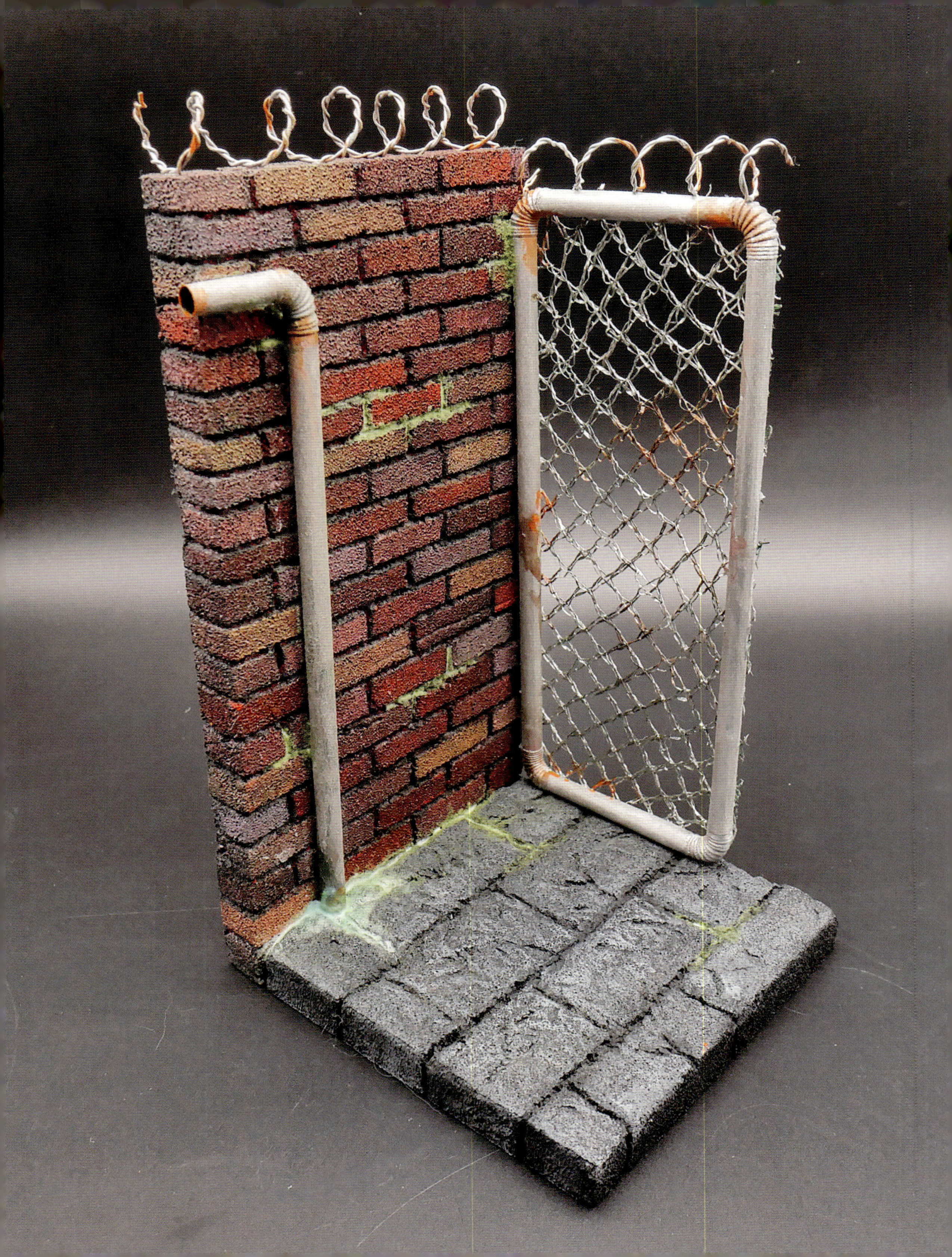

Shank Alley

Shank Alley is a lovely place if you like shanking people or people shanking you. Either way, I don't judge. Okay, maybe a little.

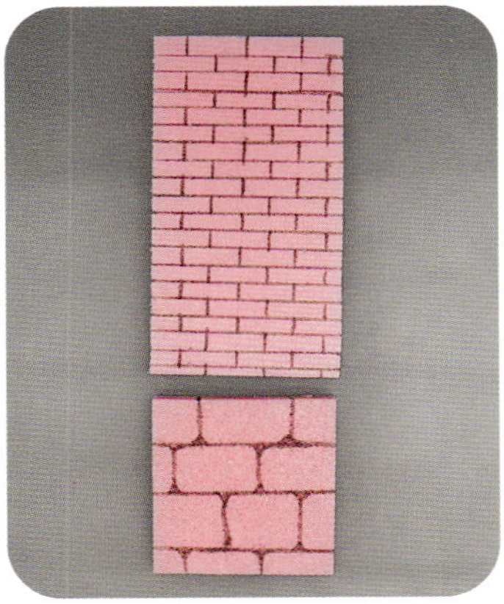

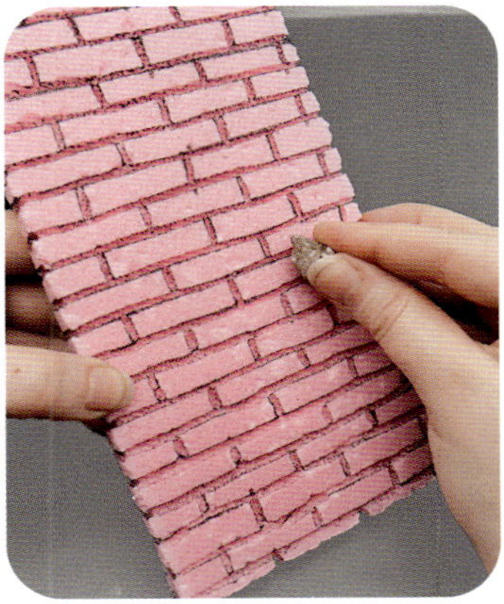

Wall/Floor

Cut the following out of XPS foam:

- **Qty: 1**—4 x 8 inches (10.2 x 20.3 cm) ***wall***
- **Qty: 1**—4 x 4 inches (10.2 x 10.2 cm) ***floor***

With a ruler and marker, draw bricks on your foam pieces. Keep them organic, no need to be perfect! Go for ¼-inch (6-mm) bricks for the wall and chunky ¾-inch (1.9-cm) bricks for the floor.

Once you're happy with the way it looks, carve the lines in the foam with a pencil or wood burner (on low). Don't forget to wrap the bricks around the edges.

For a brick-like texture, smash a rough rock along the surface of your foam. It's great for working out anger too . . .

Paint the cracks black, then layer on reds, browns, oranges for the wall and grays for the ***floor***. Let them dry.

Tip: *Using a wood burner for the cracks makes dry time shorter. It makes fewer "holes" for paint to seep into.*

Tools

- exacto knife, ruler, & cutting mat
- marker
- pencil (or wood burner)
- rough rock
- paint
- hot glue
- scissors
- silver spray paint
- superglue
- glue
- pliers/wire cutter

Wall/Floor Materials

- XPS foam
- bendy straw
- green flocking

Fence Materials

- 4 bendy straws
- mesh produce bag

Barbed Wire Material

- floral wire

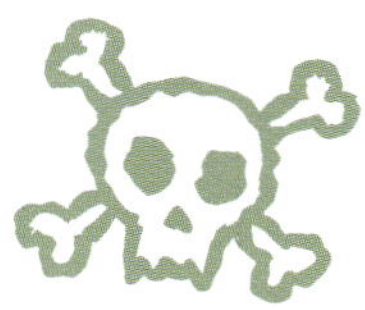

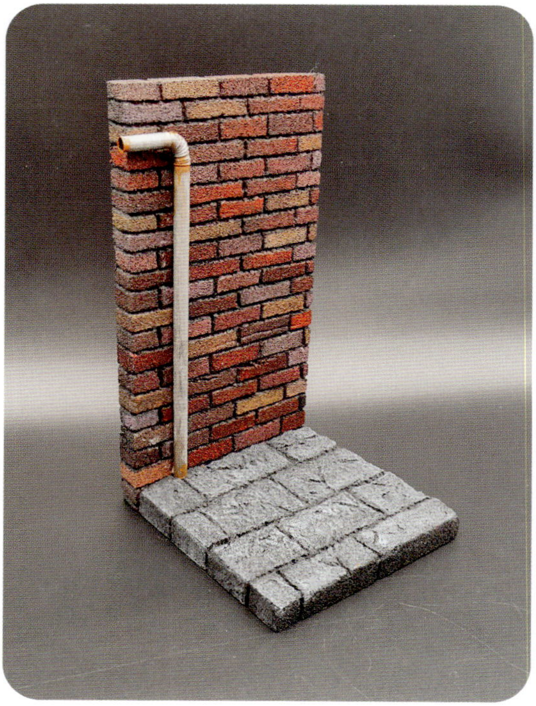

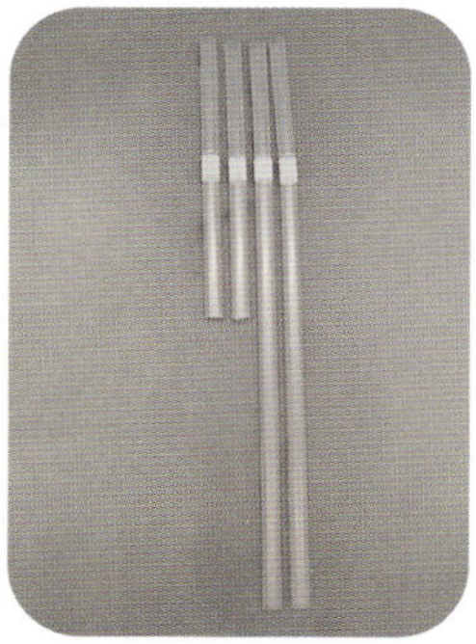

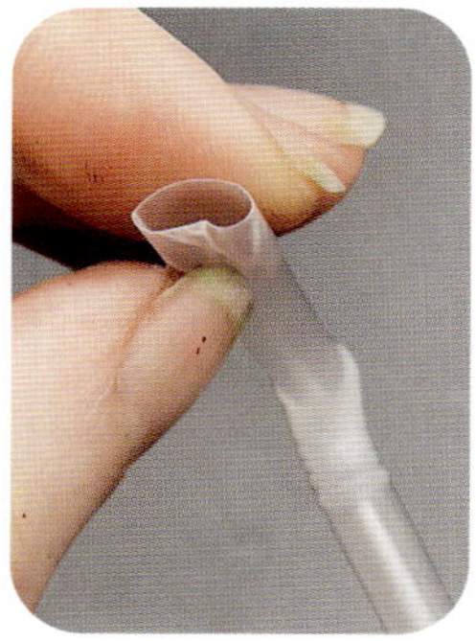

Hot glue your ***floor*** to the ***wall***.

Cut a bendy straw so that the long end nearly touches the ***floor*** of your alley. This will be a little drainage pipe.

Spray paint it silver, then dry brush orange paint on the ends of your pipe.

Glue this on your ***wall*** so that the hole on the short end is flush with the left edge of the ***wall***.

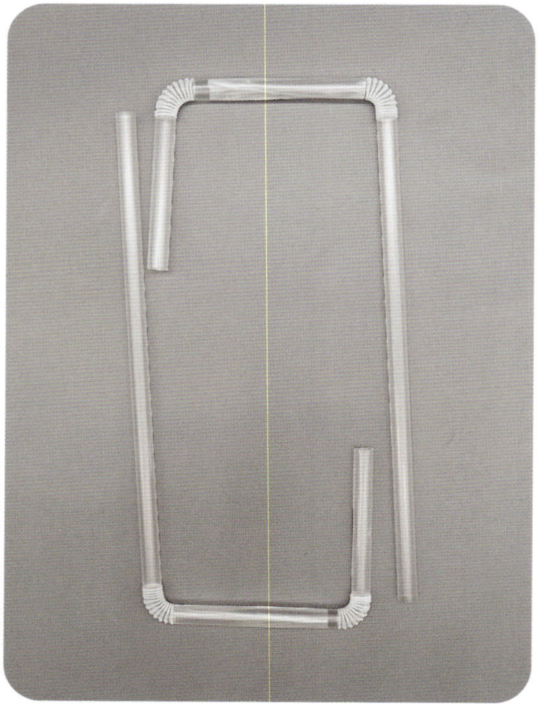

Fence

Snip the long end of a bendy straw to 2 inches (5 cm). Fold the opening of it and shove it into the short end of an uncut straw. Push it until it's as far in as possible.

Repeat this process until you have two J-shaped straws.

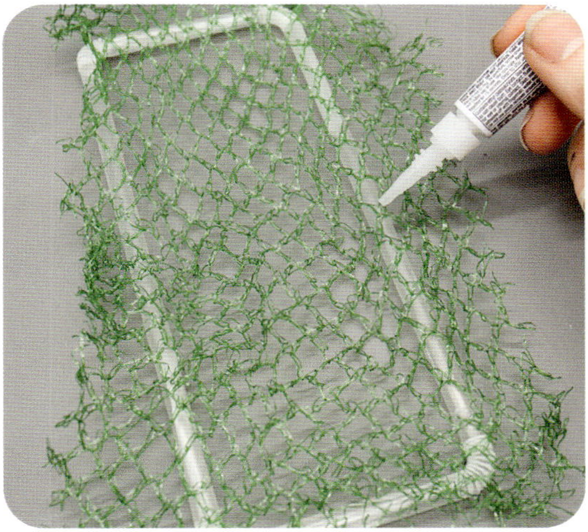

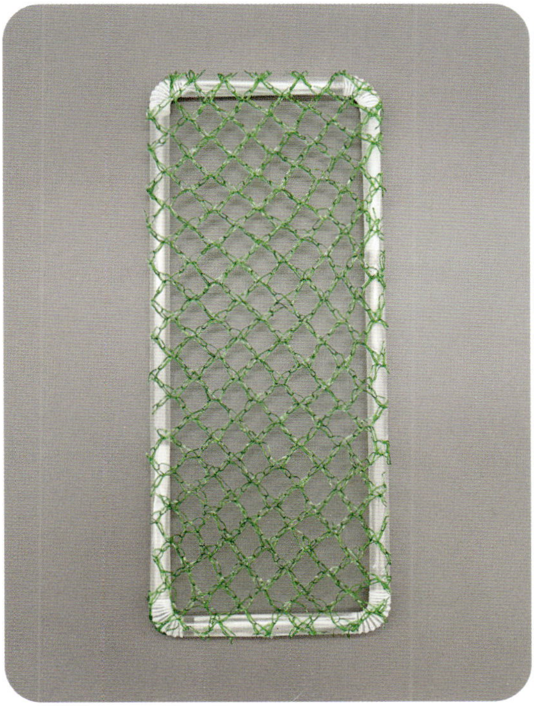

Shove your two J straws together to form a rectangle.

Take your mesh produce bag and cut it so that it's larger than your rectangle.

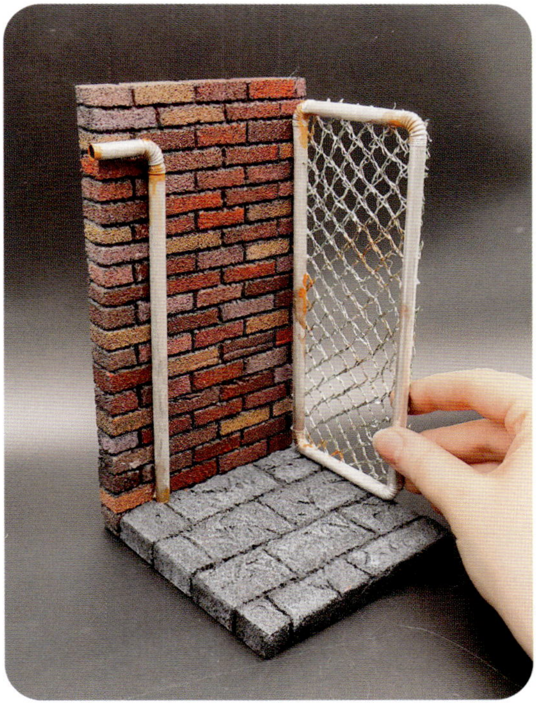

With your straw rectangle flat on the table, lay your mesh produce bag over top. Make sure it's straight. Start on the long edge and superglue each place where the bag meets the straws. You'll have to be patient because it might want to unglue itself, but once it dries, it should stay in place.

Work your way around the frame, pulling tightly as you go. Let this fully dry. This might take a while, especially if you got a little over-enthusiastic with the glue. Then trim off any excess mesh.

Spray paint both sides of your fence silver, then add a few dabs of orange and brown to make it appear rusty and worn.

Glue your finished fence on the right side of your alley.

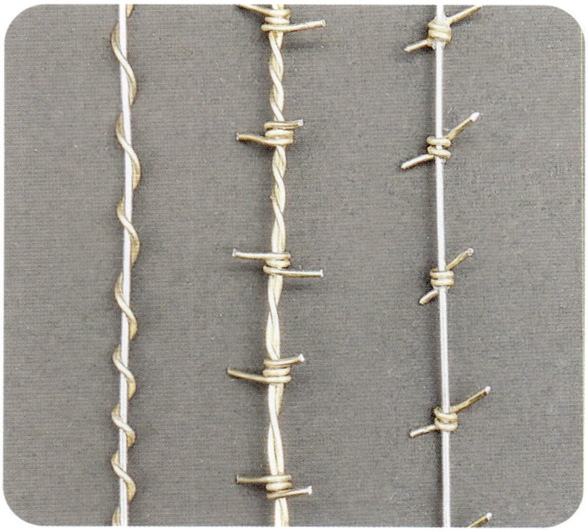

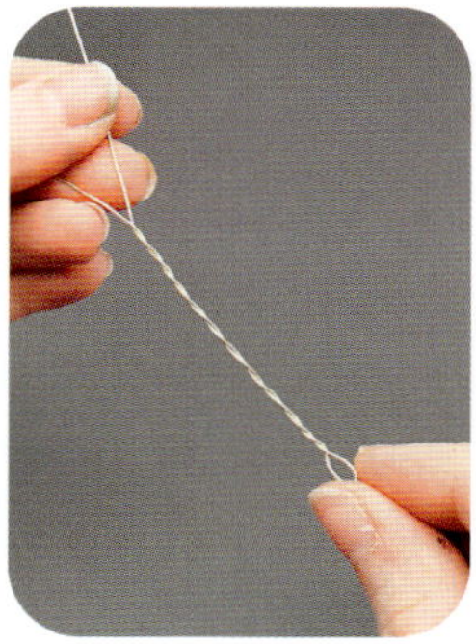

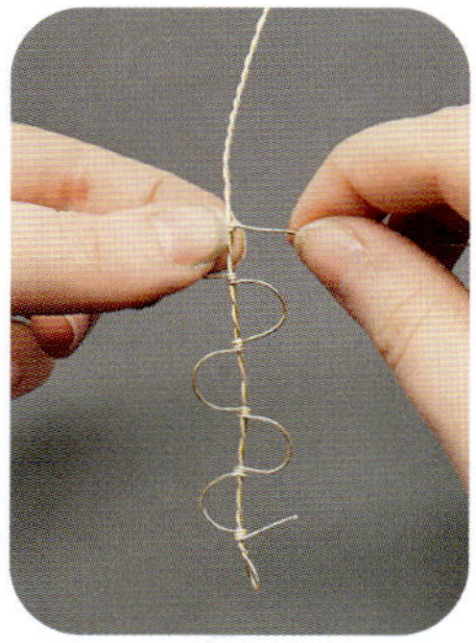

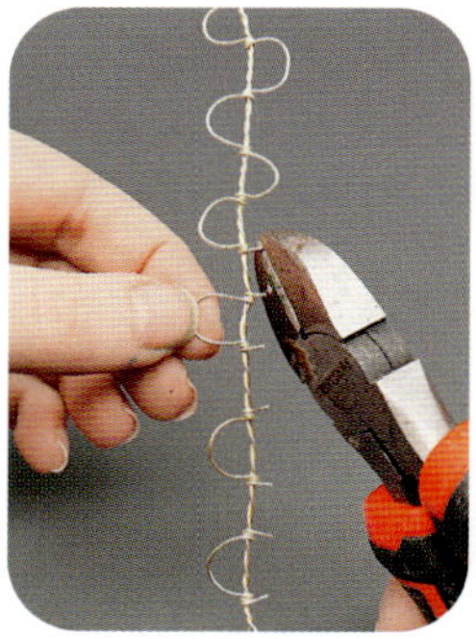

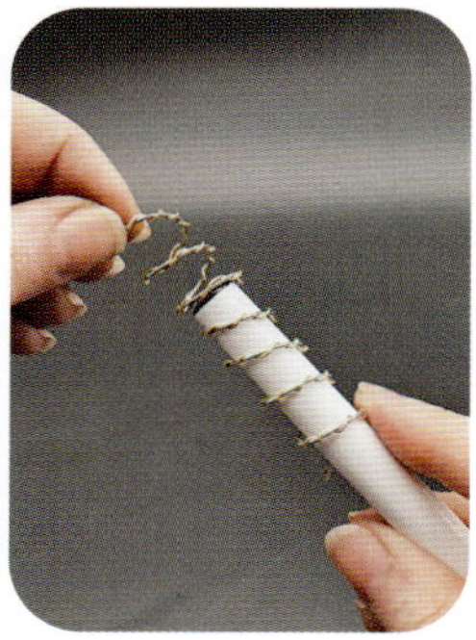

Barbed Wire

Because no shady alley is complete without barbed wire! Start with about an arm's length of floral wire and fold it in half. Twist it together all the way down. This is your basic barbed wire.

BUT, if you want something a bit more post-apocalyptic, use the same twisted wire then take another piece of floral wire and wrap it tightly around the twisted wire three times. Then make a loop and move about a finger's width down and repeat. Keep going until you reach the end. It should look like a string of $s.

Put a tiny drop of superglue on each wrapped section to hold it in place. Once your glue is dry, snip each loop in half and trim the spikes to ¼ inch (6 mm). Bend your spikes outward and you've made yourself some gnarly barbed wire!

Wrap your finished wire (either version) tightly around a thick marker, then slide it off.

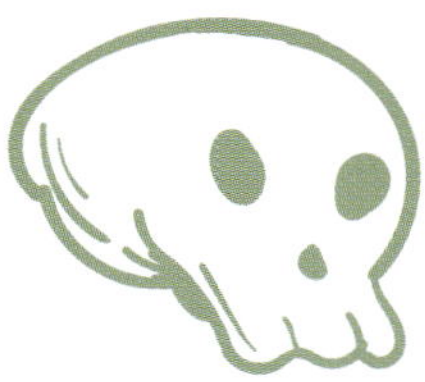

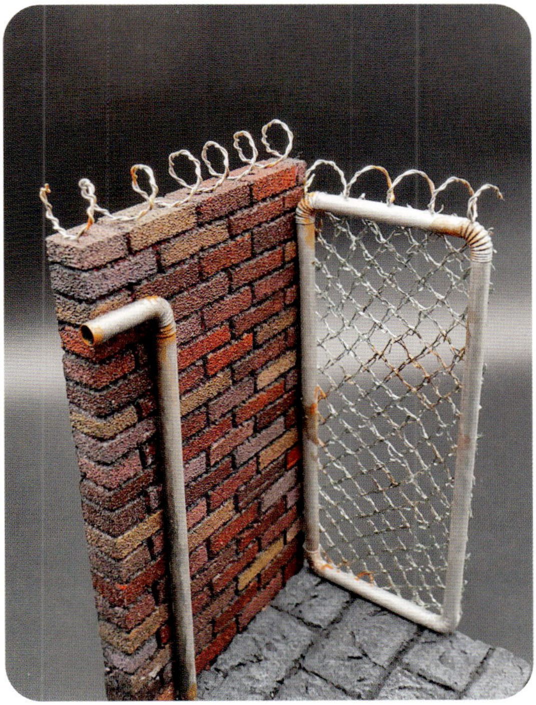

Gently pull your coils apart and glue them along your ***wall*** and fence.

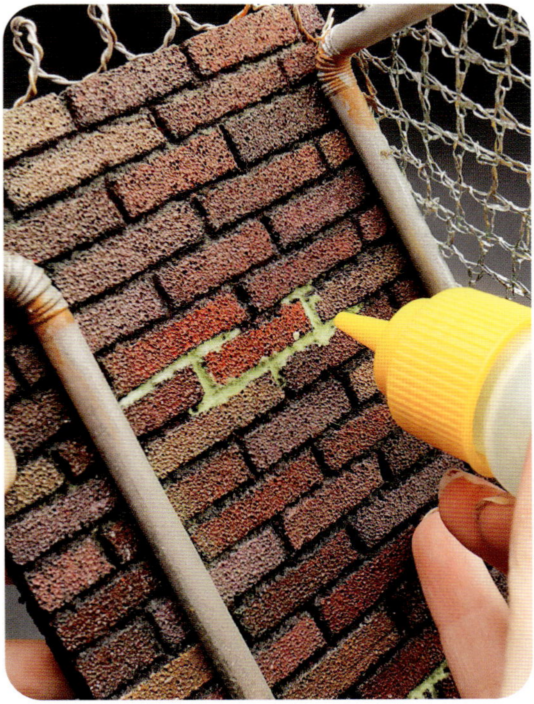

For final touches to your alley, glue green flocking in between your bricks and at the base of your drainpipe to make it look like moss. Now you're ready for some shanking in Shank Alley!

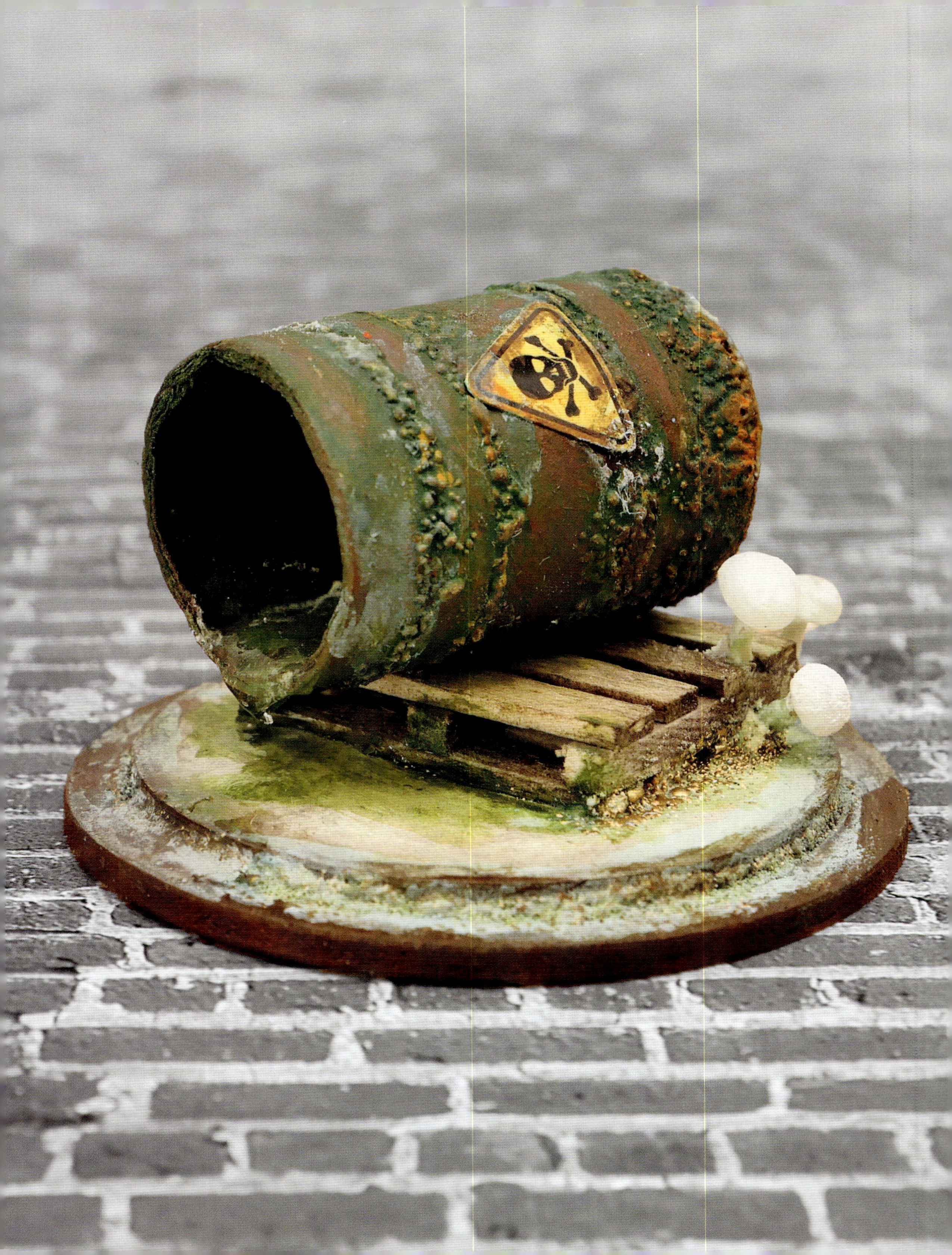

Toxic Waste Barrel

Ground zero to the apocalypse! Toxic waste in a barrel! We *could* sue whoever dumped this, but good luck! Even the lawyers are all zombies now.

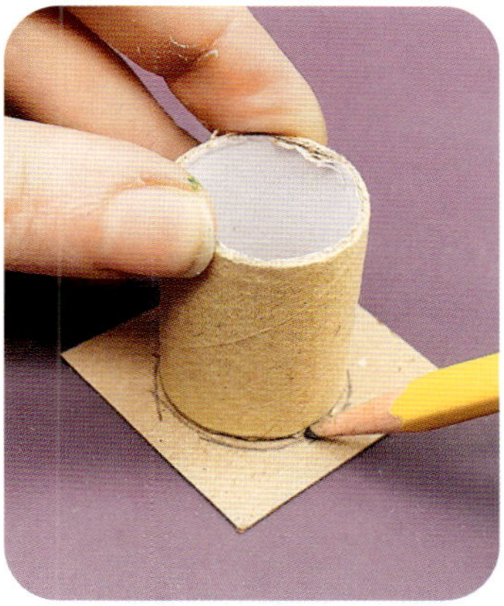

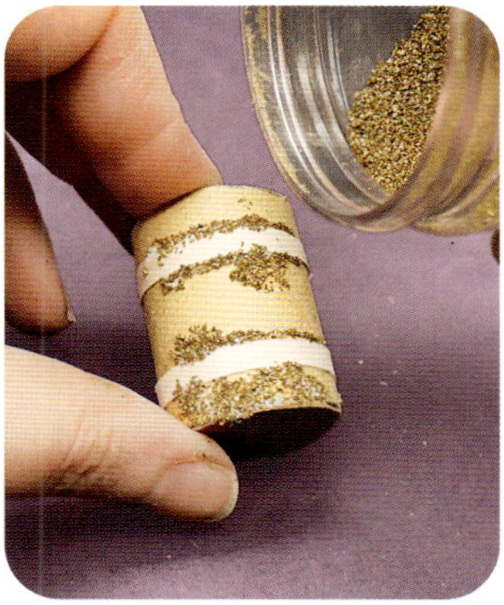

Tools

- exacto knife, ruler, & cutting mat
- pencil
- glue
- craft glue
- heat gun
- paint
- silicone mat
- hot glue
- superglue

Barrel Materials

- 1" (2.5-cm)-wide cardboard tube)
- chipboard
- paper
- coarse embossing powder
- balsa wood
- 3⁄16" (5-mm) square dowels
- 2" (5-cm) wooden circle
- clear gloss or epoxy resin (optional)

Mushrooms Materials

- hot glue
- 3 toothpicks
- glow powder (optional)

Barrel

Cut your cardboard tube so it's 2 inches (5 cm) long. This will be your barrel.

Trace the end of your cardboard tube onto a scrap of chipboard. Cut it out and glue it to the end of the tube to cap off your barrel.

Cut two thin strips of paper ¼ inch (6 mm) wide. Wrap two around the outside of your barrel about ¼ inch (6 mm) from either end.

Smear craft glue around the edges of the paper and the bottom of your barrel, then sprinkle on your coarse embossing powder. Tap off any excess powder and heat it up with a heat gun to create a raised bubbly texture.

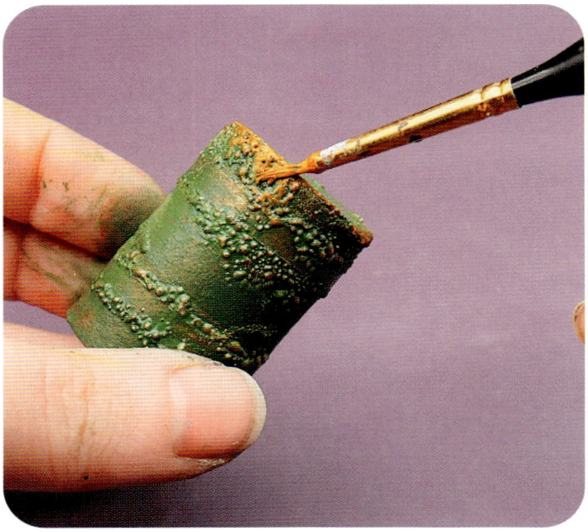

Paint the entire barrel a toxic green color and dab on some orange and brown in the bubbly areas to make it look extra rusty and corrosive.

Pallet

Let's build a pallet for the toxic waste barrel to sit on.

Cut the following out of balsa wood:

- **Qty: 8**—⅕ x 1¼ inches (6 mm x 3.2 cm)

Cut the following 3⁄16-inch (5-mm) square dowels:

- **Qty: 3**—1 inch (2.5 cm)

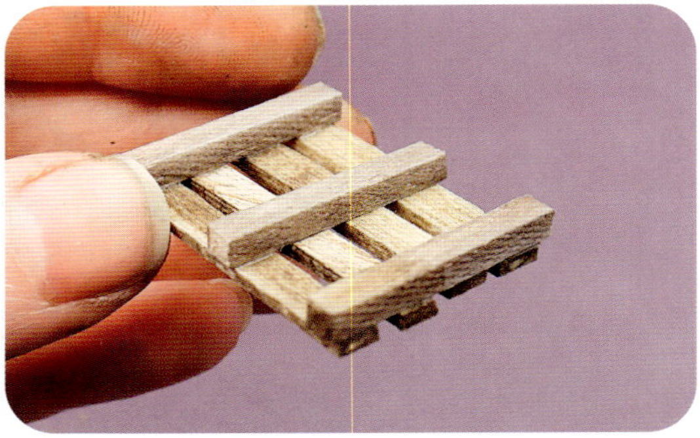

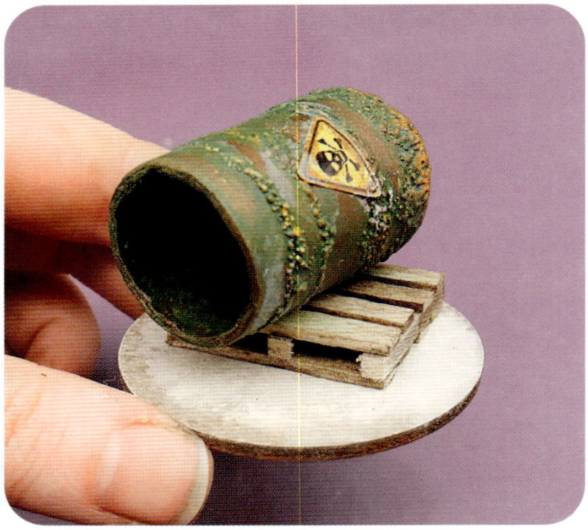

Glue the three dowels spaced evenly crisscross on top of four balsa wood strips. Then glue the remaining four balsa strips crisscross on top of the dowels to match the bottom layer. SHWABAM! Tiny pallet!

Glue your barrel on the pallet (tipped over) then glue the pallet to a 2-inch (5-cm) wooden circle.

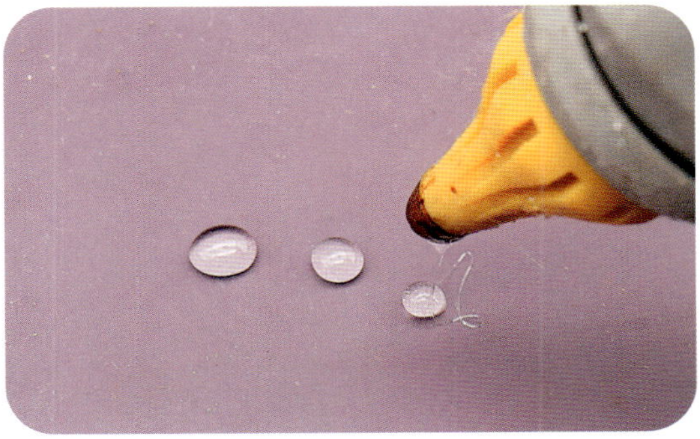

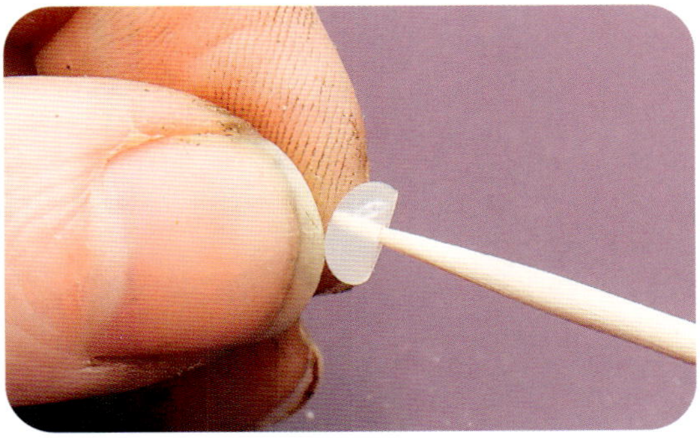

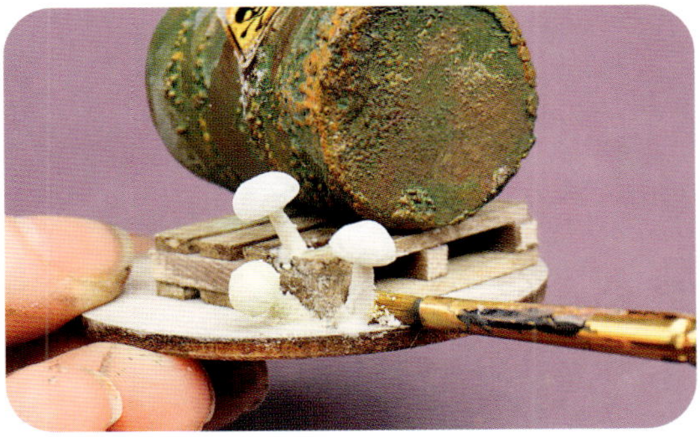

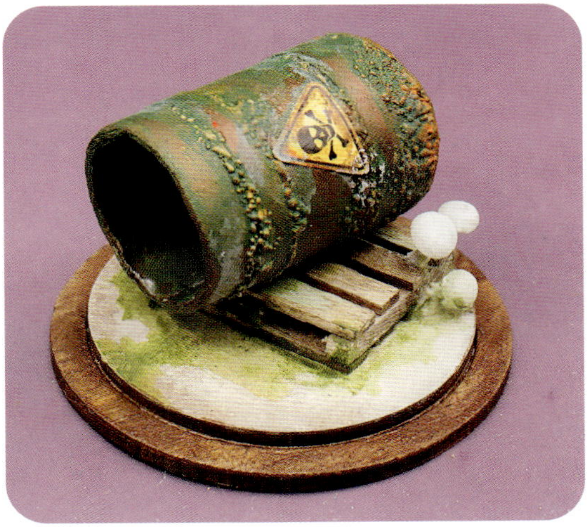

Mushrooms

I think it's time for some radioactive mushrooms! Working on your silicone mat, squeeze three to four dots of hot glue the size of pencil erasers. Let your glue cool just enough so they're not sticky. Peel them up.

Quickly before the glue hardens fully, poke the pointy end of a toothpick into the flat side of each glue dot to make a mushroom stem. Add a drop of superglue to hold each one together.

Dip your mushrooms in white paint and, while the paint is still wet, dip them in glow-in-the-dark powder if you have it. Once dry, cut your toothpicks to about ¼ inch (6 mm) and glue your mushrooms around your barrel.

For extra toxicity, add some crusty glow-in-the-dark powder along the edges of the pallet and inside your barrel.

If you want your barrel to appear like it's leaking something truly nasty, add a little gloss sealant or epoxy resin to the inside. You can even make it look like it's dripping out of the opening.

If you're worried about a lawsuit, slap on a toxic label to the side of your barrel. This will let everyone know to stay far, far away!

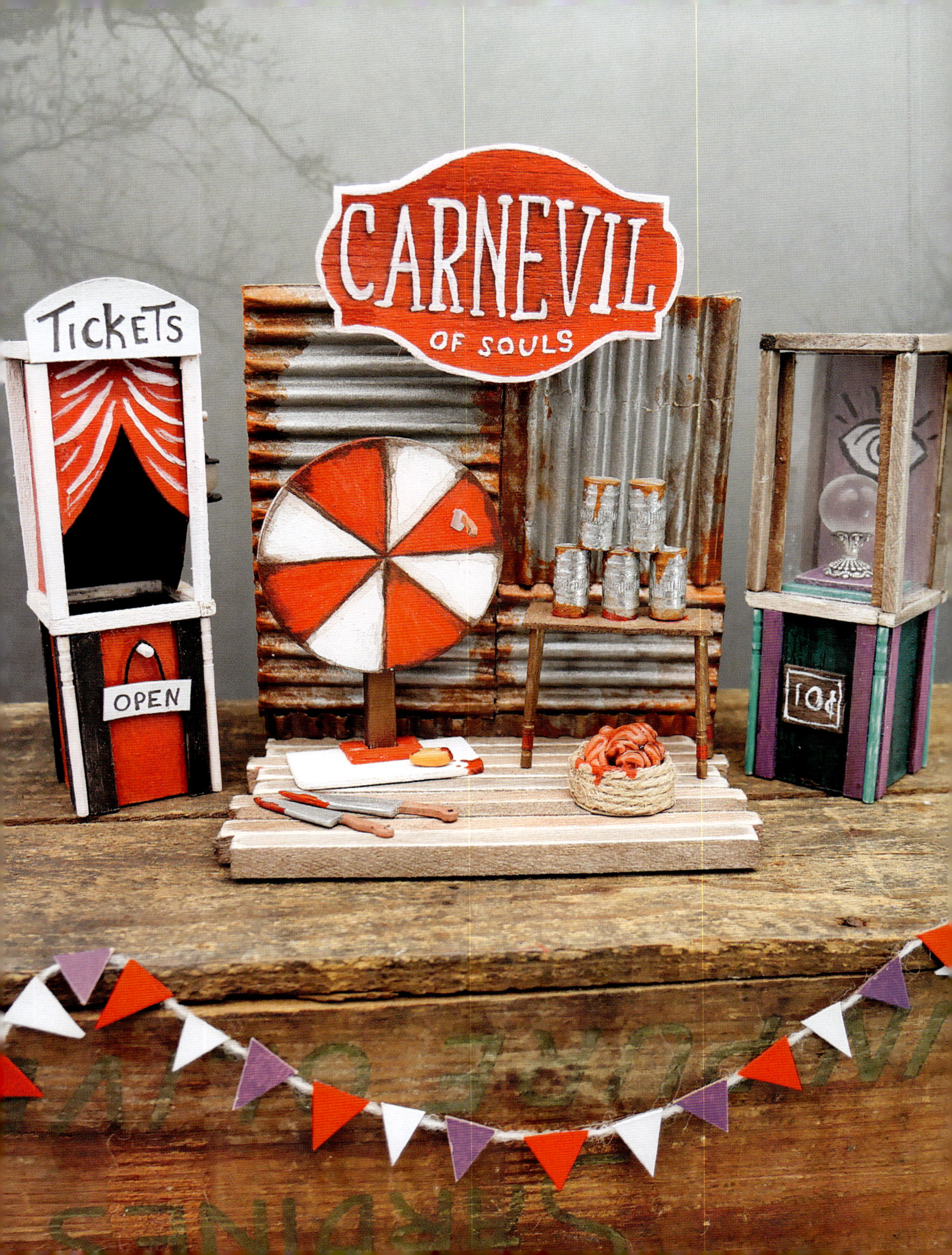
TICKETS
CARNEVIL
OF SOULS
OPEN

Carn-EVIL

If you find yourself buying a ticket to Carn-EVIL, be careful with the rides and games! You can easily lose more than just money. Legend has it the man who now runs Carn-EVIL (Steve) used to be a regular customer. Until he lost a bet!

What was the bet you ask? A game of *Brain Ball.* (Which is *totally* not rigged.) With one toss of the brain, he lost more than just his pride; he lost his soul! *Okay, but sidenote . . . touching brains is really, really icky, so it's no wonder he lost!*

Steve is now the (not so proud) owner of Carn-EVIL and is forced to collect the souls of unsuspecting players. For at Carn-EVIL, the "fun" never ends! Care to test your knife-throwing skills? How about a ride on some DOOMED balloons? No? Aww, come on! "Live" a little!

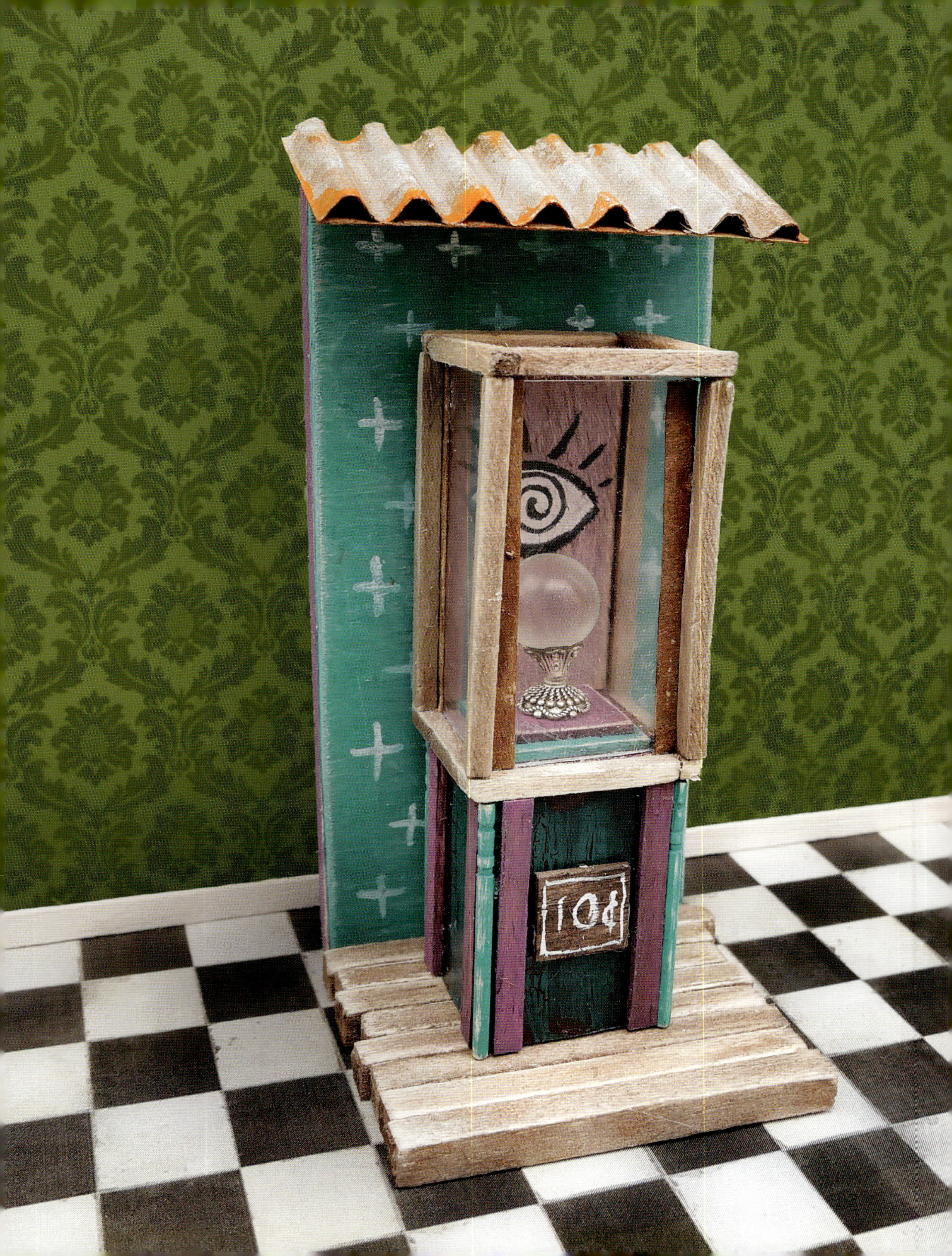
10¢

Fortune Teller

For one low, low price of 10¢, this teller will predict your fortune *and* your misfortune. WHAT A DEAL!!!

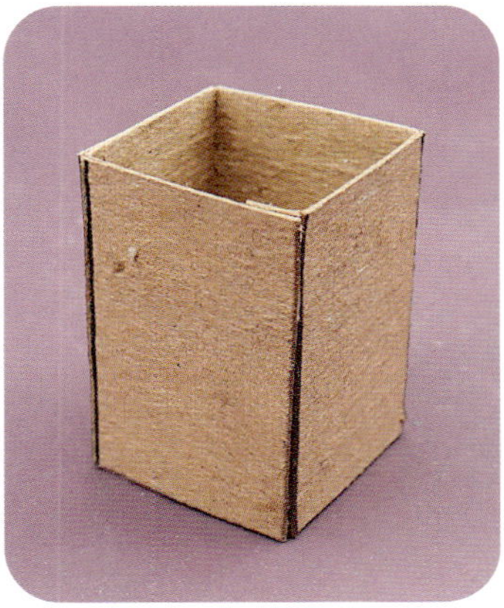

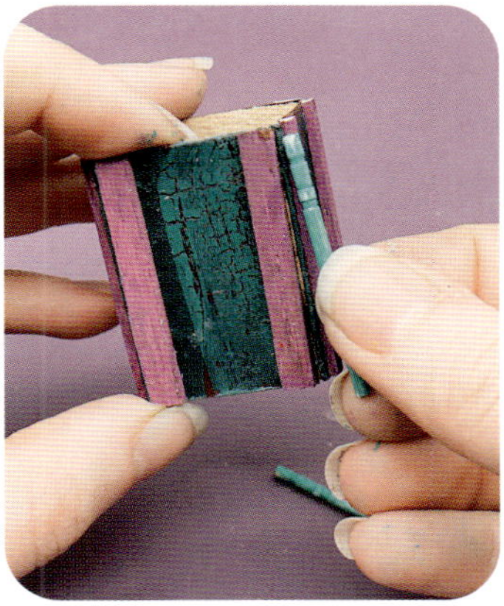

Tools

- exacto knife, ruler, & cutting mat
- glue
- paint
- superglue

Booth Materials

- chipboard
- balsa wood
- 4 toothpicks
- ⅛" (3-mm) square dowels
- thin clear plastic
- 2 bead caps
- clear marble

Stage Materials

- balsa wood
- ¼" (6-mm) square dowels
- corrugated cardboard

Booth

Cut the following out of chipboard. There's a template on page 214 for reference.

- **Qty: 1**—4¼ x 1½ inches (10.8 x 3.8 cm) ***cabinet***

Cut the following out of balsa wood:

- **Qty: 8**—1½ x ¼ (3.8 cm x 6 mm) ***cabinet edges***

On your cabinet piece, score four lines 1 inch (2.5 cm) apart, leaving a cute ¼-inch (6-mm) tab for gluing. Fold this into a cabinet cube shape and glue the tab on the inside. Paint it teal (or whatever).

Paint your eight ***cabinet edges*** purple (or whatever) and glue them along the edges of your cabinet.

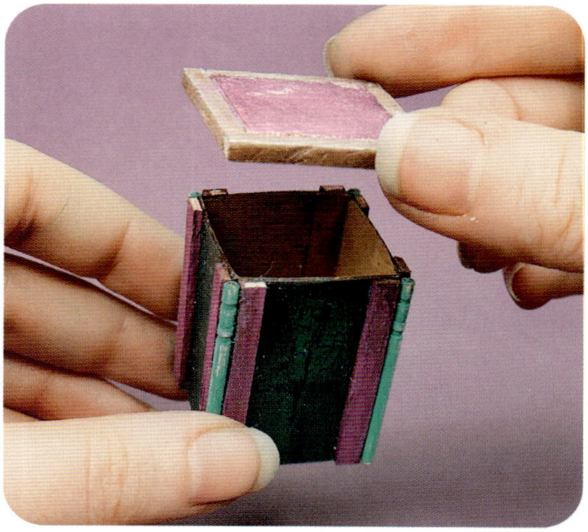

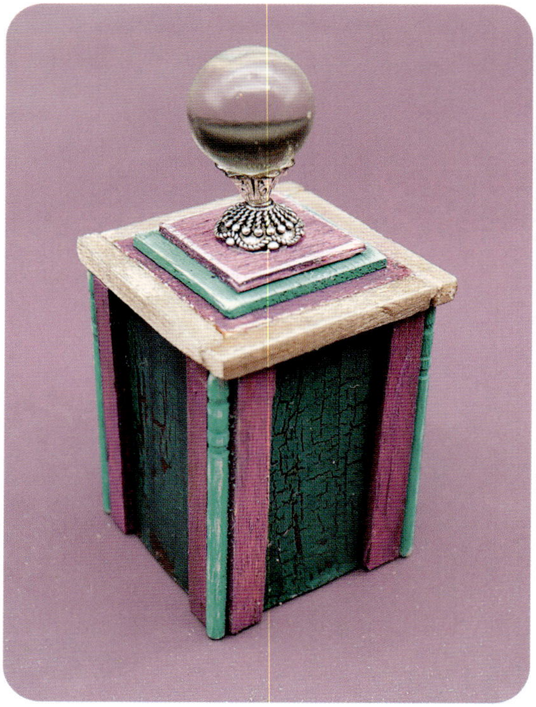

Paint four toothpicks turquoise (or whatever) and trim them to 1½ inches (3.8 cm) long. Glue them between these ***cabinet edges*** on the corners of your ***cabinet***. This will be your **cabinet base**.

Cut the following out of balsa wood:

- **Qty: 1**—1 x 1 inch (2.5 x 2.5 cm) ***tabletop***
- **Qty: 1**—⅘ x ⅘ inch (2 x 2 cm) ***large tier***
- **Qty: 1**—7⁄10 x 7⁄10 inch (1.8 x 1.8 cm) ***small tier***
- **Qty: 1**—2 x 1 inch (5 x 2.5 cm) ***case back***
- **Qty: 1**—1 x 1 inch (2.5 x 2.5 cm) ***case top***

Cut the following out of ⅛-inch (3-mm) square dowels:

- **Qty: 4**—1 inch (2.5 cm) ***table frame***
- **Qty: 4**—2 inch (5 cm) ***case edges***
- **Qty: 4**—1 inch (2.5 cm) ***top frame***

Cut the following out of chipboard:

- **Qty: 4**—2 x ¼ inch (5 cm x 6 mm) ***case joints***

Cut the following out of thin clear plastic:

- **Qty: 3**—2 x 1 inch (5 x 2.5 cm) ***case panels***

Paint your 1 x 1-inch (2.5 x 2.5-cm) ***tabletop*** piece purple and frame it with your four ***table frame*** pieces. (By frame it, I mean glue dowels around the outside of your square.) Glue it on top of your cabinet base.

Paint the ***large tier*** turquoise and ***small tier*** purple, then glue them in the center of your ***tabletop*** to create a stepped stage.

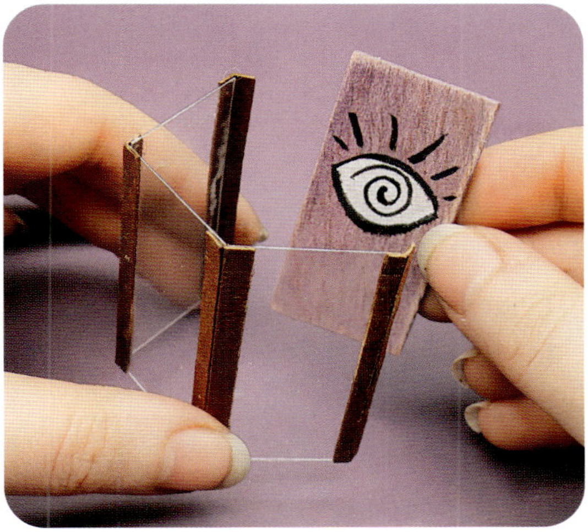

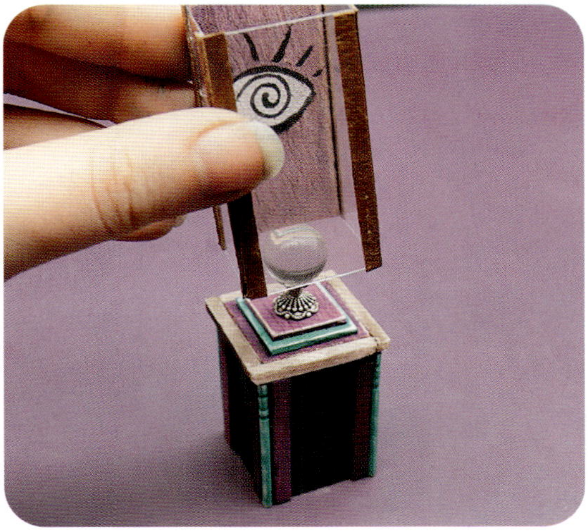

Next is the most important part: the crystal ball! Glue your two bead caps together with the small openings touching. This will be the base for the ball. Glue this onto the tabletop.

Once dry, glue your clear marble on top with superglue. Set it aside until the glue is set.

Now let's work on the case around the crystal ball.

Score your ***case joints*** down the middle. Connect your plastic ***case panels*** together with your ***case joints***.

Paint your ***case back*** either a solid color or add a design to it. I went with a weird spiral eye, but you could do a starburst or a bird . . . really anything "mystical."

Glue your ***case back*** onto your remaining two ***case joints***, making a 3D rectangle. Then glue this around your crystal ball.

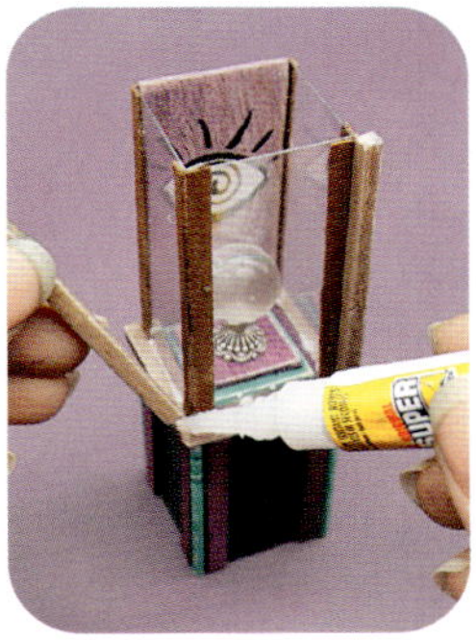

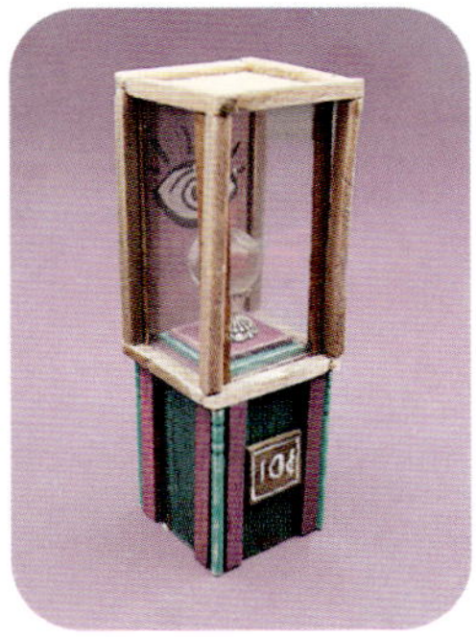

To make your case look more "fancy shmancy" glue the ***case edges*** to the corners of your case.

Top off your case with the same type of cap we made for the ***tabletop*** by framing your ***case top*** with the ***top frame*** dowels and gluing it on the top.

Add a little price sign to the outside and you have a finished Fortune Telling machine!

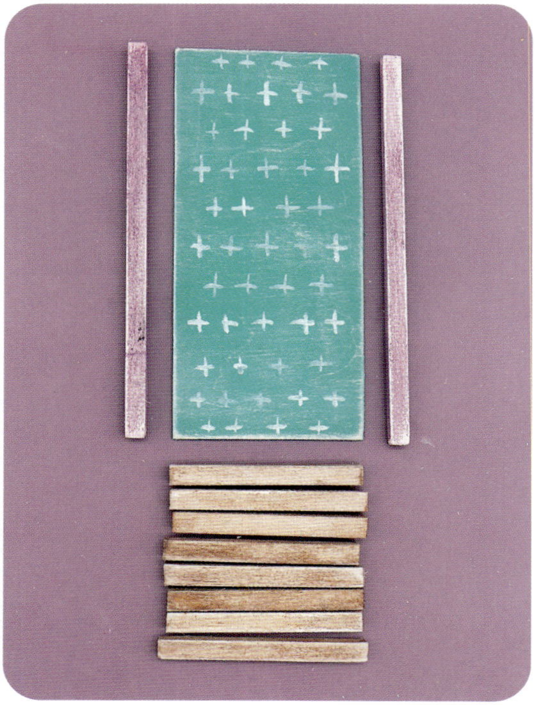

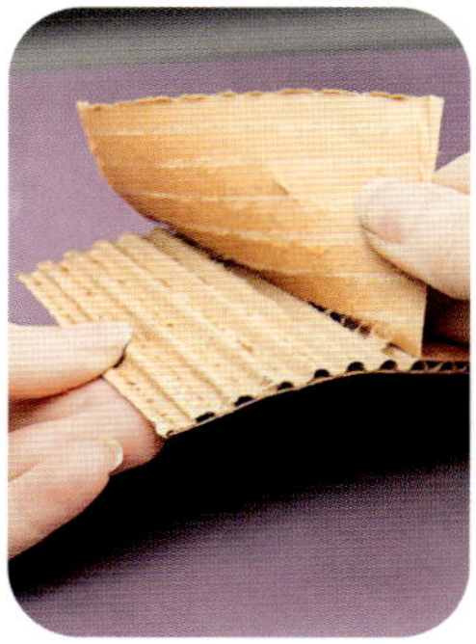

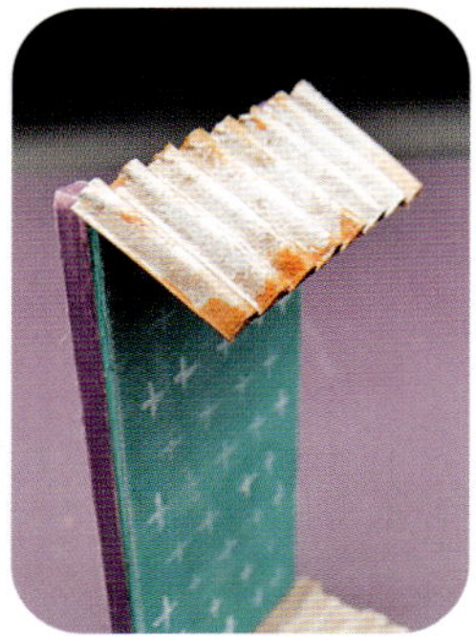

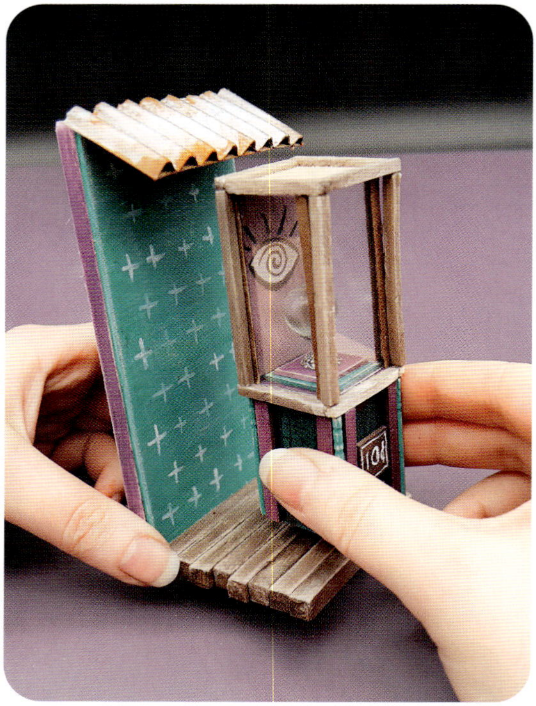

Stage

Cut and paint the following balsa wood:

- **Qty: 1**—4½ x 2 inches (11.4 x 5 cm) ***stage back***

Cut the following ¼-inch (6-mm) square dowels:

- **Qty: 8**—2 inches (5 cm) ***floor***
- **Qty: 2**—4½ inches (11.4 cm) ***back support***

Glue your eight ***floor*** dowels together side by side. Stagger each dowel a little to give it more of a homemade cobbled-together look.

Glue your two ***back support*** dowels onto the back edges of the ***stage back***.

Glue the ***floor*** to your ***stage back***.

Cut a 2 x 1–inch (5 x 2.5–cm) rectangle out of corrugated cardboard and peel off the first layer of paper to reveal the wavy bit of the corrugation.

Paint this silver and dry brush the edges orange to look like rust.

Glue your rusty corrugated cardboard to the top of your stage at an angle to make a sort of shabby-looking roof.

Voilà, you just made a stage! Put your fortune teller on your stage or make larger stages to add more Carn-EVIL things to it.

Ticket Booth

Buy a ticket to your death . . . **cough** I mean carnival!
Totally *not* death!

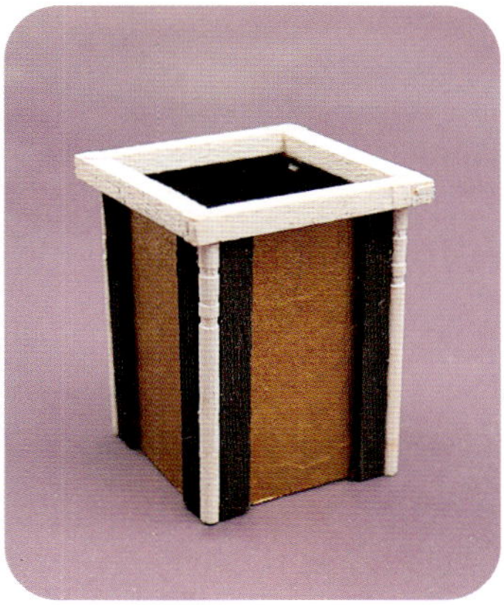

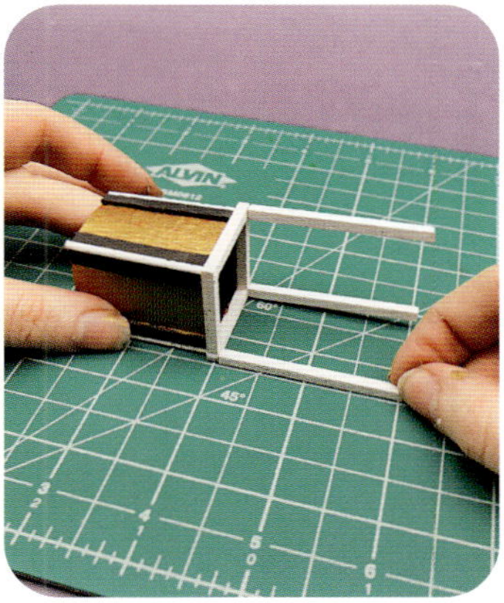

Tools

- exacto knife, ruler, & cutting mat
- paint
- glue
- pliers/wire cutter

Booth Materials

- cabinet base (page 69)
- ⅛" (3-mm) square dowels
- chipboard
- balsa wood
- 4–6 toothpicks

Lantern Materials

- pony bead (glow in the dark)
- 2 earring backs
- floral wire
- stage (page 72)

Booth

Build the **cabinet base**, just like in the Fortune Teller project on page 69.

Paint it black, white, and gold. Or pick your own color scheme.

Cut the following ⅛-inch (3-mm) square dowels:

- **Qty: 4**—2 inches (5 cm) ***curtain posts***
- **Qty: 4**—1 inch (2.5 cm) ***top frame***

Cut the following out of chipboard:

- **Qty: 1**—4¼ x 2 inches (10.8 x 5 cm) ***curtain***

Cut the following out of balsa wood:

- **Qty: 1**—1 x 1 inch (2.5 x 2.5 cm) ***top***

Glue one ***curtain post*** vertically at each corner on top of your base. To keep everything lined up and straight, use the grid lines on your cutting mat as a guide while you glue.

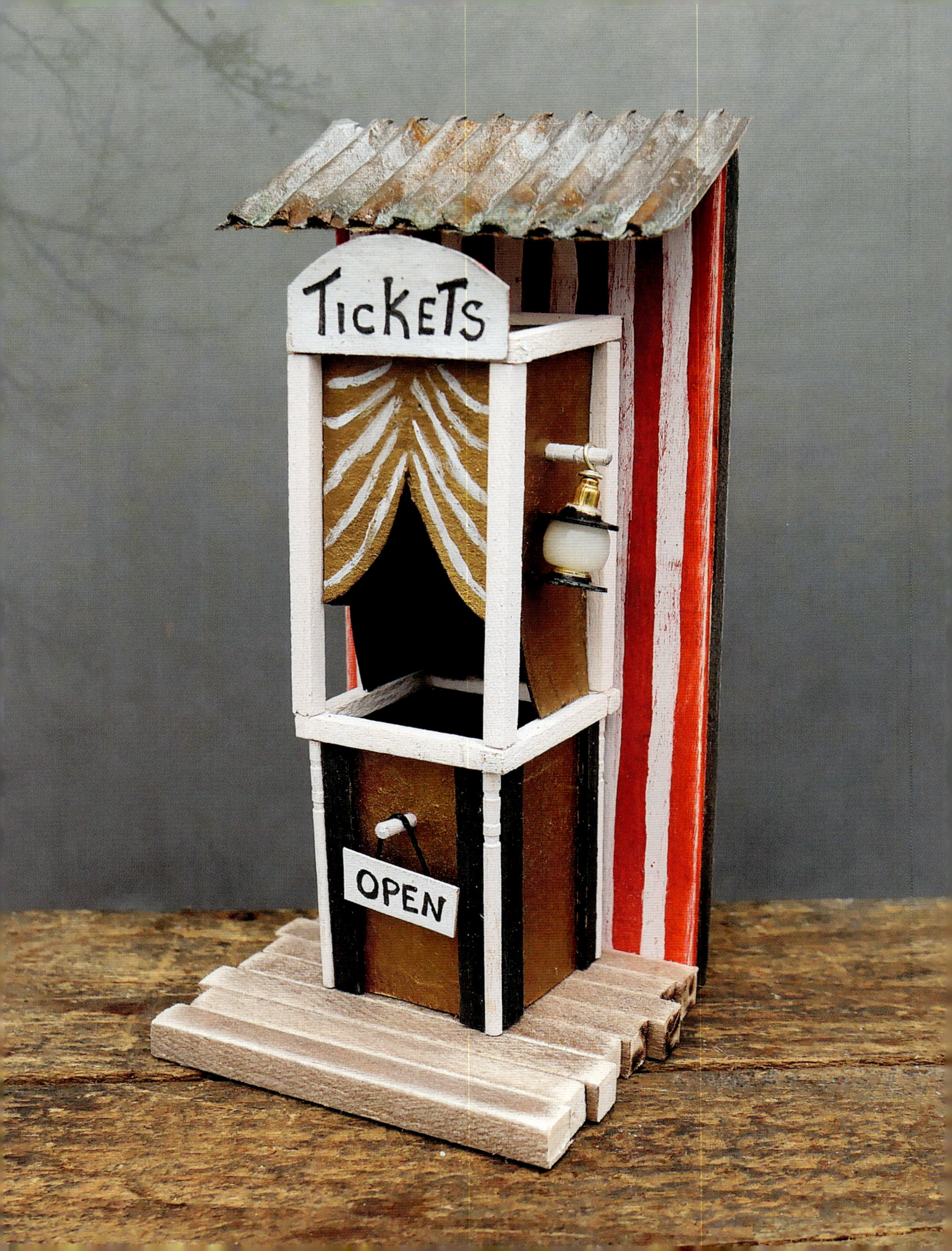
TICKETS
OPEN

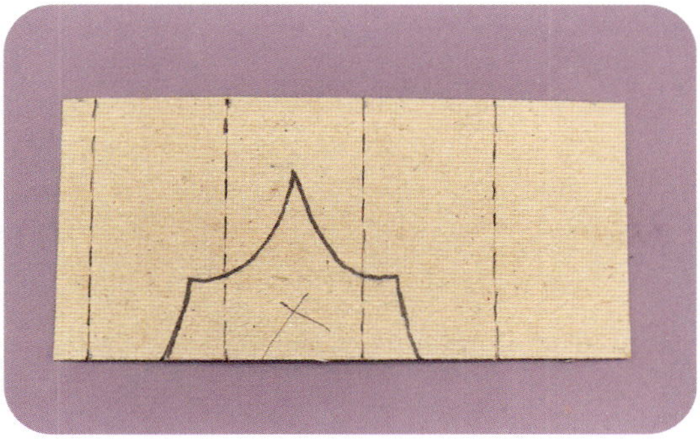

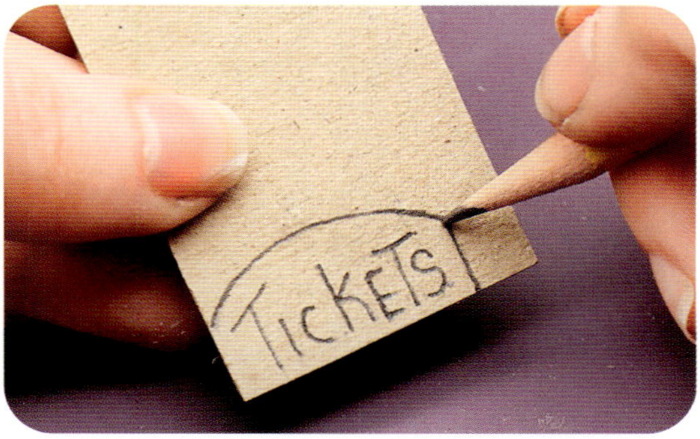

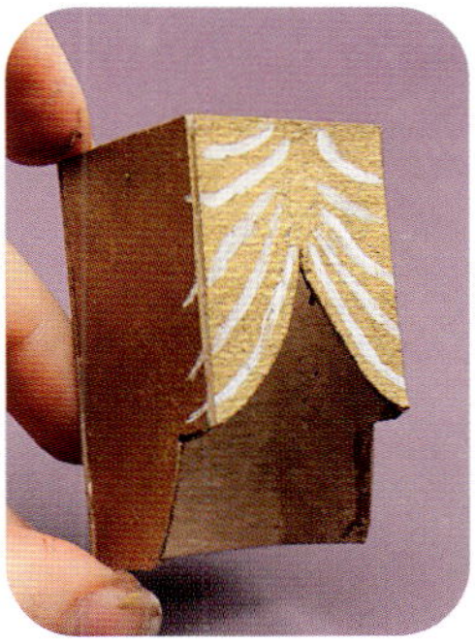

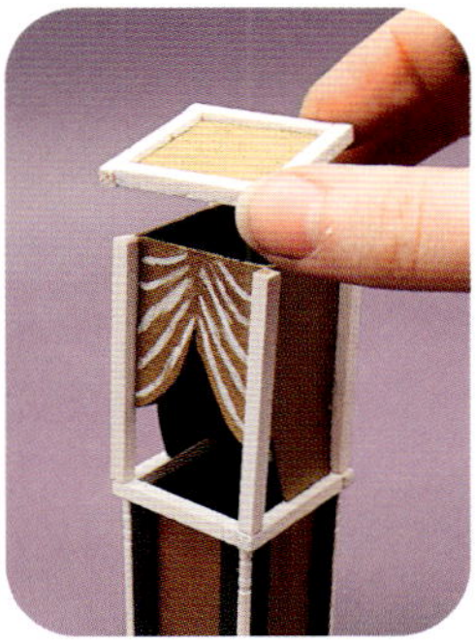

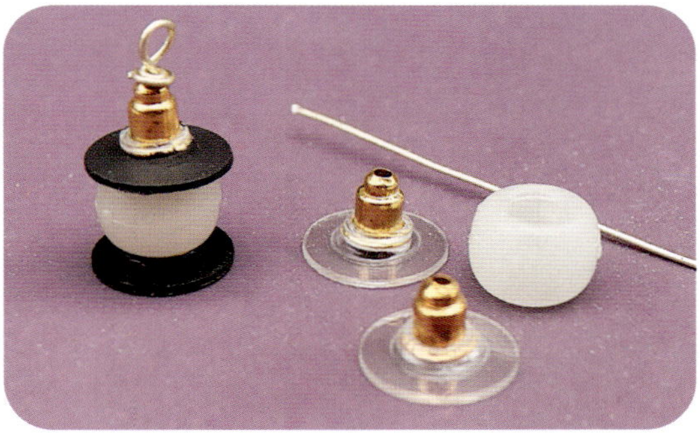

Take your ***curtain*** chipboard piece and, using an exacto knife and ruler, score three lines 1 inch (2.5 cm) apart, leaving a ¼-inch (6-mm) tab for gluing. Cut out the curtain hole according to the template on page 217.

Paint it gold and glue the ¼-inch (6-mm) tab inside to form a rectangle.

Place it between the four ***curtain posts*** and glue it into place.

Take your 1 x 1–inch (2.5 x 2.5–cm) ***top*** wood piece and frame it using the ***top frame*** dowels. Paint and glue this on top of your ***curtain posts***.

Now we need to announce what we're selling! So, let's make a sign. Cut a roughly 1 x ¾–inch (2.5 x 1.9–cm) rectangle from chipboard. Cut an arch along the top and paint the word "Tickets" on it.

Glue this to the top of your ticket booth.

Lantern

Let's make a lantern to see through the evil darkness.

Place a pony bead between two earring backs and feed a chunk of floral wire through the holes. Bend the wire on the bottom and glue it down. Loop the wire at the top so that you can hang it on a toothpick.

On the side of your ticket booth, poke a hole and glue ½ inch (1.3 cm) of the blunt end of a toothpick in it. Hang up your lantern.

Build the stage from page 72 if you want your tickets on display!

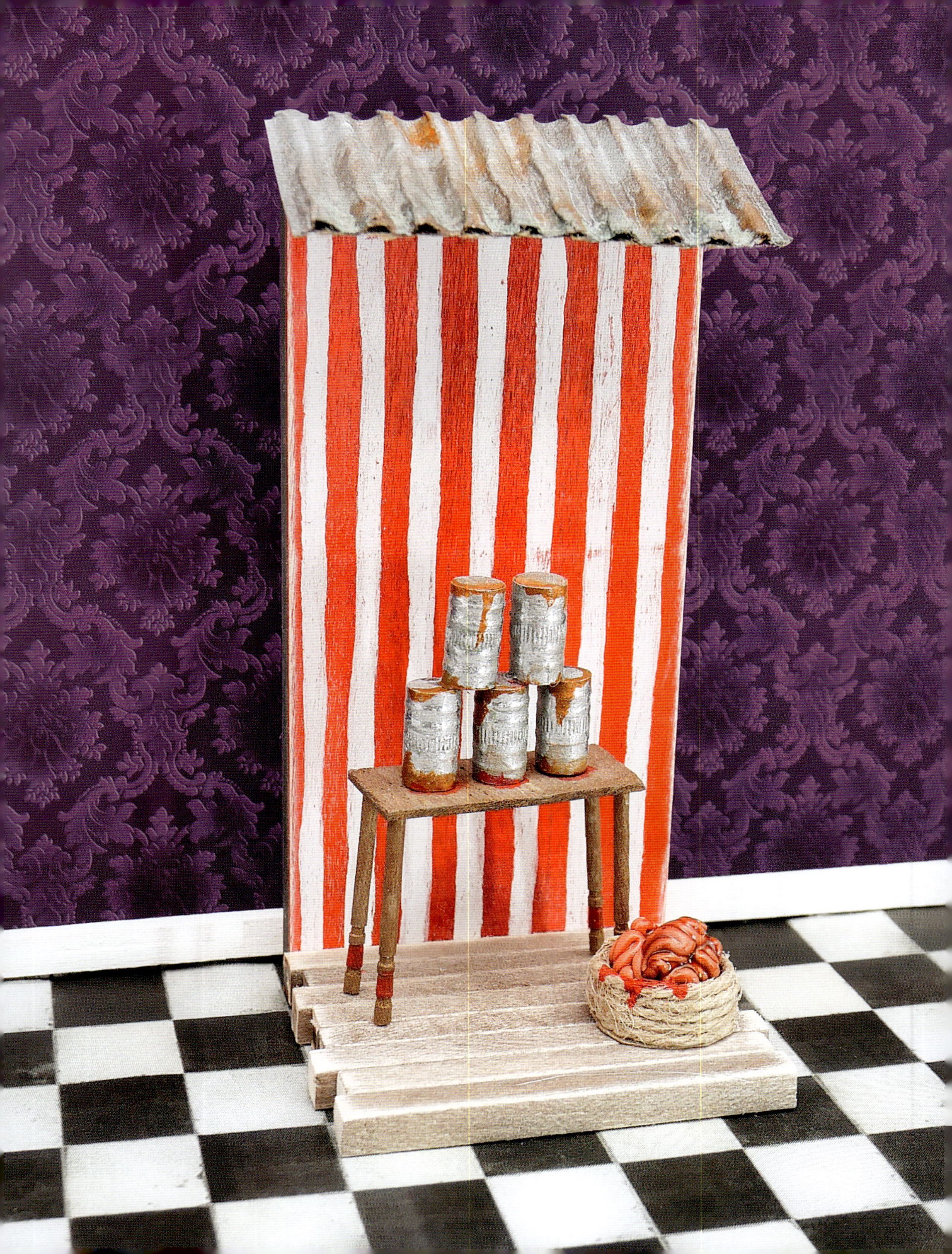

Brain Ball

Brain Ball is definitely not rigged.

Brain Ball is definitely not rigged.

Brain Ball is definitely not rigged.

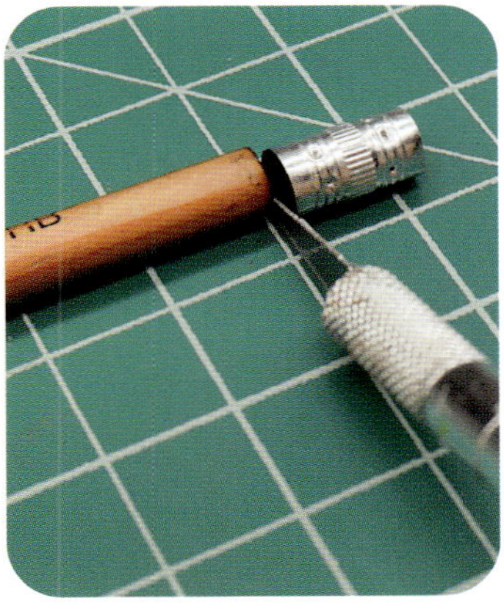

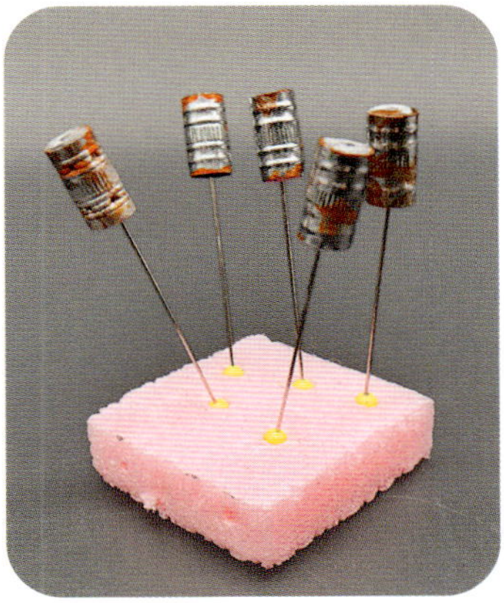

Tools

- exacto knife, ruler, & cutting mat
- sandpaper
- 3–5 straight pins
- silver spray paint (if needed)
- paint
- Styrofoam or foil
- superglue

Cans Materials

- 3–5 old pencils without erasers

Table Materials

- balsa wood
- 4 toothpicks
- 2–3 brains (page 156)
- basket (page 97)
- stage (page 72)

Cans

Using an exacto knife, cut the metal top off of three to five old pencils. *Five is better than three, but don't sacrifice any good pencils.* Sand off any excess wood or eraser that might be left over.

Once you have your three to five "cans," shove a straight pin into the eraser end to hold each one still while you spray paint them silver (if they aren't already). Dry brush orange and brown along the edges to make your cans look rusty. *Because clean cans wouldn't be spooky!*

Tip: *You can shove your pins in Styrofoam or foil to stand them up while the paint dries.*

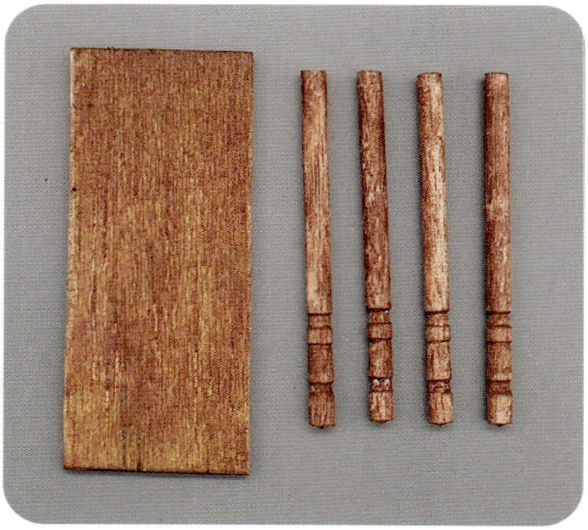

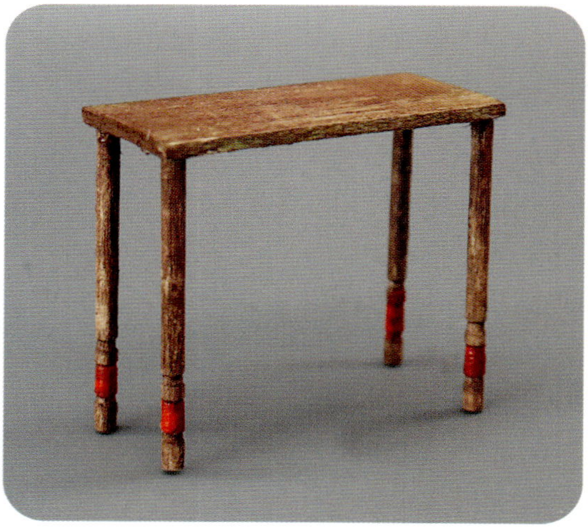

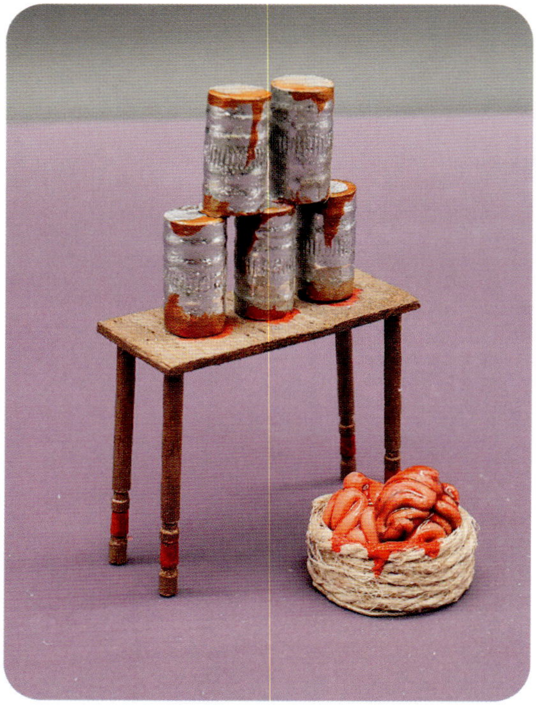

Trim the point off four toothpicks so that they are all about 1¼ inches (3.2 cm) tall for legs.

Stain everything with brown paint and let it all dry.

Using superglue, attach the legs to the bottom of your ***tabletop***. Then adhere your cans to the top of your table in a pyramid shape. *Just like they do at a real unethical carnival.*

Add your finishing touches by filling the basket with your brains and placing everything on the stage. And remember, Brain Ball is definitely not rigged!

Clay Sizer
Brains
x2

Table

Cut the following out of balsa wood:

- **Qty 1:**—2½ x ¾ inch (6.4 x 1.9 cm) ***tabletop***

Throwing Knives

WHAT! Who would let kids throw knives at a carnival?!
This is outrageous!

Ohhhh, this is Carn-EVIL? Okay, proceed.

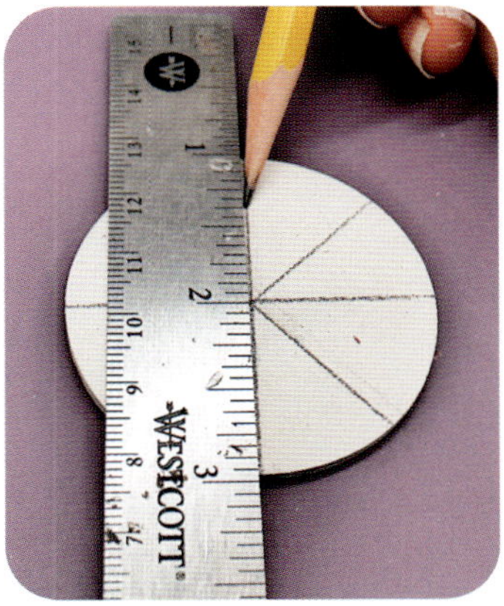

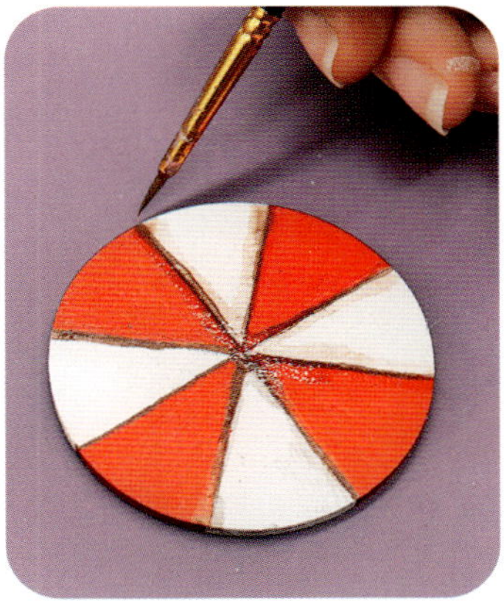

Tools

- exacto knife, ruler, & cutting mat
- paint
- pencil
- sandpaper
- glue

Wheel Materials

- chipboard
- balsa wood
- chopstick (or square dowel)

Larger Stage Materials

- chipboard
- ¼" (6-mm) or $\frac{3}{16}$" (5-mm) square dowels
- corrugated cardboard
- 2–5 knives (page 159)
- finger (page 160)

Wheel

Cut a 2-inch (5-cm) circle out of chipboard and paint it white.

Section out your circle with a ruler and pencil into eight pie slices. Paint every other slice red. If you want to add some grossness to it (and I know you do), water down brown paint and paint a few watery loose lines around your white and red sections for that grungy feel. Set it aside.

Cut a 1½ x ¾–inch (3.8 x 1.9–cm) rectangle out of balsa wood. (If you want to be fancy, sand the two front corners so they are rounded.) Paint it white.

Cut 2 inches (5 cm) off the blunt end of a wooden chopstick (or square dowel). Paint it brown.

Glue the chopstick in the back middle of your wooden rectangle. This will be the base to your wheel.

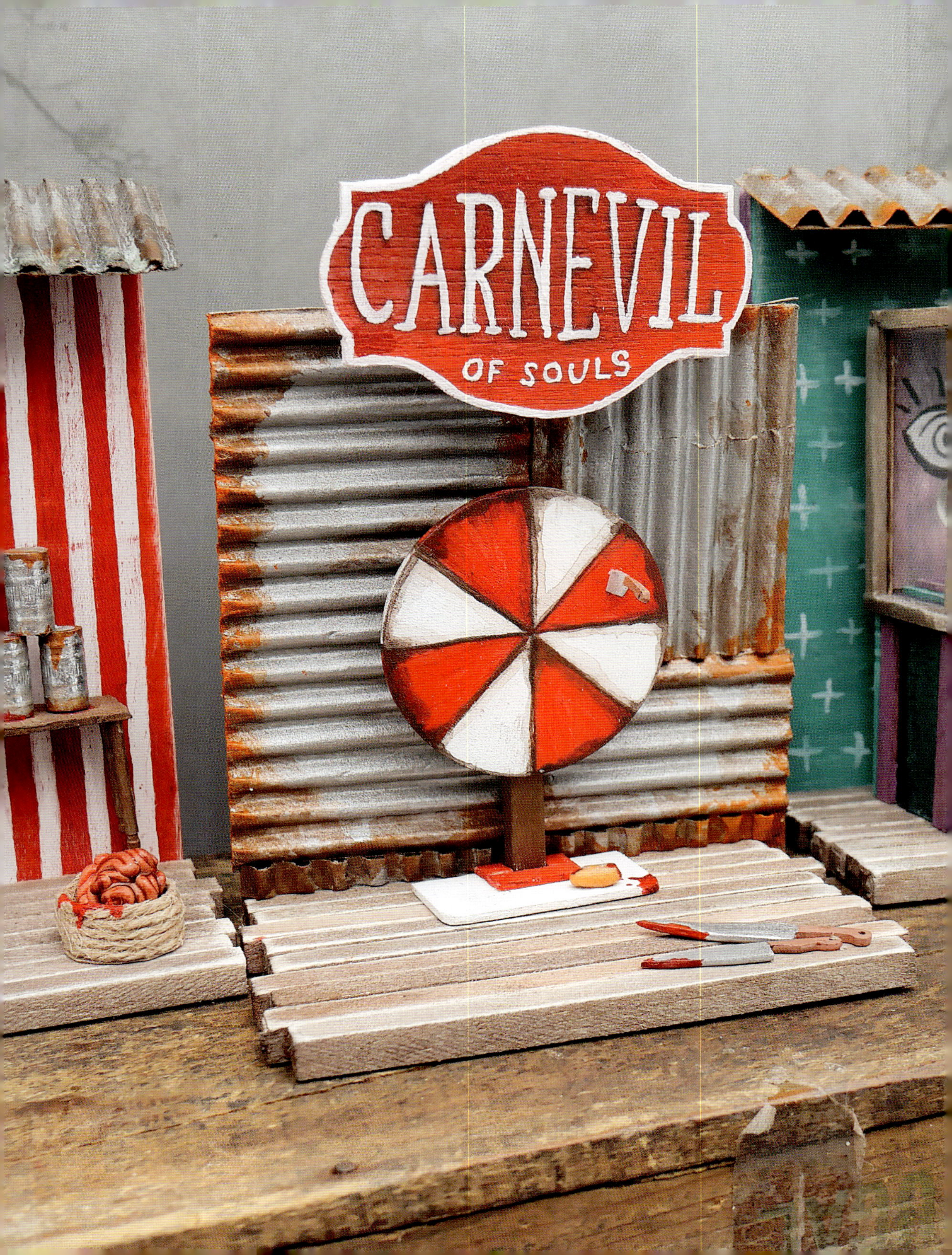
CARNEVIL
OF SOULS

Frame your chopstick on the white rectangle with a ¼-inch (6-mm) strip of red balsa wood. *You don't really need to measure, just hold it up to the chopstick and cut it with your knife. If it doesn't look perfect, it just adds to the creepy old vibe we're going with anyways.*

Lastly, glue your circle onto the front of your chopstick.

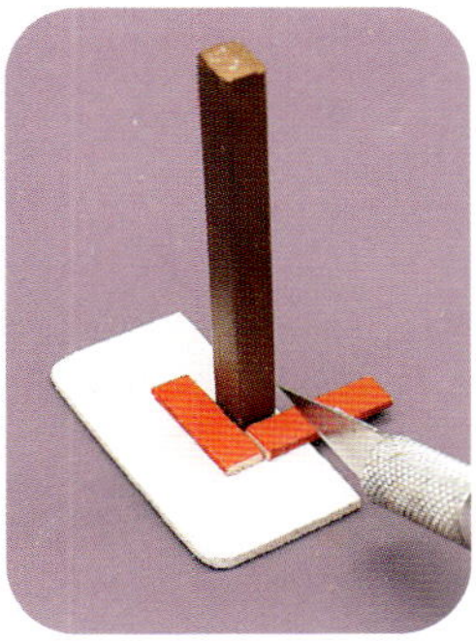

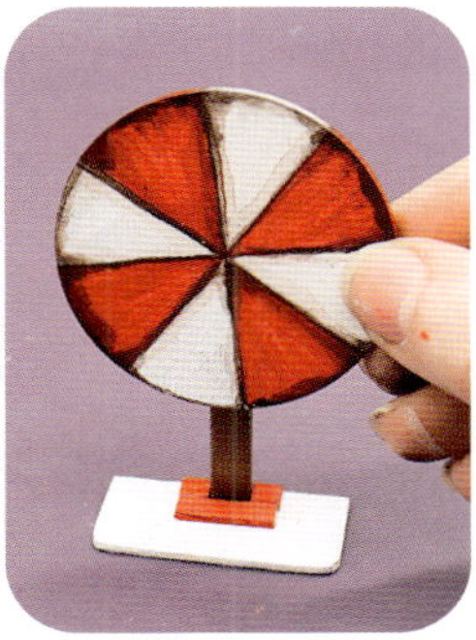

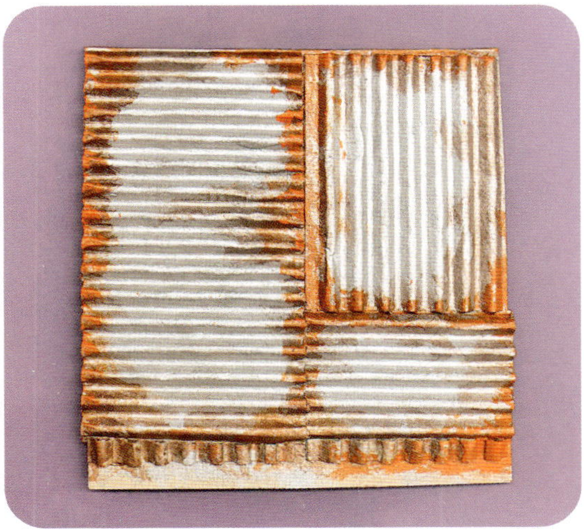

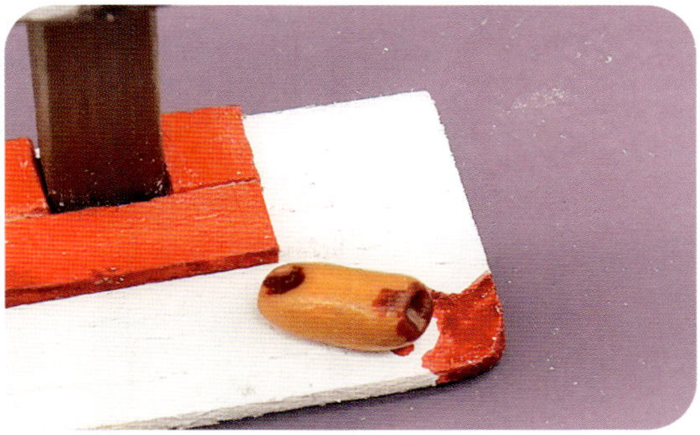

Larger Stage

Cut the following out of chipboard:

- **Qty: 1**—4 x 3¾ inches (10.2 x 9.5 cm) ***stage back***

Cut the following ¼-inch (6-mm) square dowels:

- **Qty: 9**—3¾ inches (9.5 cm) ***floor***
- **Qty: 2**—4 inches (10.2 cm) ***back support***

Paint your nine floor dowels brown and glue them together to make a floor. Stagger each one a bit to give it that same homemade cobbled look we did on the other stages. Set it aside.

Take your corrugated cardboard and rip the first layer off. Cut it and glue it onto the ***stage back*** leaving a ¼-inch (6-mm) gap on the bottom so we can glue it onto the floor. You can do one big piece to cover the whole back or a few little pieces and rotate for a hodgepodge look. Paint this to look like old rusty metal.

Glue the edge of your ***floor*** onto the ¼-inch (6-mm) gap on your ***stage back***. Glue the two ***back*** supports onto the back to help keep the back straight.

If you want to get fancy, make a Carn-EVIL sign using the template on page 217 and glue it to the top of your ***stage back***. You can paint one on wood, or if that sounds like too much work (and I totally get it), print one out.

Add your wheel to your stage and scatter a few knives around the floor from page 159 and severed fingers from page 160. Now you're ready for the danger!

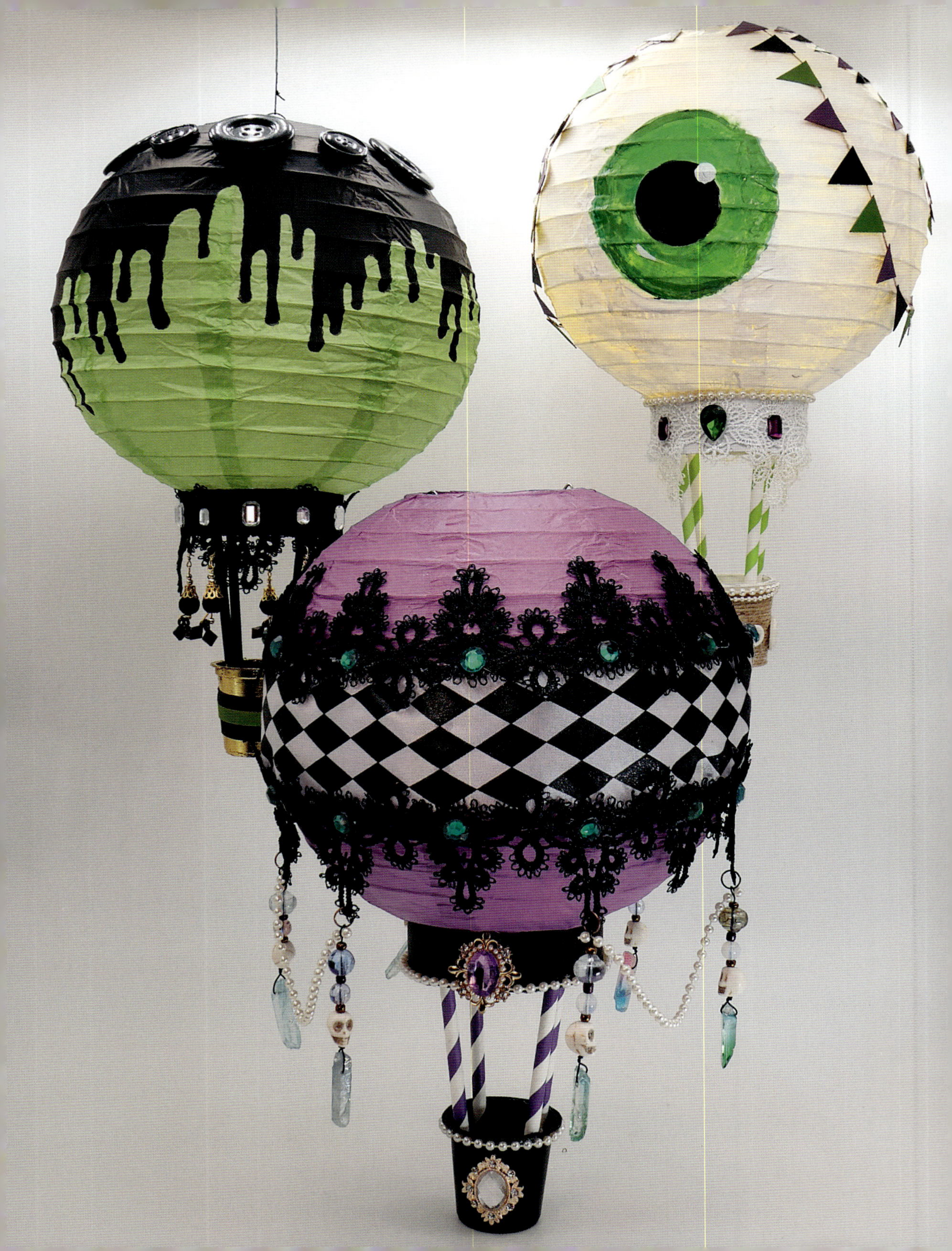

DOOMED Balloons

Ride in a hot air balloon, they said. It will be fun, they said. Once in a lifetime experience, they said. Wait a minute, who are THEY and why don't THEY take a spin on a ride called "DOOMED Balloons"?

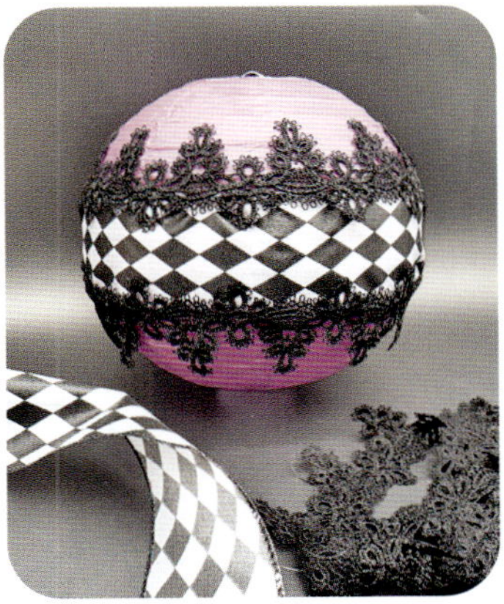

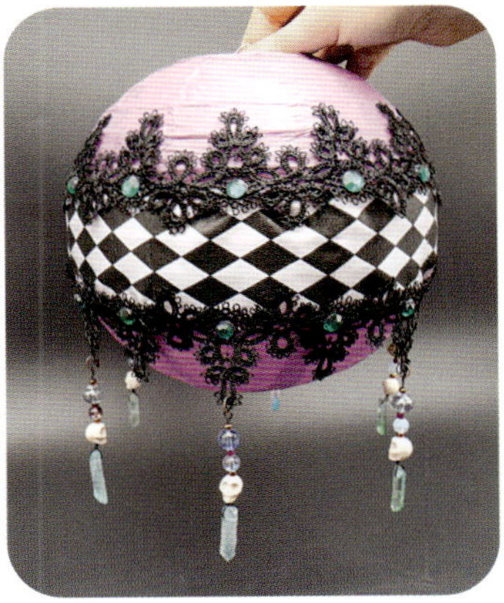

Tools

- hot glue
- scissors
- pliers/wire cutter
- paint
- glue

Materials

- various laces and ribbons
- hanging lantern
- various beads or charms (optional)
- floral wire (optional)
- empty painter's tape cardboard
- random shiny bedazzle
- 4 straws
- coffee pod (cleaned out)

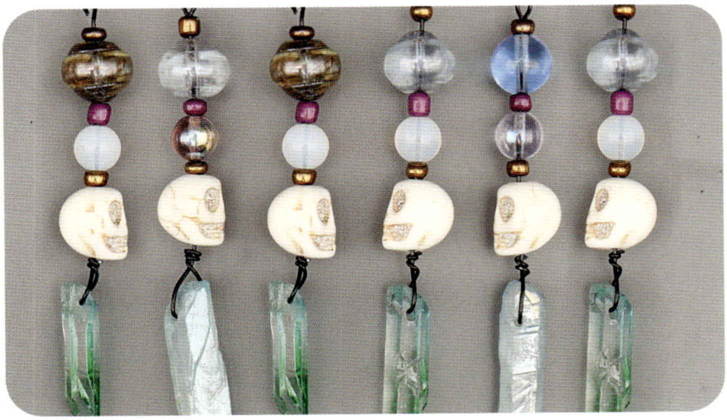

Start by hot gluing ribbon and lace around the middle of your lantern. Yours won't look exactly like mine, and that's okay!

Optional: *Add dangly bits, like beads or charms, with floral wire around your lace. Really challenge yourself to not buy new. See what you have lying around the house first.*

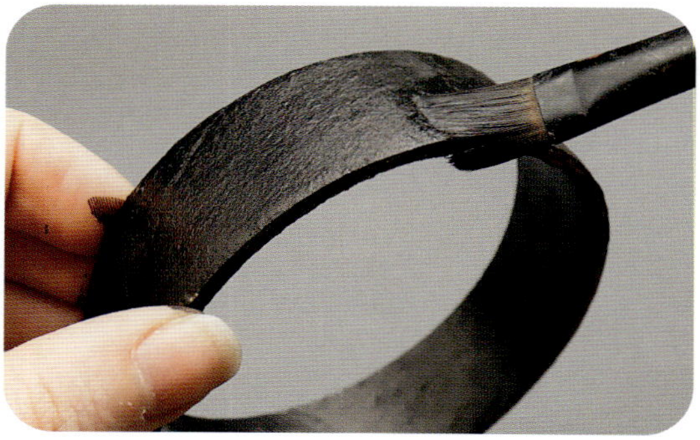

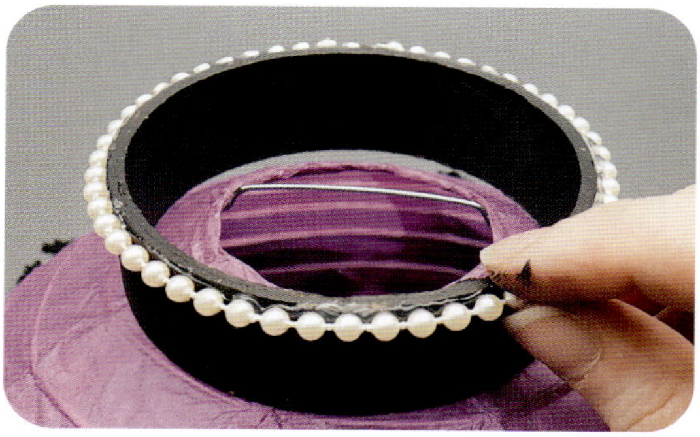

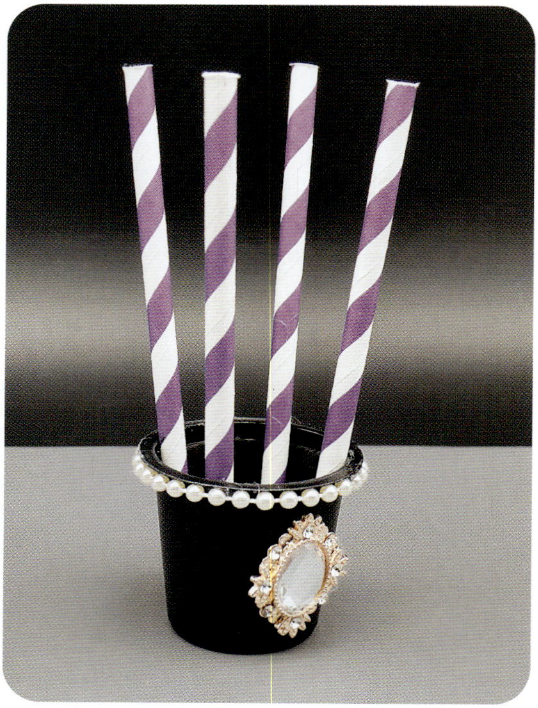

Take the cardboard ring from a used tape roll and paint it black. Bedazzle it with shiny things, like a string of pearls or gems, or just do more lace or ribbons. No need to make it complicated!

Glue this to the bottom of your lantern, around your lantern hole. Set it aside.

Take your four straws and cut them about 6 inches (15.2 cm) long. *You may need to adjust this based on the size of your lantern hole and coffee pod.*

Hot glue the four straws inside the four corners of your coffee pod. *Look, it's a circle and not a square, I know shapes! But pretend for half a second that it's a square and imagine where those corners would be and glue them there, okay!*

Tip: *Make sure your coffee pod is cleaned out. On second thought, dirty things are creepy, so I guess don't worry about it!*

Flip your lantern upside down so its bottom hole is facing straight up.

Hold the coffee pod so the ends of the straws rest inside the opening of the lantern. If it fits well, hot glue the crap out of it! If it doesn't fit, trim your straws a bit and try again.

Keep the lantern upside down until the glue hardens so that any drips go inside the lantern and not down the sides.

YAY! You just made a hot air balloon! I made a whole fleet of them to hang in my daughter's room. She even helped make them. This is a great craft to do with kids! Just be careful they don't burn their little fingers on the hot glue gun!

"Prize" Counter

Sure, the prizes here are a bit "questionable" at best, but consider yourself lucky if you win! Because losing is a whole lot worse at Carn-EVIL!

Shelf

Let's add a shelf in the counter from page 199. Cut a 1 x 2½–inch (2.5 x 6.4–cm) piece of balsa wood and glue a ⅛-inch (3-mm) square dowel along one long edge. Attach this shelf inside your counter roughly ⅗ inch (1.5 cm) down from the top. Angle it slightly sloping toward the front. Paint it.

Stage

Make the stage from the Fortune Teller project on page 69, but skip the roof and use these dimensions instead:

Cut the following out of balsa wood:

- **Qty: 1**—6 x 3 inches (15.2 x 7.6 cm) ***stage back***

Cut the following ¼-inch (6-mm) square dowels:

- **Qty: 8**—3¼ inches (8.3 cm) ***floor***
- **Qty: 2**—6 inches (15.2 cm) ***back support***

Paint the word "PRIZES" on a 1 x 3–inch (2.5 x 7.6–cm) piece of balsa wood and dirty the edges with paint. Glue this onto a painted piece of chipboard that's 1¼ x 3¼ inches (3.2 x 8.3 cm). Glue a dowel onto the back so that it pops off the stage a little, then glue that puppy to the top of your stage.

Tools

- exacto knife, ruler, & cutting mat
- glue
- paint
- scissors
- pliers/wire cutter

Shelf & Stage Materials

- counter (page 199)
- balsa wood
- ⅛" (3-mm) and ¼" (6-mm) square dowels
- chipboard
- 8 toothpicks

Prizes Materials

- 1 ice box (page 155)
- 4–5 skull beads
- balsa wood
- 3 fingers (page 160)
- 4 toy cars (page 140)
- 2 knives (page 159)
- 2 baseball bats (page 39)

Axe Materials

- 2 toothpicks
- floral wire
- shrink plastic

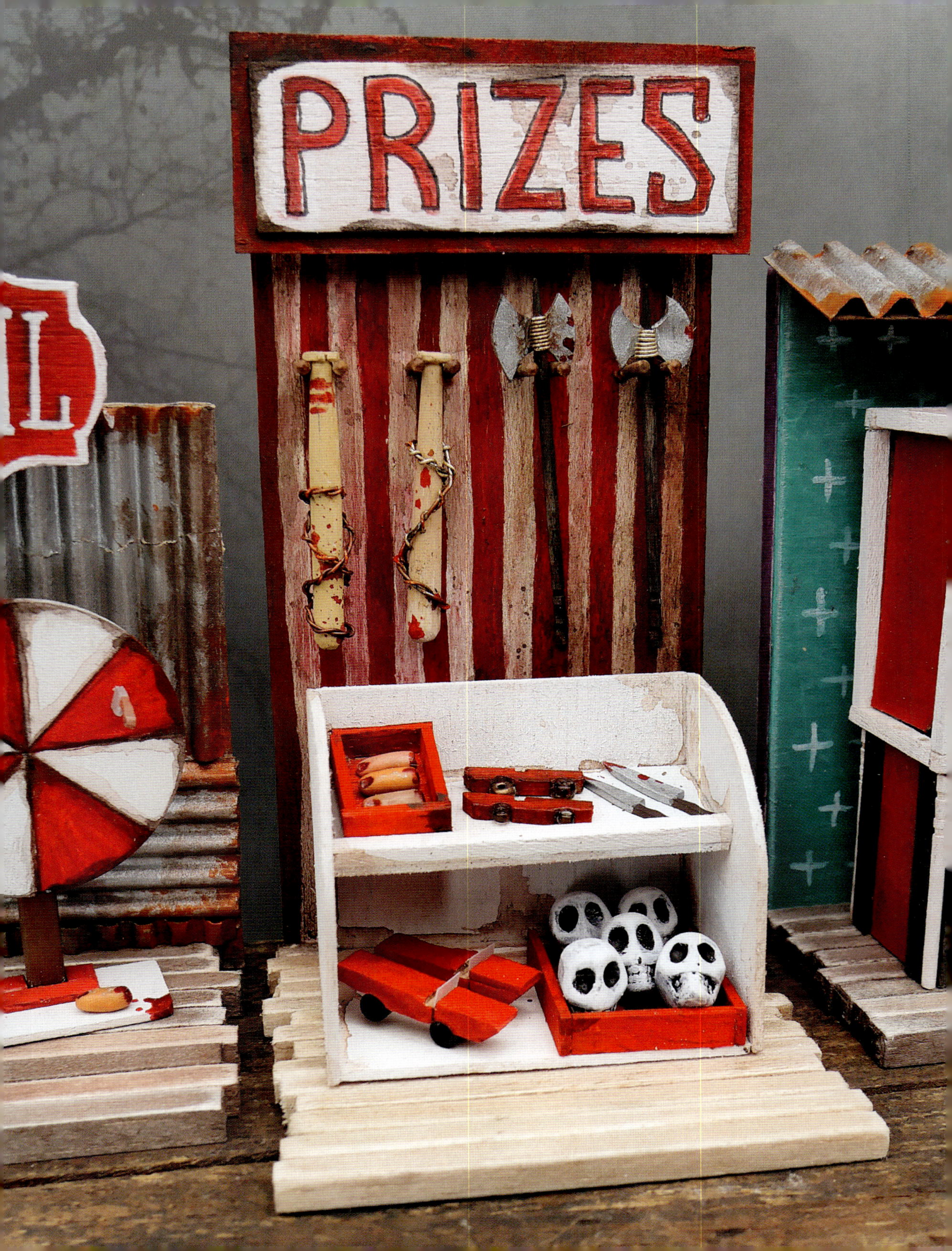
PRIZES

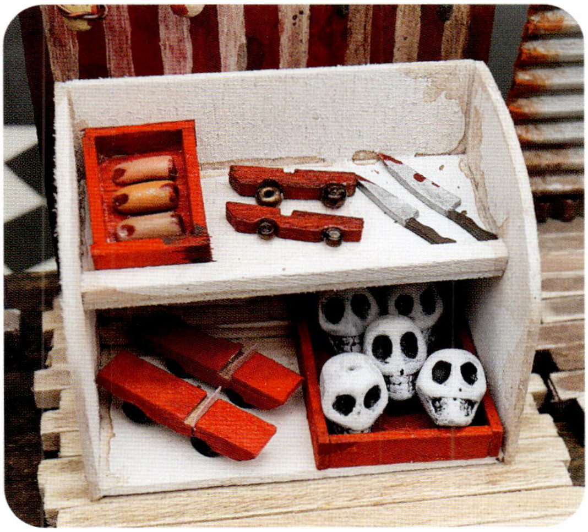

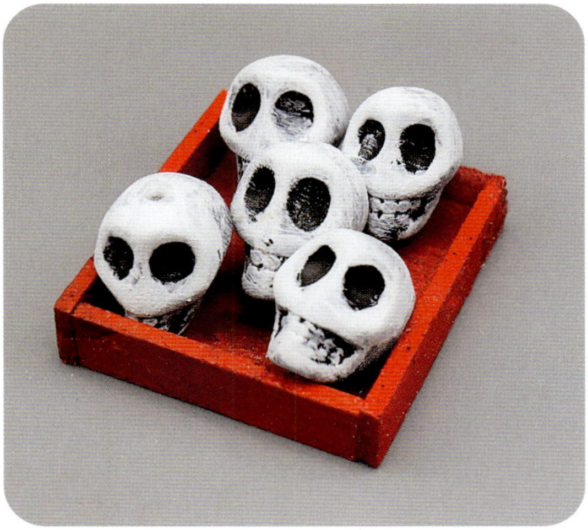

Prizes

Let's stock those questionable prizes! Feel free to move these items around wherever you like. This is just my placement.

Take your box from page 155 and paint it red. Glue 4 to 5 skull beads in your box and SHA-SHAAA! Box of skulls! Place it on the right bottom shelf.

Next, make another box from balsa wood, using the same ice box method, but sized ¾ x ½ inch (1.9 x 1.3 cm) and fill it with fingers from page 160. Place it on the top shelf on the left side.

Make four toy cars from page 140. Optionally, you can add variants with different sized clothespins. Place two on the top middle shelf and two on the bottom.

Take your two knives from page 159 and put them next to the cars on the top shelf.

Axe

Paint a toothpick brown and about ⅖ inch (1 cm) from the pointy end, wrap floral wire tightly around it eight-ish times.

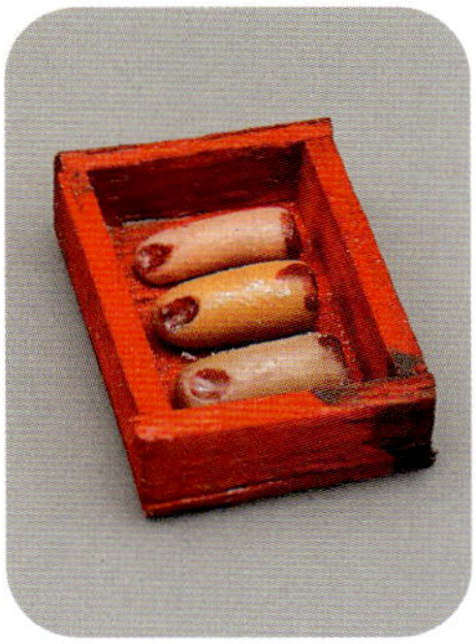

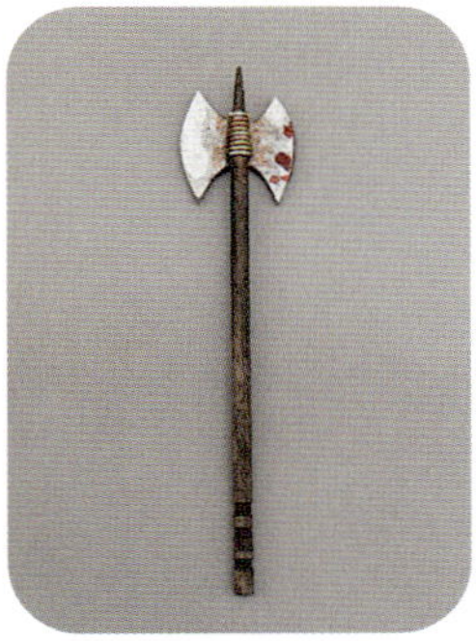

Trace and cut out the axe blade template on page 213 onto shrink plastic and shrink it.

Paint the blade silver and add red "stains" for that extra bloody look.

Glue the middle of the blade onto your wrapped wire. Repeat the process so you have two axes.

To mount them to the wall, decide where they will go, then glue the blunt ends of two toothpicks under each blade to hold them up.

Mount your two baseball bats from page 39 the same way. Which prize do you want to take home?

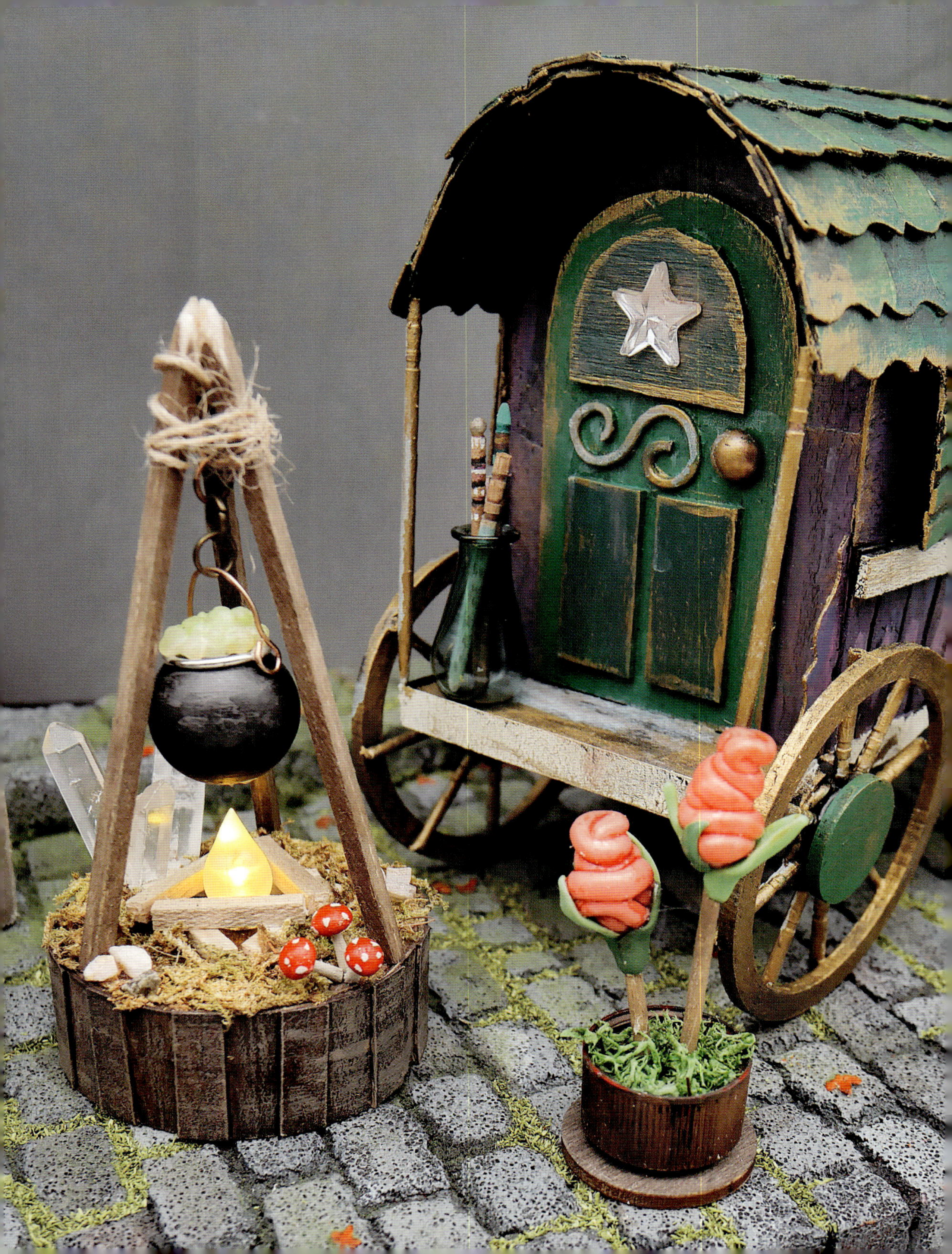

Magic Town

Here in Magic Town, the witches have a very strict set of rules:

1. All wands are to be polished and stored in approved racks and jars.
2. Magical items must be contained under glass domes when not in use.
3. No blocking any circle window at any time.
4. Mutant plants must be tamed and limited to consuming one human per week.

But most importantly, the humans must not know that Magic Town is full of witches. It's a good thing that humans are clueless meat bags, because with a name like *Magic Town*, it's pretty obvious. For the most part, it wasn't an issue until Wilma the Witch ruined everything!

It started when she left her wand out on the lawn (she was busy making fleas do synchronized acrobatics, which *was* pretty cool), but if you remember rule #1, "the grass" was not an approved storage location. So, the WOA (Witch Owners Association) wrote her up.

Strike two happened when Wilma left the dome off of her magical rose. In her defense, she only left it uncovered for like 2 minutes while she ran to the bathroom. But unfortunately, the WOA was already outside her circle window, writing a ticket for her wagon!

And then Wilma's poor mutant plant, Bruce, caught a case of Mad Plant Disease and went on a human snacking spree! By noon, it had consumed three humans (WAY over the limit)! Naturally, the WOA was forced to kick Wilma out. Totally unfair!

So, Wilma packed up her mutant plants into her witchy wagon and took off for Lonely Lane, leaving only her specimen shelf behind!

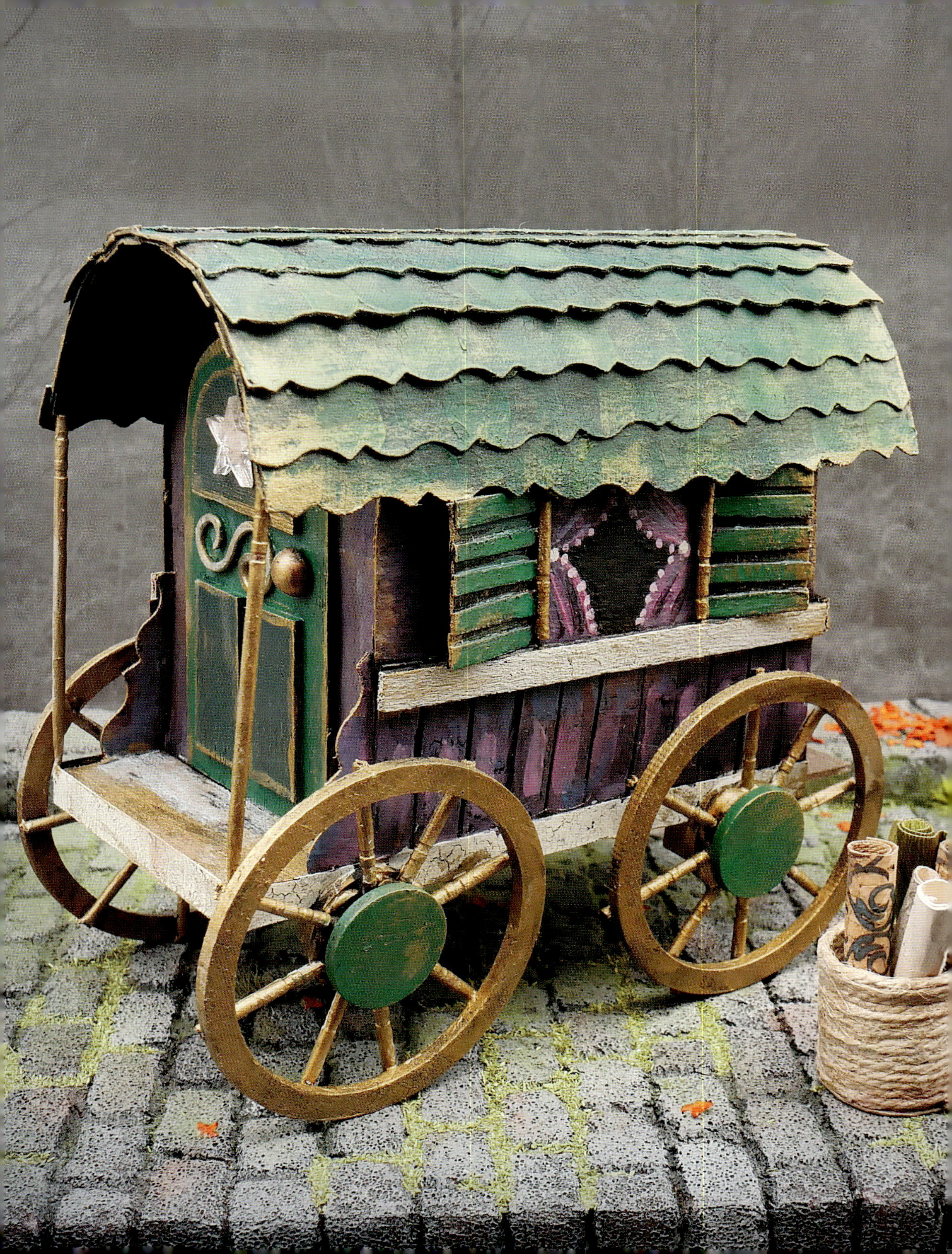

A Wagon Full of Witches

How many witches do you think can fit in a *witch wagon*? Three? Four? Thirty-two tops!

Tools

- tape
- scissors
- exacto knife, ruler, & cutting mat
- hot glue
- "fun" scissors
- pencil
- glue
- pliers/wire cutter
- silicone mat
- matte black spray paint
- paint
- craft glue

Wagon Materials

- 2 spray paint caps
- chipboard
- foam core
- 32–40 toothpicks
- balsa wood
- round metal brad
- floral wire
- cap (~1" [2.5 cm])
- 4 (¼" [6-mm]) flat circles
- 8 (½" [1.3-cm]) flat circles
- 4 (2" [5-cm]) hoops (wood or wire)

Basket Materials

- smooth plastic cap
- hemp/twine
- chipboard

Wagon

Tape together the ends of two spray paint caps.

Arch a piece of chipboard around your caps long enough to wrap around the top curve and come down in a U shape. Hot glue it in place, making sure the two ends of the U are even.

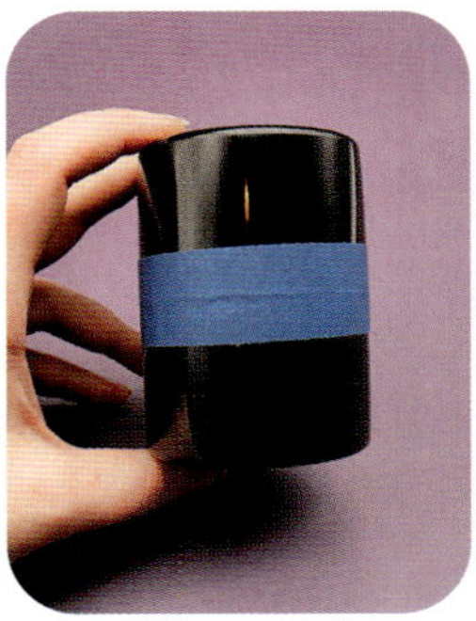

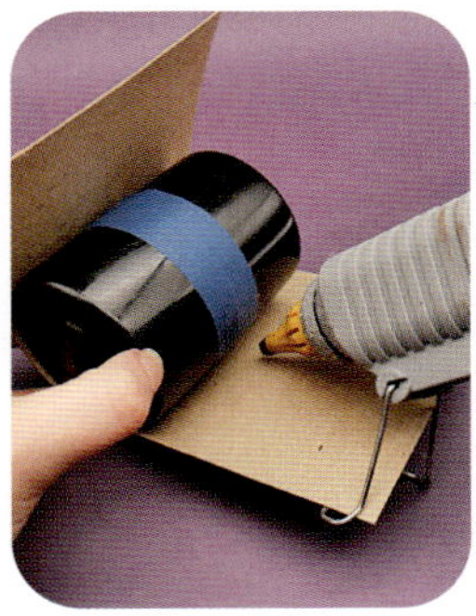

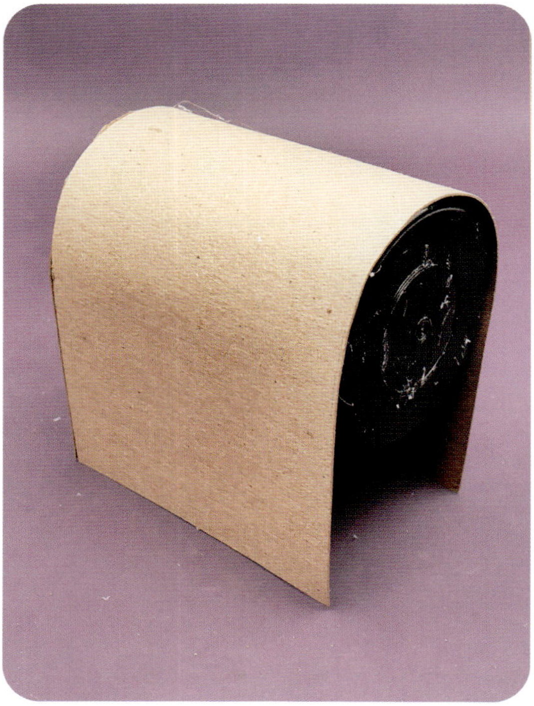

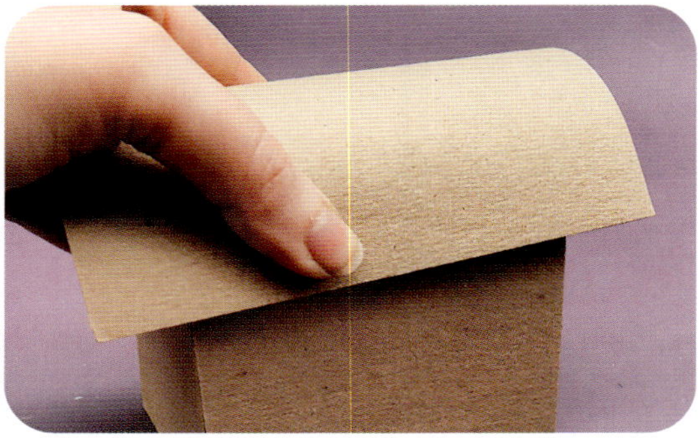

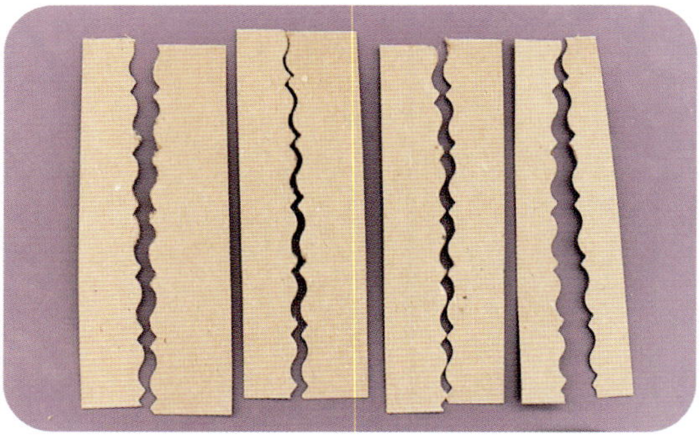

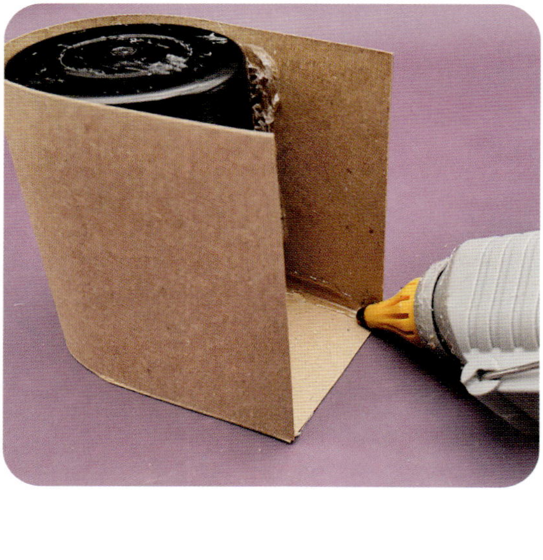

Flip your U face down onto a piece of chipboard, trace the shape, and cut two identical U pieces to cap the ends. Hot glue them in place, then hot glue the inside edges so there are no gaps.

Roof time! Curve another piece of chipboard over the top of your wagon. Trim it so it hangs about ¾ inch (1.9 cm) over on both sides and 2 inches (5 cm) down. It should be roughly 4 x 5 inches (10.2 x 12.7 cm), but yours might be different depending on your caps.

Let's shingle the wagon. Cut six to seven strips of chipboard, each as long as your roof and 1 to 2 inches (2.5 to 5 cm) wide. Using your "fun" scissors, cut them down the middle.

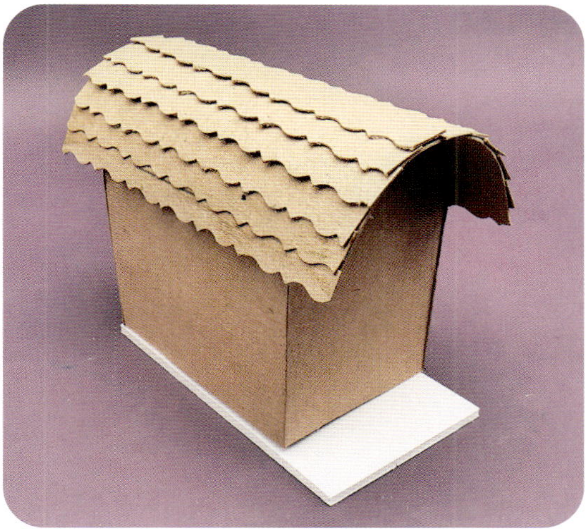

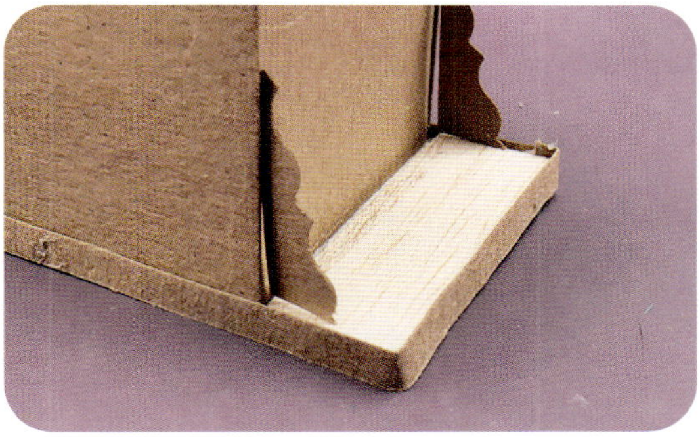

Starting on the bottom of your roof, glue your strips with the "fun" edge facing down. Overlap as you work your way to the top. Repeat on the other side.

The top's looking rough, so let's cover it up with a strip of shingles that's "fun" on both sides.

Place your wagon on foam core and trace the bottom. Extend one of the short ends by ¾ inch (1.9 cm) and cut it out. Hot glue this to the bottom of your wagon. Cover the edge by gluing a thin strip of chipboard.

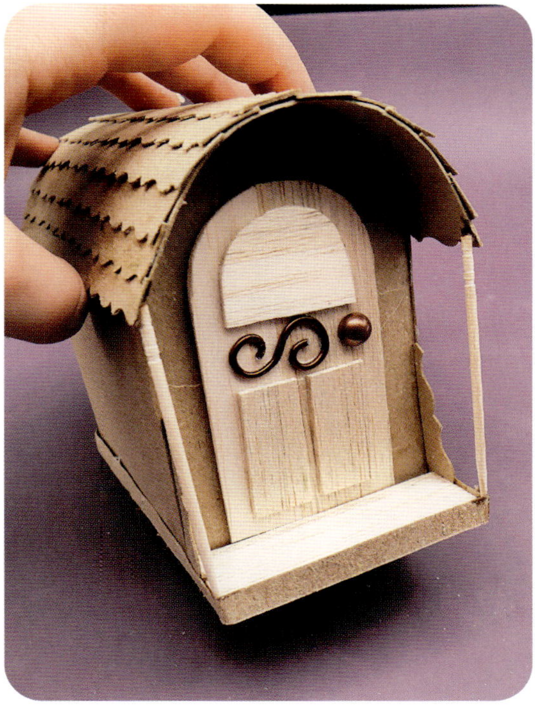

The longer end is your porch or "emergency exit." Let's make it look more welcoming by adding two chipboard triangles between the porch and the wall. Add toothpicks for columns to make your porch look more structurally sound.

Don't forget the door! It's very important for emergency exiting purposes!

Cut a 3 x 1¾-inch (7.6 x 4.5-cm) rectangle of balsa wood and round the top to complement your roof shape. Glue on some chipboard rectangles for paneling and a metal brad for the handle. Decorate your door with bent floral wire.

Hot glue your exit door onto the porch side.

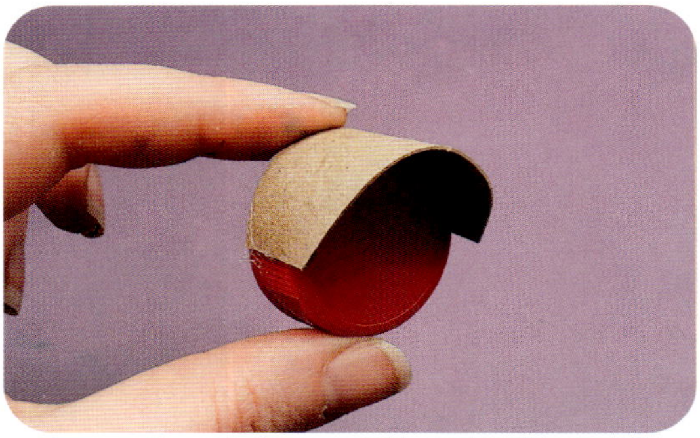

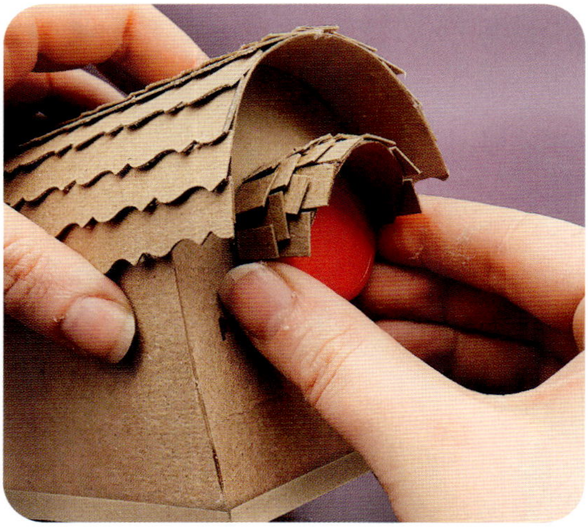

Next is the most important part of the wagon! The wheels? Nope! The CIRCLE WINDOW!

Take a cap (about 1-inch [2.5-cm]-wide) from something that you're preferably done using and cut a piece of chipboard that's big enough to curve around the top half of your cap and hang over the front about ½ inch (1.3 cm). Cut your chipboard so that it slightly arches on the front and hot glue it in place.

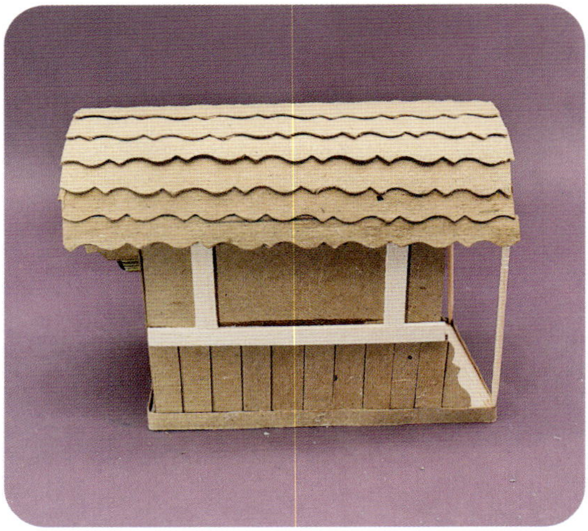

Add little overlapping chipboard rectangles as shingles. *Perfection is overrated. It's supposed to look wonky, so let it look wonky if it wants.*

Hot glue your charming, amazing circle window on the opposite side of your wagon.

Next let's jazz up those boring bland walls with paneling! Cut a bunch of chipboard strips roughly 1 x ¼ inch (2.5 cm x 6 mm). Glue these vertically along the bottom of your wagon's side walls.

On top of this paneling, cover up the ends with a horizontal strip of balsa wood going the length of the wagon.

Glue two vertical balsa wood strips coming up from the horizontal strip, 1 inch (2.5 cm) in on either outside edge.

Repeat on the opposite wall.

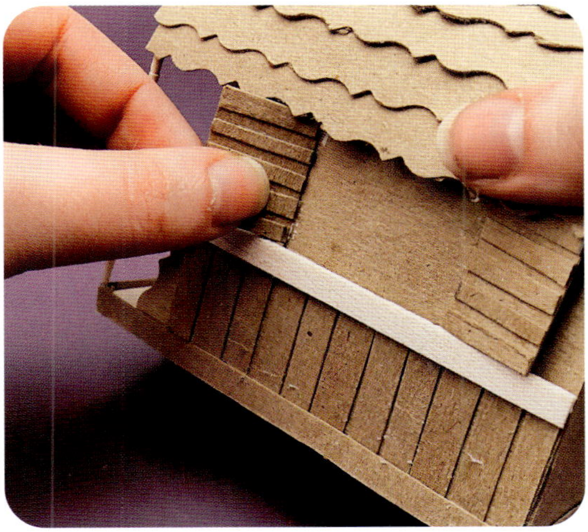

In case of tornadoes, we'll need some shutters. Cut four chipboard rectangles roughly ¾ x 1 inch (1.9 x 2.5 cm). Glue skinny strips of chipboard horizontally onto your four rectangle shutters.

Glue your shutters over the vertical strips you just added to your cart. If you glue along one edge and angle your shutter, they look hinged.

Now we're going to do the wheels. If you'd like a simpler wheel, you can just use four 2-inch (5-cm) jar lids. But they won't look quite as "wagony."

> **Note:** *We'll need to work fast, so have everything ready before you start. Also crank your glue gun temperature up a little (if you can). Be careful not to burn yourself!*

On your silicone mat, squeeze a drop of hot glue about ¼ inch (6 mm) wide.

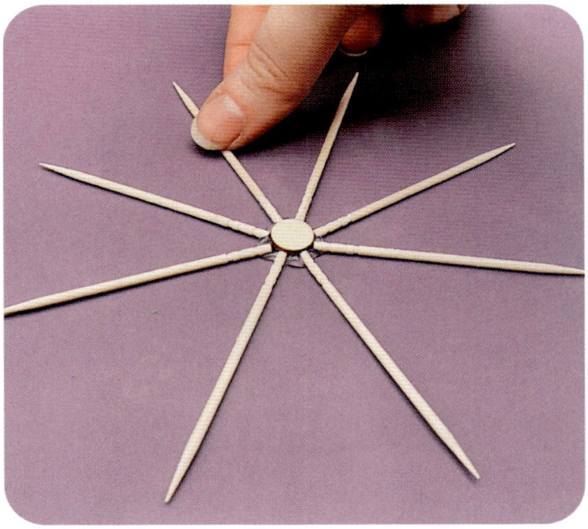

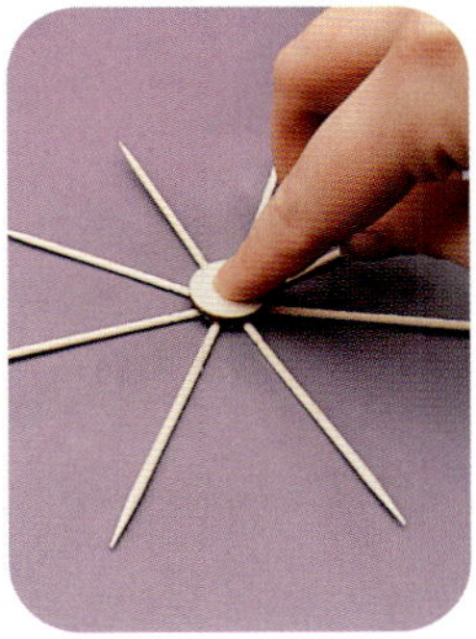

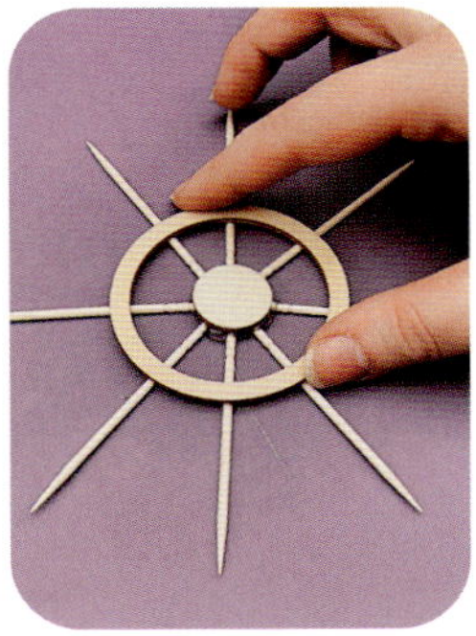

Quickly press a ¼-inch (6-mm) round (button or wooden circle) into the glue so that it squishes out.

In the squished-out glue, place eight toothpicks radiating out as spokes. (Start with the top and bottom, then the sides, then fill in between.) Let this cool but do NOT peel up yet.

Hot glue a ½-inch (1.3-cm) round object on top of the center, then glue a 2-inch (5-cm) hoop over the spoke ends.

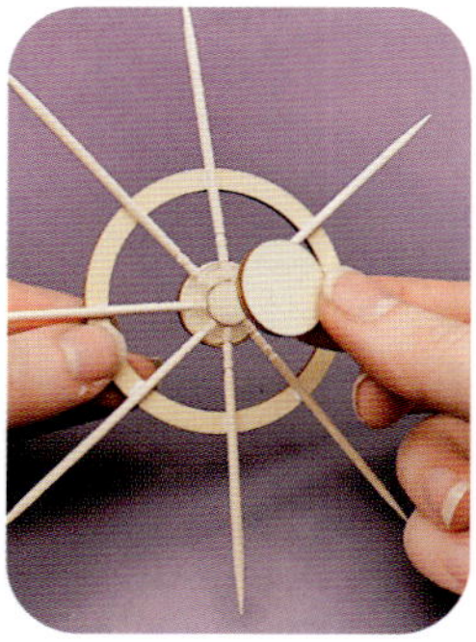

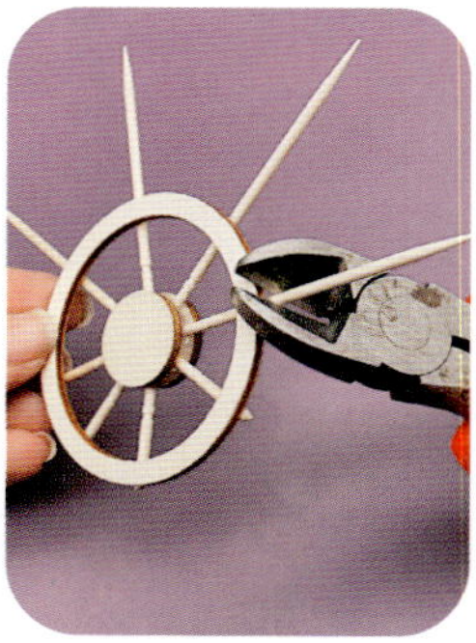

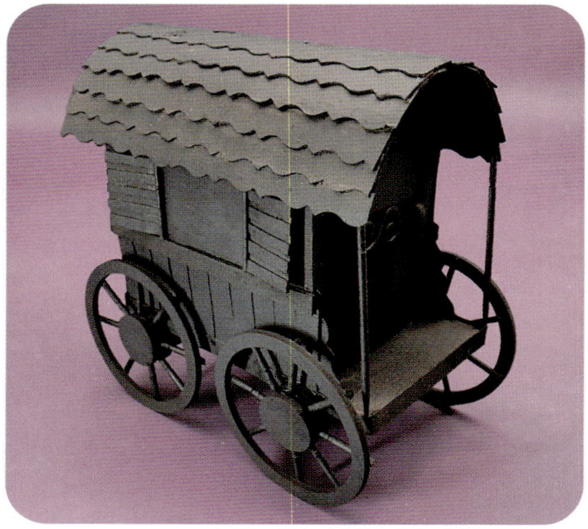

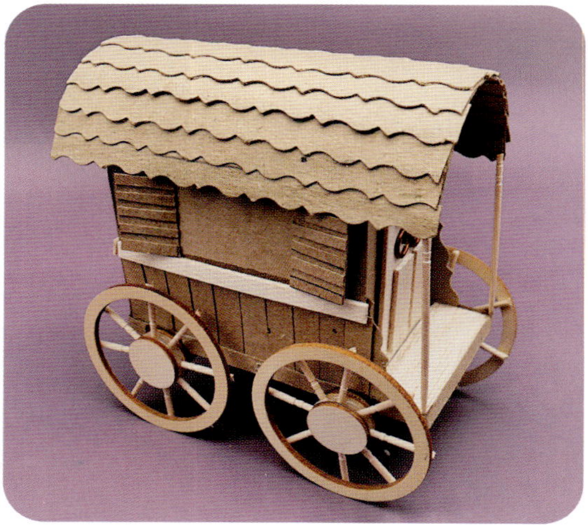

Note: *If you don't have a wooden hoop, you can bend a thick piece of wire around a 2-inch (5-cm) cylinder to make a hoop.*

Okay, now you may peel your wheel off the silicone mat! Glue another ½-inch (1.3-cm) circle on the back to finish it off.

With a wire cutter, trim your toothpicks to the 2-inch (5-cm) hoop. Repeat for four wheels.

Hot glue your four wagon wheels to your wagon.

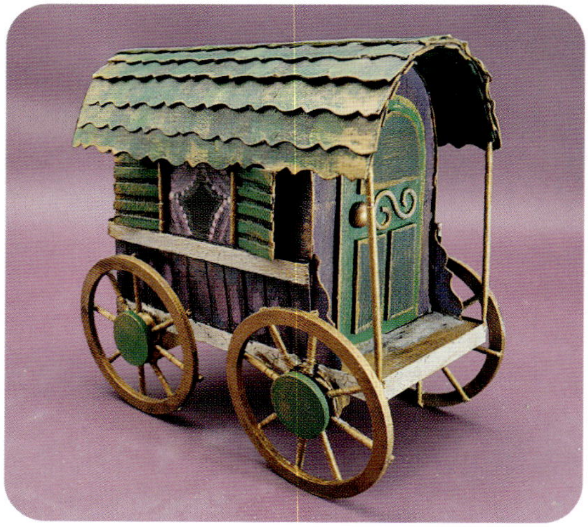

Now comes the scary part, but don't worry! I'll hold your hand! Spray paint the whole thing matte black. I know it seems odd because we're going to be painting on top of this, but trust me, it makes it 100000% easier!

After your spray paint is dry, paint your wagon. Add curtains, cracks, dirt, the whole sha-bang!

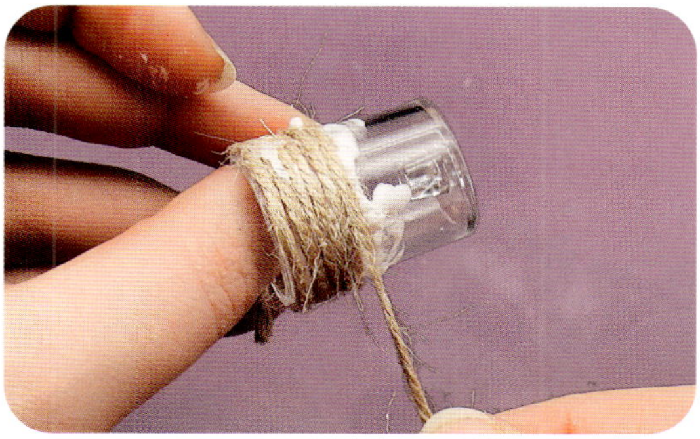

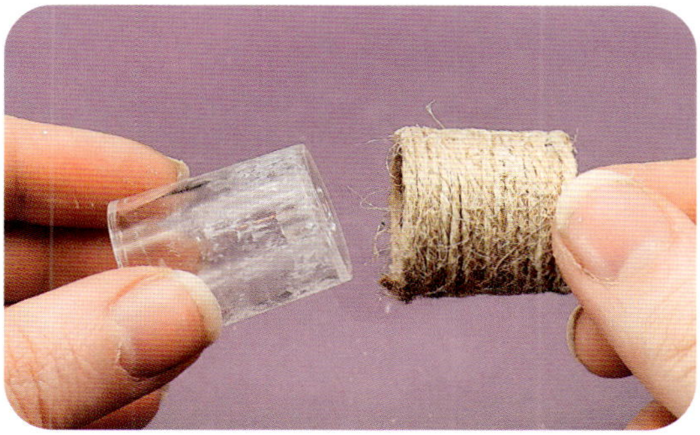

Basket

Use a smooth cap as a mold for your basket. A squirt bottle cap works well.

Tie a loop of hemp around your cap and craft glue it into place. Smear craft glue over the cap and wrap hemp around it until the basket is as tall as you want it. Tie it off and let the glue get tacky.

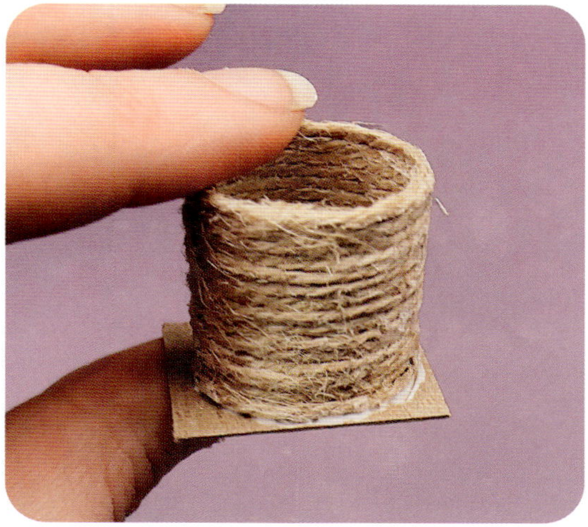

Once tacky, gently scooch the hemp off the cap. You may need to reshape it once you get it off, especially if you want an oval basket.

Glue one end of your freshly made basket to the chipboard and let it dry. Trim the excess chipboard off to make a bottom to your basket. Fill it with tiny goodies! Glue little handles to the top if you're feeling ambitious.

If you don't mind OSHA fining you for blocking a fire exit, glue the basket to your front porch. Or attach a little back ledge on the other end just for your basket. It's like its own little seat back there!

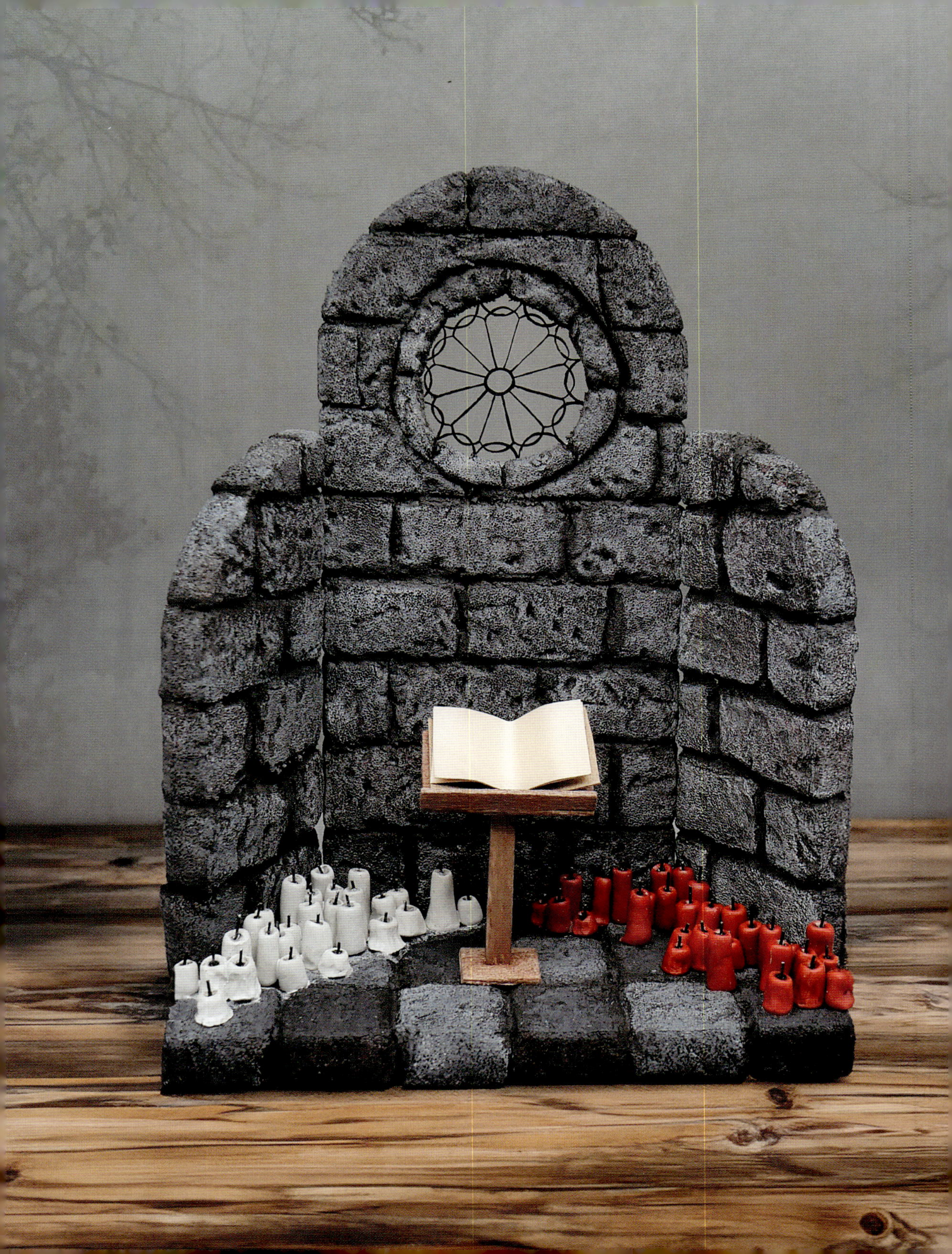

Circle Window

Circle windows are essential! I hear the light that shines through a circle window makes spells 42% more effective. Yes, exactly 42%!

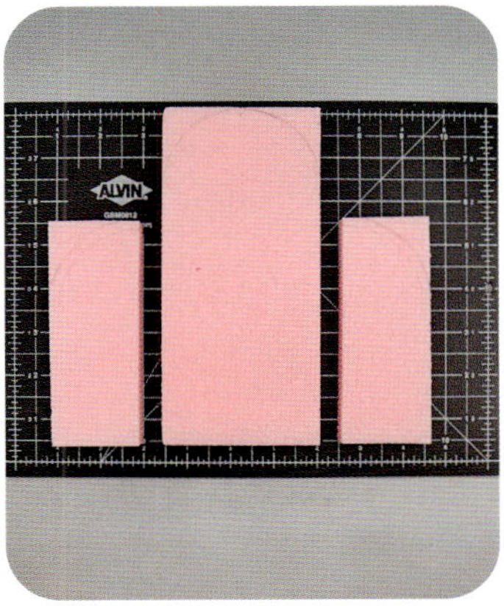

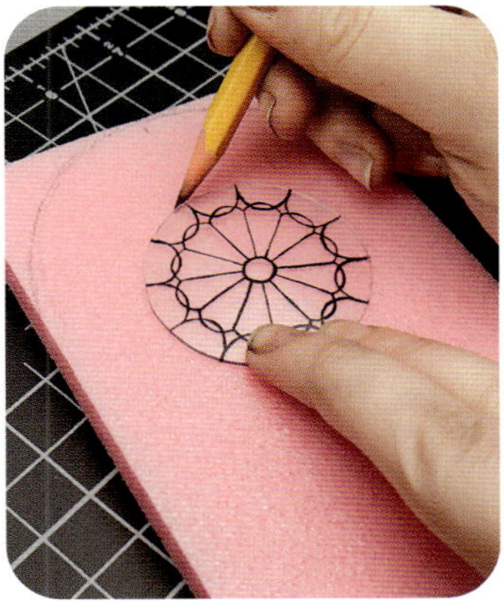

Window

Trace the amazing circle window template on page 216 on shrink plastic with a black marker. Make it dazzle with color or keep it simple like mine. The choice is yours. Cut it out and shrink it.

Cut the following out of XPS foam:

- **Qty: 1**—3½ x 7½ inches (8.9 x 19.1 cm) ***center***
- **Qty: 2**—2 x 5 inches (5 x 12.7 cm) ***edges***
- **Qty: 1**—5½ x 2¾ inches (14 x 7 cm) ***floor***

On the ***center*** piece, trace your shrunken circle window 1½ inches (3.8 cm) down from the top middle.

Tools

- black marker
- scissors
- pencil
- exacto knife, ruler, & cutting mat
- sandpaper
- wood burner (or pointy object)
- small rough rock
- paint
- hot glue
- ball sculpting tool
- glue

Window Materials

- shrink plastic
- XPS foam

Candle Materials

- your favorite clay
- floral wire

Book & Lectern Materials

- square dowels (or chopsticks)
- balsa wood
- chipboard
- paper

Inside that circle, doodle a slightly smaller circle. We will want a little ledge to attach the window to. Cut the smaller circle out with an exacto knife. Cut the corners off the top of your ***center*** piece and round them to enhance your circle window.

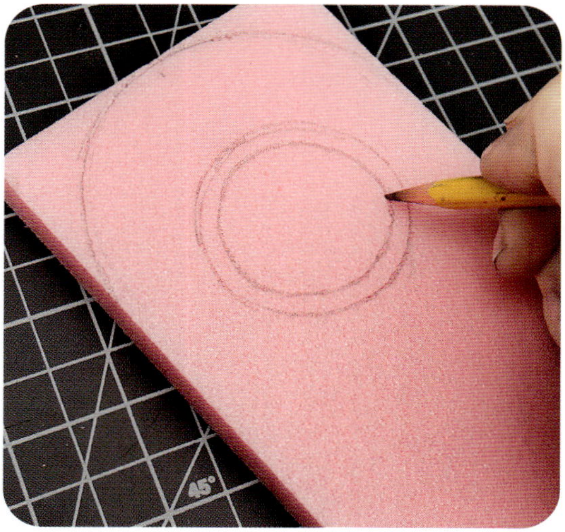

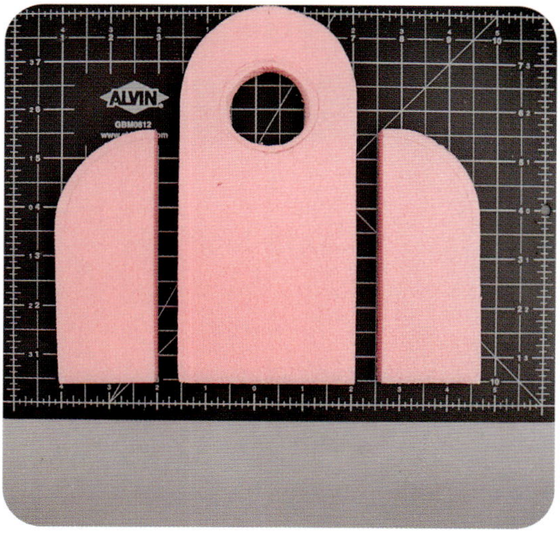

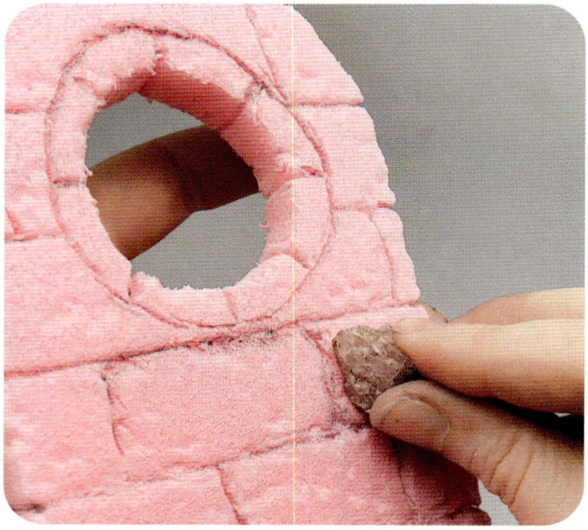

On the two ***edge*** pieces, round off just one of the top corners to make an arch.

Use sandpaper to smooth any imperfections on your foam.

Detailing! Use a ruler and marker to sketch your brick design onto your foam. I went with large bricks on the walls and, because I'm obsessed with *Alice in Wonderland*, I did a checkerboard for the floor.

If you happen to have a wood-burning tool, carefully brand your design into the foam. If you don't because you're a "normal" person who doesn't pick up hobbies like they're groceries, use a pointy object like a pencil and push the design in the foam. Don't forget to go carry your design around the edges.

Take your roughest, toughest rock and work out your anger by whacking it on the foam. Rotate your rock while you whack to keep the texture from getting repetitive.

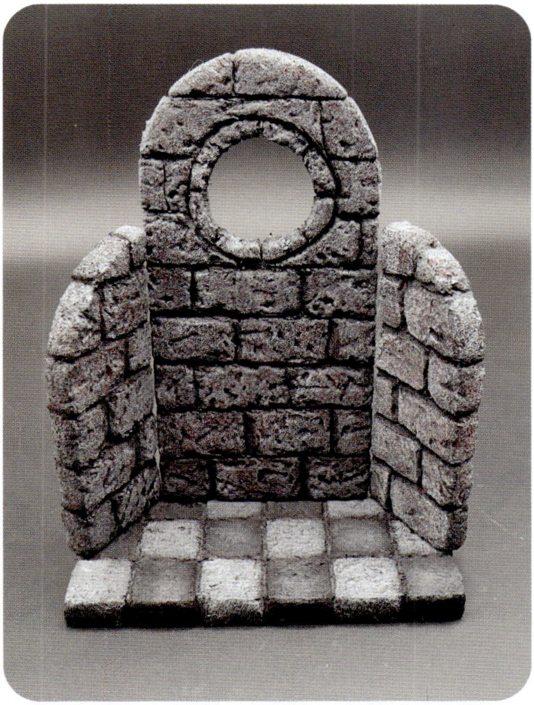

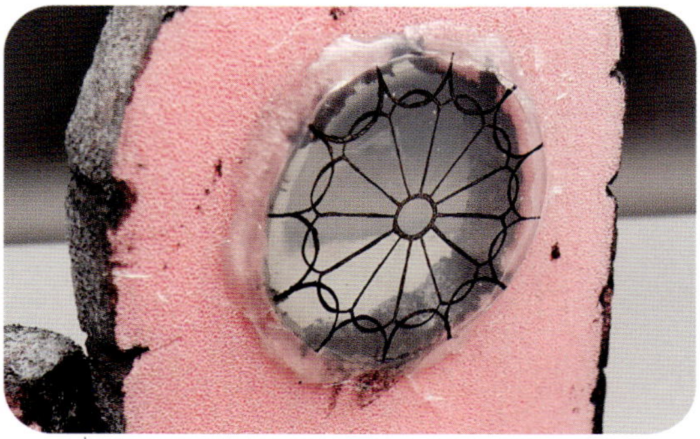

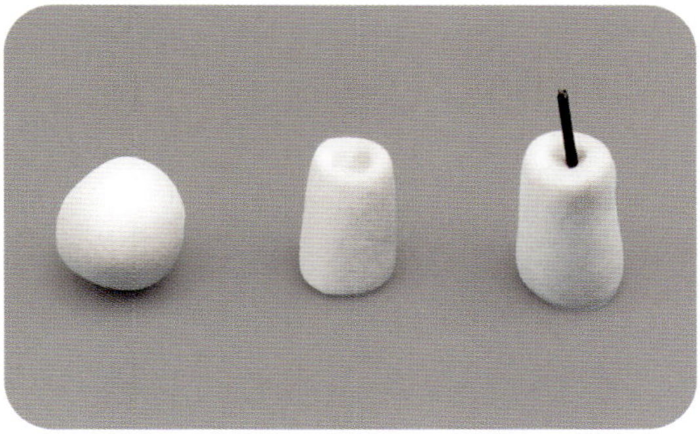

Paint all of your foam pieces black. Get it into all the nooks and crannies first. Foam drinks paint like a sponge, so drying can take 1 or 2 hours! Spray paint is faster, but beware, for some strange and probably science-y reasons, spray paint eats foam.

Once your paint is mostly dry, dry brush gray overtop. On the floor, I only dry brushed the gray on every other square because . . . Alice . . .

If your hot glue gun has a temperature setting, make sure it isn't set to "the depths of hell." You will melt your foam! Opt for a "warm bath" setting instead.

Hot glue the ***center*** on top of the back middle of the floor. Then glue the ***edges*** on either side of the ***center*** at an angle. Sort of like a folding mirror.

Let's get that circle window installed! Hot glue your circle window to the back of the circle hole.

Clay Sizer
Candle
Lots

Candles

Now that the stage is set, let's fill it with . . . stage-y things? Like candles.

Using the candle sizer, roll out a ball of clay and shape it into a cylinder.

Stand it up and make a dent in the top with a ball sculpting tool.

Shove a tiny piece of floral wire into the dent. This is your wick.

Repeat about 30-ish times. Make different sizes and cluster a few together for that witchy vibe.

Make another set of candles in red (or paint them afterward if you don't have red clay).

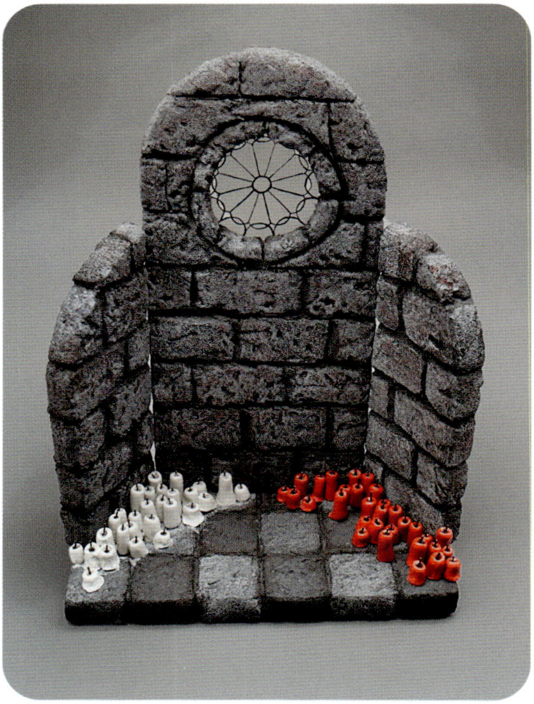

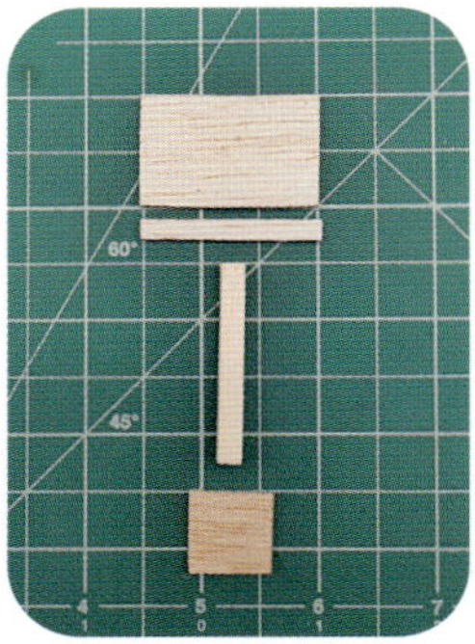

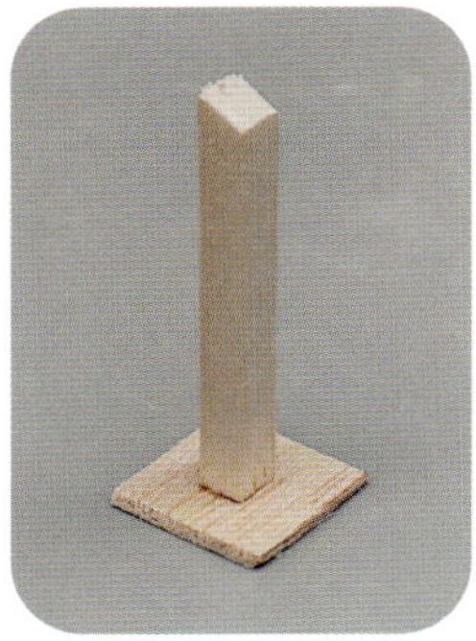

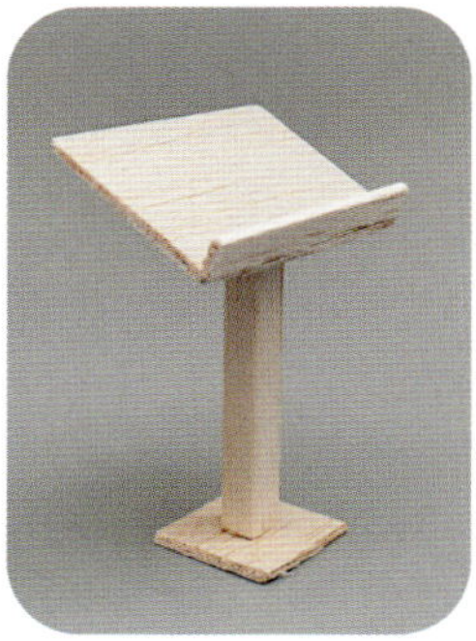

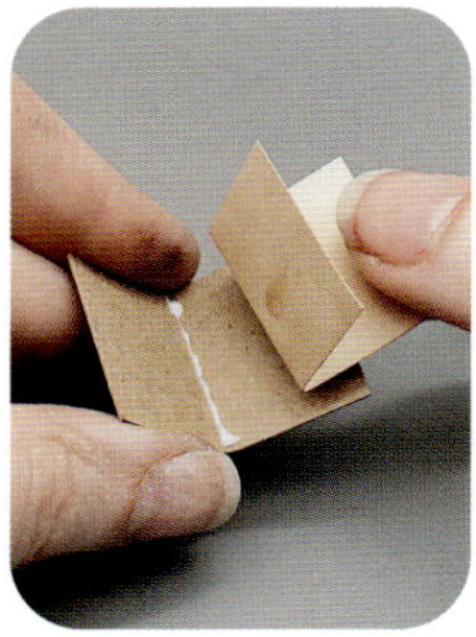

Harden your clay candles according to the package instructions.

Paint the top of each candle with watered-down black paint to make them look used.

Then make your stage look extra occult-y by gluing them along the walls. (Superglue works well.)

Book and Lectern

We're gonna need to cast spells from something!

Cut the following square dowel or chopstick:

- **Qty: 1**—1¾ inches (4.5 cm) ***shaft***

Cut the following out of balsa wood:

- **Qty: 1**— ¾ x ¾ inch (1.9 x 1.9 cm) ***base***
- **Qty: 1**—1½ x 1 inch (3.8 x 2.5 cm) ***tabletop***
- **Qty: 1**—1½ x ⅛ inch (3.8 cm x 3 mm) ***pencil stopper***

Take the ***shaft*** and sand one end at a slight angle. Glue the flat end of the ***shaft*** in the middle of the ***base***. Glue the angle part of the ***shaft*** in the back middle of the ***tabletop***. Glue the ***pencil stopper*** at the lowest end of the ***tabletop*** at a 90° angle. Paint it brown and set it aside.

Cut the following out of chipboard:

- **Qty: 1**—1½ x 1 inch (3.8 x 2.5 cm) ***cover***

Cut the following out of paper:

- **Qty: 2**—1½ x 1 inch (3.8 x 2.5 cm) ***pages***

For the book, fold the ***cover*** and both ***pages*** in half. Glue the two folded ***pages*** inside the ***cover*** and lay it open on the lectern.

Position the lectern in the middle of your stage. Now you have your very own amazing circle window!

Bubbling Cauldron

Double, double, toil and trouble.

Every witch needs a cauldron and as a bonus, this one won't burn down your craft table!

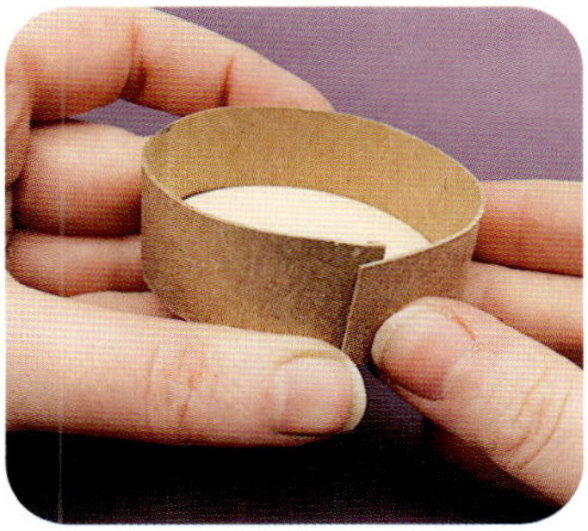

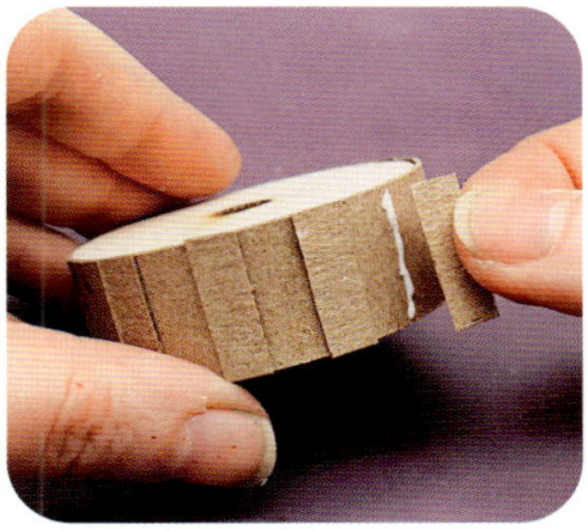

Tools

- exacto knife, ruler, & cutting mat
- drill or wood burner
- glue
- paint
- sandpaper
- pliers/wire cutter
- silicone mat
- hot glue
- glow-in-the-dark paint (optional)
- superglue

Materials

- chipboard
- ⅛" (3-mm) square dowels
- wooden circle (~2" [5 cm])
- electric tea candle
- moss
- 1" (2.5-cm) wooden bead (with wide opening)
- hoop ring (size to fit bead opening)
- floral wire
- silica gel packet
- short chain
- twine/hemp
- 3 mushrooms (unpainted) (page 65)
- 3 small quartz crystals
- pebbles (optional)

Cut the following out of chipboard:

- **Qty: 1**—6½ x ¾ inch (16.5 x 1.9 cm) ***base wall***
- **Qty: 15-ish**—⅛ x ¾ inch (3 mm x 1.9 cm) ***paneling***

Cut the following out of ⅛-inch (3-mm) square dowels:

- **Qty: 6**—1 inch (2.5 cm) ***firewood***
- **Qty: 3**—3½ inches (8.9 cm) ***poles***

Using a drill or wood burner, make a hole in the center of your 2-inch (5-cm) wooden circle. The hole should be just big enough to fit the light of your tea candle.

Tip: *If your candle's "flame" cover can be removed, measure only the bulb portion. If not, size your hole for the whole flame.*

Wrap the ***base wall*** around your wooden circle so it sits flush and glue it in place.

Glue the ***paneling*** strips vertically around the outside of the ***base wall***. Space them evenly-ish with a space in between. It doesn't have to be perfect; this is supposed to be made by witches, not IKEA®!

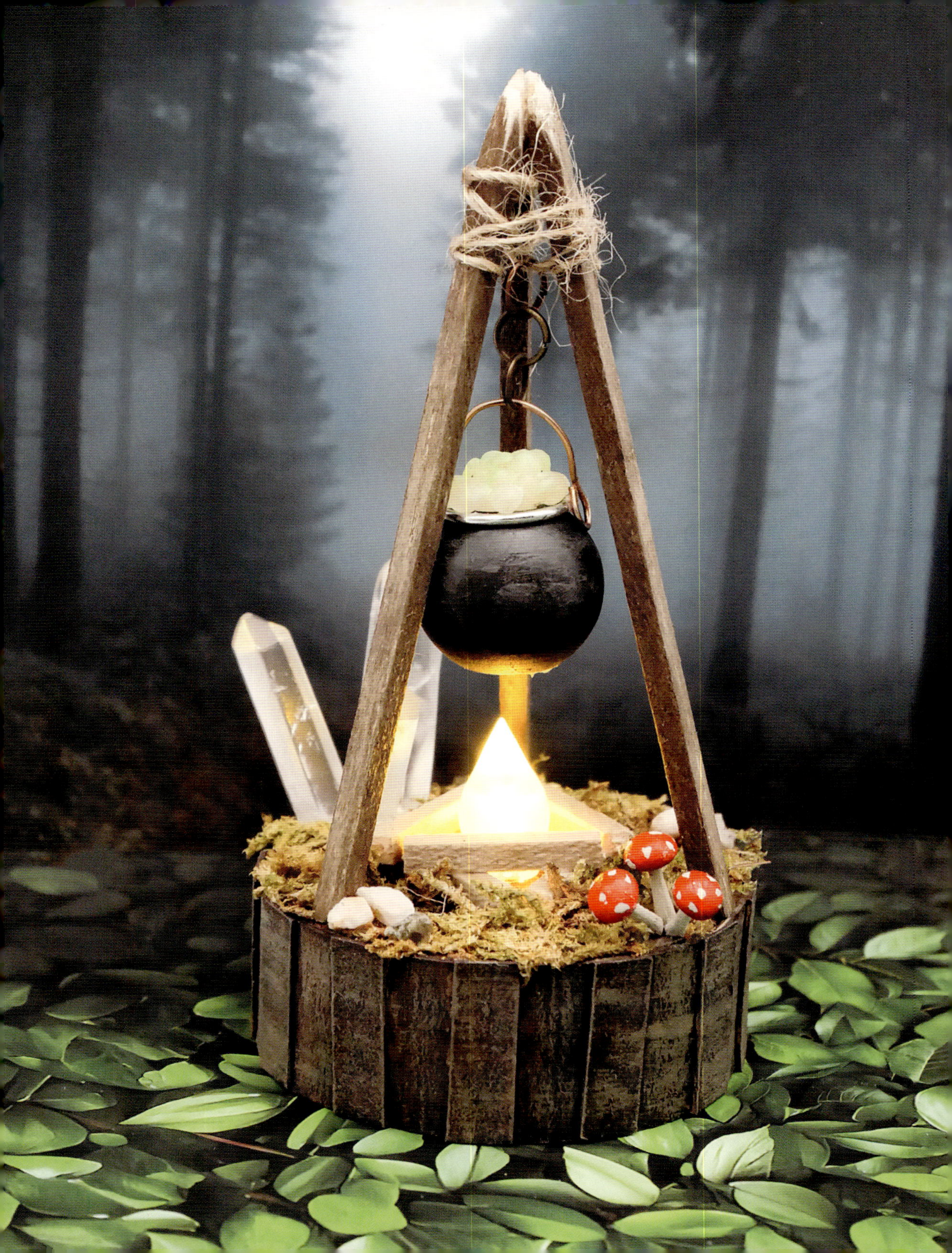

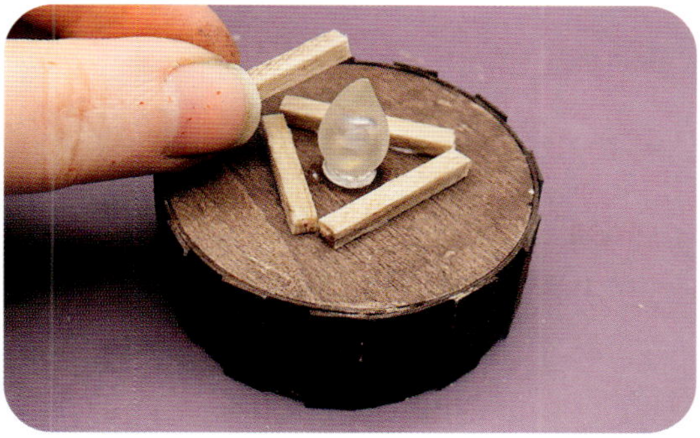

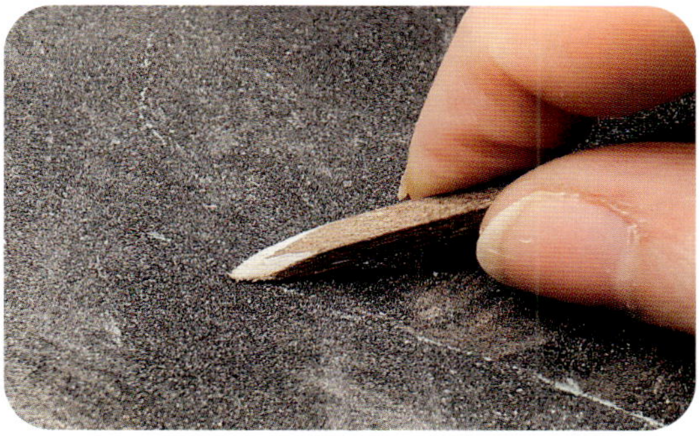

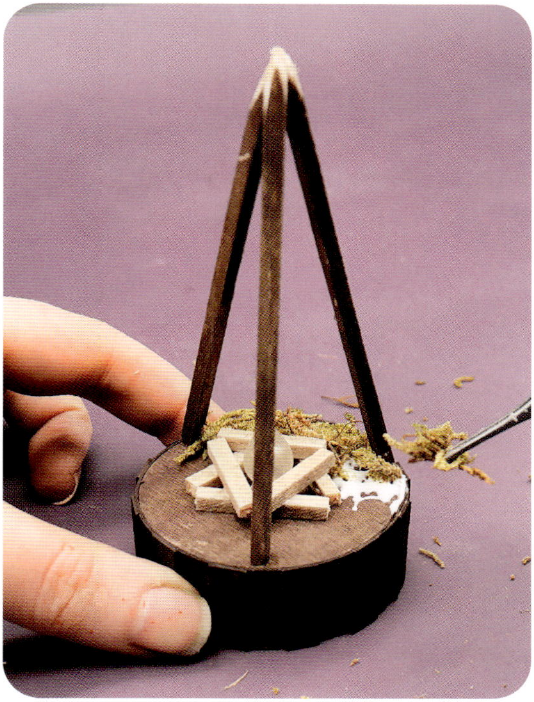

Paint this whole contraption a nice earthy brown.

Slide your candle flame/bulb into the hole and reattach the flame cover (if it has one).

Stain the ***firewood*** with watered-down brown paint.

Glue three ***firewood*** sticks in a triangle around the flame. Glue three more crisscrossing the first.

Paint the three ***poles*** dark brown and let them dry. Sand one end of each into a point so that they look like they could stab someone's eye out. *But don't test this!*

Glue the ***poles*** upright on the base in a wide tepee shape over the flame.

Glue moss around your ***firewood*** for a forest floor look. Set it aside.

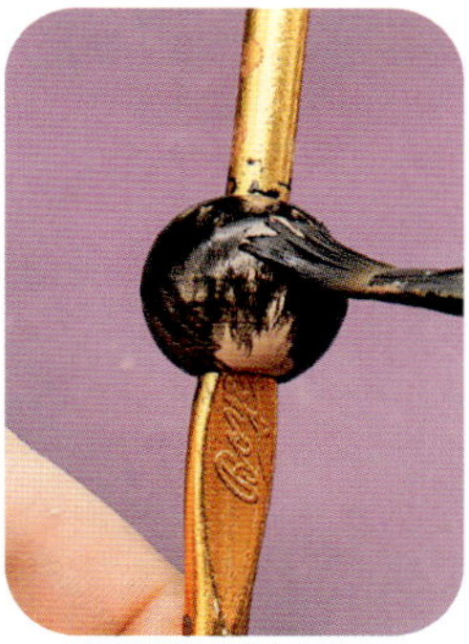

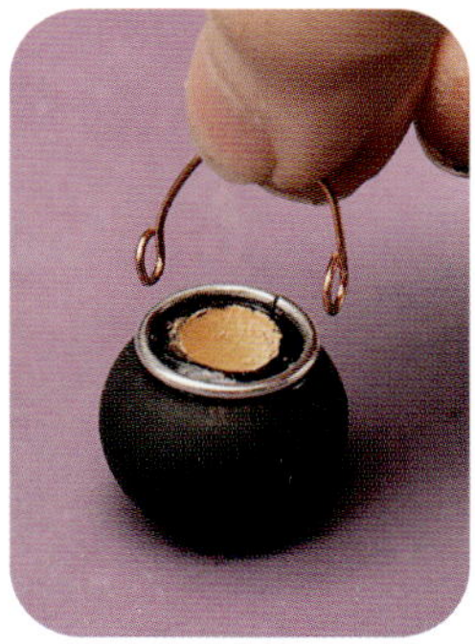

Summon your inner witch and we'll start brewing up a cauldron! Paint your wooden bead black.

Tip: *To keep your bead from running away, skewer it on a stick while you paint it.*

Once the bead is dry, glue your hoop ring or wire around the hole of the bead.

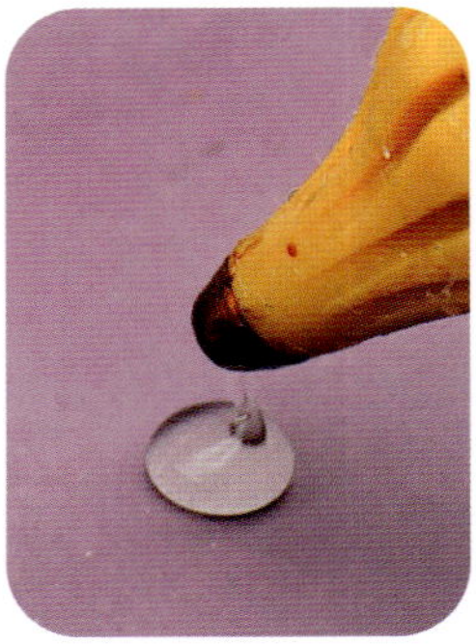

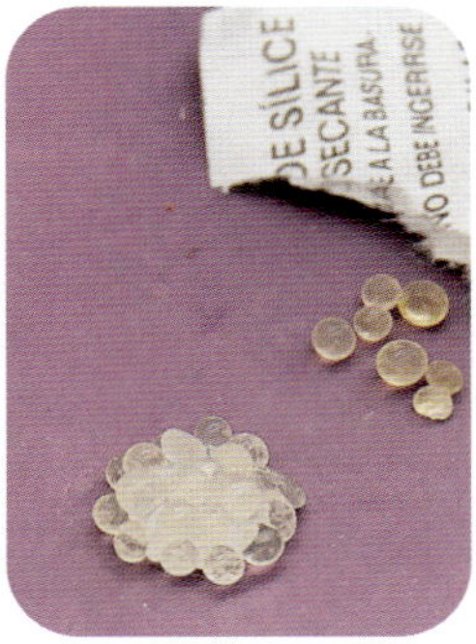

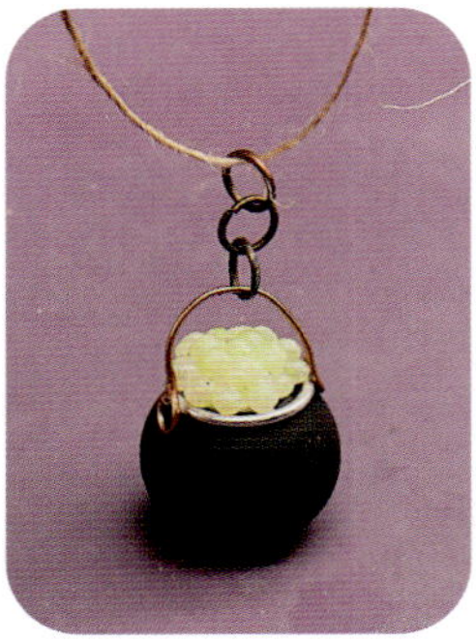

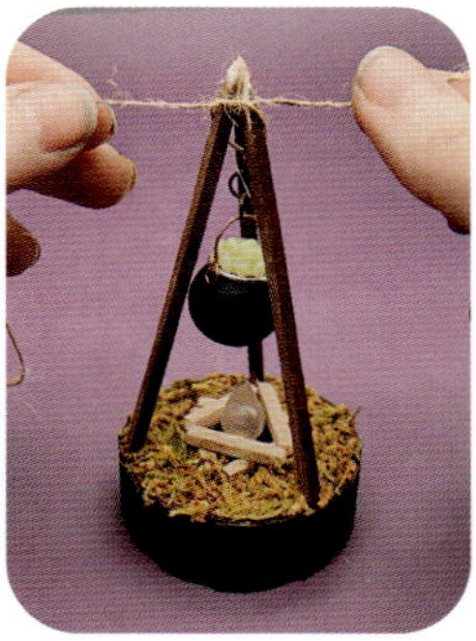

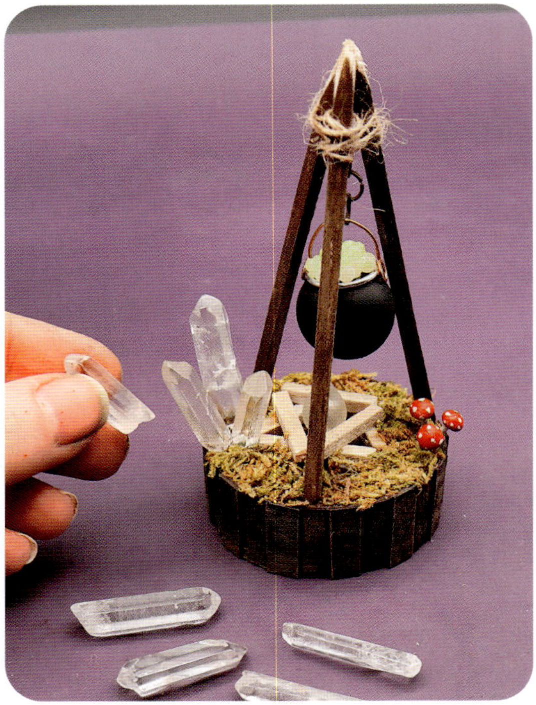

Cut a 2-inch (5-cm) piece of floral wire and bend it into a U. Curl the ends into small loops. Glue these loops onto opposite sides of the hoop ring to form a handle. Set it aside to dry.

On a silicone mat, squeeze a round puddle of hot glue about the size of the bead's opening. Before it hardens, sprinkle your silica gel beads (DON'T eat the silica packets. They don't taste good.) on top and kind of squish them into the glue a little. Let it cool.

If you have it, paint this bubble cluster with glow-in-the-dark paint.

Once dry, peel it off the mat and glue it onto your bead like a bubbling cauldron. Boom! You have a bubbling cauldron! Resist the urge to cackle. Unless you're home alone, then cackle away!!!

Attach the cauldron handle to a short chain (or improvise with a few small hoop rings).

Tie twine to the last link and secure it to the tops of your three poles so that your cauldron dangles above the flame.

Now, we could stop here and call it "done." But are you here for "done"? Heck no! We're here for MAGIC!

Paint the three mushrooms (page 65) red with white spots and superglue these, the three quartz crystals, and pebbles around your poles for that extra witchy magic!

Mutant Plants

Most plants need sunlight and water. However, these plants need much, much more!

Companionship!

What? Did you think I'd say blood?

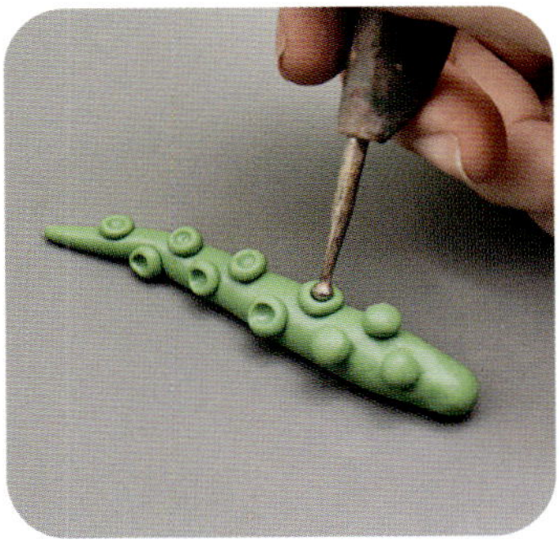

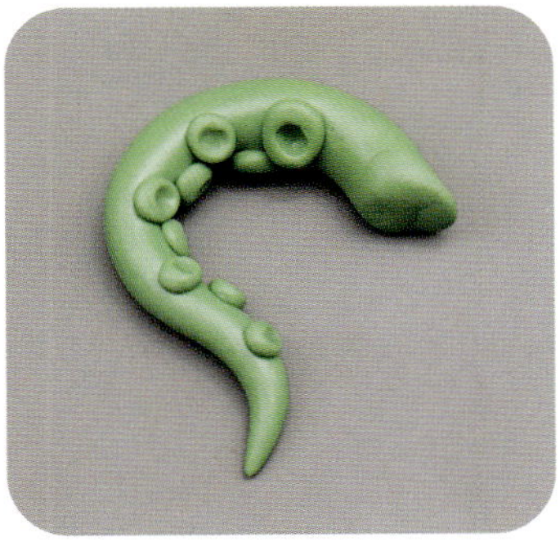

Tools

- ball sculpting tool
- hot glue
- paint
- clear gloss
- toothpick
- superglue

Materials

- polymer clay
- 3 small caps (for pots)
- 2 toothpicks
- moss
- wooden circles (if needed)
- crates (page 161)

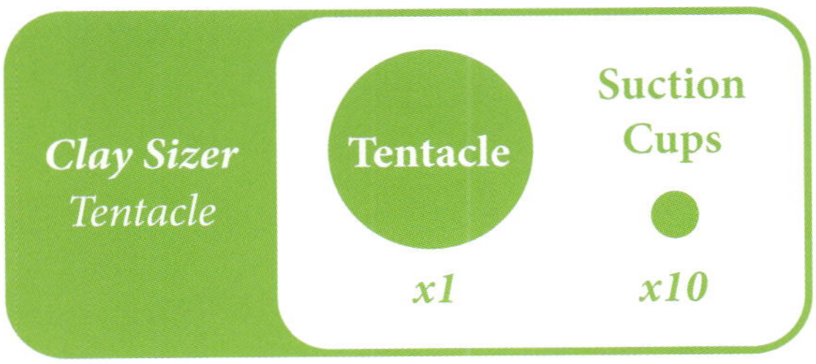

Tentacle Plant

It doesn't need sunlight . . . just victims!!

Roll out tentacle clay balls in green (or whatever color you want).

Take the largest ball and roll it into a snake with a tapered end roughly 2 to 3 inches (5 to 7.6 cm) long. This is your main tentacle.

Place your ten smaller balls along one side of the tentacle in a zigzag pattern and push a dent into each ball with a ball sculpting tool to make suction cups.

Bend your tentacle in a short S shape with the suction cups facing inward.

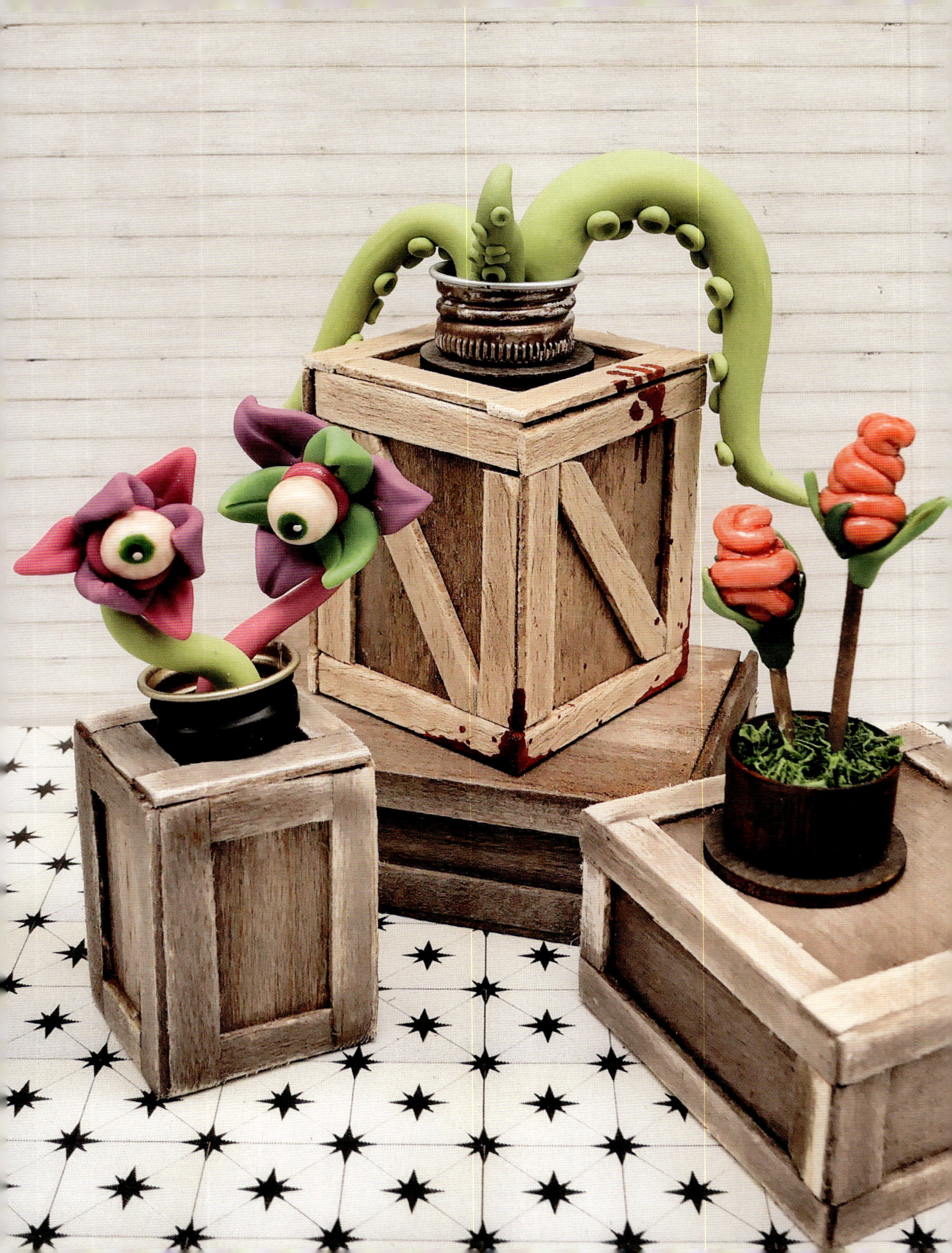

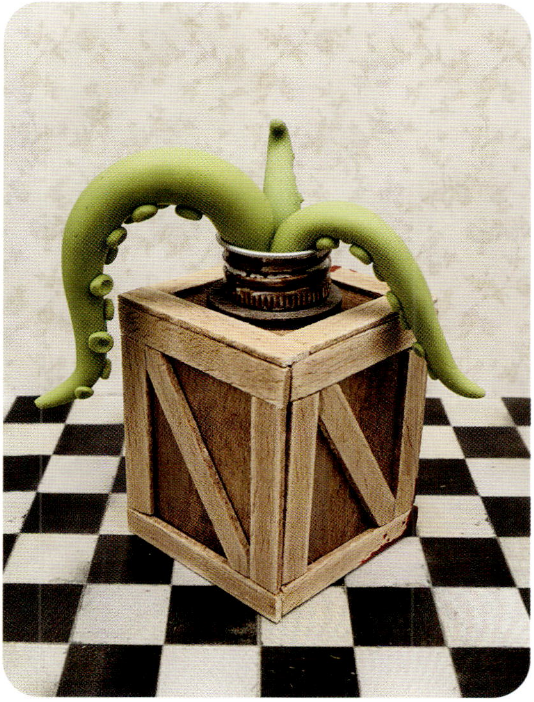

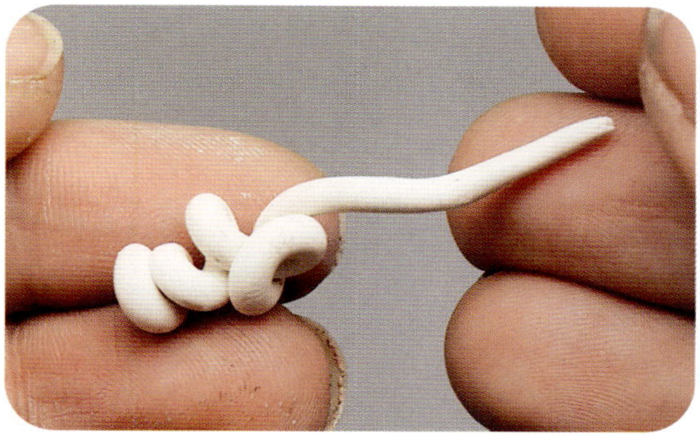

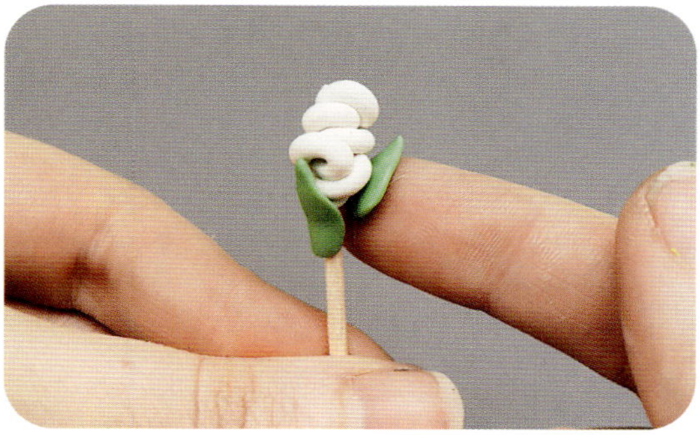

Repeat until you have three tentacles total. These other two should be smaller with slightly different curves. The variety makes it feel more alive.

Bake to harden according to the package instructions.

In one of your caps, hot glue the tentacles so that it looks like a mutant potted plant. Some of the tentacles may droop over the side and hang lower than the pot.

Brain Plant

This plant is smarter than it looks!

Roll out the following clay balls for your brain plant.

Roll the largest ball into a long, skinny snake, about the width of a phone charger. Spiral it into loopy kinks and gently press together to make a long brain.

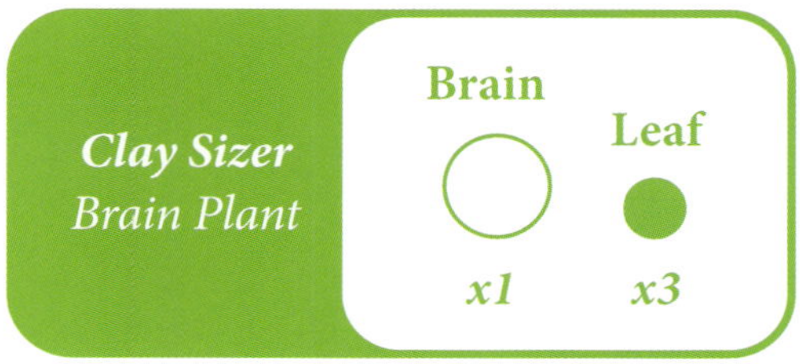

Poke a toothpick through the center to make a stem.

Take one of your smaller balls and flatten it between your fingers. Pinch one end to make a leaf shape and wrap it around the bottom of your brain flower where the brain meets the toothpick. Repeat and make two more leaves also wrapping around the bottom of the flower.

Make a second brain flower the same way and harden both.

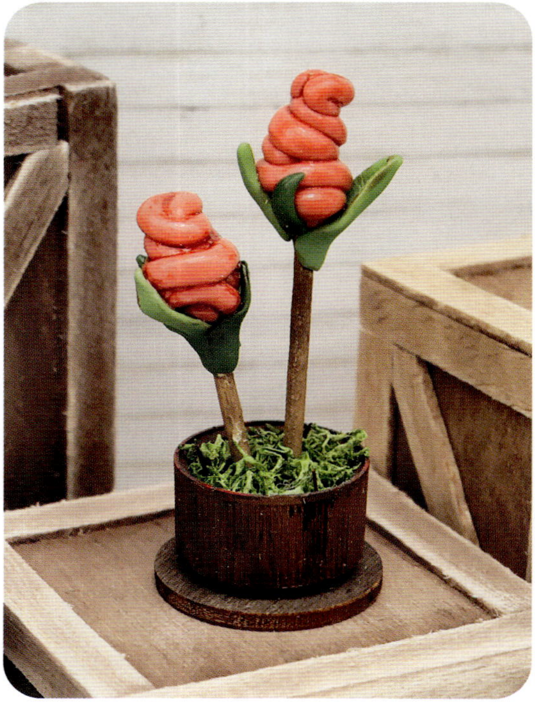

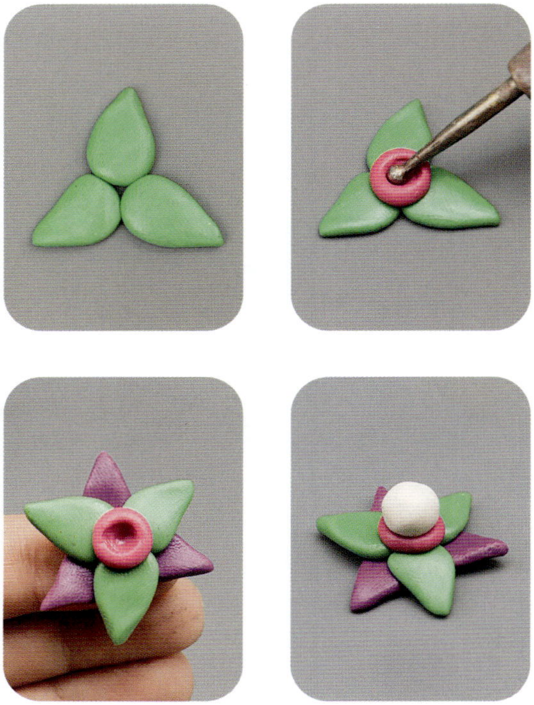

Clay Sizer *Eye Plant*	Tentacle	Eye	Eye Socket	Leaf	Petal
	x1	*x1*	*x1*	*x3*	*x3*

If you have white clay like I did, paint the white clay by mixing red with clear gloss. This will give it a juicy look.

Paint the toothpicks brown and snap them to size.

Fill a cap halfway with hot glue and stick the stems in. Hold until it hardens. Top with moss to hide that gross hot glue.

Eye Plant

It sees everything . . . even that weird thing you did in the kitchen.

Roll out your eye plant clay balls.

Flatten the three ***leaf*** balls into teardrop shapes and push their butts together to make a triangle.

Place the ***eye socket*** ball in the center of your leaf triangle and push a dent in the center.

Shape the three ***petal*** balls into teardrops and add them around the back of your leaf triangle.

Place the ***eye*** ball in the eye socket.

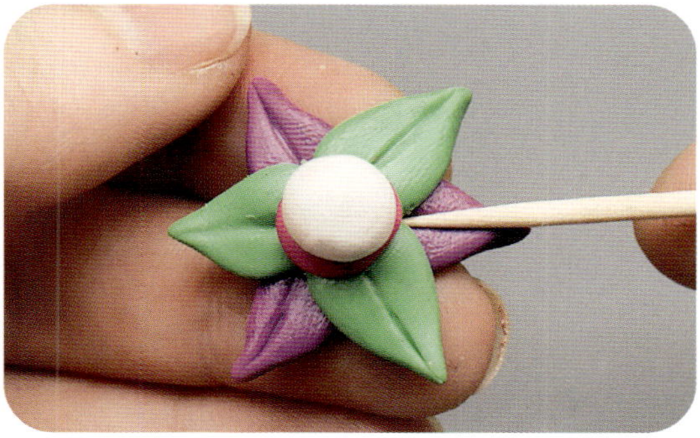

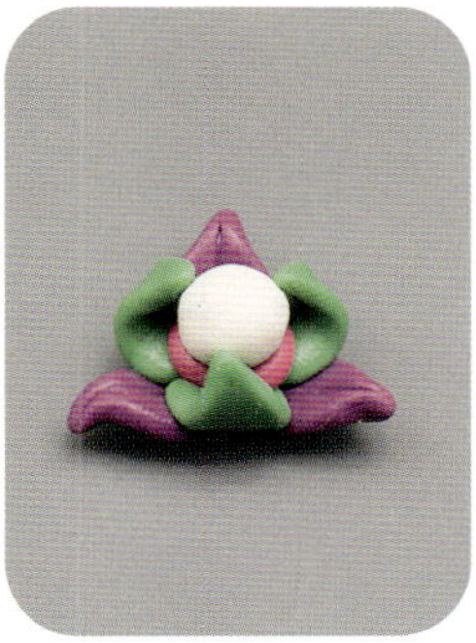

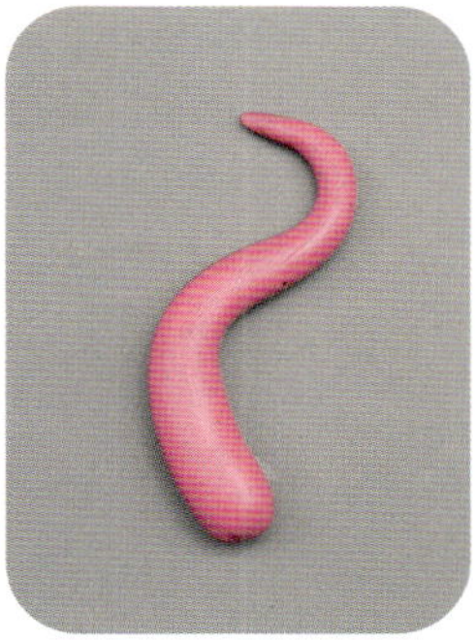

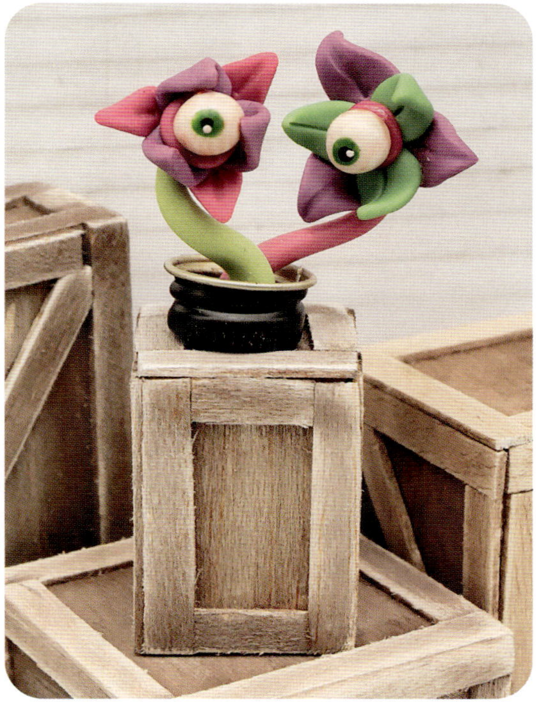

Use a toothpick tip to score veins in the middle of each leaf and petal. Curve your leaves toward the eye and petals away. Set it aside.

Take a ***tentacle*** ball and roll it into a skinny S-shaped tentacle just like we did for the tentacle plant.

Repeat so you have two flowers and two tentacles. Harden everything.

Paint an iris on your eyeball. Use the blunt end of a toothpick for the pupil and highlights.

Coat the whole eye with clear gloss for maximum shine. Add red to your gloss if you want your eyes to be bloodshot. And I'm guessing you do.

Superglue a flower onto the skinny end of each tentacle.

Fill your cap halfway with hot glue and plant your new horrors inside. Cover the glue with moss if needed.

Note: *Wooden flat circles that are slightly larger than your pot can be added to the bottom to help stabilize your plant.*

If you want to set the scene, perch your new mutant plants on top of wooden crates from page 161. Are you going for a strange little shop of horrors or perhaps just a witchy garden?

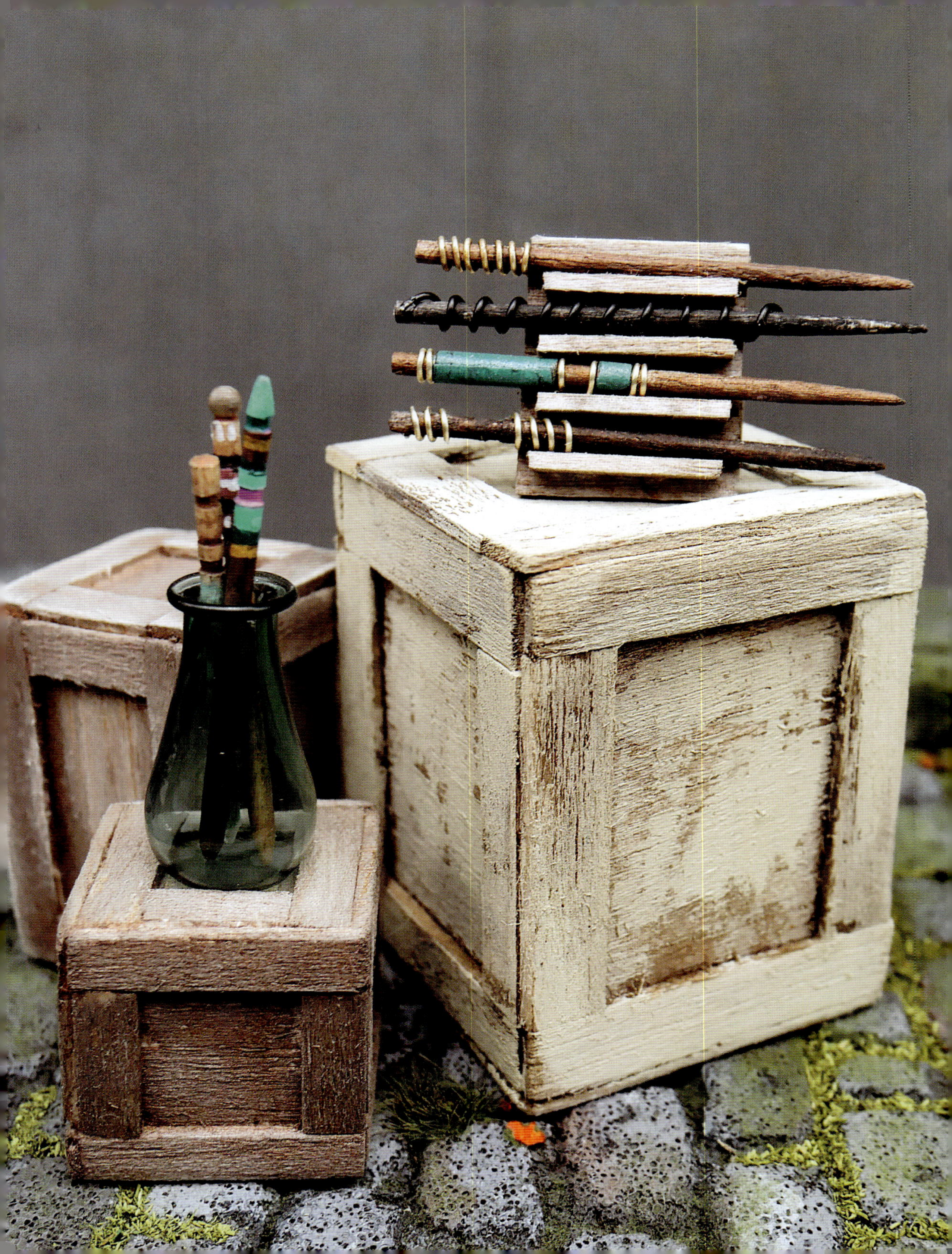

Wand Storage

Wand storage is a very important part of safe wand ownership. If your wands are just rolling around everywhere, someone's bound to get an eye poked!

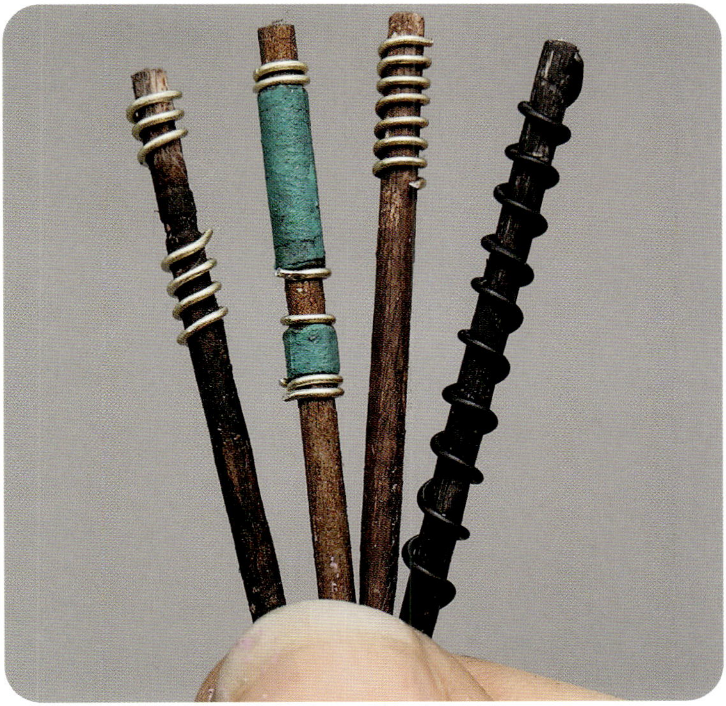

Tools

- paint
- exacto knife, ruler, & cutting mat
- sandpaper
- glue

Wands & Holder Materials

- 4 toothpicks (aka mini wands)
- floral wire
- beads
- paper
- balsa wood

Wands

Paint your four toothpicks various shades of brown. *Or all the same shade if you want to be boring.*

Cut them to roughly 1½ inches (3.8 cm) long, keeping the pointy end.

Sand the points so they're "magically pointy" and not "ouchy pointy."

Decorate! Wrap floral wire around them, add beads to the top, or glue colorful paper around various bits to create different thicknesses. *The more decorated they are, the more powerful the spells . . . probably.*

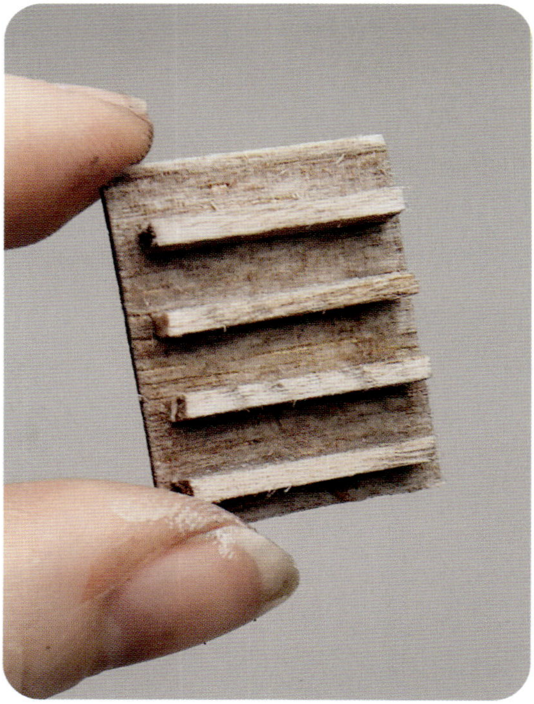

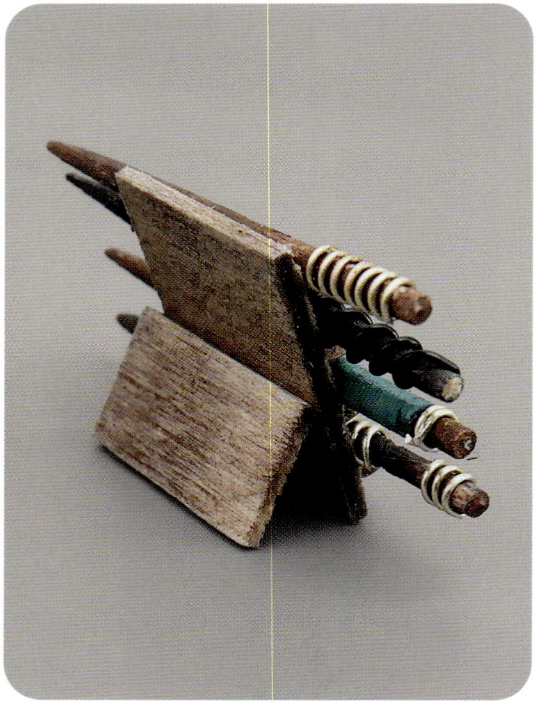

Holder

This is what makes them look more like wands rather than tiny chopsticks.

Cut and stain brown the following balsa wood. A template is on page 213 for reference.

- **Qty: 4**—⅛ x 7⁄10 inch (3 mm x 1.8 cm) ***shelves***
- **Qty: 1**—¾ x 1 inch (1.9 x 2.5 cm) ***backer***
- **Qty: 1**—¾ x ½ inch (1.9 x 1.3 cm) ***stand***

Glue your four ***shelves*** evenly spaced across the ***backer*** at 90° angles. *It doesn't have to be perfect. Crooked racks give off strong haunted vibes. Which is good!*

Glue the ***stand*** at an angle to the back of the ***backer*** so that your wand stand sits slanted but upright.

For variety, you can also plop your wands into a little glass jar. Which is just as magically cute! There you have it! A proper wand rack for proper wand safety!

Magic Rose

Is that a magic rose AND a mirrored circle window? Heck yes, it is! Just remember to keep your magic roses covered. Otherwise, the WOA (Witch Owners Association) will fine you 42 toadstools for the violations!

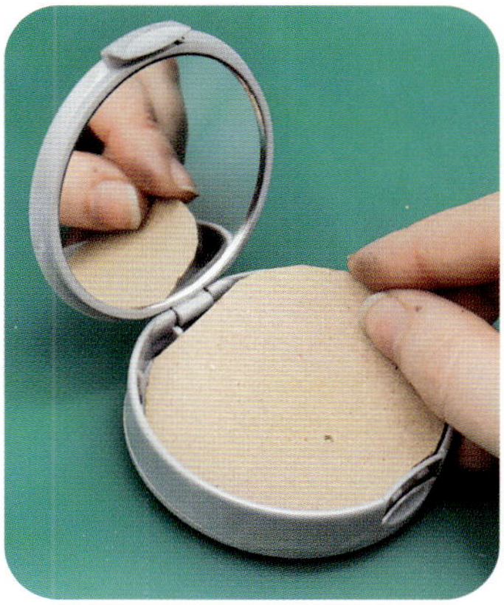

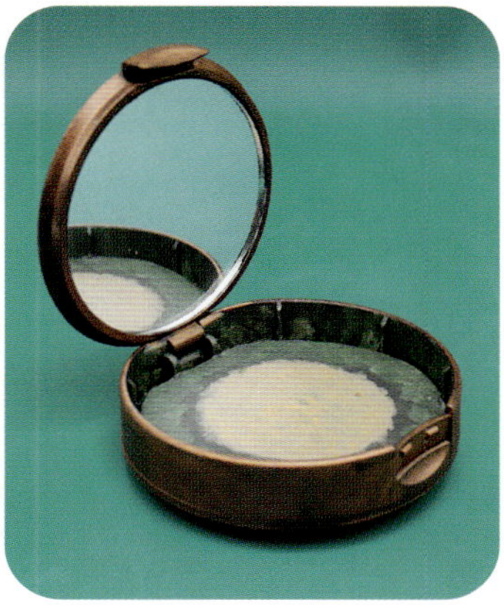

Tools

- exacto knife, ruler, & cutting mat
- hot glue
- paint
- sandpaper
- glue
- pliers/wire cutter
- superglue
- craft glue

Base Materials

- empty compact with mirror
- chipboard
- small pebbles
- 10 mushrooms (page 65)
- green flocking (optional)

Rose Materials

- polymer clay
- toothpick
- green paper

Table Materials

- 2 snap fastener posts (or earring backs)
- floral wire
- wooden circle (larger than capsule opening)
- bead cap
- clear plastic capsule (or vial)
- barbed wire (page 60)

Base

With an exacto knife or other slim object, carefully pry the metal piece from the base of your compact where the makeup would have been. With enough yelling and prying, it will eventually pop out.

Cut and hot glue a piece of chipboard to fit in the bottom of your compact.

Dab green and black paint along the edges of your chipboard and the inside wall to make it look like foliage. Paint a light tan center "clearing." This is where the rose will set.

Lightly sand the outside of your compact and smother (paint) it in bronze.

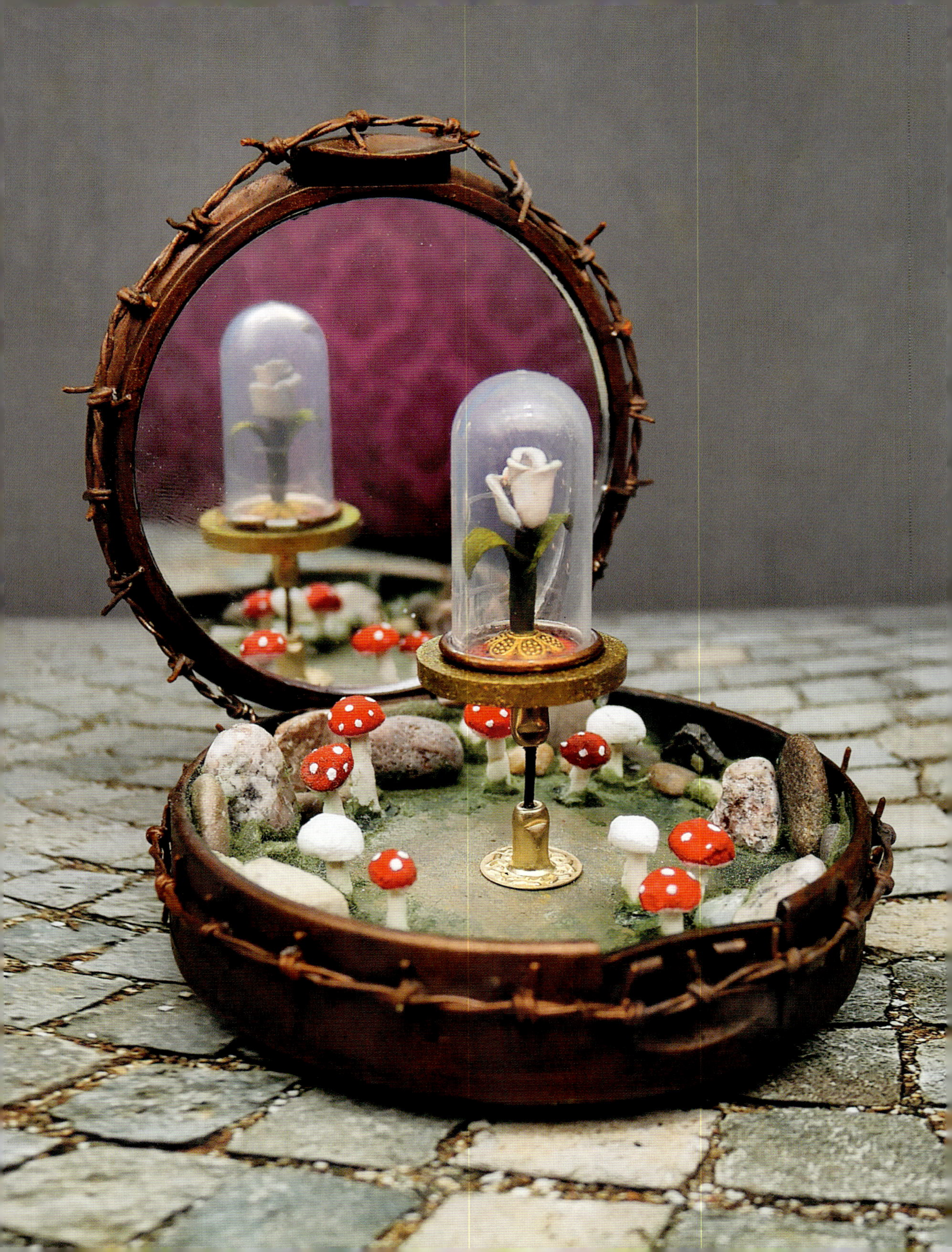

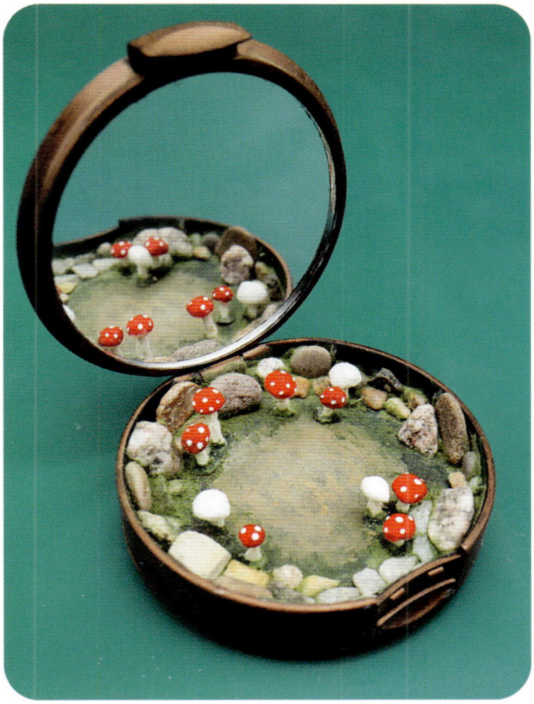

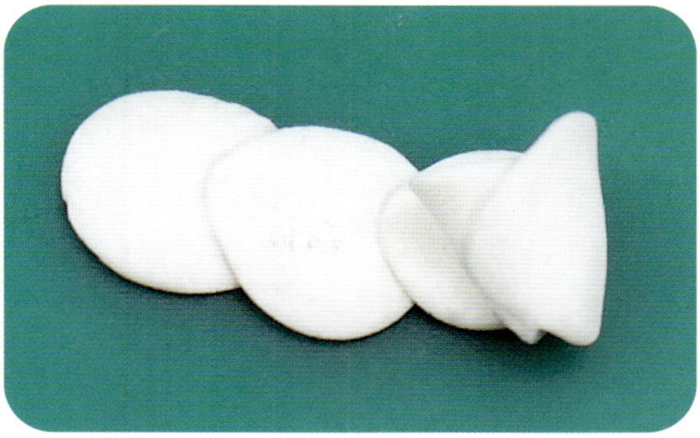

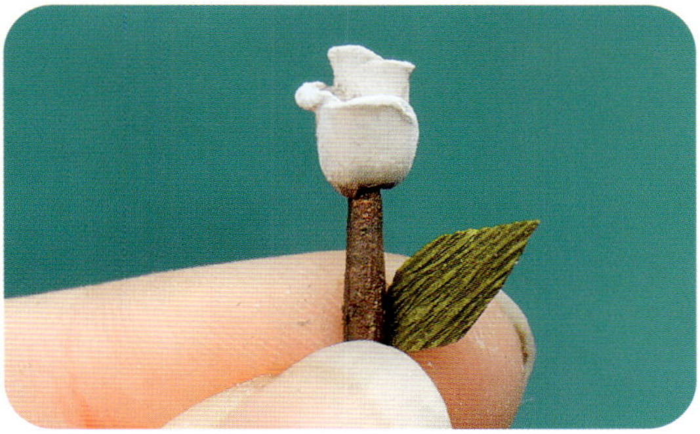

Clay Sizer
Rose Petals
x5

Around the inside edge, glue a circle of pebbles and a few mushrooms from page 65. Have fun with your mushrooms, they don't all have to be white. Try painting a few red with spots or heck, paint them any color you like!

Glue flocking around the pebbles and shrooms. *If you don't have flocking (because admittedly that's not a normal thing to have), no worries! It looks fine without it too.* Set it aside.

Rose

Flatten five pea-sized balls of clay into disks and lay each disk in a line with edges slightly overlapping. Like a row of magical dragon scales.

Carefully roll up your scales into a rose shape. This might take a few tries before you get the hang of it. Don't give up, I believe in you!

Gently push the point of a toothpick into the bottom of your rose and cure according to the package instructions.

> **Tip:** *If you're afraid your rose will become misshapen while curing, push your toothpicks into a ball of aluminum foil to keep it upright.*

Once your rose is hard, paint the toothpick brown and cut two leaf shapes out of your green paper. Curl them around your exacto knife handle to give them more shape, then glue them around the toothpick. Set this aside.

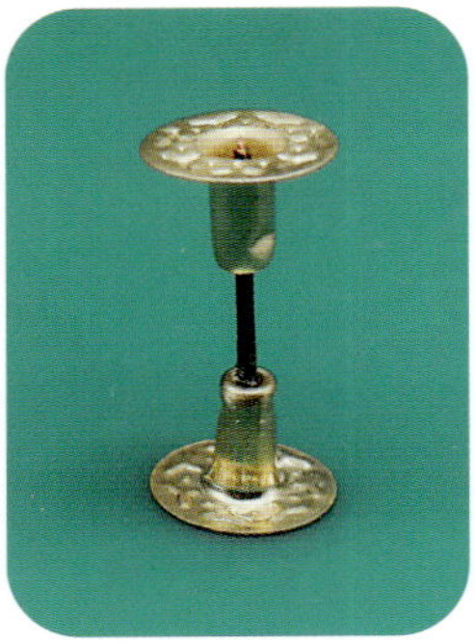

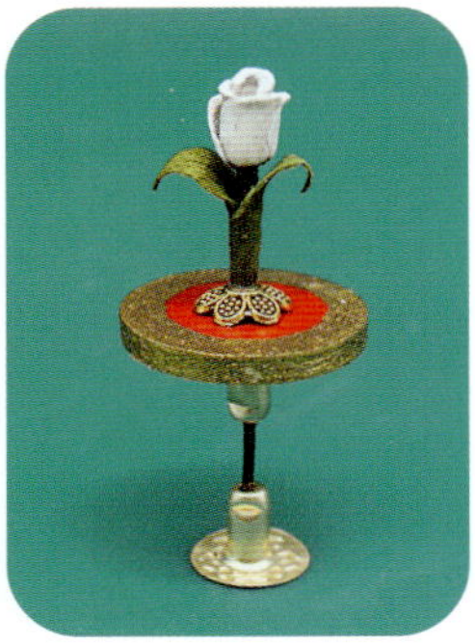

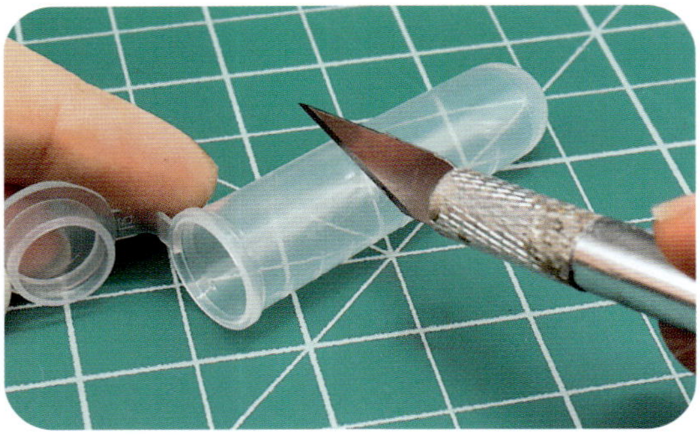

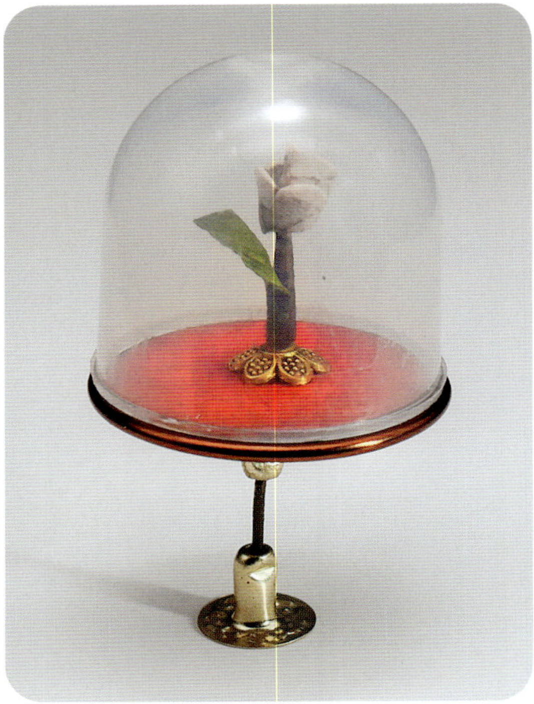

Table

Take your two snap fastener posts (or flat earring backs) and push a wire that's about 1½ inches (3.8 cm) long through the bump end of each post. Superglue in place.

Superglue the end of one snap fastener post to the center of your wooden circle.

Paint your wood circle any way you like. I went with a royal look with gold and red.

Nobody likes a floppy flower! Glue a bead cap in the center of your table. *Don't have a bead cap? Just use a bead, as long as your toothpick fits inside.*

Glue your rose in the bead cap.

We need to cover the rose, otherwise the witching community will come for us!

Cut your vial or capsule to length if needed and glue it over your rose with craft glue.

Superglue will fog the plastic.

Are your capsule edges rough from cutting? Keep it a secret by wrapping a wire around the bottom.

Glue this in the center of your compact.

Optionally, you can decorate the edges of your compact with barbed wire from page 60.

My Specimens

You can look, but don't touch! My specimens might appear innocent, but those eyes rolled right out from the "Chest of Secrets," and trust me, you don't want to know where that butterfly came from.

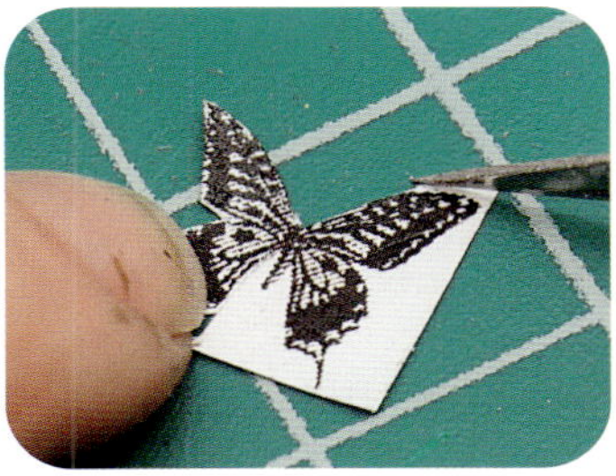

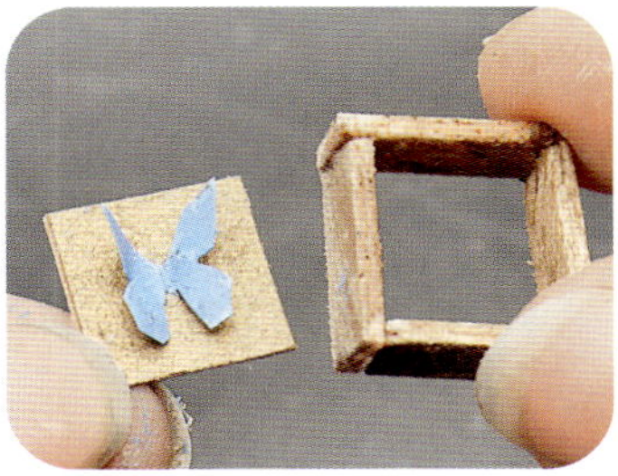

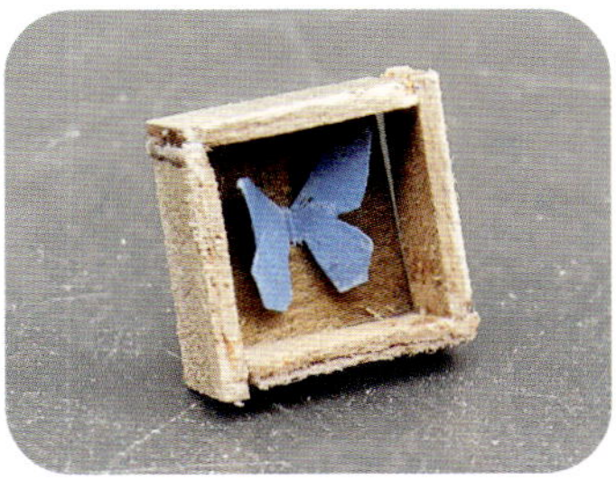

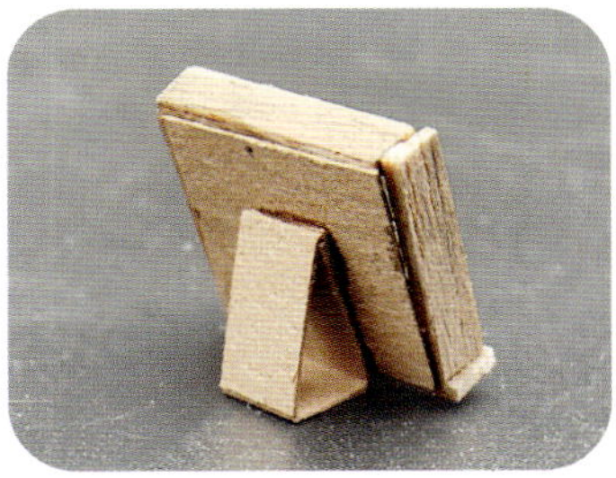

Tools

- exacto knife, ruler, & cutting mat
- glue
- paint
- toothpick

Butterfly Materials

- butterfly image (<¼" [6 mm])
- chipboard
- balsa wood

Eyeball Materials

- chipboard
- silica gel packet
- balsa wood
- shelf (page 45; instead of four shelves, do three spaced 1½ inches [3.8 cm] apart)

Butterfly

Using an exacto knife, trim around your image of a butterfly.

On a ½-inch (1.3-cm) square piece of chipboard, glue only the belly of your butterfly in the center.

Frame your butterfly with four strips of stained brown balsa wood ½ inch (1.3 cm) long by about ⅛ inch (3 mm) wide. For framing help, follow the gluing guide on page 218 to see how to glue the end-grain edges to the face-grain edges.

Fold a little strip of chipboard into a triangle and glue it on the back to keep it from flopping over.

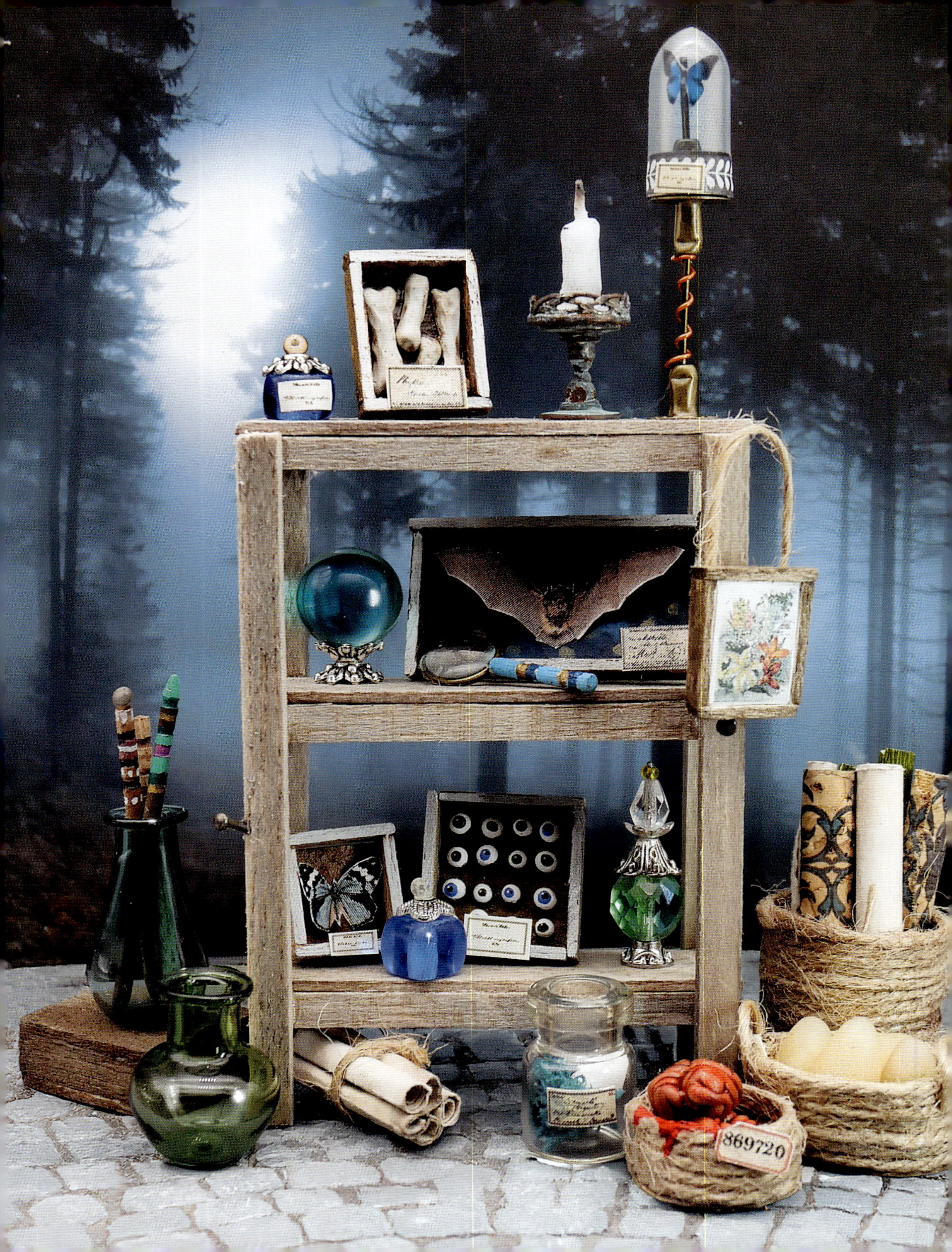
869720

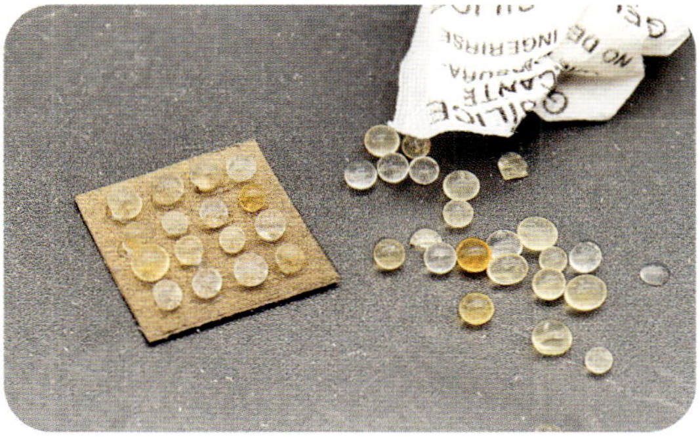
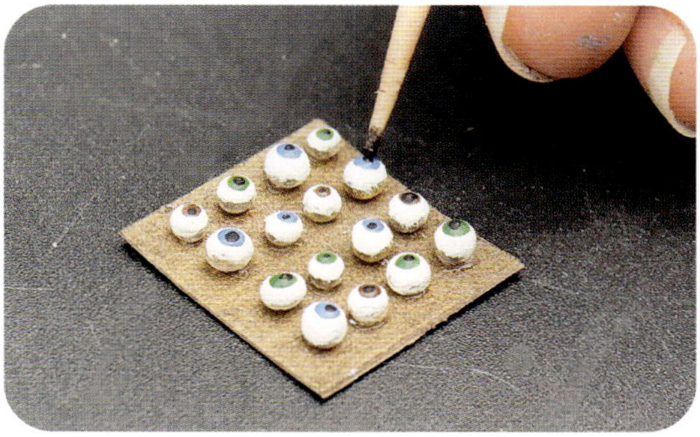
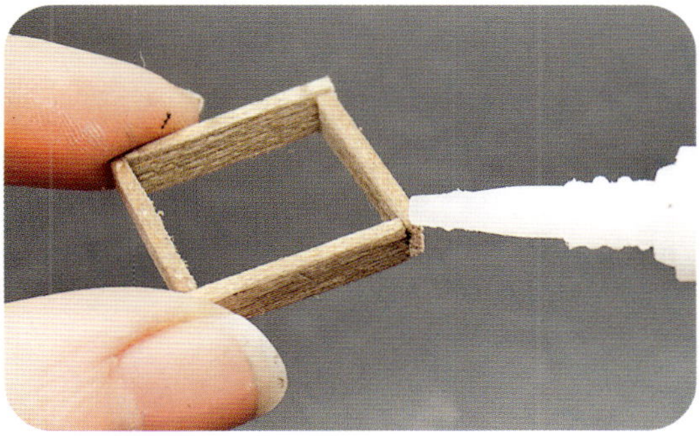
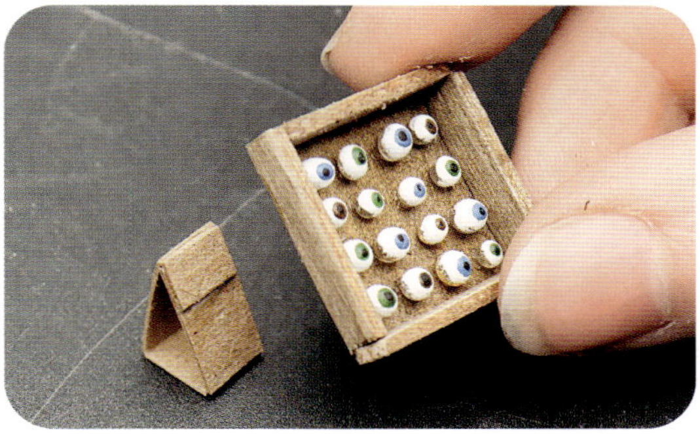

Eyeball

On a ¾-inch (1.9-cm) square piece of chipboard, glue a grid of silica balls in four rows of four.

Once your glue is 100% dry (you don't want to dislodge the balls while painting), paint the tops of each ball white.

Dip the blunt end of a toothpick in colorful paint and dab an iris on the top of each ball. Avoid boring eyes by alternating colors.

Once dry, use the pointy end of a toothpick to stab the pupils in black.

Just like with the butterfly, make a frame out of strips of balsa wood to glue around your eyes. Don't forget about the triangle stand to keep your eyes upright and not lazy.

Add these along with other framed things using the same framing method onto your specimen shelf. Bats, sculpted bones, spiders . . . What would you keep on your specimen shelf?

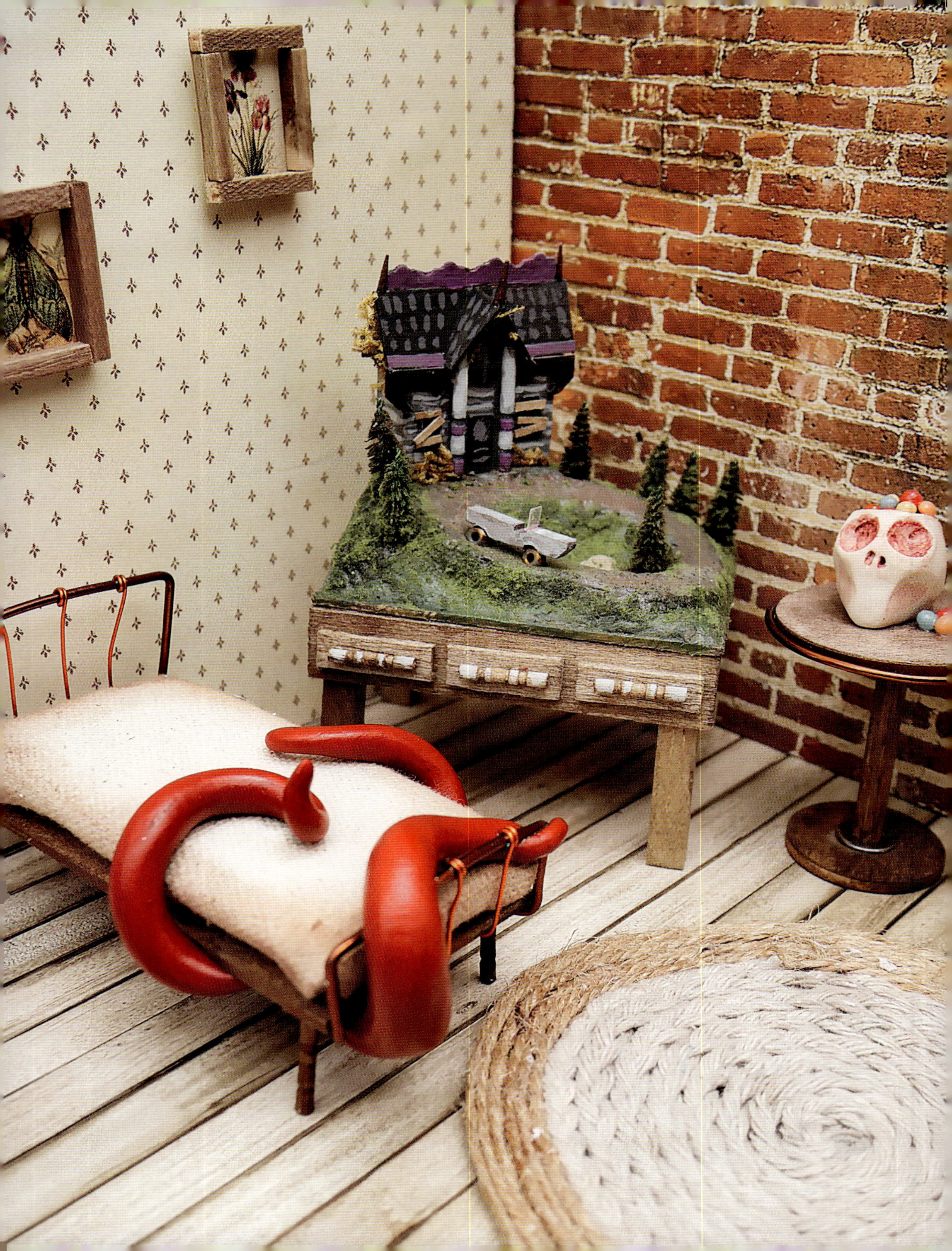

Child's Play

When little Clayton turned 12, he finally got his very first sleepover birthday party! His parents went all out. Balloons, cake, candy, even those party hats with glitter . . . the glitter that sticks to EVERYTHING! But what Clayton wanted most was a carousel. Stupidly, Clayton's parents said yes.

Now mind you, Clayton's parents didn't exactly have "carousel money," so they struck a deal with a sketchy traveling carnival. However, what Clayton's parents didn't know was that this carnival was in cahoots with the devil himself and, you guessed it, the carousel they purchased was very much EVIL! With a capital E. V. I. L.!

At first, the party went great. Music, cake, games, gifts! But as soon as the carousel started spinning, things got . . . weird. The birthday cake sprouted eyeballs. Clayton's brand-new dollhouse sang "yadhtriB yppaH." The candy bowl turned into a skull and tasted like . . . brains? But only the kids noticed. The adults were much too busy talking about adult things, like taxes or something, and just like in *every* scary movie *ever,* they didn't believe a word the kids said!

Then came the sleepover portion. While the kids drifted off to sleep, Clayton's room came to life with evil tentacles! Grabbing the children and pulling them under his bed into the dark nothingness. By morning . . . well, let's just say there were a few less children than the night before.

And to think, if only Clayton's parents had told him "no" every once in a while . . .

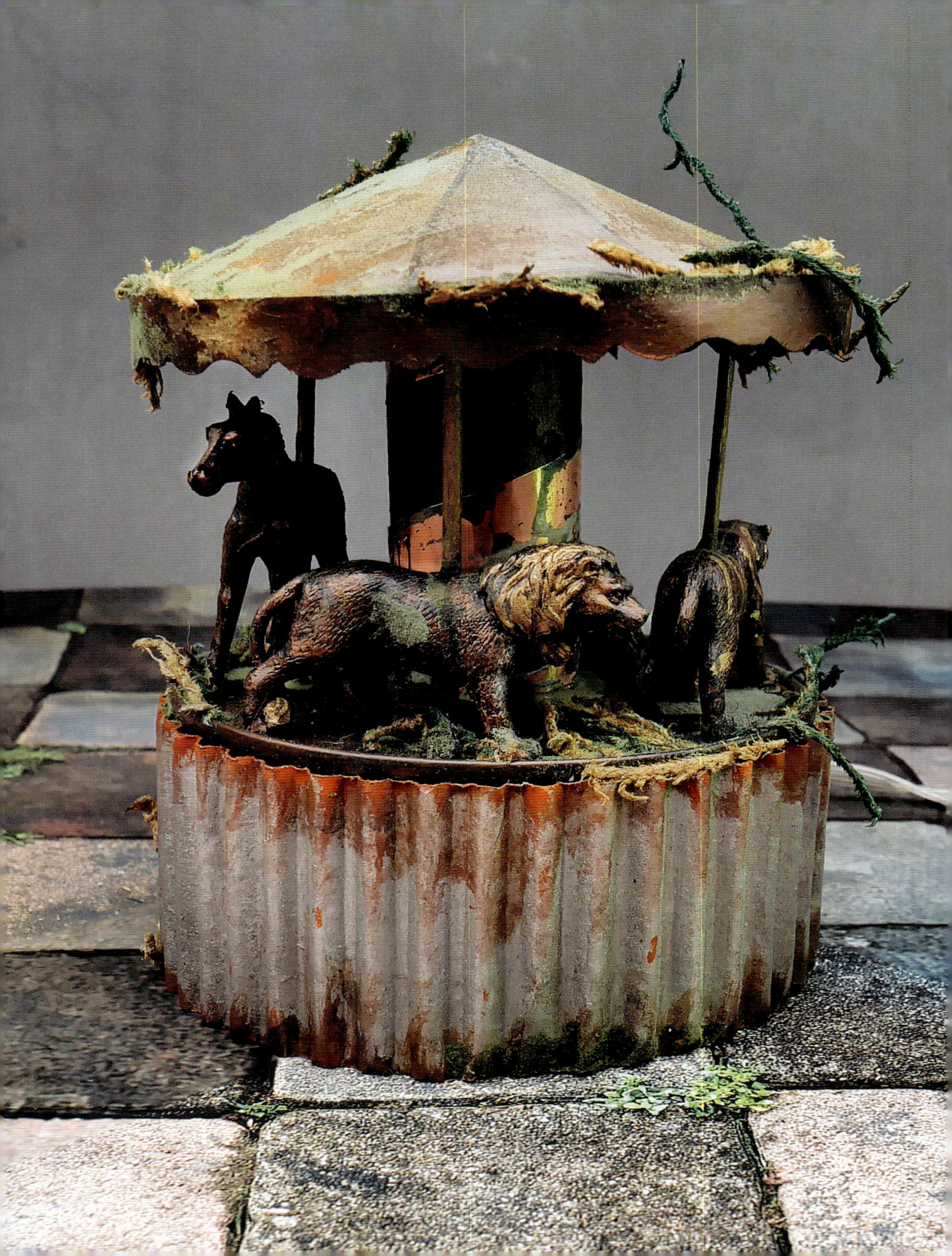

Carousel of EVIL

Nobody rides the Carousel of EVIL anymore. But on certain nights, they say you can still hear its song . . . or maybe that's my phone. Either way, it's pretty spooky! I mean, who calls anymore!

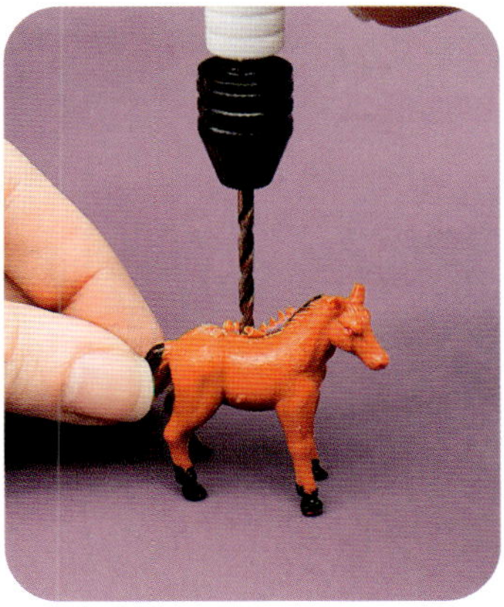

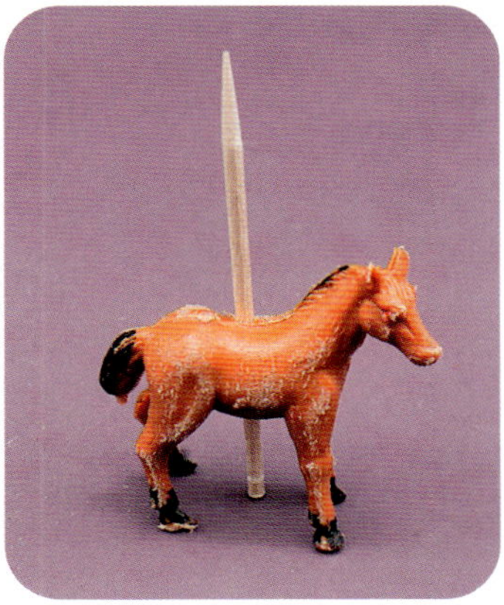

Choose your three to four plastic animals by deciding which ones are the most evil. By only using evil animals, you can ensure that your carousel will be haunted. Which is important!

Using a drill (I used a hand drill because I don't trust myself around power tools after "the incident"), drill a hole in each animal's back. **Keep it as straight as possible.** Your hole should be just big enough for a toothpick.

Skewer each animal with a toothpick. Push it through so the blunt end is touching the table and superglue it in place. Set the prepared animals aside.

Tools

- drill
- superglue
- pencil
- glue
- exacto knife, ruler, & cutting mat
- matte black spray paint
- paint
- hot glue
- "fun" scissors (if you have them)

Materials

- 3–4 small plastic animals
- 4 toothpicks
- tuna can
- balsa wood
- 1" (2.5-cm)-wide x 3" (7.6-cm)-long cardboard tube
- decorative tape (if you have it)
- black cardstock
- corrugated cardboard
- moss and/or green flocking (if you have it)

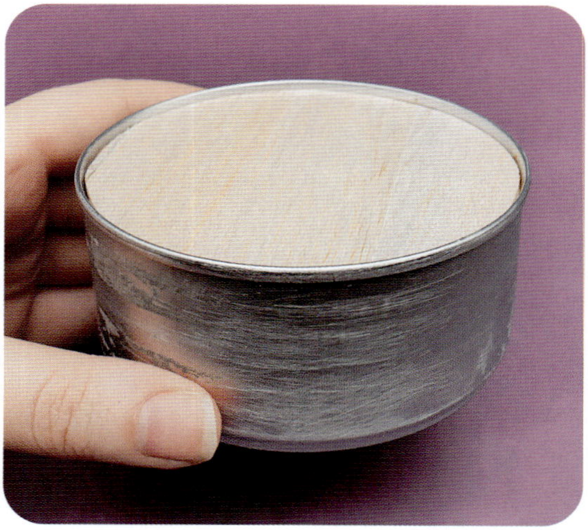

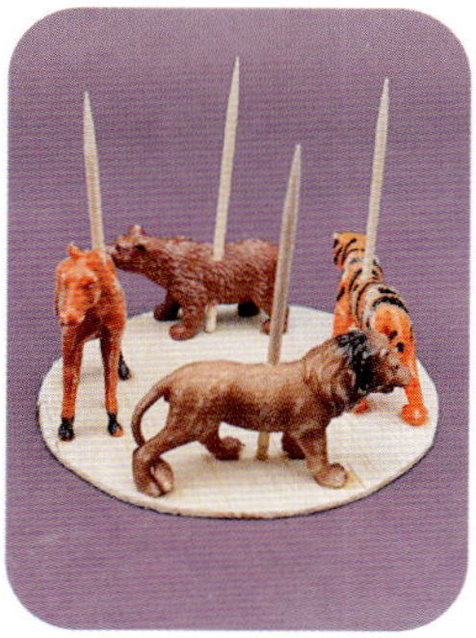

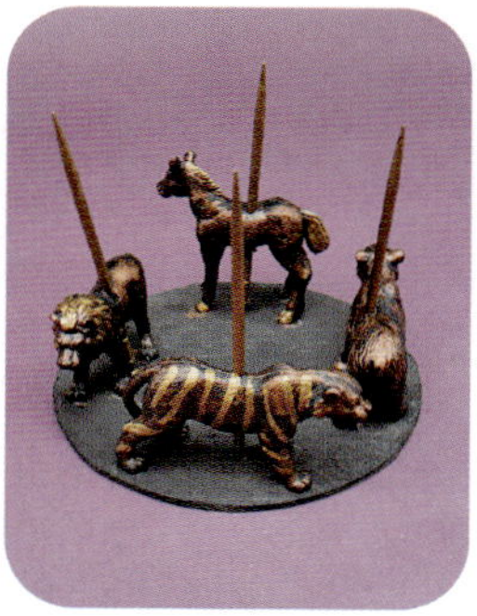

Trace the top of your empty tuna can onto a sheet of balsa wood and cut the circle out slightly smaller. It should be small enough to sit in the lip of the can but large enough that it doesn't fall in.

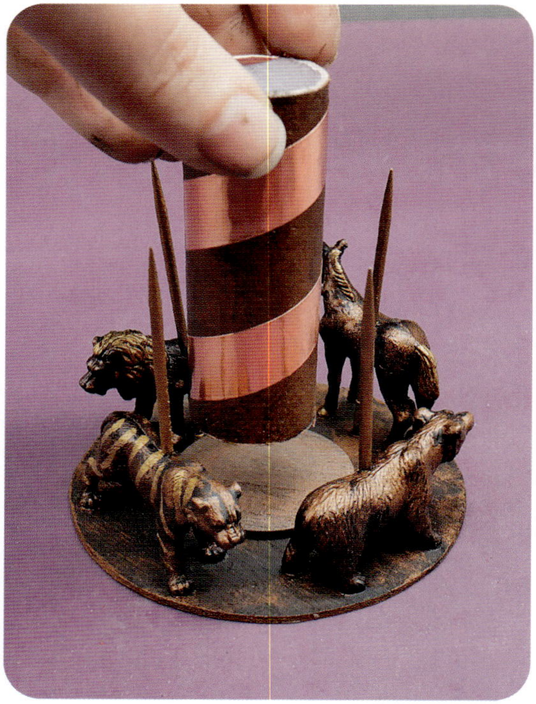

Grasp your evil animals before they run away again and imprison them by supergluing them on top of the wooden circle. Make sure they are all facing the same direction.

Spray paint them to match their souls . . . matte black. Once dry, dry brush them with a dark bronze and add golden details, like stripes on the zebra, hair on the lion's mane, etc.

Paint your cardboard tube black to match. If you have decorative tape, swirl it around your tube like a demented circus pole.

Glue it in the middle of your animals.

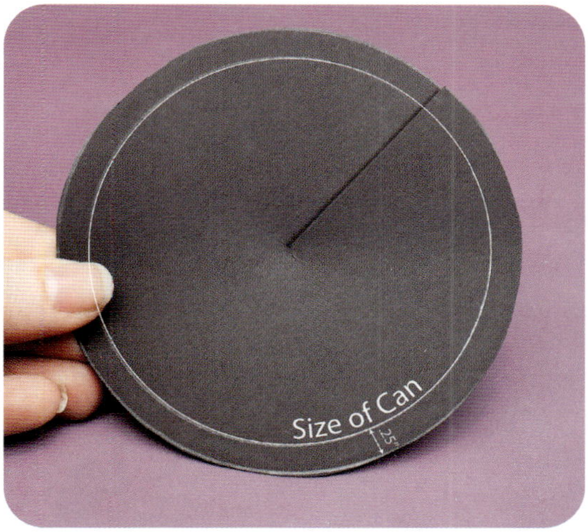

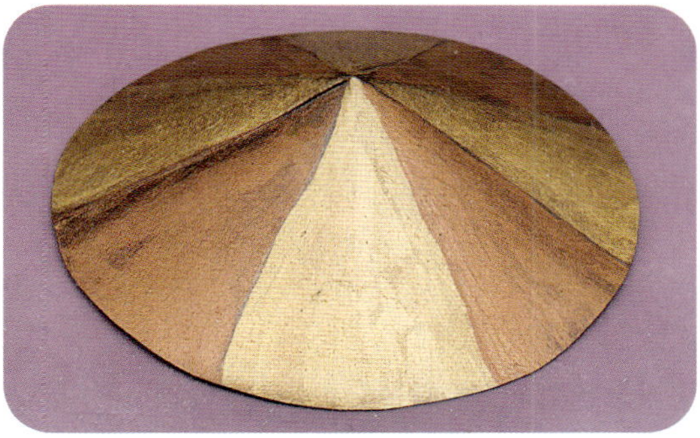

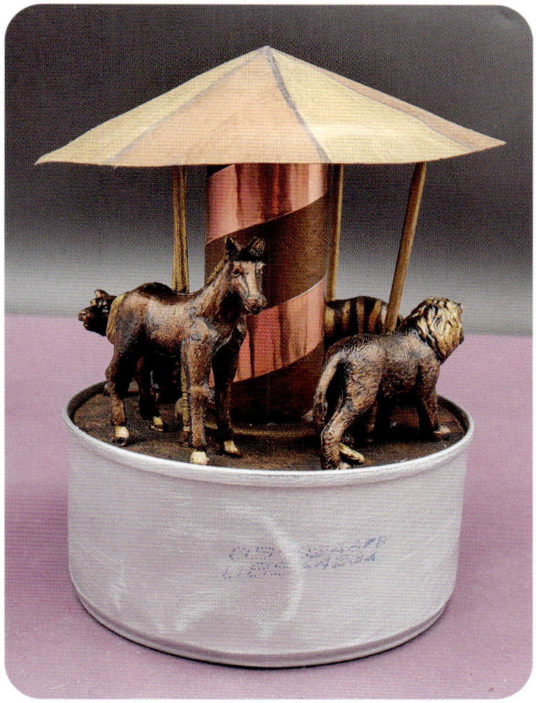

Trace your tuna can onto a sheet of preferably black cardstock. Measure ¼ inch (6 mm) out from your tracing and draw a larger circle. Cut it out, along with a straight line from the middle of the circle to the edge.

Overlapping the edges slightly, bend it into a very shallow cone and glue it.

Paint the top of your cone any way you like. I went with a pie shape pattern, but you could do a spiral or polka dots . . . whatever.

Hot glue this on top of your tube. If the toothpicks prevent it from resting fully on the cardboard tube, trim it.

Glue your animals on top of your tuna can.

The last step is to decorate it. Rip the top layer off of your corrugated cardboard and wrap it around your tuna can. Paint it to look like metal. Use "fun" scissors to add a strip of decorative cardstock around the umbrella. Top it all off with moss or flocking to make overgrown plants. Have fun with it. Add your own little touches.

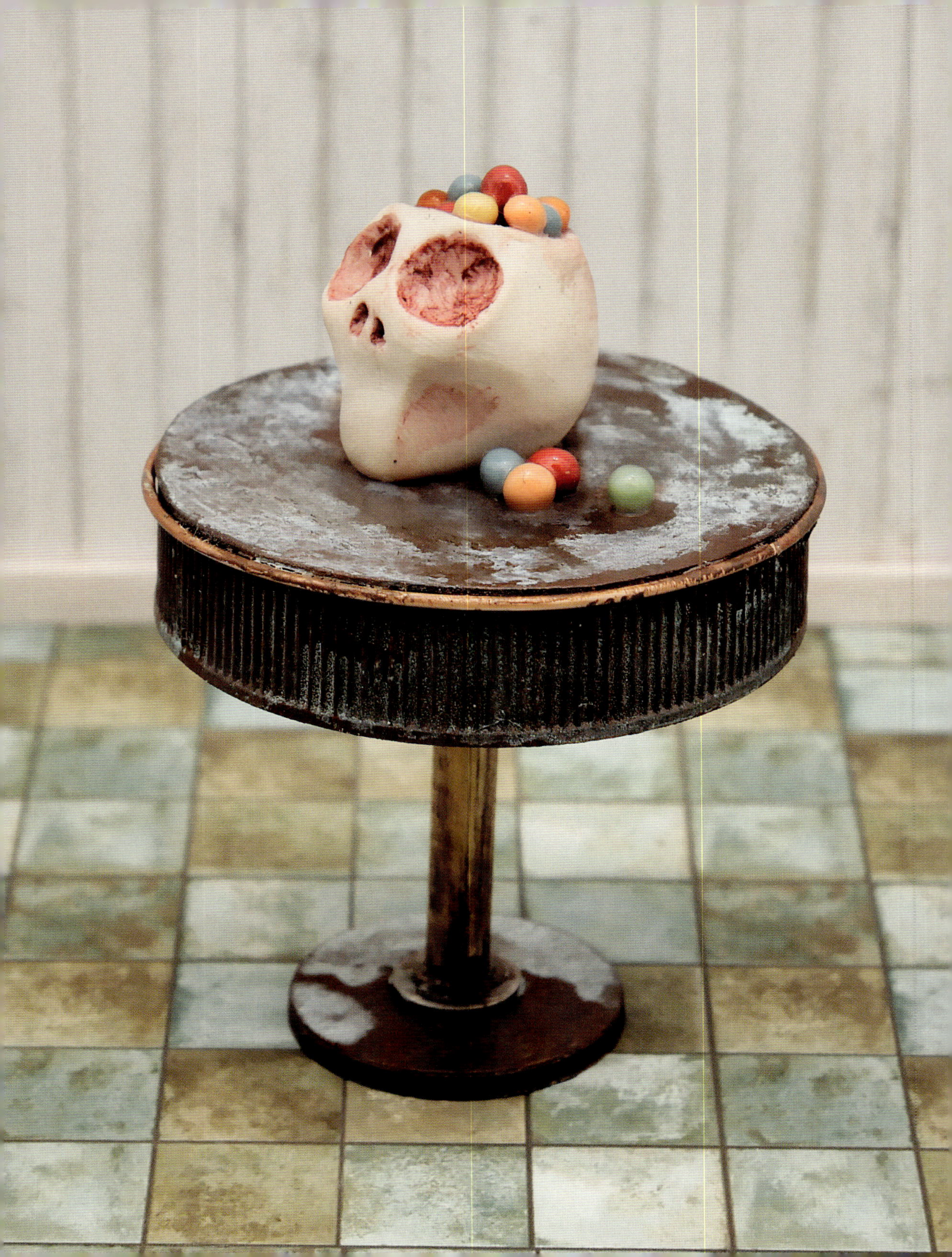

Skull Candy

Oh riiight! The skull candy. The candy for the skull. The candy chosen specially to be stored in the skull. The skull candy . . . that candy skull?

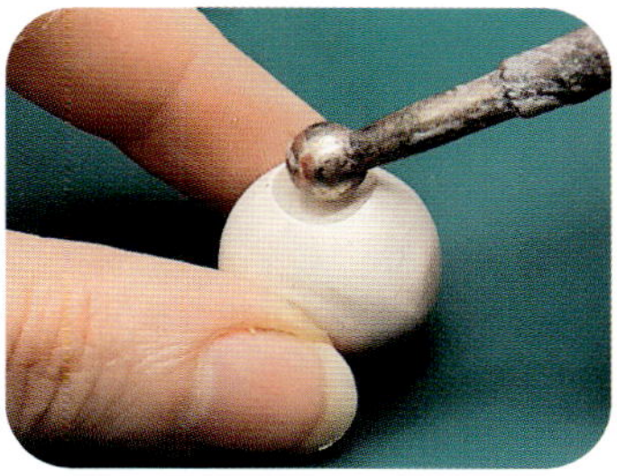

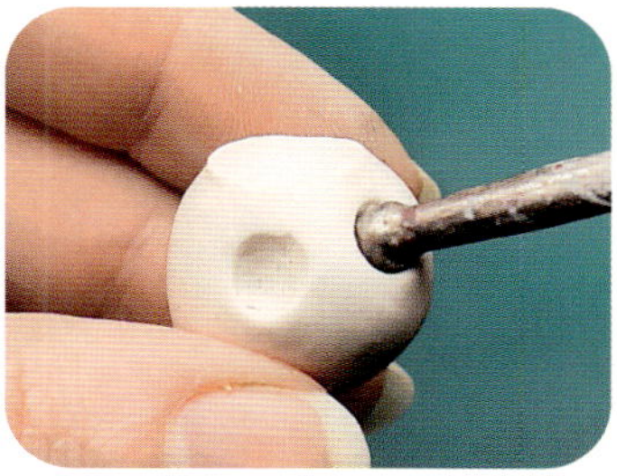

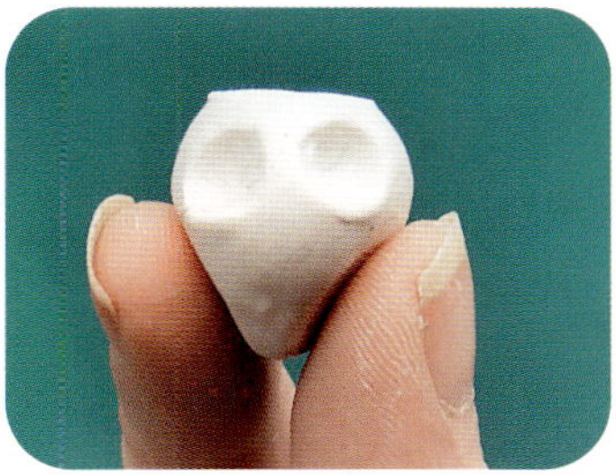

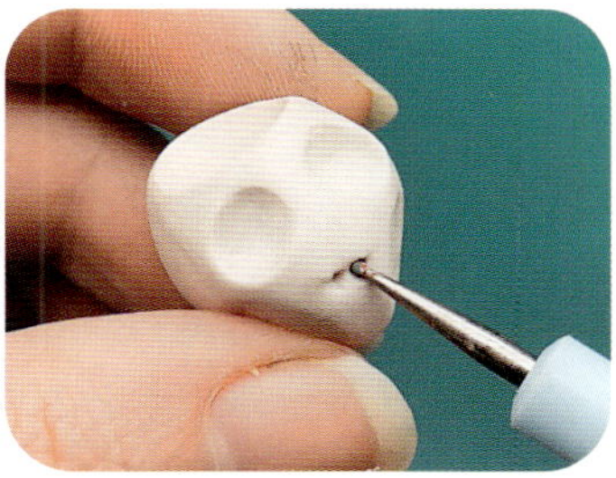

Clay Sizer
Skull Candy

Skull	Candies (Multi-color)
x1	*x20ish*

Tools

- ball sculpting tool
- toothpick
- paint
- craft glue
- superglue
- hot glue

Skull Material

- polymer clay

Table Materials

- medicine cap or wooden circle (~1½" [3.8 cm])
- wooden circle (~1" [2.5 cm])
- 2" (5-cm)-long wooden dowel (or chopstick)
- wire (~12 gauge)
- small washer (hole as big as wooden dowel)

Skull

Roll a white ball of clay to the size shown. Take your ball sculpting tool and make a round cavity on the top of your ball. This is the top of your skull.

Make two eye sockets with the same tool.

With your thumb and pointer finger, gently squeeze the bottom of your skull to make a jaw line.

Using a toothpick, jab in two nostrils. Your ball should be looking more skull-y now. Set it aside.

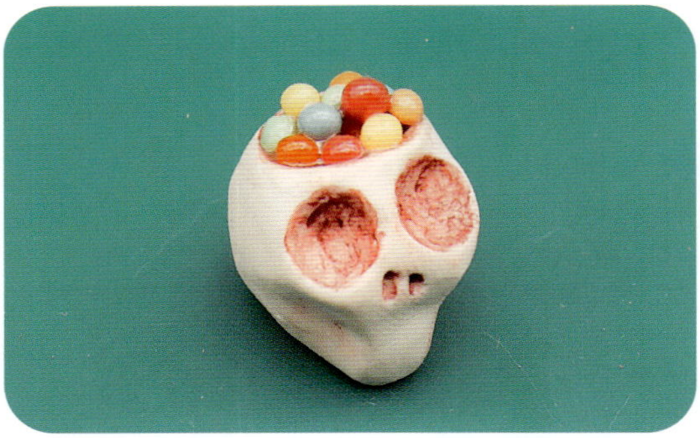

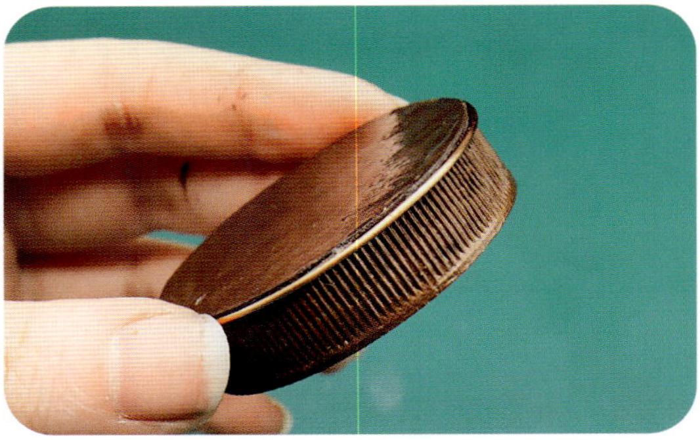

Next, roll out 20-ish small balls (using the clay sizer) in various colors in the size shown. These will be the candies. Yummy!

Cure the skull and candies according to the package instructions. If you'd like, you can start on the table or wait for your skull and candies to be done.

Once everything is nice and hard, paint all the skull's cavities maroon. Before the paint dries, wipe it off. This gives it a "worn" appearance.

Using craft glue, glue enough candies to be slightly heaping inside the cavity of your skull. (Save a few for the table.) Coat the top of the candies in craft glue. This gives them a glossy appearance.

Table

Tip: *If your medicine cap doesn't have a flat top (some caps have embossed text), glue a chipboard circle to the top.*

Paint your medicine cap, 1-inch (2.5-cm) wooden circle, and 2-inch (5-cm) wooden dowel bronze or brown. Let them dry.

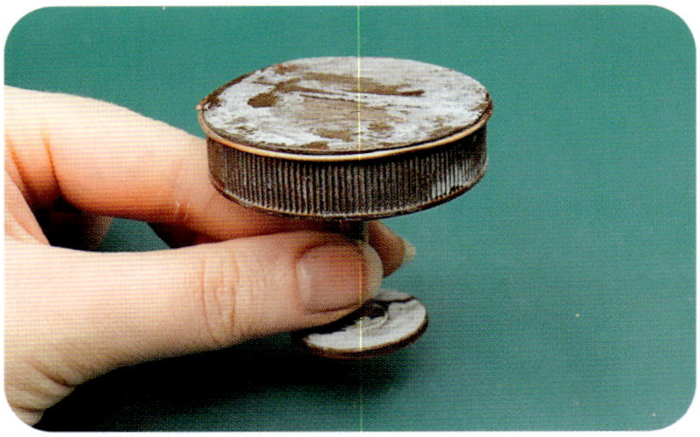

Wrap the top edge of your medicine cap once with wire and superglue it in place.

Flip your cap over and, on the underside, squeeze a blob of hot glue and glue your dowel in as straight as possible. This is the table leg.

Take your 1-inch (2.5-cm) circle and glue your washer in the middle. Then glue the table leg in the middle of the washer.

Plop your skull onto the table. Add a little pile of candies next to the skull, like someone spilled them while trying to find the flavor they wanted.

A Desk Mate

Imagine if you had an octopus desk mate. I hear octopuses are pretty smart; maybe I would have gotten better grades in school. I'd just have to keep it fed, otherwise it'd eat my homework . . . or me!

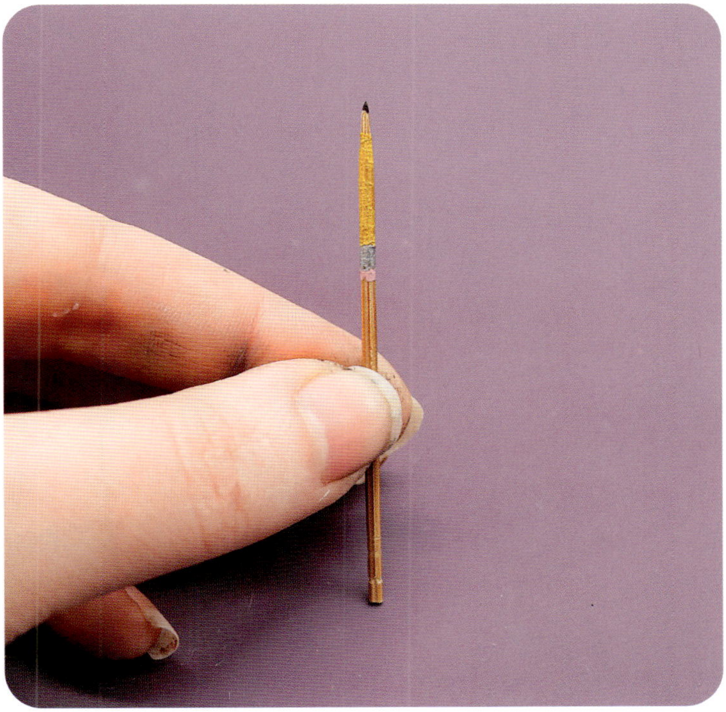

Tools

- paint
- pliers/wire cutter
- superglue
- pencil
- exacto knife, ruler, & cutting mat
- glue
- gloves & silicone mat (for clay)

Pencil Material

- toothpick

Desk Materials

- wire (~14 gauge)
- empty dip container
- balsa wood
- paper

Octopus Materials

- Apoxie® Sculpt clay (preferably red)
- medium bead
- small feather

Pencil

Every desk needs a pencil! Paint the pointy end of a toothpick to look like a pencil and trim off the excess with pliers or a wire cutter. Set it aside. We're going to need it in a minute.

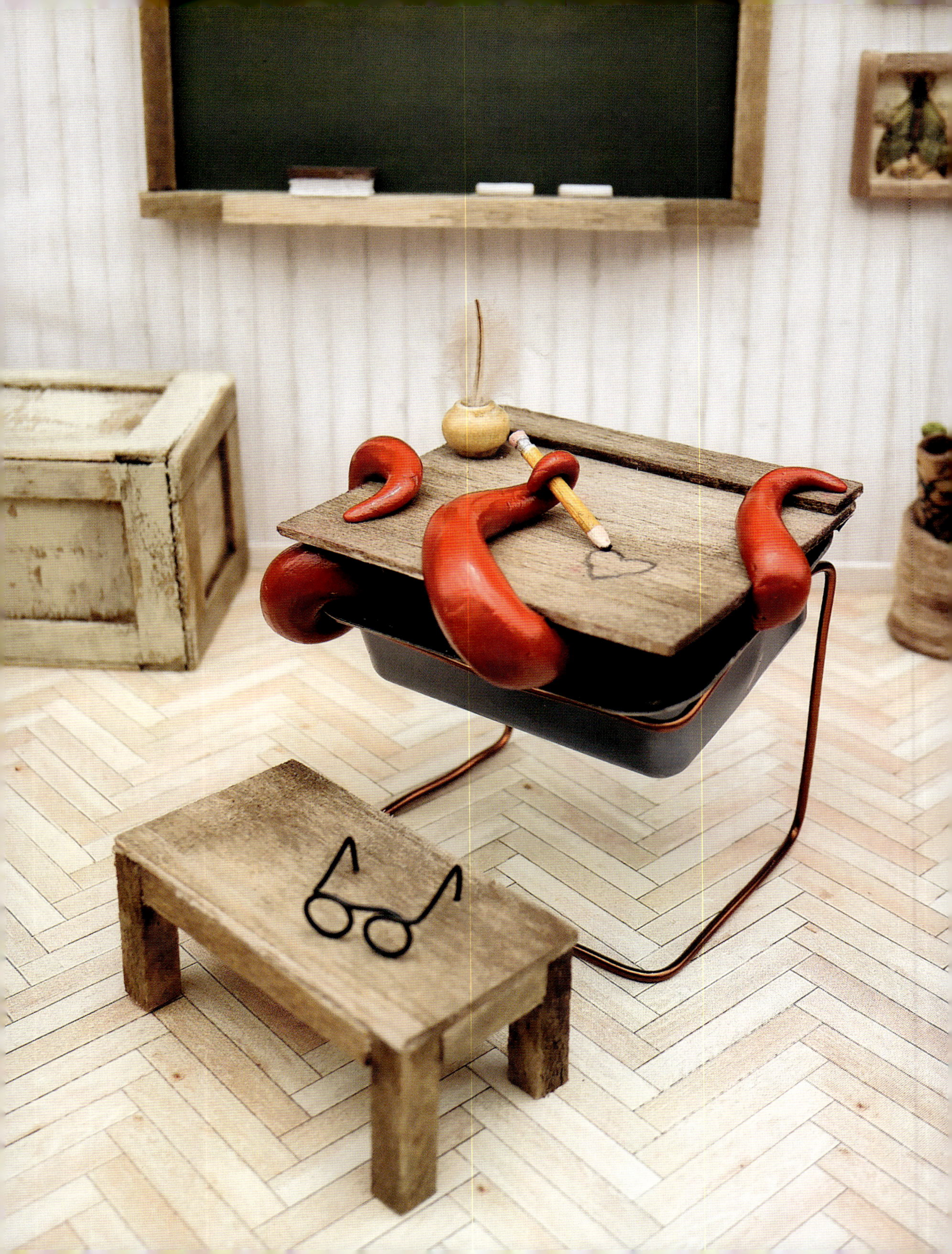

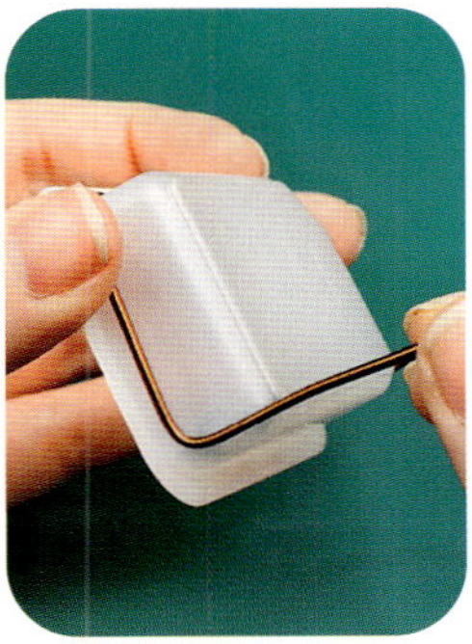
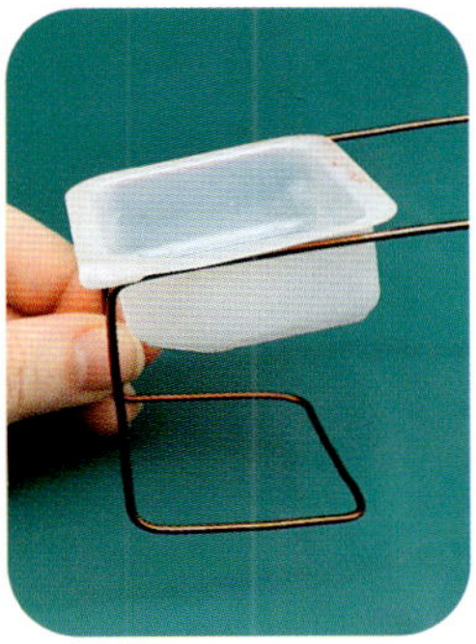
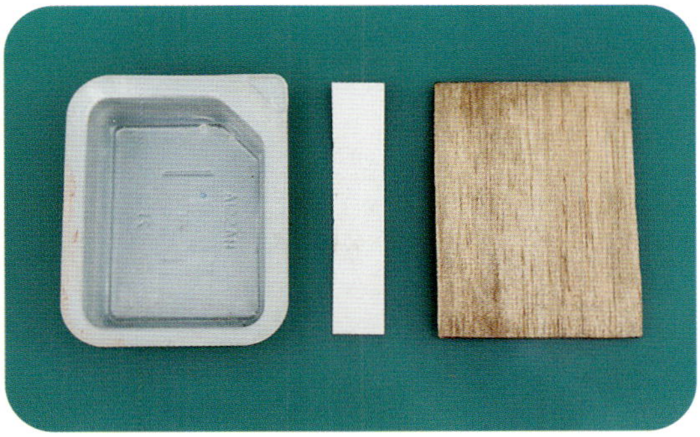
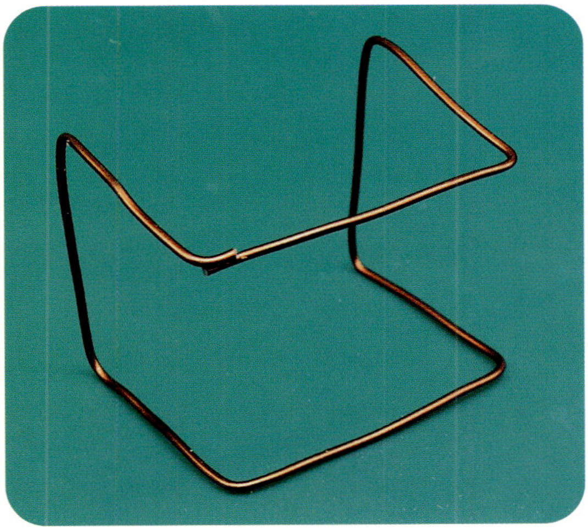

Desk

Cut a roughly 16-inch (40.6-cm) length of wire. *Everyone's dip container will be different, so this may be overkill on the wire but better too much than too little.*

Starting from the center of your wire, wrap it around the long edge of your dip container then around the two short edges to make a [shape.

On the two short edges, bend your wire at a 90° angle.

Remove your dip container and set it aside. You should have two long wire ends sticking straight up. Measure 1½ inches (3.8 cm) up from each wire and make another 90° angle bend mirroring the bottom bends.

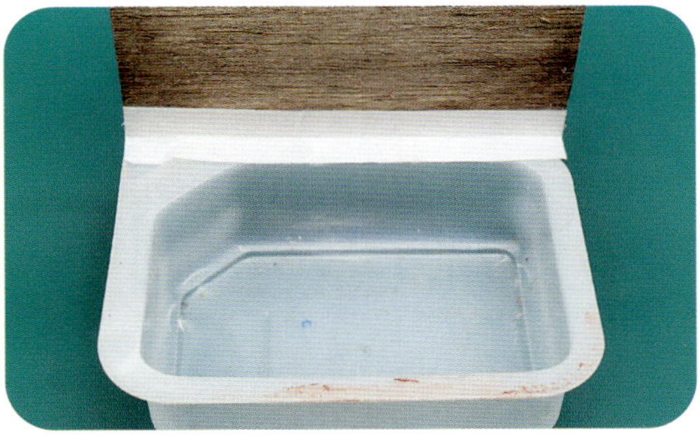

Grab your container again and place it between the 90° bends and wrap your wire around the back of the container.

Your ends should now be touching/overlapping. Trim the excess off but leave some wire overlapping. Superglue the overlapping wires. Set it aside.

Let's make a top for the desk. Trace the top of your container on balsa wood. Cut out and stain it with brown paint.

Cut a strip of paper the same length as your container and about ¼ inch (6 mm) wide. Crease the middle (taco style). This is the hinge for your desk.

Glue along the top long edge of your container and let this dry. Then glue the other side onto the long edge of your wood rectangle to make a folding desktop.

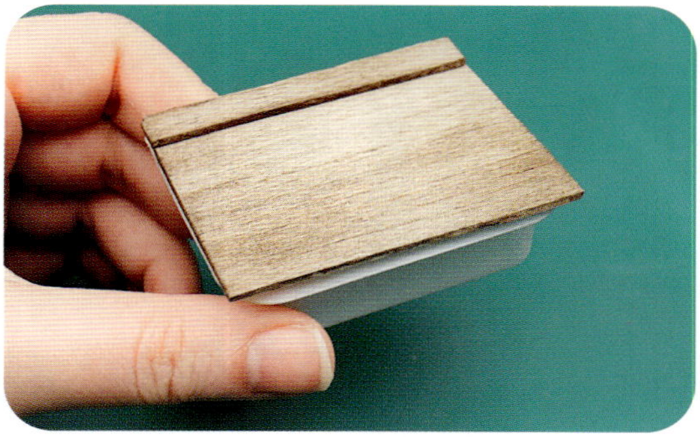

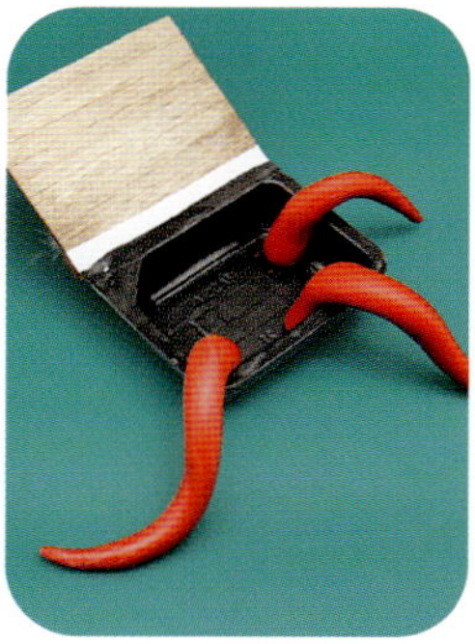

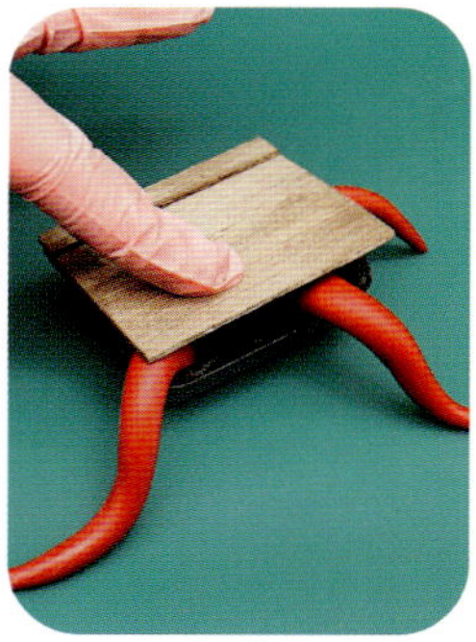

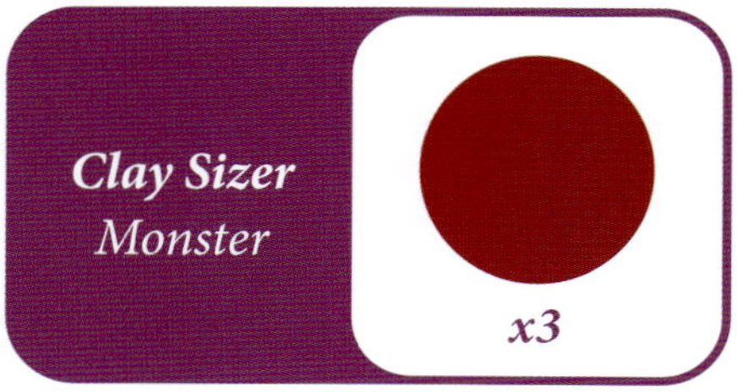

Glue a painted strip of wood to the top of your desktop as a pencil ledge.

Paint your dip container black if it's not already.

Octopus/Monster

Put on your gloves and lay out your silicone mat. Mix up your Apoxie Sculpt clay into three balls, sized according to the graphic.

Roll each ball into a long octopus tentacle shape, about 3 inches (7.6 cm) long.

Smash the larger end of each tentacle inside your desk.

Flip the lid over and gently squish the tentacles (not too much, you don't want them to appear squished, you just want the wood to grip the clay).

Wrap your tentacles around the edges of your desk.

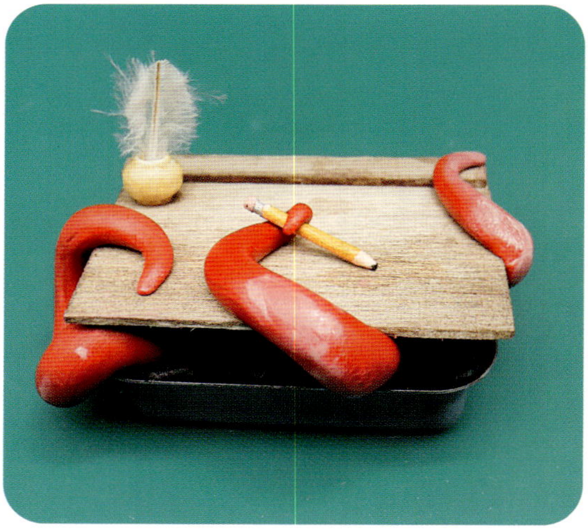

Remember that pencil? Wrap one tentacle end around that. Make it look like the tentacle is drawing on the desk. *Naughty octopus!*

A medium-sized bead and small feather make for a great ink and quill! I mean, come on! An octopus would obviously use ink!

Lastly, set your desk in the wire frame we made earlier and tilt the top slightly toward the front. If you need to, you can glue this in, but it should hold on its own if you tilt it far enough.

Haunted Toy House

Did you see the lights turn on inside that dollhouse? Of course not because it's just a toy, right?

Tools

- glue
- exacto knife, ruler, & cutting mat
- pencil
- "fun" scissors (optional)
- paint
- pliers/wire cutter
- hot glue
- gloves (for clay)
- ball sculpting tool
- rough rock

House Materials

- 6 wooden cubes (~⅖" [1 cm])
- chipboard
- 3–5 toothpicks
- bread tag
- moss

Tiny Trees Materials

- pipe cleaner (brown)
- green paint

Tabletop Materials

- balsa wood
- aluminum foil
- Apoxie Sculpt clay (preferably brown)
- small rocks
- ¼" (6-mm) or 3⁄16" (5-mm) square dowels

Car Materials

- small clothespin
- 2 small beads (or Q-tips® cotton swab shaft)
- thin clear plastic

House

Glue six ⅖-inch (1-cm) wooden cubes in two rows of three. This will be the base of the haunted house.

Cut a 1 x 1½–inch (2.5 x 3.8–cm) rectangle out of chipboard. Score down the middle chili-dog style and crease in a V shape. This will be your haunted house roof.

Glue your haunted house roof on, you guessed it, your haunted house!

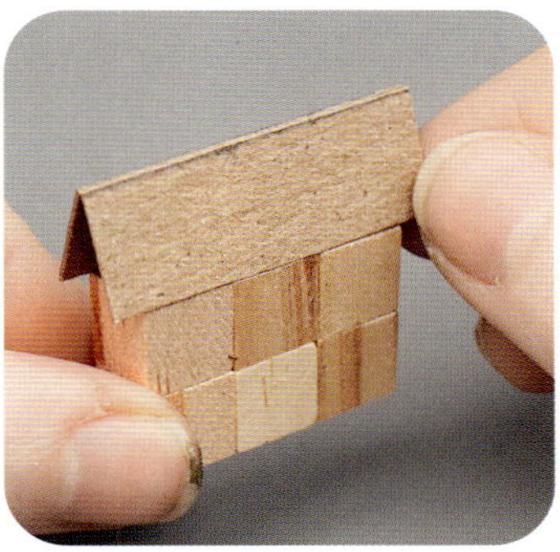

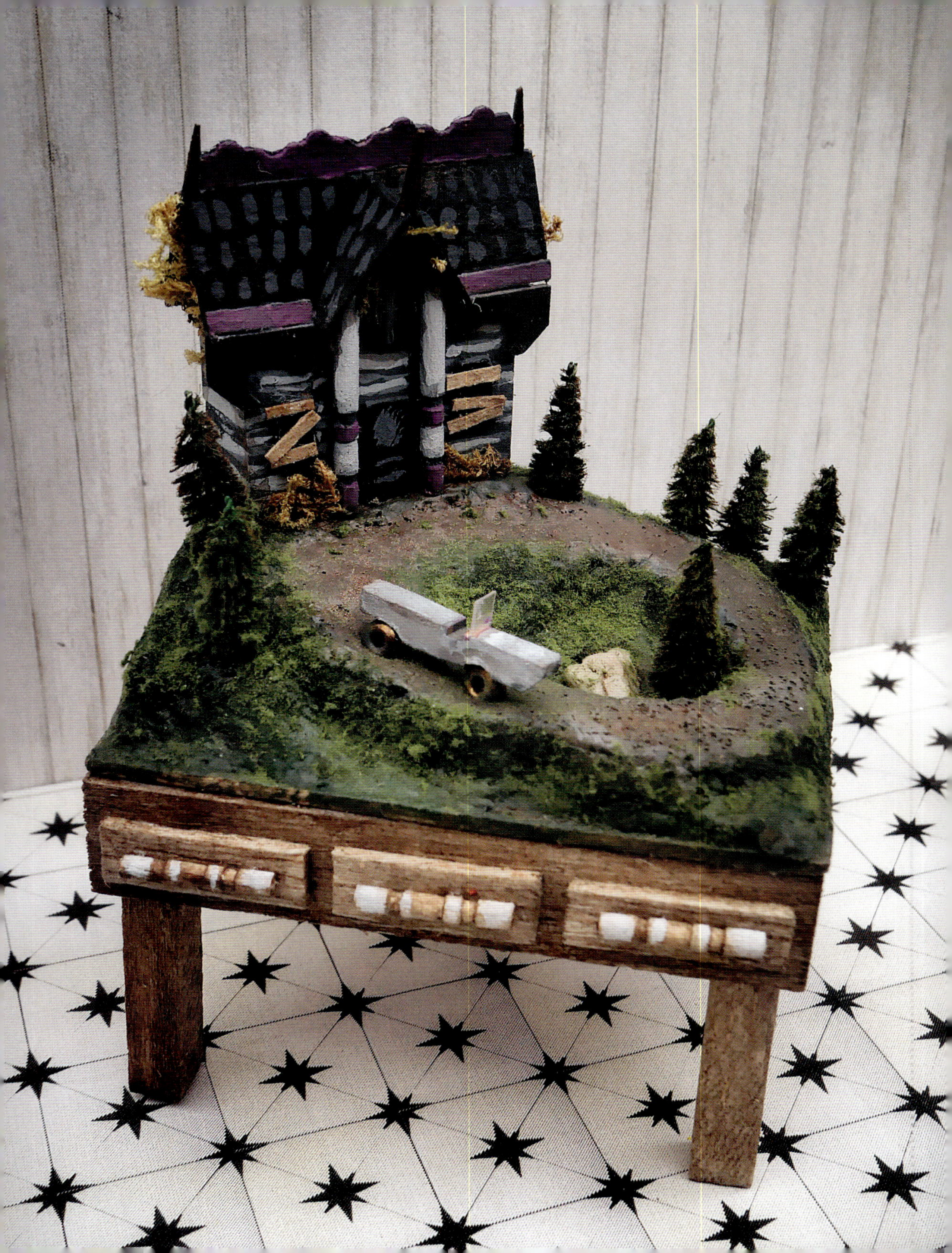

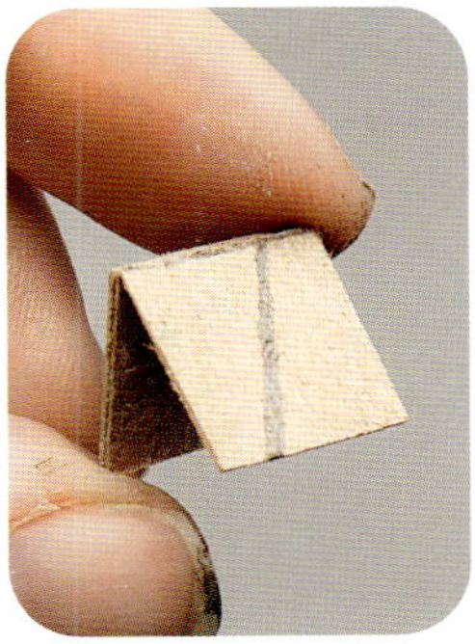

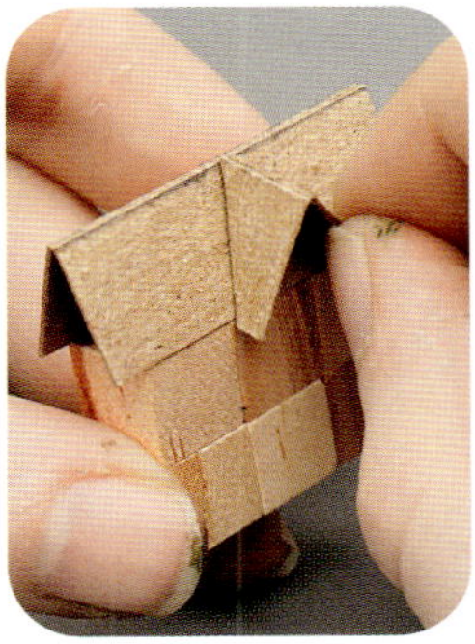

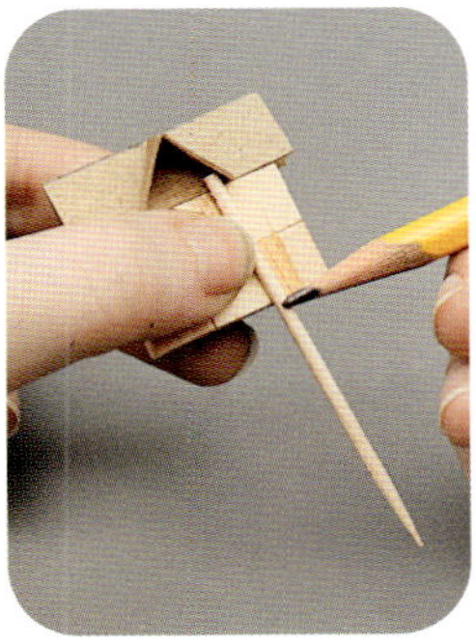

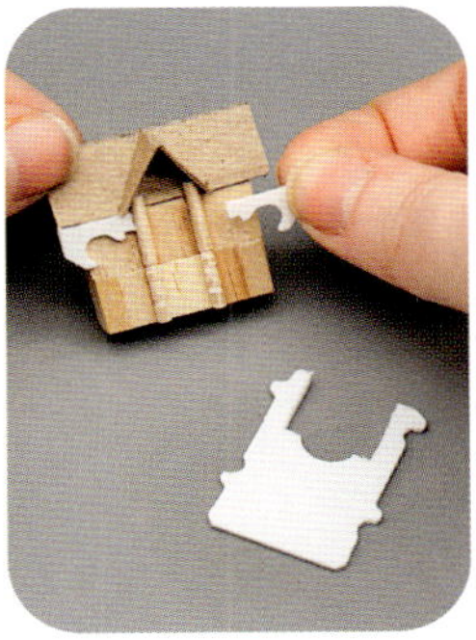

Cut a ½ x 1–inch (1.3 x 2.5–cm) rectangle out of chipboard. Score and fold down the middle, salmon-burger style. (Which is healthier.)

While folded flat, draw a diagonal line from almost corner to corner but a little in on either side. Cut through both sides along this line.

Glue in the middle of your haunted roof as a littler haunted roof.

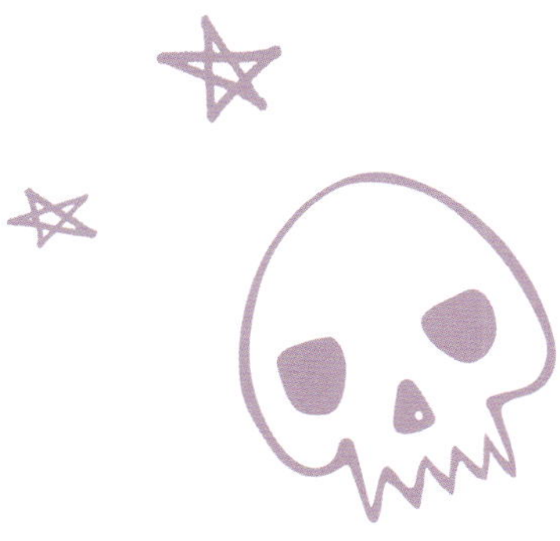

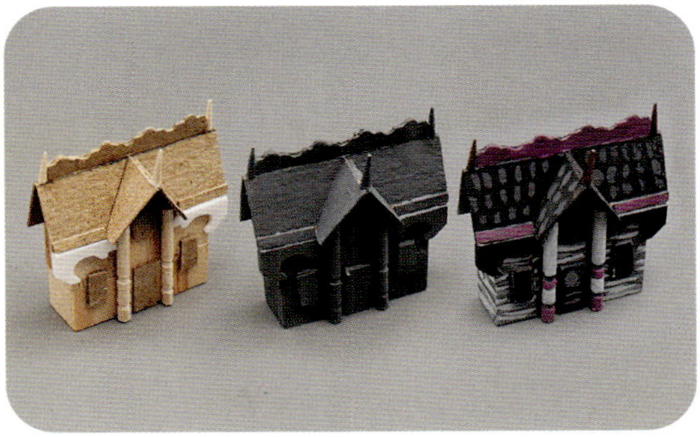

Trim and glue two toothpicks to fit under this littler haunted roof, as if these toothpicks will be holding its weight.

We can't have a drab haunted house, so let's add some decor! Pretend you're on the show *Curb Appeal* and spice this house up!

Curb Appeal **Suggestions**

- Cut the hooks off a bread tag to add eaves onto your roof.
- Toothpick points make great spires.
- Add windows and doors with scraps of chipboard.
- Using "fun" scissors, you can add flair to the peak.
- Don't forget the CIRCLE WINDOW!

Once you have played exterior decorator to your heart's content, cover your entire house in black paint. Then add details with gray and purple, such as siding, shingles, or windows.

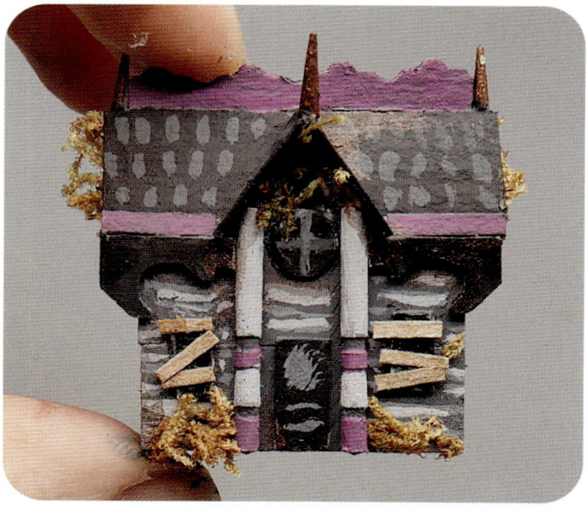

At this point, your house is probably looking a little too HOA homeowner-y. So, let's make Karen angry! Board up those windows with scraps of chipboard. No one's brave enough to clean those gutters, so add moss under your roofs. Set it aside.

Tiny Trees

Next, we need to make a lot for *"our house in the middle of the street"* to live.

Take a pipe cleaner and trim it to a point. Hey, like a tree!

Paint or dip the pointed end in dark green, roughly ⅘ inch (2 cm) down. Then snip it with a wire cutter.

Keep going until you have seven to eight trees. (You always lose one.) Set them aside to dry.

Tabletop

Cut the following out of balsa wood. A template is on page 218 for reference.

- **Qty: 1**—2 x 2½ inches (5 x 6.4 cm) ***top***
- **Qty: 2**—2 x ½ inch (5 x 1.3 cm) ***sides***
- **Qty: 2**—2½ x ½ inch (6.4 x 1.3 cm) ***sides***
- **Qty: 3**—¼ x ¾ inch (6 mm x 1.9 cm) ***drawers***

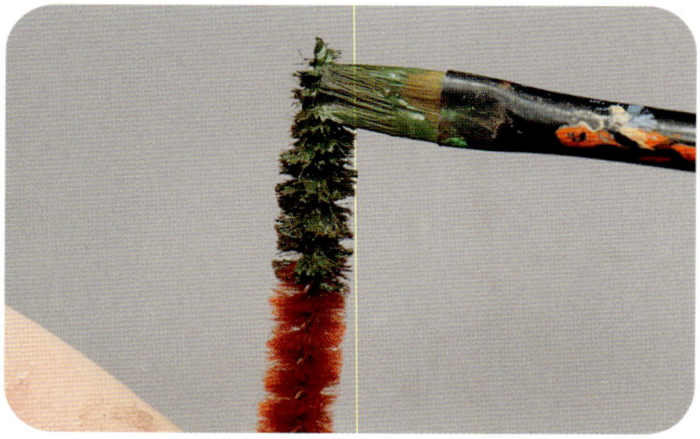

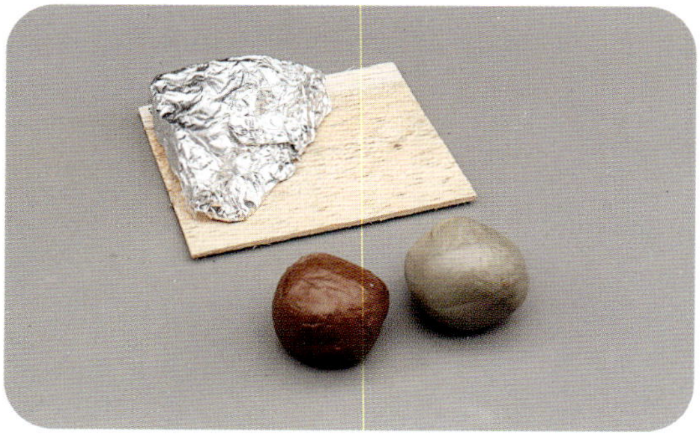

Stain everything with watered-down brown paint.

Because ALL haunted houses are on top of hills, let's make one for this house! Take a small piece of aluminum foil and crumple it up into a 90° triangular wedge, with the sides sloping toward the long edge.

Hot glue this in the corner of your ***top***. Make sure it's large enough that your house will live comfortably on it.

Mix together a small amount of Apoxie Sculpt clay, just enough to cover the top with your hill. Smooth it out in a thin layer over the top.

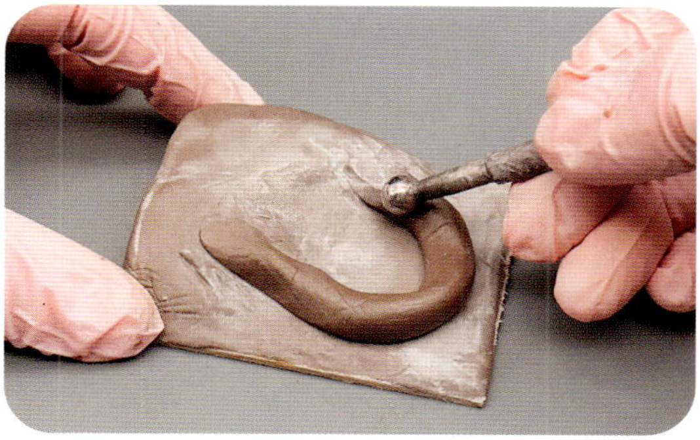

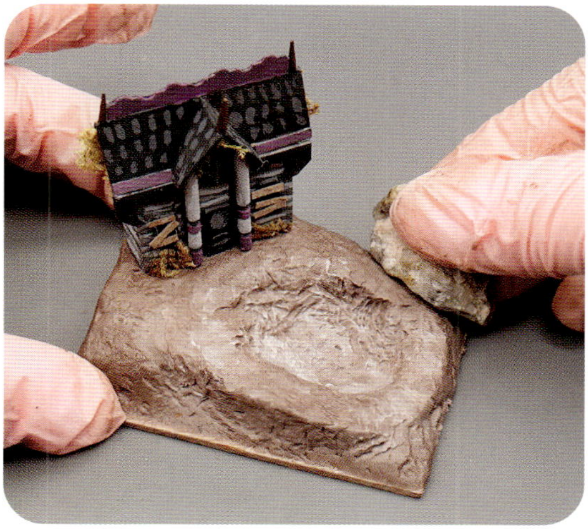

Because fancy haunted houses have circle driveways, let's get fancy! Mix a small amount of Apoxie Sculpt clay and roll it into a 3- to 4-inch (7.6- to 10.2-cm) tube. Make a U shape and attach it to your hill.

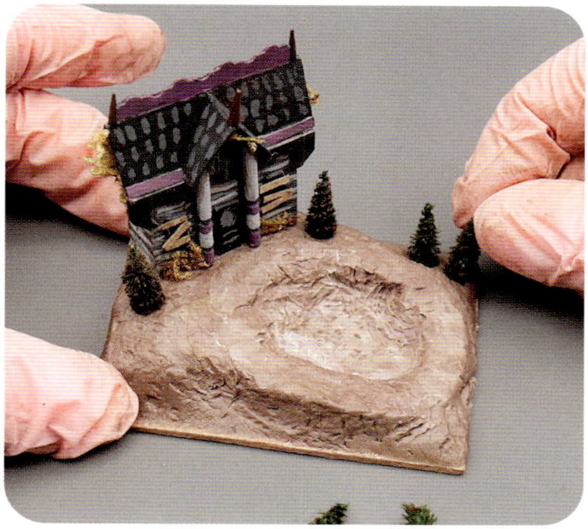

Smooth out the seams of your driveway with your ball sculpting tool. Flatten the top of your driveway so that it looks like a car could drive on it and not roll off. *This doesn't have to be perfect.*

We need texture! Take a rough rock and smack your clay over and over until you've smacked all the demons out. I mean . . . until it looks like rough ground.

Here's the exciting part! Push your house into the clay hilltop.

Before your clay hardens, grab your tiny trees, and push them in around the driveway and house. Add small rocks for boulders.

Paint your ground green and the driveway brown. Set it aside to harden/dry.

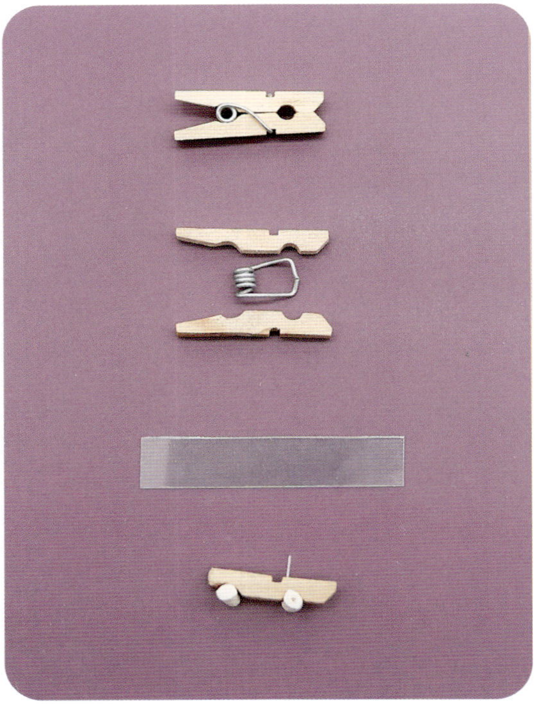

Car

Pull your small clothespin apart. *Save the spring for other projects.*

With an exacto knife, trim the handle on one of the wooden pieces a little before the back dimple. *There should be two dimples, aka tire holes.*

Paint your car. *I went with gray because, as a millennial, what's more haunting than millennial gray?*

Glue two beads into the two dimples to make tires. *Don't have the right sized beads? Cutting the shaft of a Q-tip into two cylinders the width of your car works pretty well.*

Glue a tiny scrap of clear plastic as a windshield.

Glue your car onto your haunted driveway.

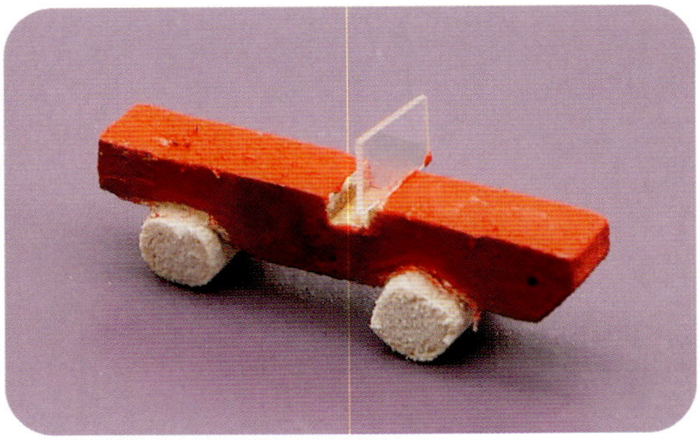

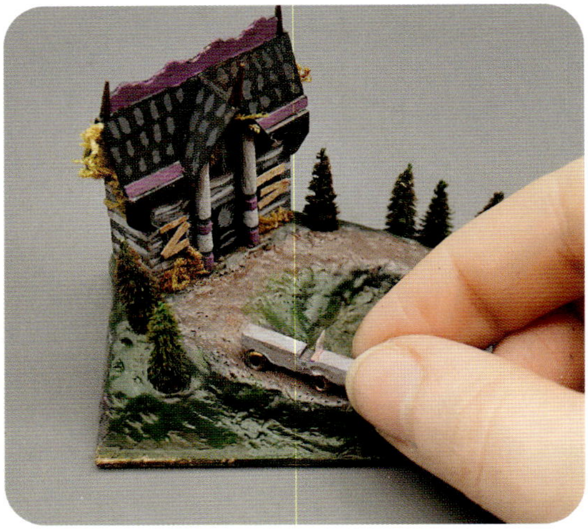

Tabletop *Continued*

Once you have your tabletop just the way you want it and the clay has cured, the last step is to make your tabletop into a table.

Glue the four ***sides*** under the ***top*** to make a box. Set it on its side while the glue dries.

Once your glue is dry enough that it won't fall apart when you touch it, glue on the three drawers evenly spaced on to the front face of your table. Trimmed toothpicks make great handles if you wanna be fancy.

Cut a square dowel into four 2-inch (5-cm) lengths and stain them to match. Glue them on as legs.

Eye Cake

Watching your diet can be a hassle. But what if your diet watched you back?

No thank yooou!

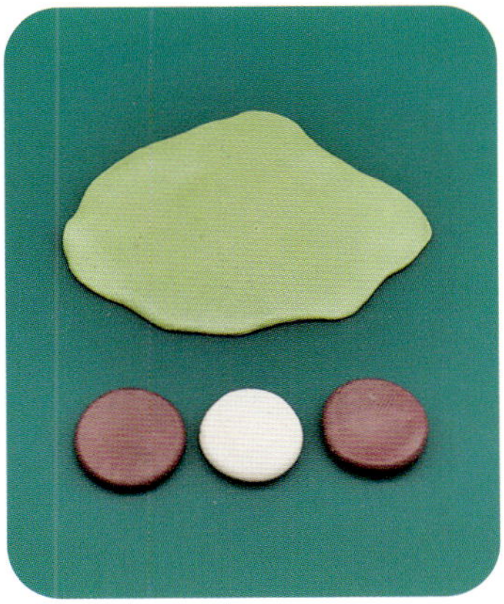

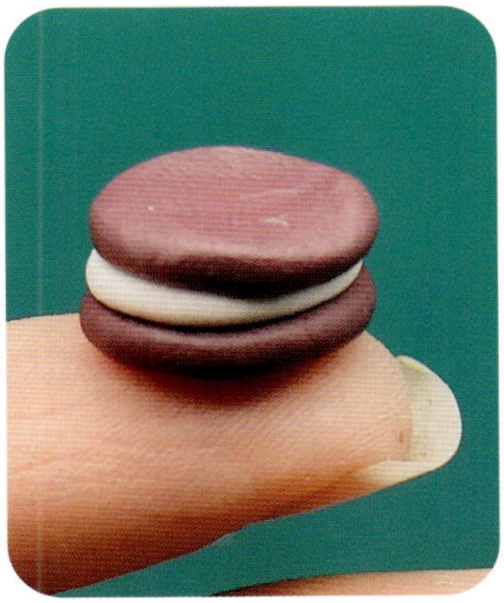

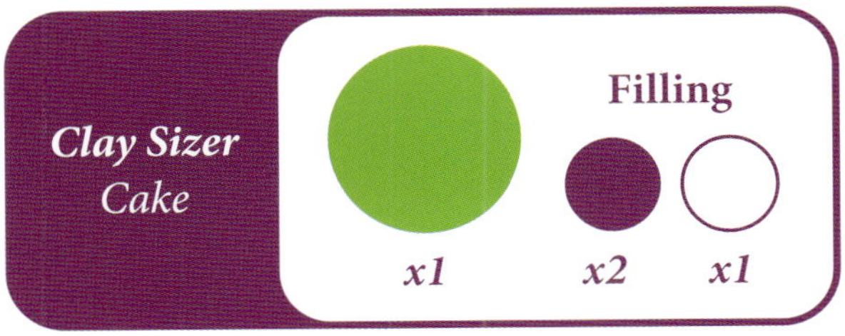

Tools

- rolling pin for clay
- exacto knife, ruler, & cutting mat
- ball sculpting tool
- wire brush (or toothbrush)
- paint
- clear gloss
- glue
- sandpaper, if needed

Cake Materials

- polymer clay
- 3 eyeballs (page 121)
- 1" (2.5-cm) wooden circle
- 4/5" (2-cm) wooden circle

Table Materials

- 16 wooden cubes (~2/5" [1 cm])
- 1/8" (3-mm) square dowels
- 1/4" (6-mm) square dowels

Cake

Roll your clay into four balls using the sizes and colors above.

Squish your two purple balls and one white ball so that they are about double in size and make a little clay sandwich.

With either your hands or a clay rolling pin, flatten your larger green ball of clay as thin as you can while still being able to pick it up without ripping it.

Lay your "sandwich" on top of your flat green clay and cut around it with an exacto knife. Flip your sandwich and repeat with other side.

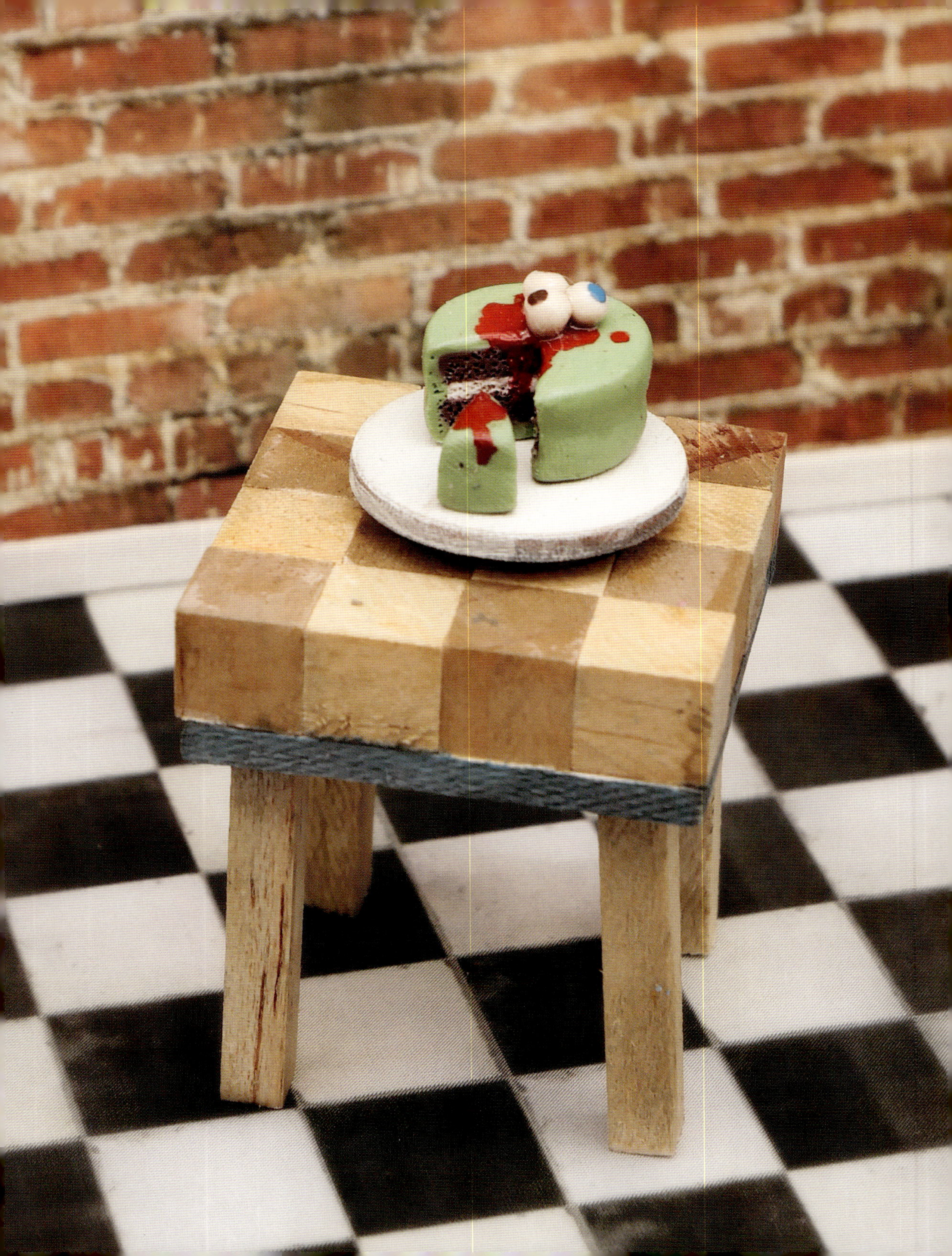

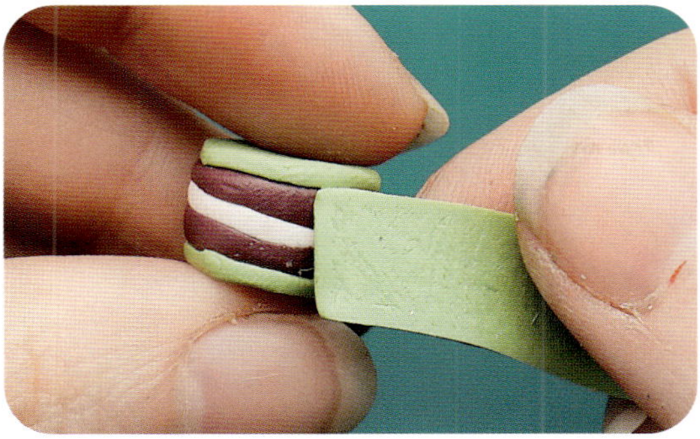

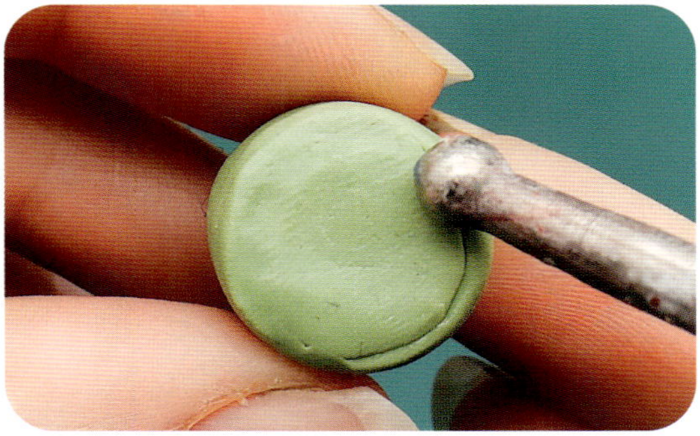

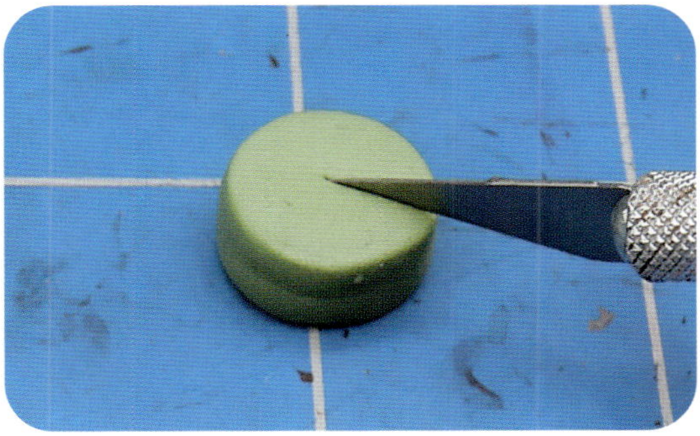

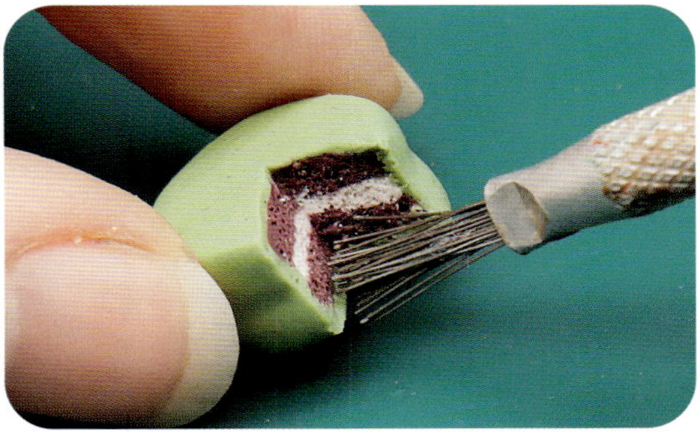

Take the excess green clay and re-ball it. Flatten it into a long skinny piece.

Cut a strip as wide as your cake. Wrap this strip around the midsection of your cake until it meets the other end. Trim off any excess overlapage.

Smooth out the seams with a ball sculpting tool.

Throw this in the freezer for less than 30 minutes. (Okay, maybe don't throw it.) In the meantime, you can skip to the table if you like.

Once your cake is chilled, it'll cut clean. Using your exacto knife, cut a cake slice out of your cake.

Take a wire brush (or toothbrush) and roughen the cut surface on both the pieces to make it look like moist cakey cakeyness.

If you don't have extra eyes from your various other projects, turn to page 121 and make three or four.

Bake according to the package instructions and cool.

Mix red paint and clear gloss to make the *"raspberry sauce."* Paint a splotch of it on top of your cake and glue your eyeballs in the middle like a garnish. You can make some of the *"strawberry sauce"* drip down if you like. Put some of that *"cherry sauce"* on your cake slice as well. *Okay, the sauce isn't sauce at all but blood . . . There, I said it . . . We can move on now.*

Glue your 1-inch (2.5-cm) wooden circle in the middle of your ⅘-inch (2-cm) wooden circle and paint them white.

Glue your cake and slice in the middle of the larger circle. Set it aside.

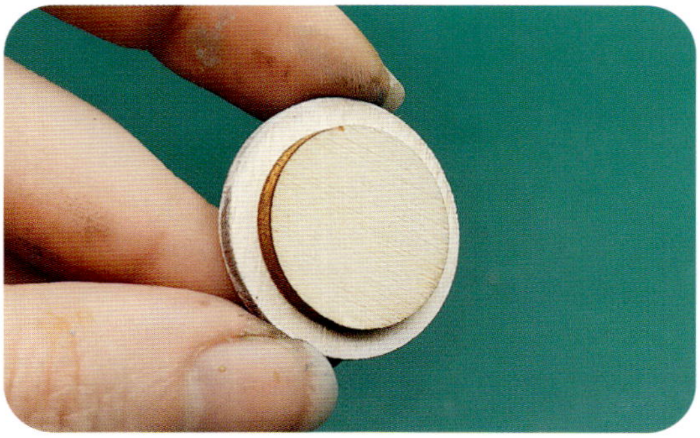

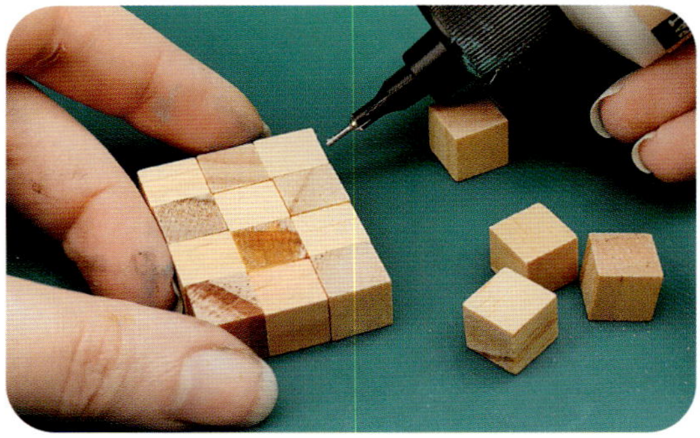

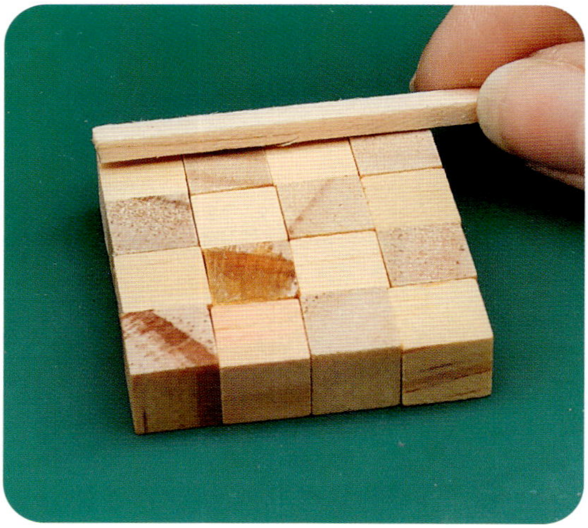

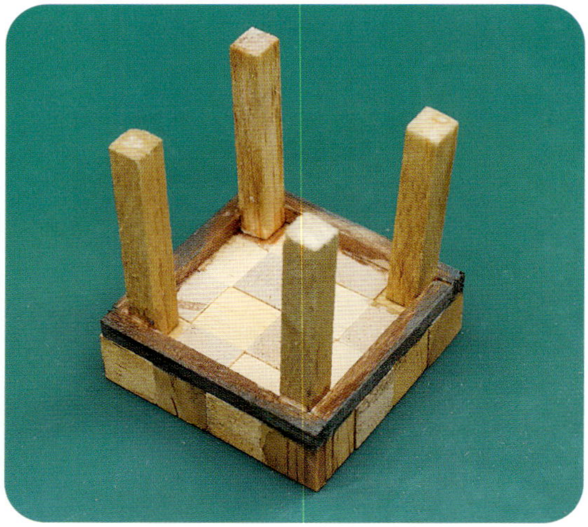

Table

Glue your ⅖-inch (1-cm) cubes into a flat square that's four cubes by four cubes. Turn each cube to alternate the grain pattern, making a checkerboard.

Frame the bottom of your table with ⅛-inch (3-mm) square dowels.

Cut your ¼-inch (6-mm) dowels into four 2-inch (5-cm) sticks and glue these under as legs.

Paint your table with super watered-down tan paint.

Place your delicious eye cake to your table and get ready to serve up some "side-eye" . . . or is that a side of eyes?

> **Tip:** *If you have any spots that paint won't stick to, it just means you got a bit messy with the glue, no biggie. Sand and try again.*

A Monster's Under My Bed!

Little Clayton didn't know there was a monster under his bed. Little Clayton still doesn't know there's a monster under his bed because he's been ate-in.

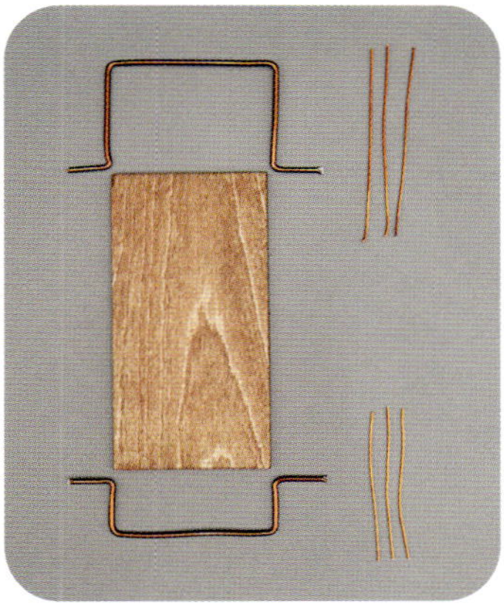

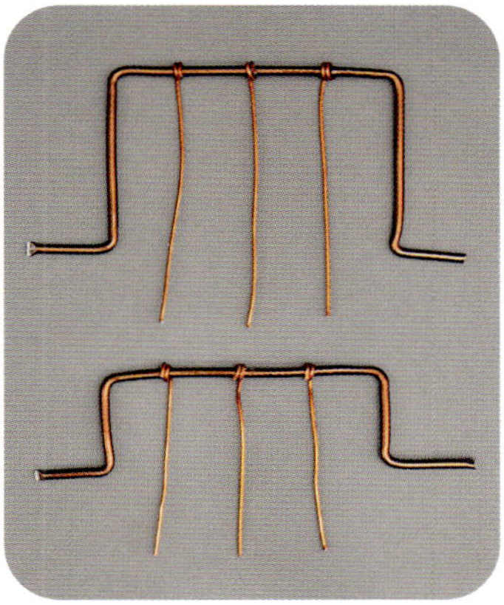

Tools

- pliers/wire cutter
- superglue
- exacto knife, ruler, & cutting mat
- paint
- glue
- hot glue
- gloves & silicone mat (for clay)

Materials

- wire (~14 gauge)
- floral wire
- balsa wood
- 4 toothpicks
- corrugated cardboard
- fabric
- brown eye shadow
- Apoxie Sculpt clay (preferably red)

Cut 3½ inches (8.9 cm) and 4½ inches (11.4 cm) out of about 14-gauge wire. Bend the two wires to match the template on page 219.

Cut six strands of floral wire roughly 2½ inches (6.4 cm) long.

Wrap the ends of three strands around the middle of each thicker wire twice and evenly space them across. This will be the headboard and footboard of your bed.

> **Tip:** *If your wires keep moving around, put a single drop of superglue on each wrap to help secure them in place.*

Out of balsa wood, cut a 1½ x 3–inch (3.8 x 7.6–cm) rectangle and stain it brown. A template is on page 219 if needed. This will be the bed part of your bed. *Unless you consider the mattress as "the bed part of your bed," in which case, this will be where "the bed part of your bed" will rest.*

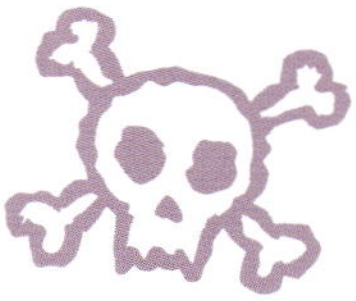

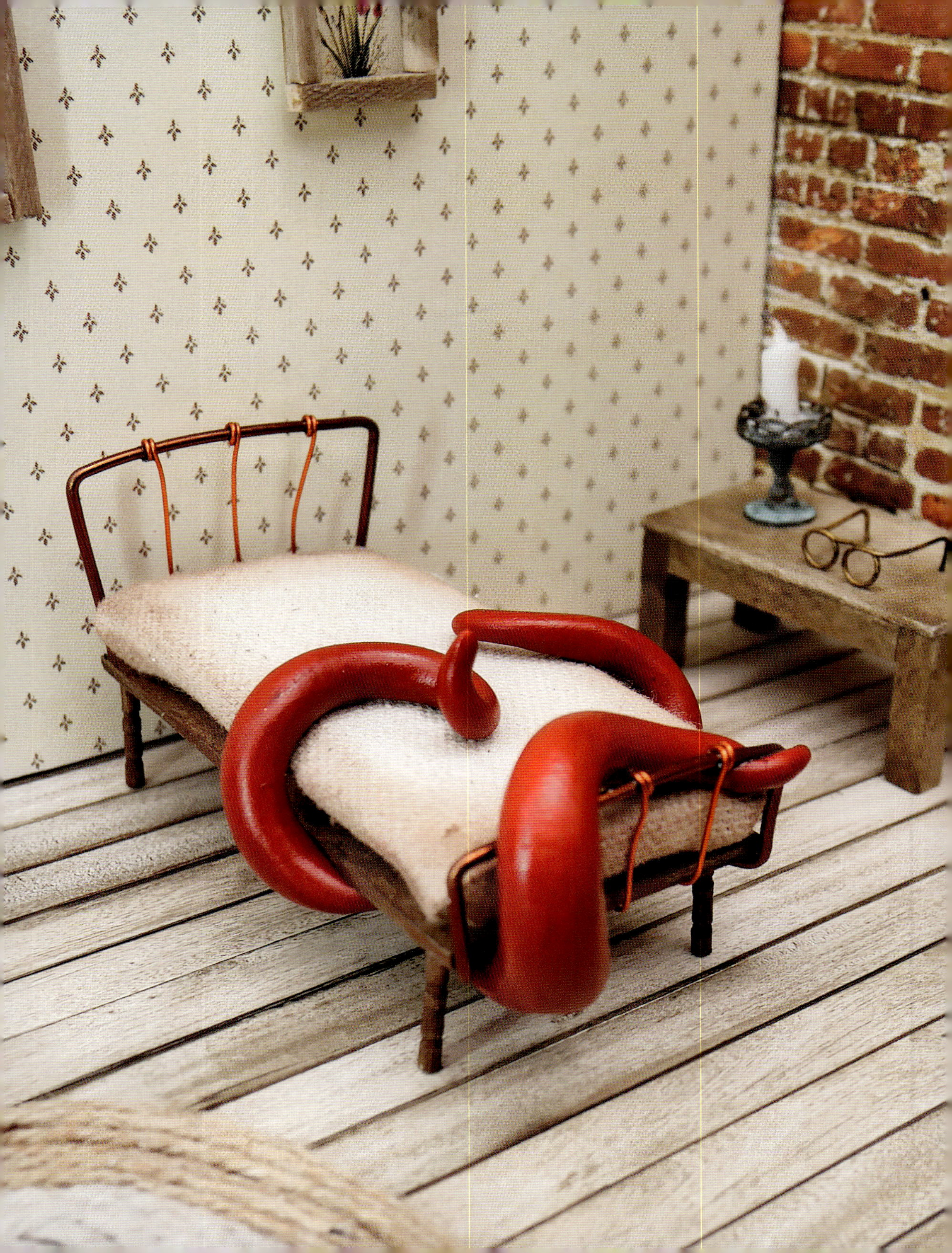

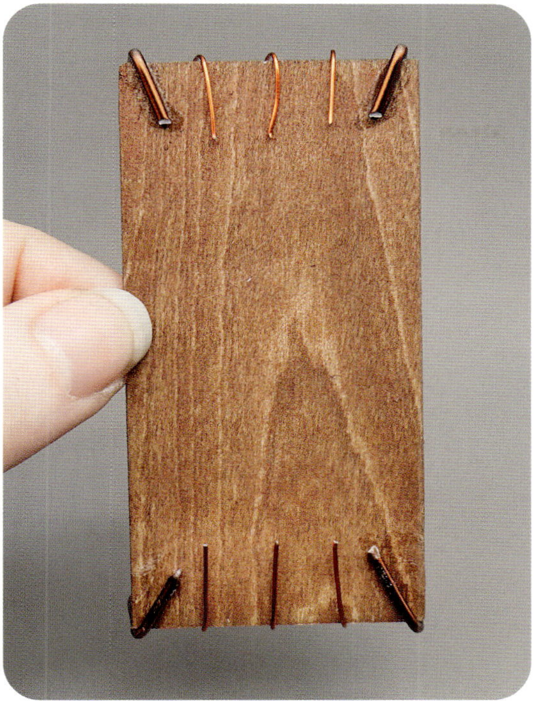

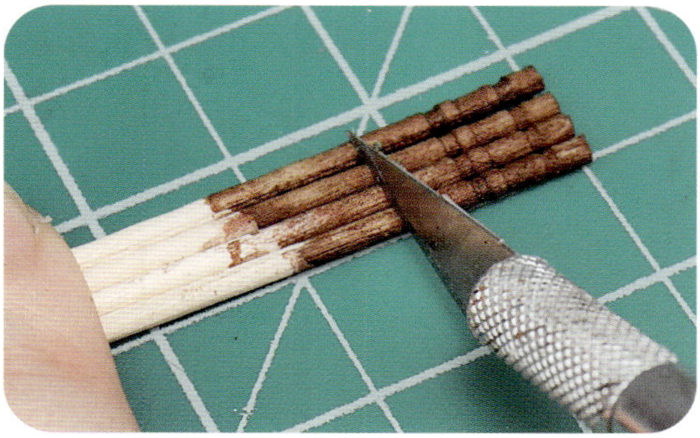

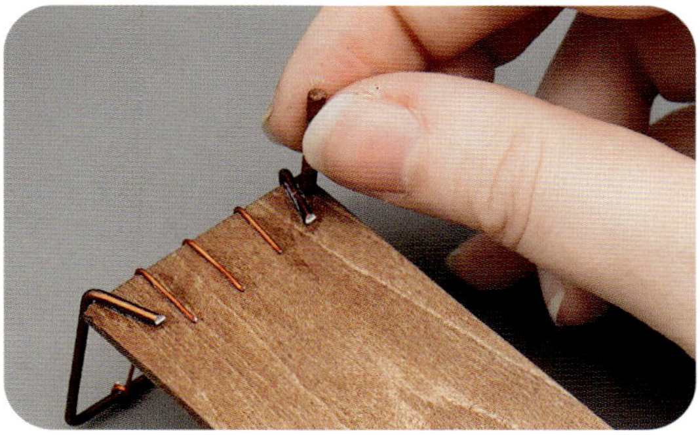

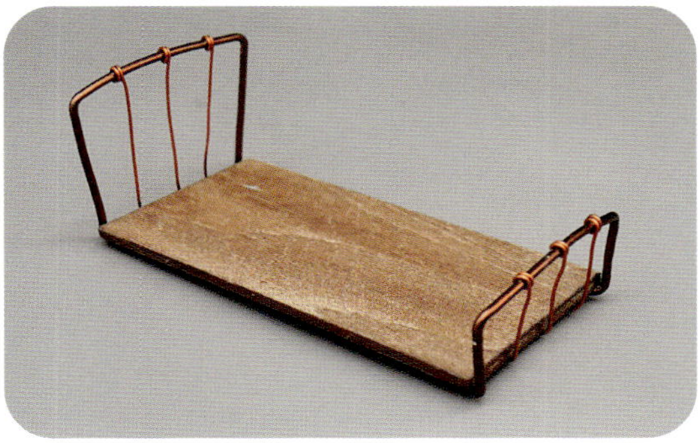

Bend the ends of your headboard and footboard inward toward the middle. Superglue these ends under the short edges of your bed.

Bend the six floral wires around the bottom as well and superglue them in place.

Paint four toothpicks and trim them to ½ inch (1.3 cm). Glue these to the bottom four corners. *These are the bed's legs, but not its only "legs" ::evil laugh::*

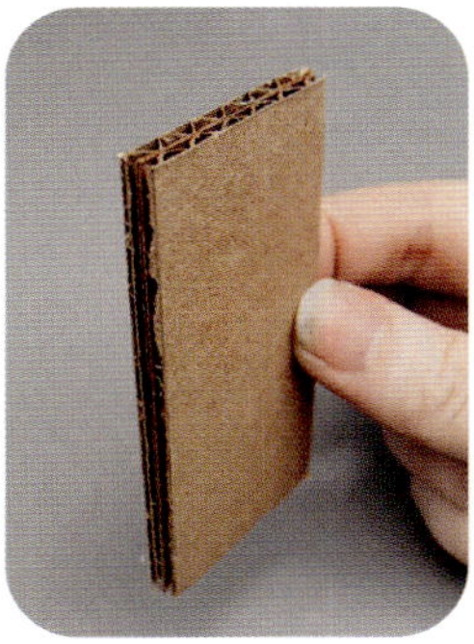

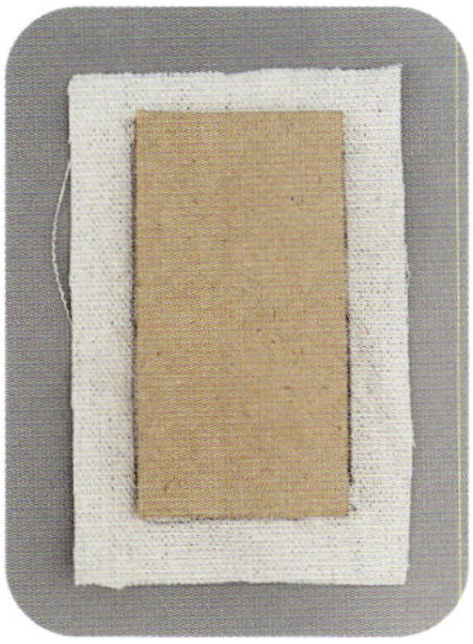

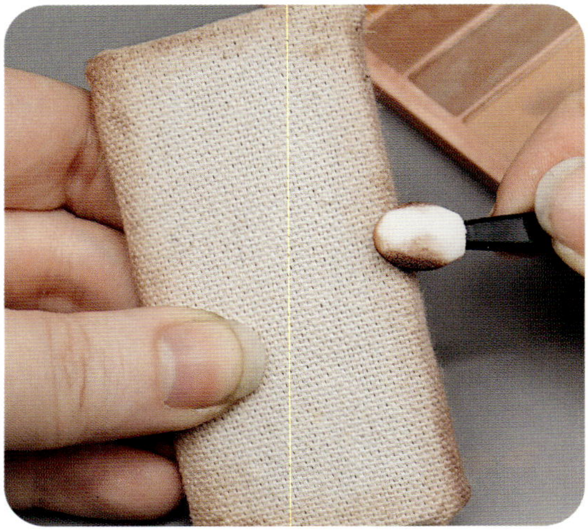

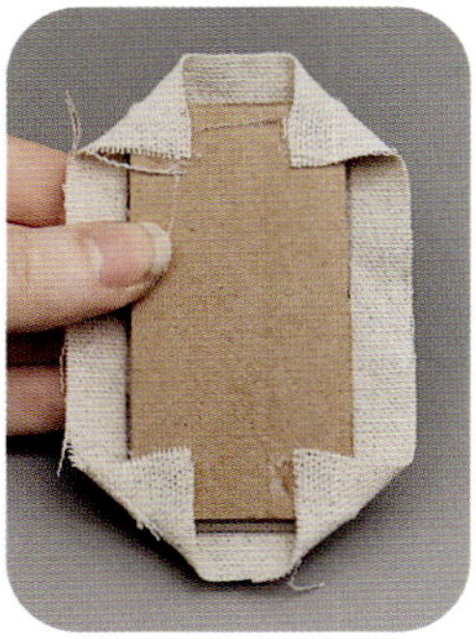

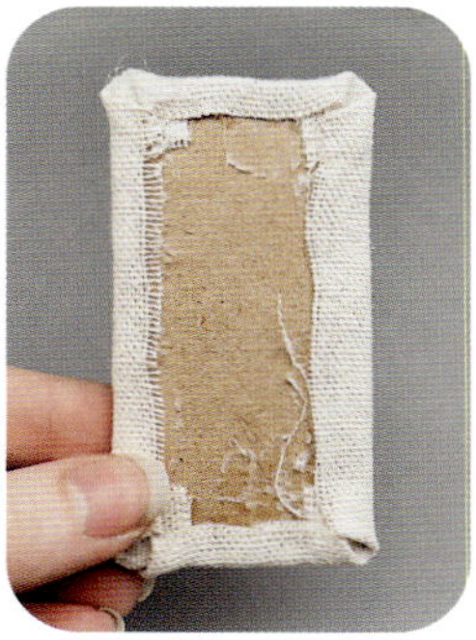

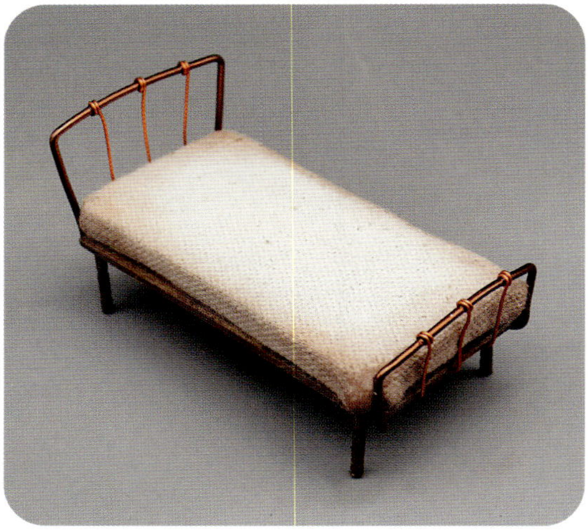

Now for the mattress. Cut two 1½ x 3–inch (3.8 x 7.6–cm) rectangles out of corrugated cardboard and glue them together.

Lay your cardboard in the center of your fabric and cut a rectangle out that is roughly ½ inch (1.3 cm) larger on each side.

Fold the corners toward the middle and hot glue them in place.

Then fold the sides toward the middle and hot glue them in place. Keep your fabric tight while gluing.

Rub each edge of your mattress with brown eye shadow. This will make your bed look dirty. Because a clean bed isn't scary! Place your mattress on top of your bed.

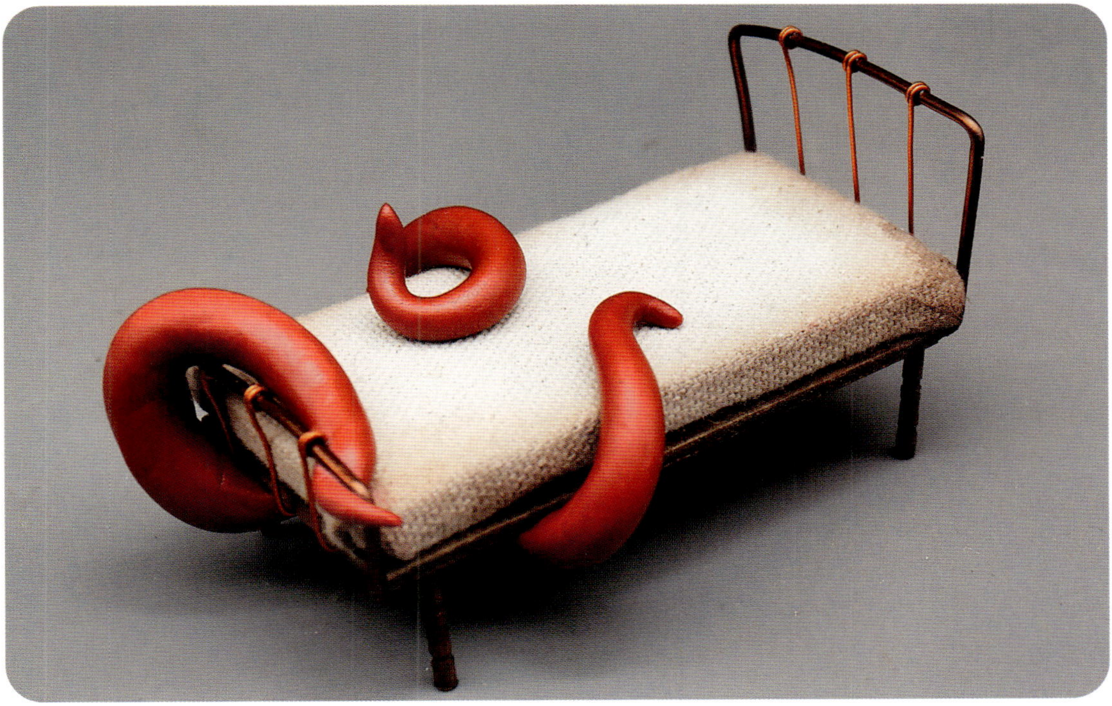

You could stop here if dirty sheets are terrifying enough for you. Otherwise, let's add a monster!

Put on your gloves, and while working atop your silicone mat, mix together a small amount of Apoxie Sculpt clay. Roll your clay into a rope with a tapered end. In other words, a tentacle shape, because SURPRISE, they're tentacles!

Forcefully smash the thicker side of your tentacle onto the bottom of your bed and wrap the rest up onto your bed. Try to imagine the monster under there and how its tentacles might move and look as you wrap it.

Add as many tentacles as your little heart desires! Wrap them around the headboard or footboard. Heck, wrap them around the legs. It's really your choice and it's up to you to come up with your own story.

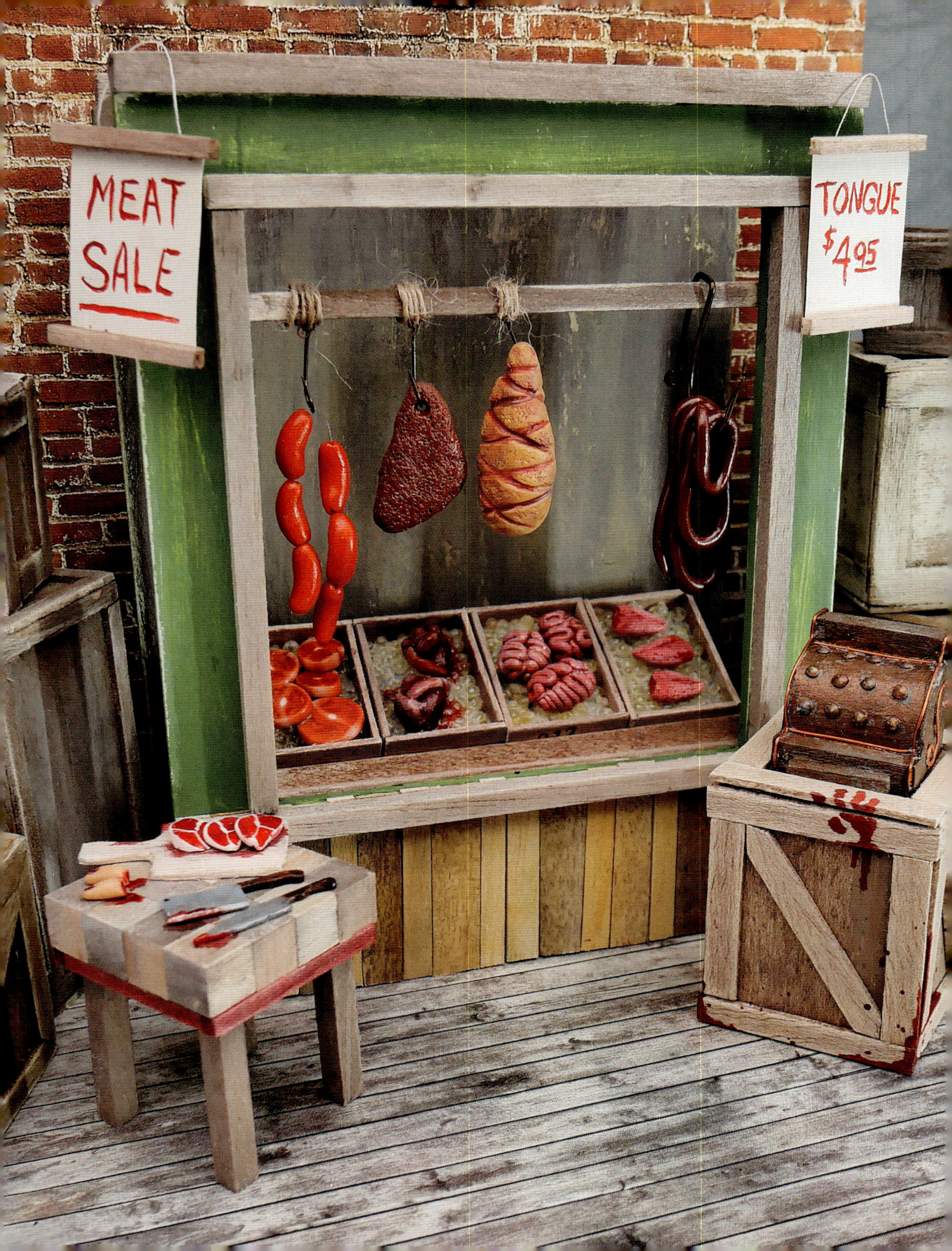
MEAT SALE
TONGUE $4.95

The Butcher

Everyone in town knows Marvin's Butcher Shop is a bit . . . unusual. It's open at strange hours and the service has always been a bit . . . lacking. However, the meat Marvin sells has always been the highest quality and the most exotic! In fact, people flock from all over the world to try and get their hands on Marvin's meat!

What makes this meat taste so good? Well, a very determined detective named Charlie was going to find out.

Late one night, Charlie crept through the empty streets in town to sneak into the butcher shop. But when he arrived, he was surprised to find the butcher shop open. I mean, it was 2 a.m.! Who in their right mind is buying meat at two in the morning?

Against Charlie's better judgment, he decided to enter the shop. He was greeted by Marvin himself. Well, I say greeted, but what Marvin really did was grunt in his general direction. Charlie started asking a lot of questions. Too many questions. He asked, "What kind of meat is that? Where does your meat come from? Why does it twitch like that? What's your favorite color?" And on and on he went. Marvin, a man of few words, simply replied, "Stew?" Charlie, not one to pass up on free mystery stew, accepted.

Marvin's Mystery Stew made Charlie mysteriously sleepy. (Imagine that!) Did Marvin mix something in for some peace and quiet, or was Charlie just sleep-deprived? Either way, Charlie fell asleep face-first in his bowl of stew and woke up the next day in the street. Minus one kidney. And the strangest part is nothing remained of Marvin's Butcher Shop except a single empty mouse trap.

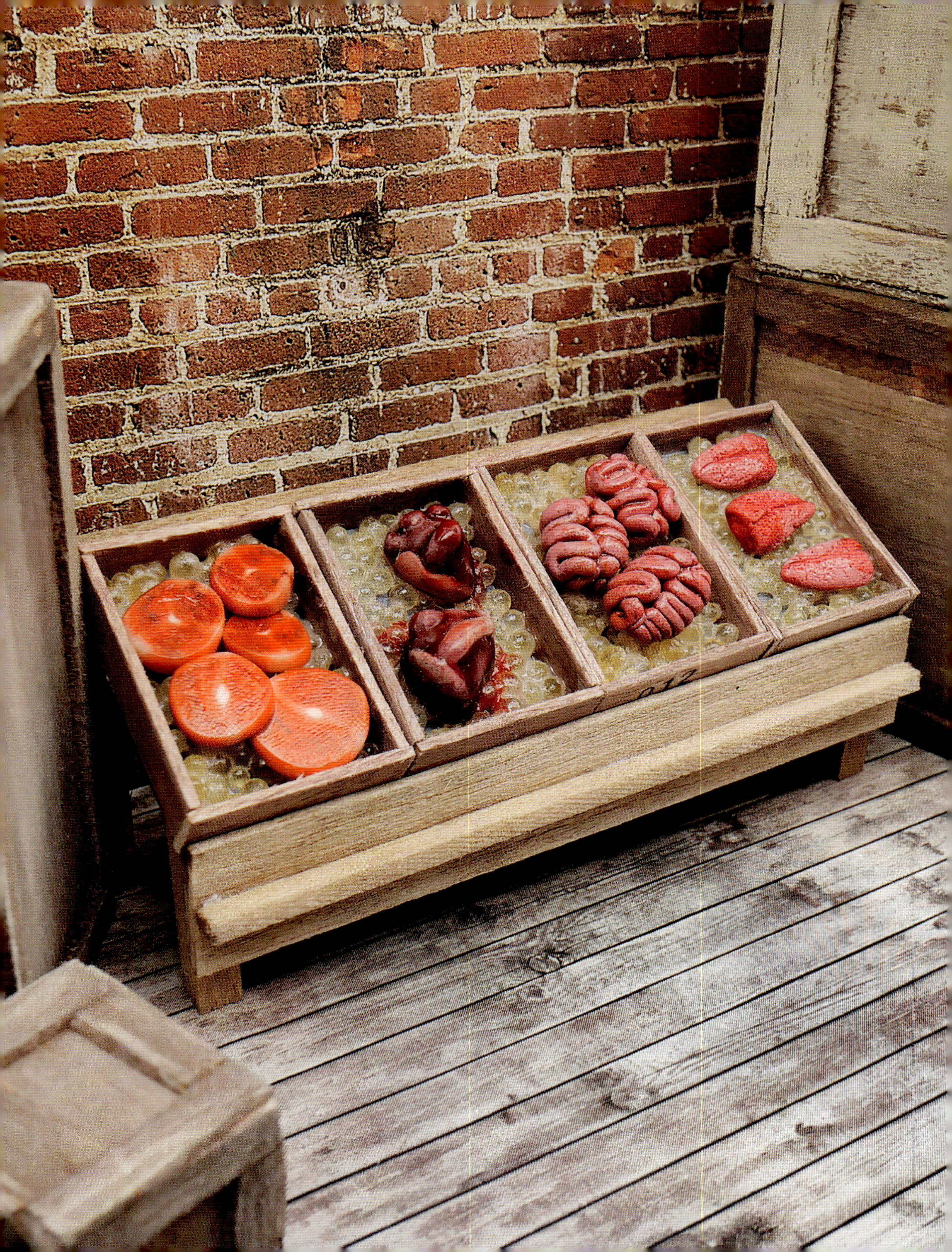

Ice Boxes

Perfect for keeping Charlie's harvested kidney nice and fresh! I mean, we can only take so many trips to candy mountain before the liopleurodon eats us!

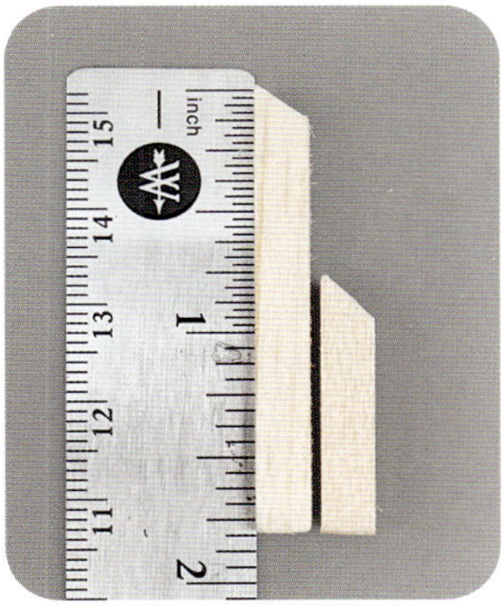

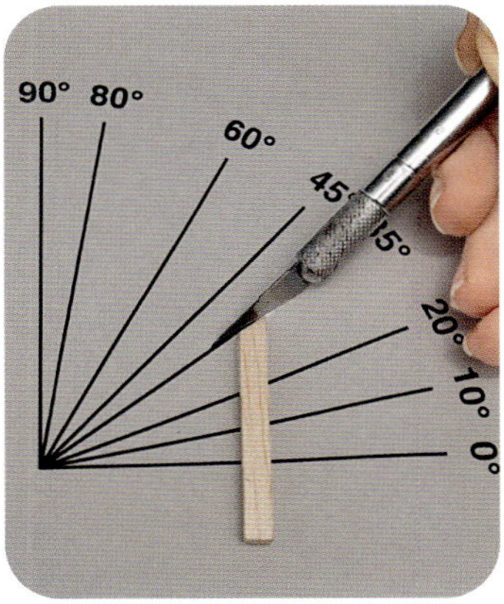

Tools

- exacto knife, ruler, & cutting mat
- paint
- glue
- craft glue
- toothpick
- wire brush (or toothbrush)
- ball sculpting tool
- clear gloss

Rack Materials

- ¼" (6-mm) or 3/16" (5-mm) square dowel
- balsa wood

Tray & Meat Materials

- balsa wood
- silica gel pack
- polymer clay
- 4–6 meats (page 47)

Rack

Cut the following ¼-inch (6-mm) or 3/16-inch (5-mm) square dowels:

- **Qty: 2**— 1¾ inches (4.5 cm) ***back legs***
- **Qty: 2**— 1 inch (2.5 cm) ***front legs***

Cut and paint the following balsa wood. Use the template on page 221 if needed.

- **Qty: 1**—4¼ x 1 inch (10.8 x 2.5 cm) ***back***
- **Qty: 1**—4¼ x 1¾ inches (10.8 x 4.5 cm) ***top***
- **Qty: 1**—4¼ x ½ inch (10.8 x 1.3 cm) ***front***
- **Qty: 1**—4¼ x 3/5 inch (10.8 x 1.5 cm) ***finished front***

Cut one end on each of the ***legs*** at a 35° angle using the angle reference on page 220.

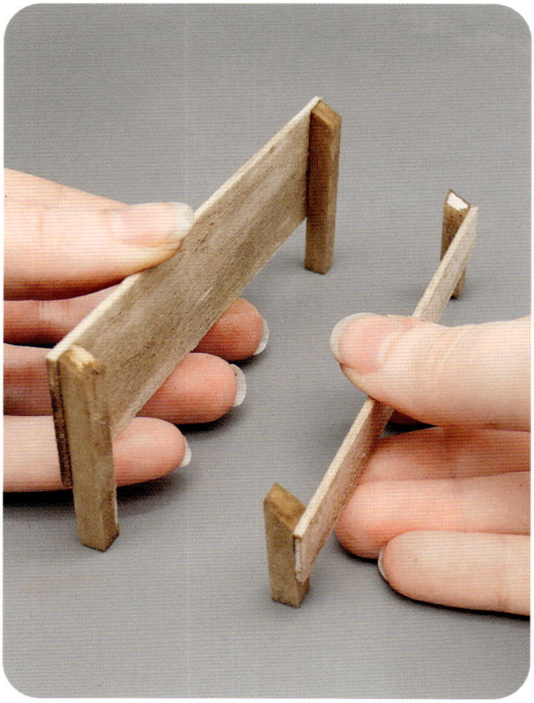

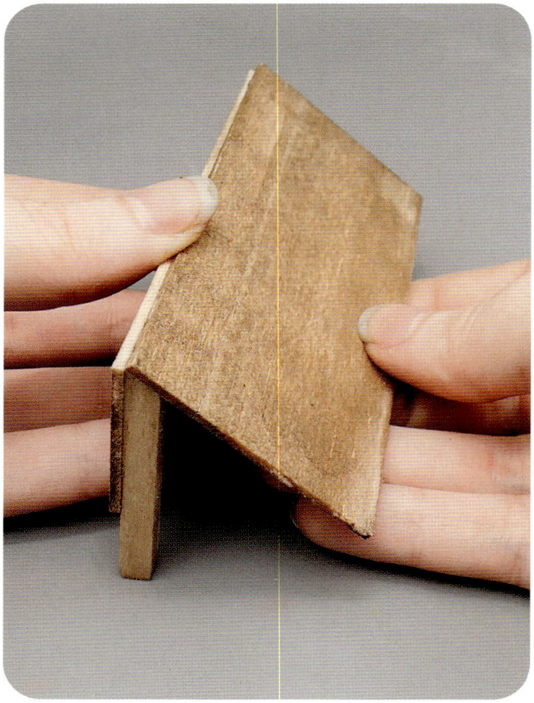

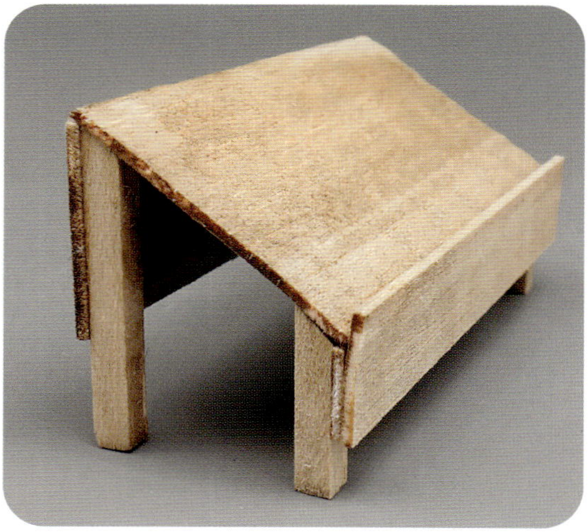

Glue the ***back legs*** flush with the short edge of the ***back*** piece. The top angle of the leg should be flush with the top of the ***back*** piece.

Glue the ***front legs*** flush with the short edge of the ***front*** piece. The bottom of the angle on the legs should be flush with the top of the ***front*** piece.

Glue the ***top*** piece on top of the ***back*** and ***front*** pieces.

Glue the ***finished front*** piece onto the ***front*** piece so that it sticks up over the rack. This is so that the trays won't slide off.

Finish off the rack with a 4¼-inch (10.8-cm) strip of balsa wood or dowel across the front for decor. Set it aside.

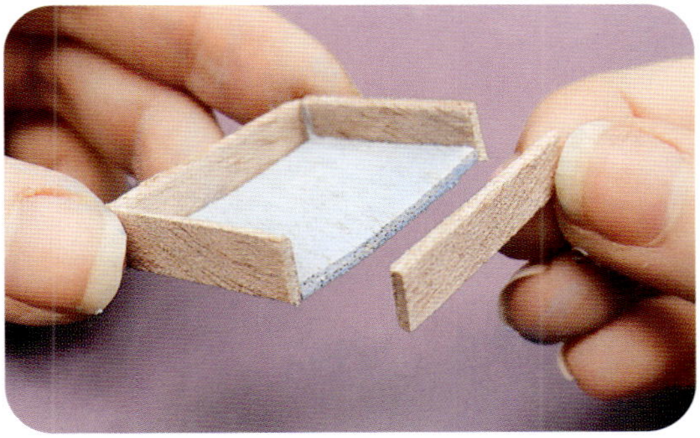

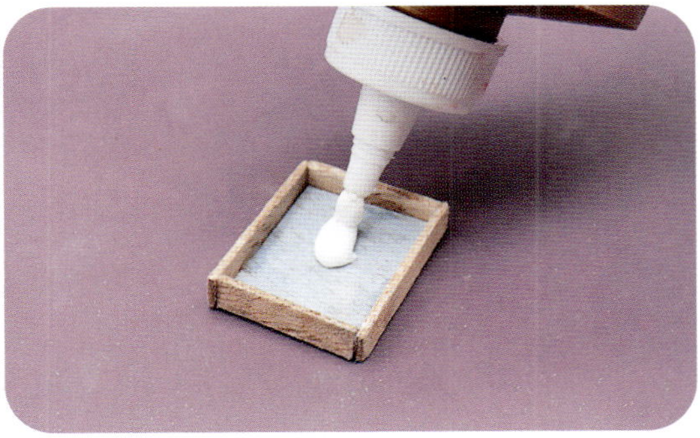

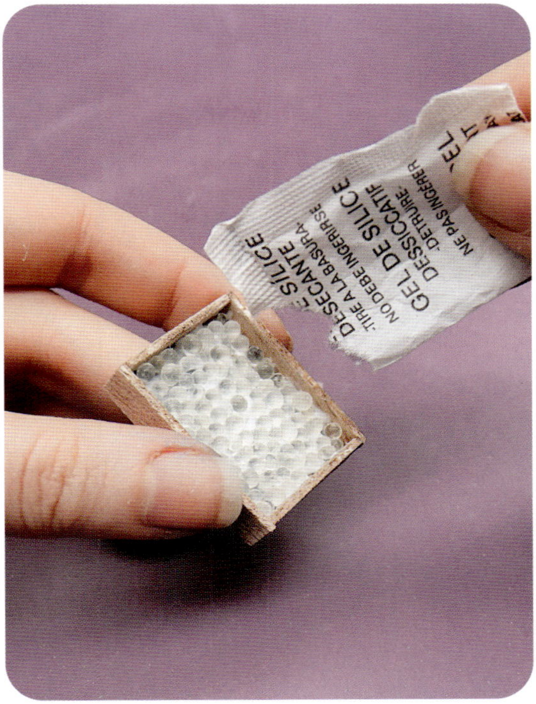

Trays

Cut and paint the following balsa wood. Use the template on page 220 if needed.

- **Qty: 4**—1 x 1½ inches (2.5 x 3.8 cm) ***bottom***
- **Qty: 8**—1 x ¼ inch (2.5 cm x 6 mm) ***front***
- **Qty: 8**—1⅗ x ¼ inch (4.1 cm x 6 mm) ***side***

Take a ***bottom*** piece and frame it by gluing two ***front*** pieces and two ***side*** pieces along the cut edge of the ***bottom*** piece.

Make sure you're gluing along the cut edges of the bottom and not on top of it.

Repeat until you have four trays.

Coat the bottom of a tray with craft glue. Use your finger to smooth it out. Before the glue dries, pour a single layer of silica gel balls. Use your finger to push balls into every corner for maximum ball-age! This is the ice.

Do this to all four trays. Set them aside.

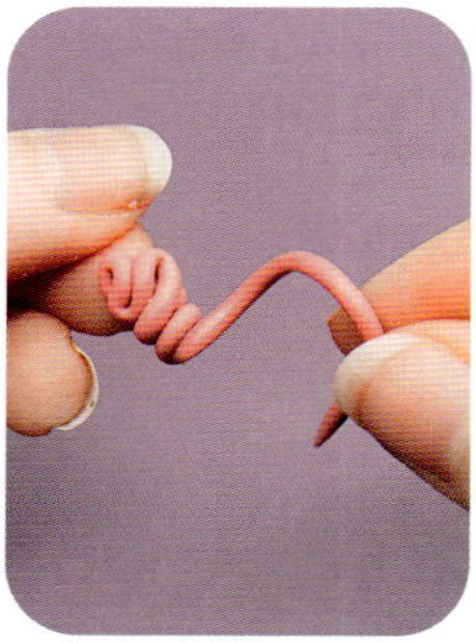
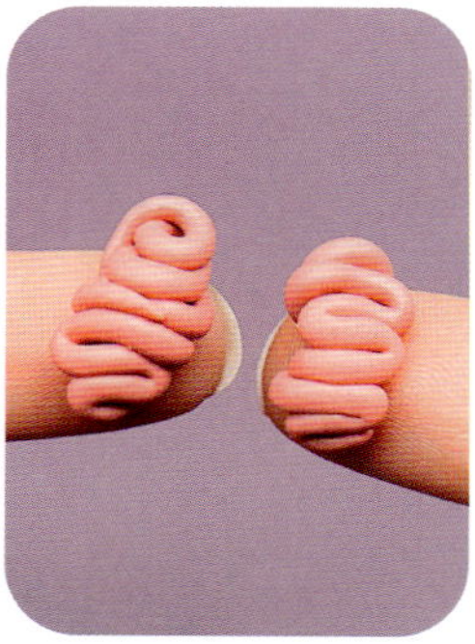
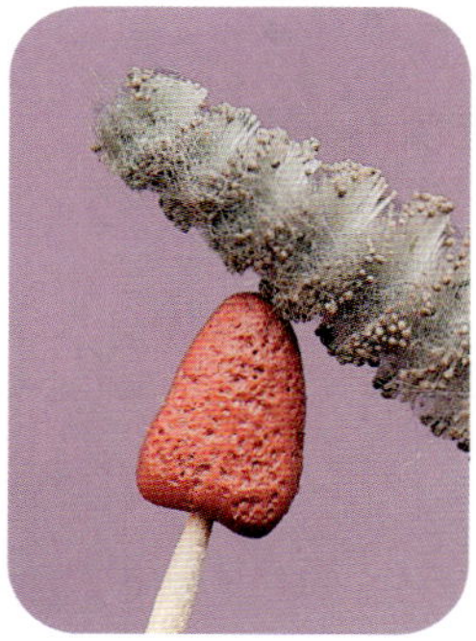
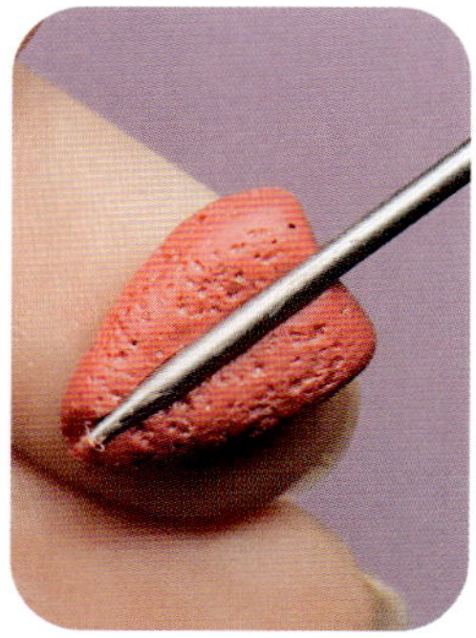
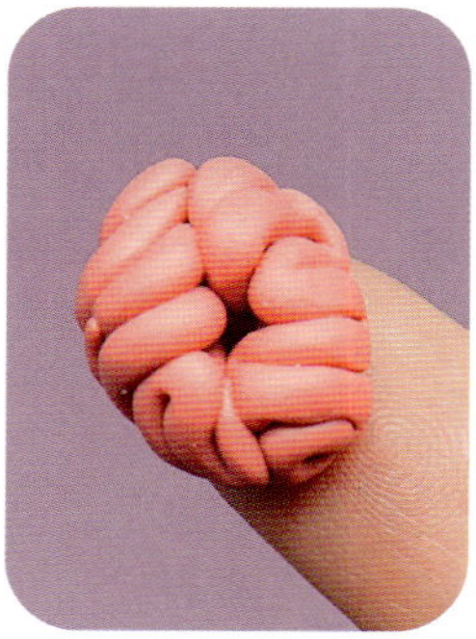
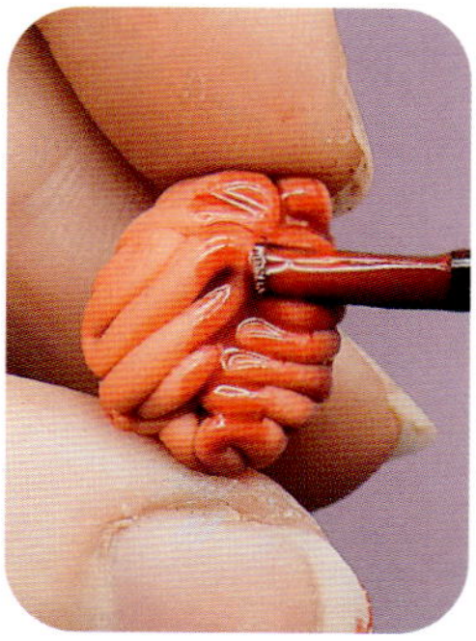
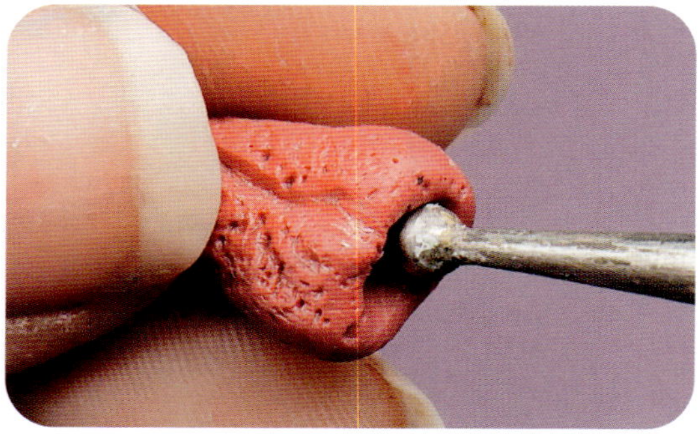

Clay Sizer
Brains
x2

Clay Sizer
Tongue

Brain

Roll out your two brain balls in clay and make them into a long, super skinny snake about as thick as a Q-tip cotton swab handle.

Twist the clay snake back and forth into a squiggly oval. Repeat so you have two.

Gently squish your two brain halves together.

Do this until you have at least three brains, then harden them according to the package instructions. Set them aside.

Tongue

Roll out your tongue ball and gently flatten it to half the width.

Pinch the top to make a rounded triangle shape.

Stab a toothpick into the bottom so that you can hold it while texturing it with a wire brush or toothbrush. Take your toothpick out and use it to add a line down the middle of your tongue. With a ball sculpting tool, make a dimple in the bottom.

Do this until you have at least three tongues, then harden them according to the package instructions. Set them aside.

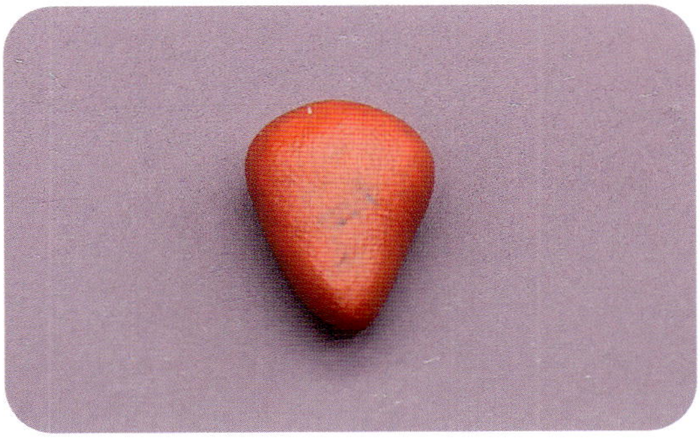

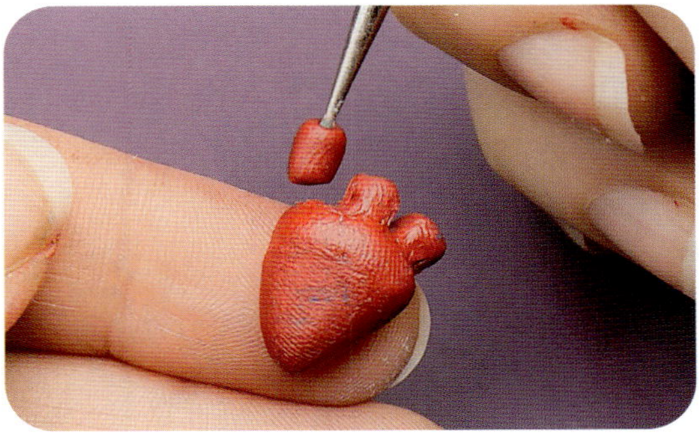

Heart

Roll out your six heart clay balls.

Holding your ***base*** clay ball, gently flatten it to half the width.

Gently pinch the bottom to make a rounded triangle shape. Set it aside.

Take your three ***nub*** balls and gently roll them in one direction to make fat cylinders.

Place each ***nub*** in a row on top of your ***base***. Smooth the seam between the ***nubs*** and ***base*** with a rounded sculpting tool. Poke holes into the top of each ***nub***.

Take your ***artery*** ball and gently roll it in one direction to make a long cylinder about the width of your heart. Place it across the middle of your heart.

Flatten your ***side*** ball into an oval and stick it to the left side of your heart.

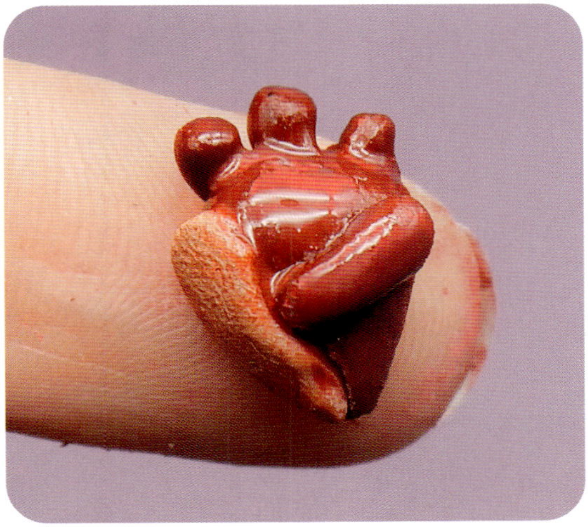

Do this until you have at least two hearts, then harden them according to the package instructions. Set them aside.

You should now have brains, tongues, and hearts! Add the four to six slices of meat from page 47 and you have four different meats for your four trays. Glue in each meat into its own tray and cover with a clear gloss. Tint your gloss with just a little red to make it look like meat juices.

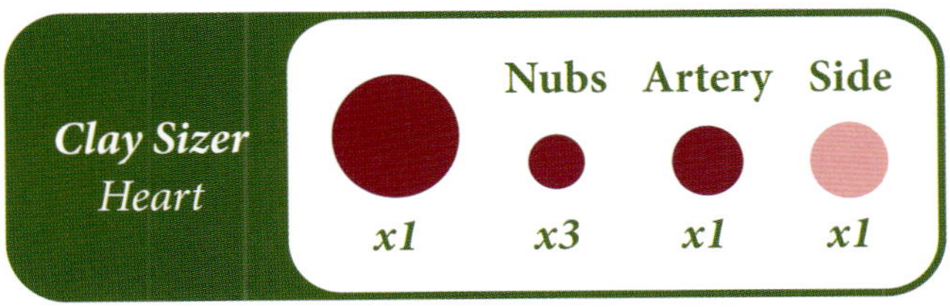

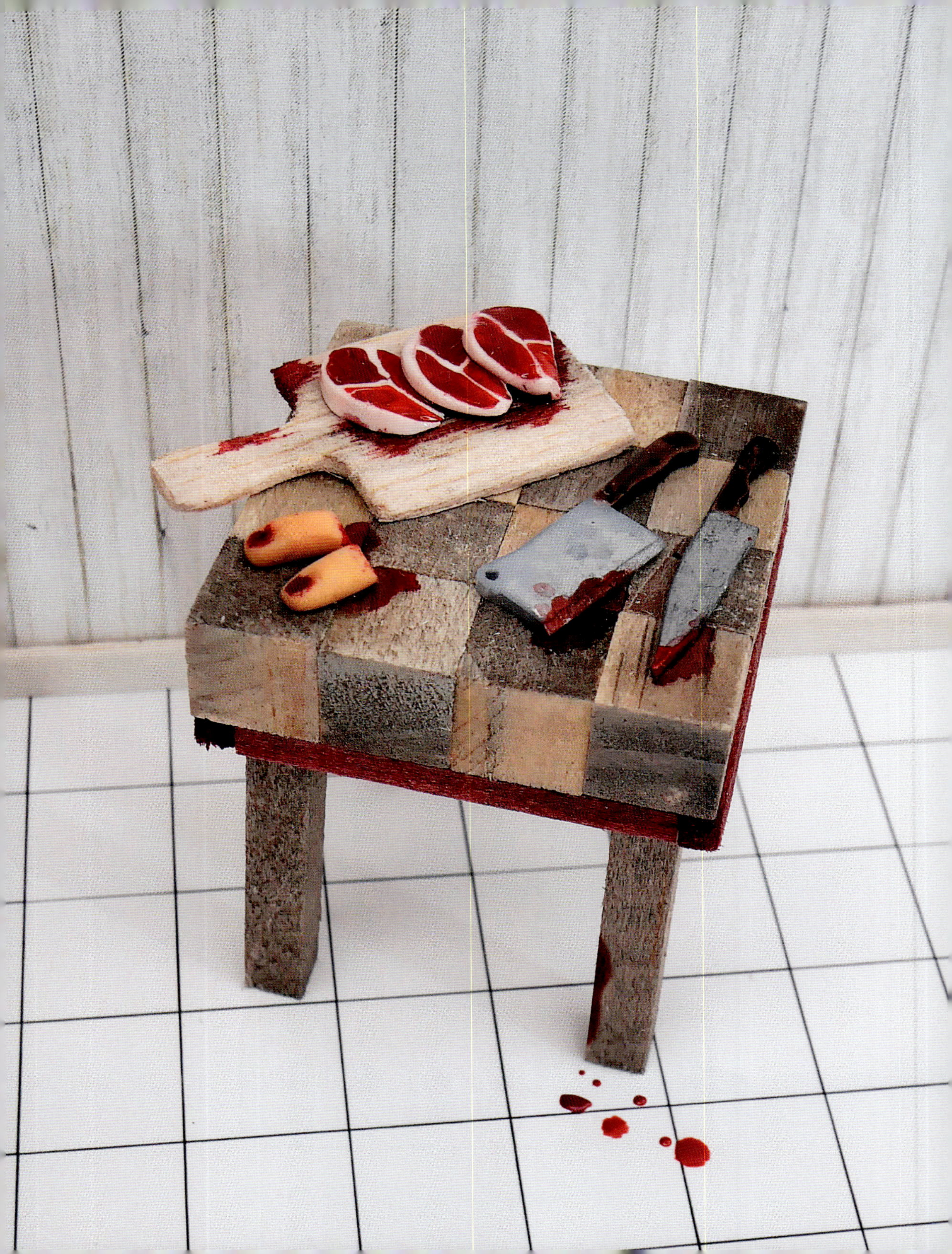

Chopping Block

Chopping your fingers off is just one of the many hazards of being a butcher. Just don't get it mixed up with the meat!

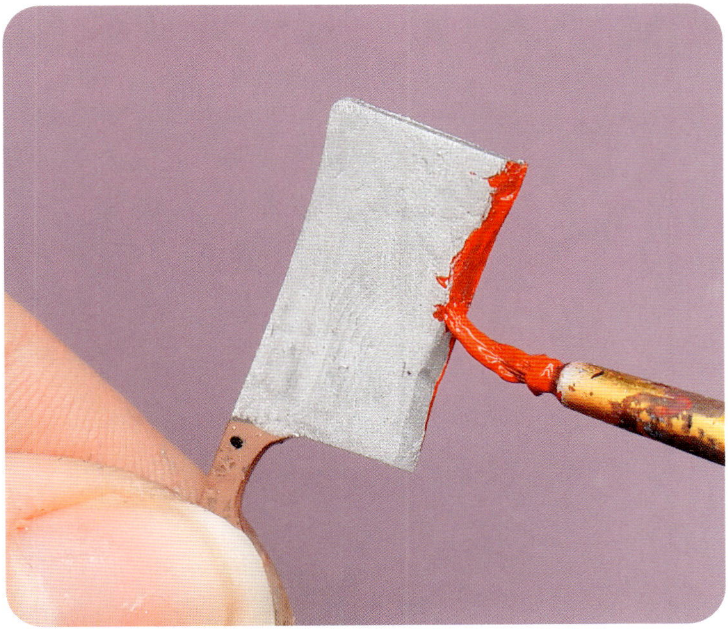

Tools

- pencil
- scissors
- paint
- ball sculpting tool
- exacto knife, ruler, & cutting mat
- sandpaper (or file)
- glue

Knives Material

- shrink plastic

Fingers Material

- polymer clay

Cutting Board Materials

- balsa wood
- polymer clay
- meat (page 47)
- table (page 144)

Knives

Trace the knife templates on page 219 onto shrink plastic. Cut them out and shrink them.

Paint your knives with silver paint for the sharp bits, brown for the handle bits, and . . . *Oh my, someone's been cutting beets because there's red dripping down the edge of the blade!*

Set them aside.

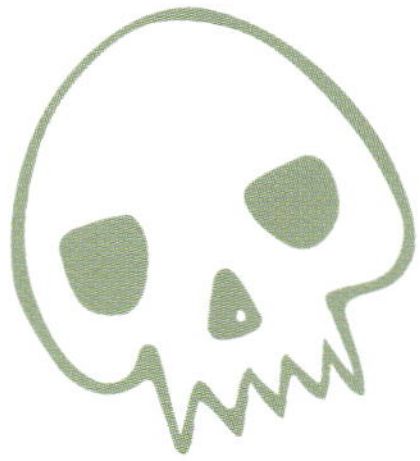

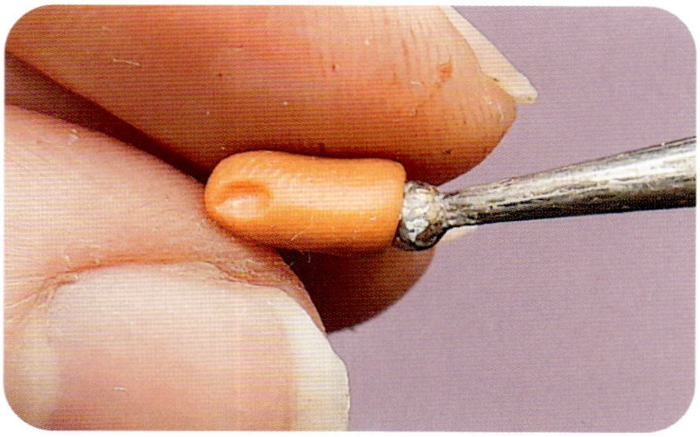

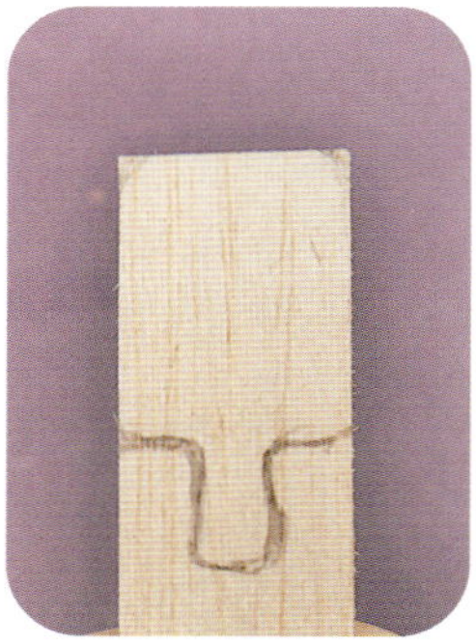

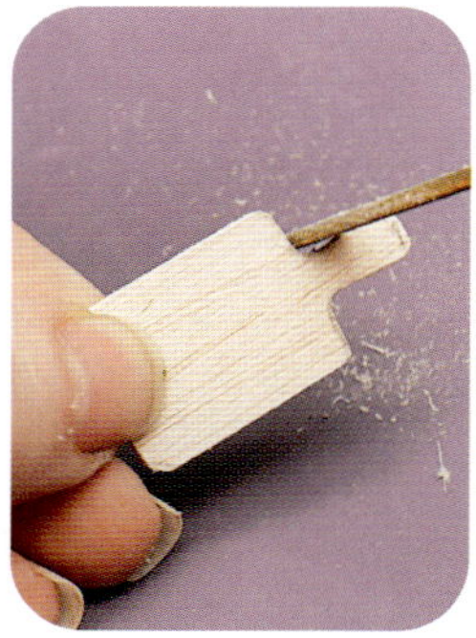

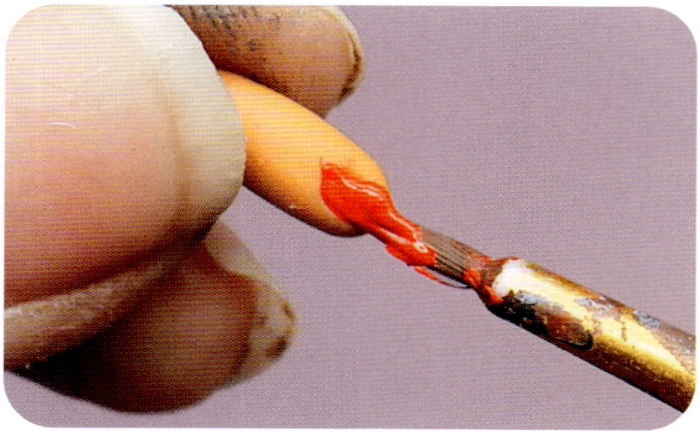

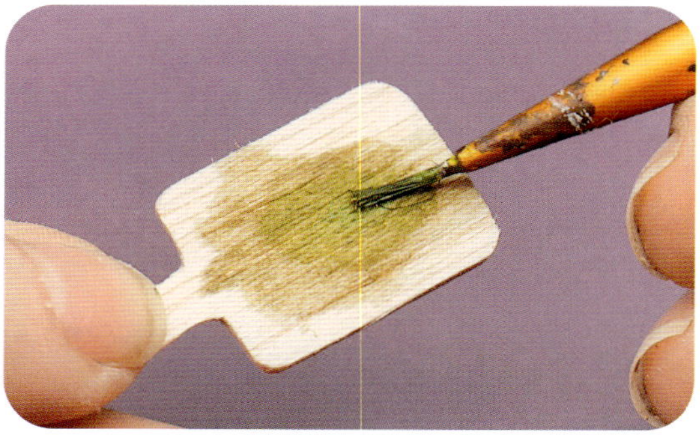

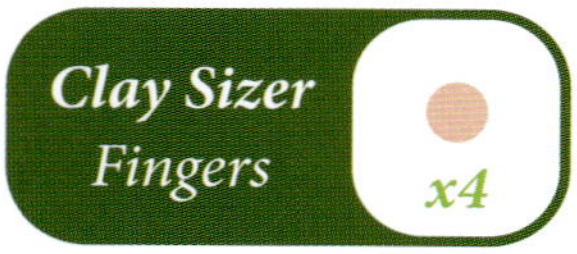

Fingers

Roll two to four finger clay balls into little, short, tiny sausages.

Take a ball sculpting tool and press an indent on the top for a nail bed and on the end for a severed finger look. Cure according to the package instructions.

Paint both dents with dark red paint. Set them aside.

Cutting Board

Sketch a cutting board, roughly ¾ x 1 inch (1.9 x 2.5 cm), onto a sheet of balsa wood.

Cut your cutting board out and round the edges with sandpaper and/or a file.

Paint a green stain in the middle. Gross!

Glue the meat from page 47 to the cutting board. Then glue this to the table from page 144. Scatter your knives and fingers around and you're ready to cut your own meat!

Crate & Cash Register

Great for cashing and registering! Registering for what, I don't know. But you can now do both the cashing and registering on your tiny cash register!

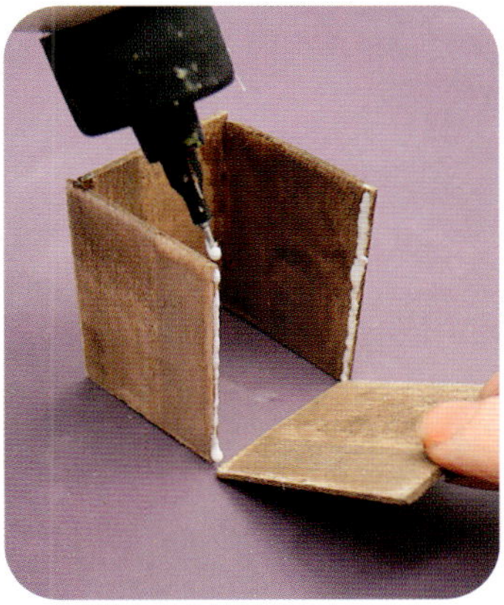

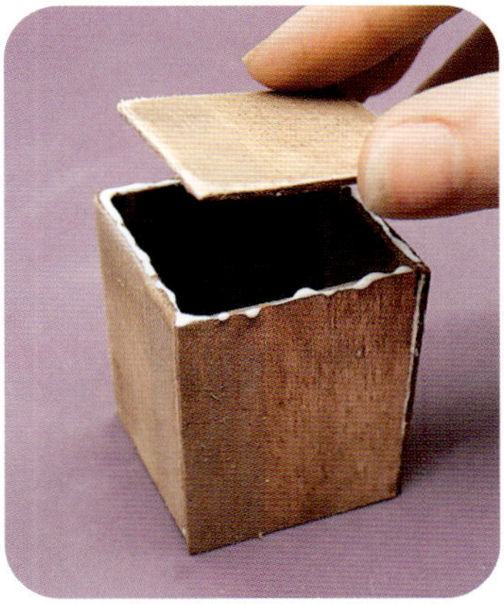

Tools

- exacto knife, ruler, & cutting mat
- paint
- glue
- pencil

Crate & Cash Register Materials

- balsa wood
- ¼" (6-mm) or 3⁄16" (5-mm) square dowels
- chipboard
- 12 diamond drills (or puff paint)
- floral wire

Crate

Cut and stain brown the following balsa wood:

- **Qty: 4**—1½ x 2 inches (3.8 x 5 cm) ***sides***
- **Qty: 2**—1½ x 1½ inches (3.8 x 3.8 cm) ***ends***

Start by gluing your four ***sides*** along the long end into a cube. Make sure each side has one end-grain edge glued onto the face-grain next to it. (See the diagram on page 218.)

Glue on the two ***ends*** to make a box. Let this sit for a few minutes to be sure it doesn't fall apart.

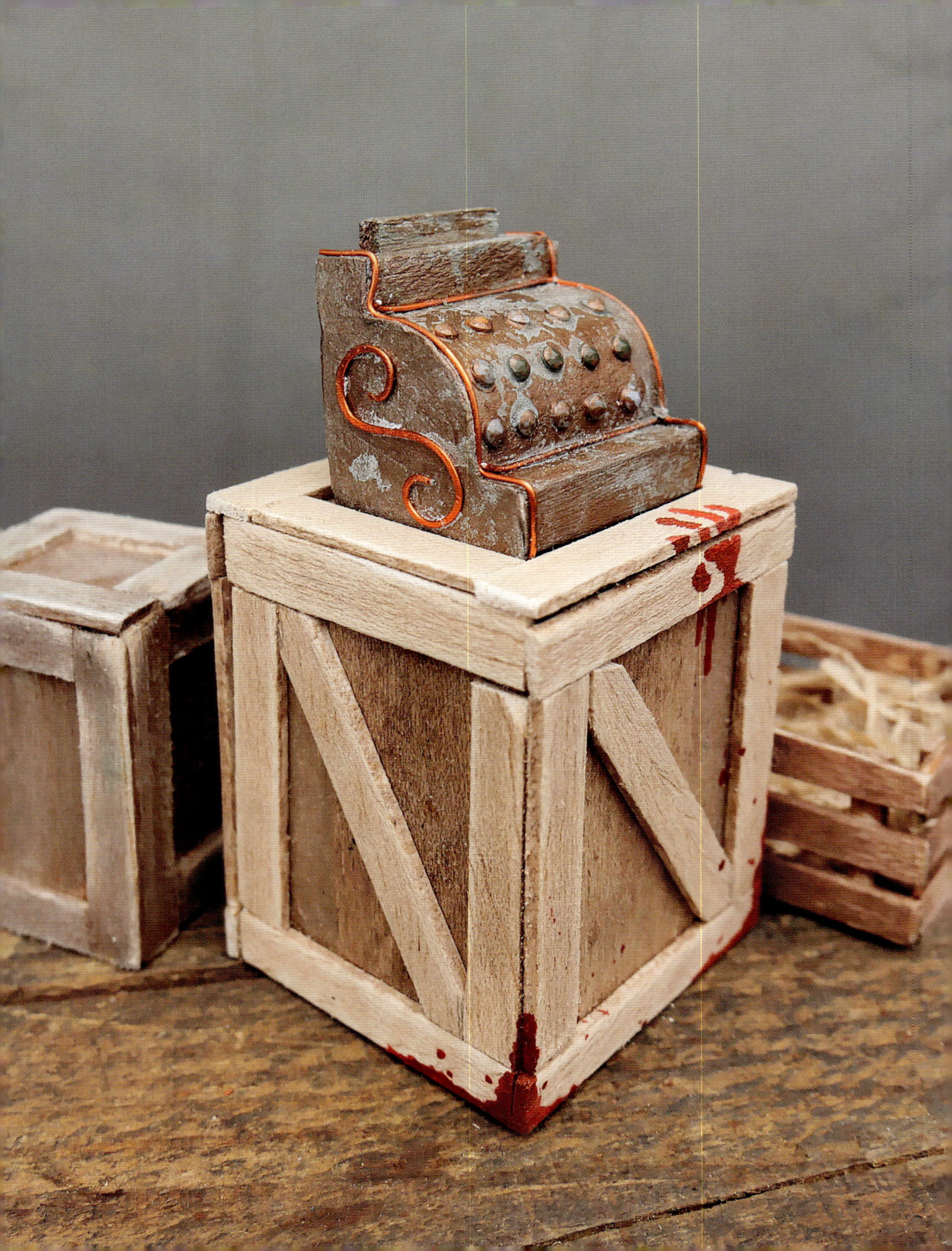

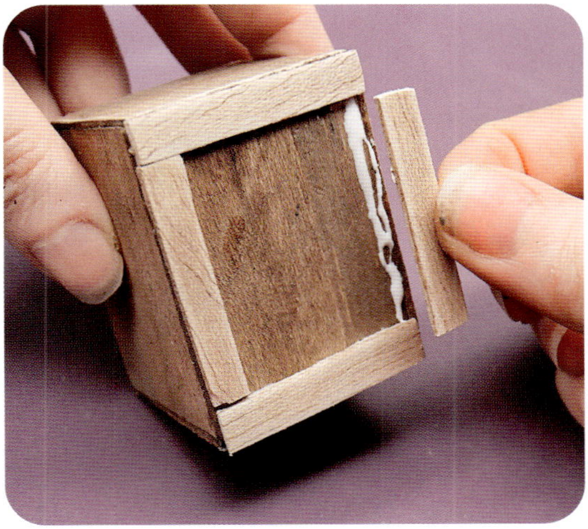

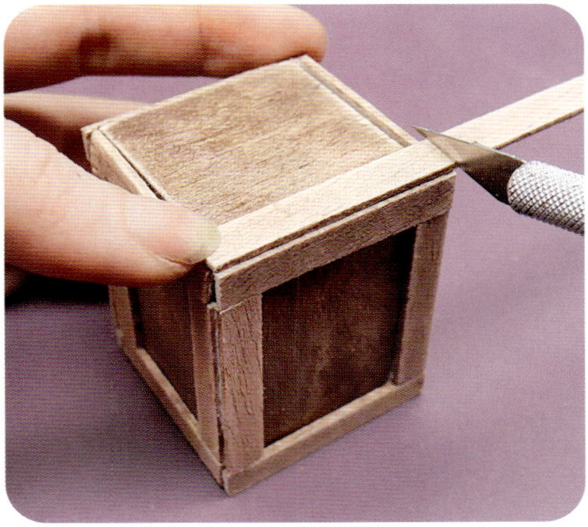

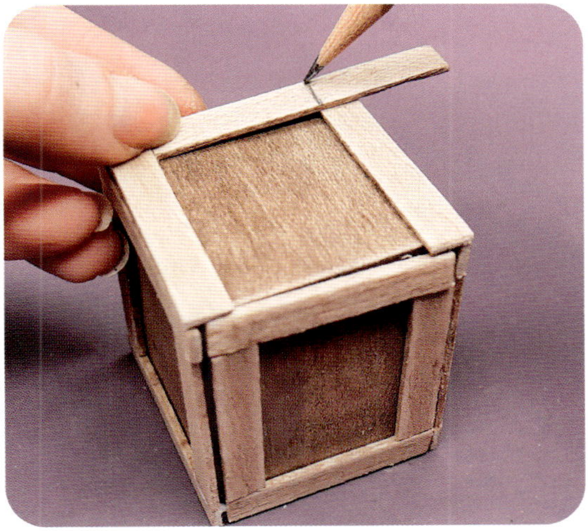

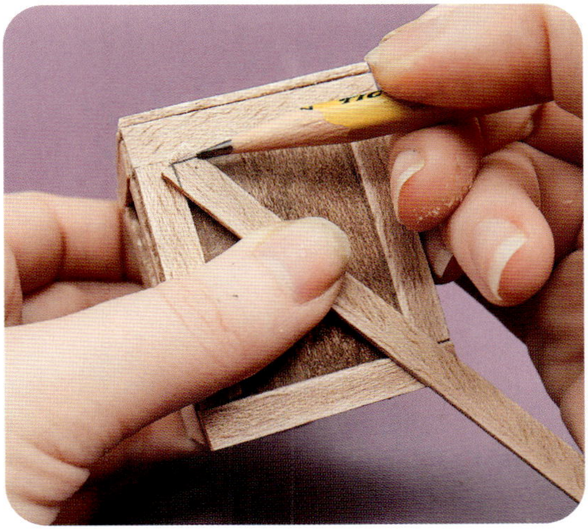

Cut a long (about ¼-inch [6-mm]) strip of balsa wood and start framing your sides. *There's no need to measure. Just hold your strip up to the side, mark it with a pencil and cut. Start with short edges first, then do the long edges. It doesn't have to be perfect because it's supposed to look old. You will get the hang of it once you get going.*

There's no need to frame the bottom unless you're feeling *"extra."*

If you want to be fancy, add a crossbeam diagonally on each side, or if you've had enough with this stupid crate, leave it blank. It looks good either way.

Optionally, splatter some blood around the edges to make it look like it's leaking something icky.

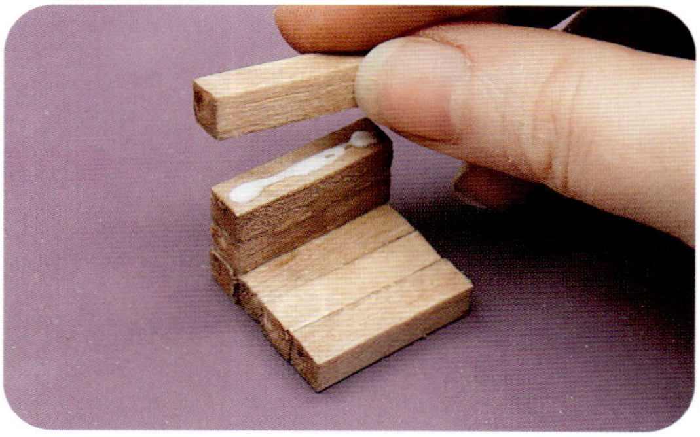

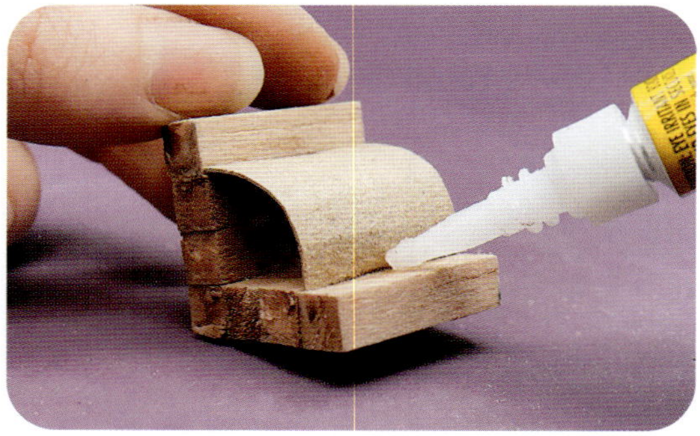

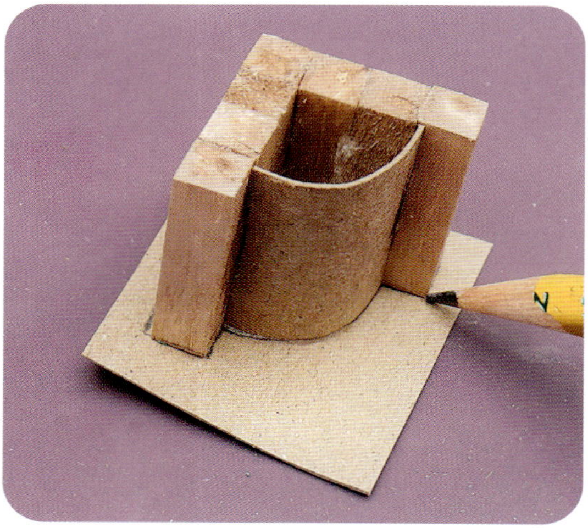

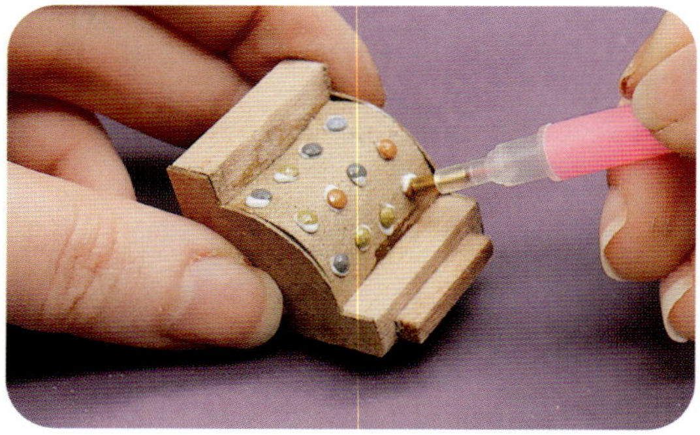

Lay the side of your register onto a scrap of chipboard. Trace it with a pencil and cut out two.

Glue them onto either side of your register.

If you have diamond drills, glue them onto your curved cardboard in a 4 x 3 grid. *If you don't, you can use drips of glue or puff paint instead. Just be sure the glue dries before you move on to the next step.*

Paint your cash register bronze or brown.

Jazz it up with some floral wire around the edges and swirls on the side.

Printing out little dollar bills and crumpling them up adds a touch of realism. Just avoid printing them at normal size. You might get arrested.

Cash Register

Stain your square dowel with watered-down brown paint and cut seven sticks 1¼ inches (3.2 cm) long.

Glue them on top of each other in an L shape.

Cut a square out of chipboard that's 1¼ x 1¼ inches (3.2 x 3.2 cm) and curve it around something round like a marker to make it curl a bit.

Put your curved chipboard inside the L so that the top of it touches the bottom of the first dowel and the bottom touches the top of the last dowel. Glue and hold it in place.

Pot of "Mystery Stew"

It's not what's in the "Mystery Stew" . . . It's *who's* in the "Mystery Stew."

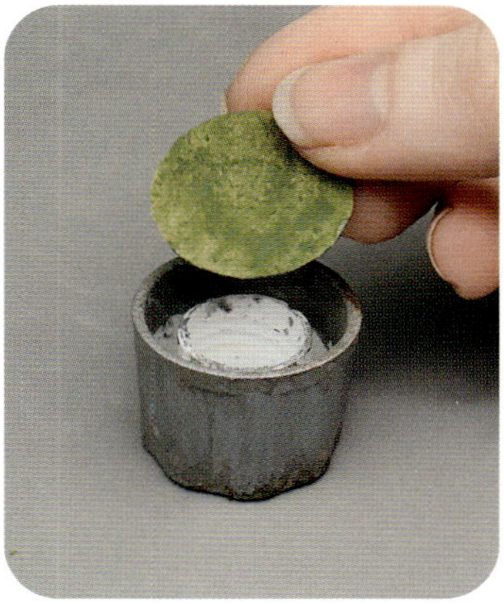

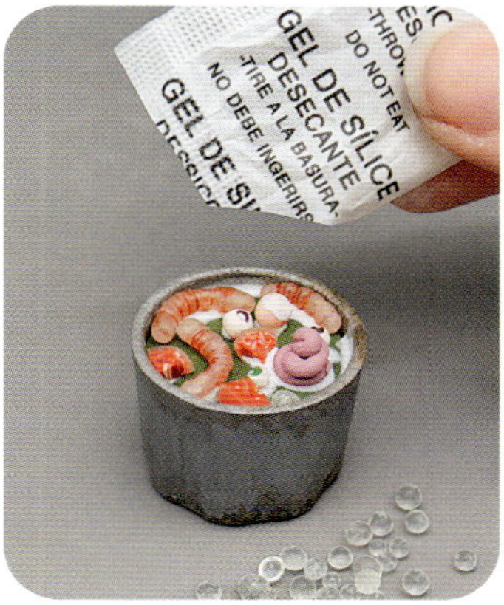

Paint your tall cap silver and stipple some brown/orange around the edges to make it look rust-alicious.

Cut a circle of chipboard just big enough to set below the rim of your cap. Paint it green and hot glue it in place.

Note: *My cap had a center that I could glue this to, but if yours doesn't, then pack it with aluminum foil and glue your chipboard to that.*

Glue the maggots, eyeballs, sliced meat, and brain ball into your pot. Sprinkle a silica gel pack on top. Wait for the glue to dry.

Tools

- paint
- scissors
- hot glue
- glue
- pliers/wire cutter

Materials

- tall cap (~1" [2.5 cm] wide)
- chipboard
- aluminum foil, if needed
- 3 maggots (page 181)
- 3–5 eyeballs (page 121)
- meat (sliced) (page 47)
- brain ball (page 156)
- silica gel pack
- green epoxy dye (or glow powder)
- epoxy resin
- paper clip
- shank button (optional lid)
- table (page 144)

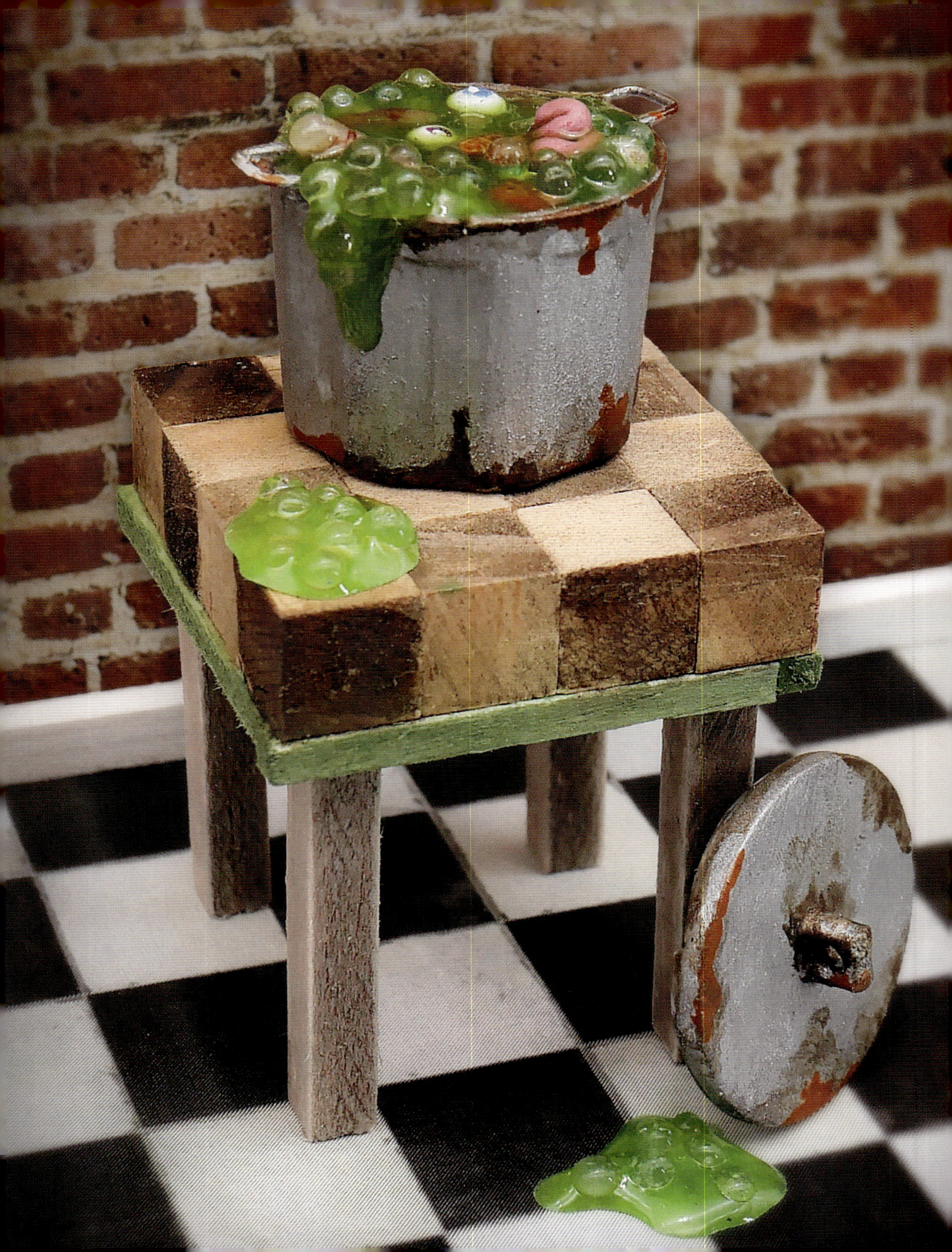

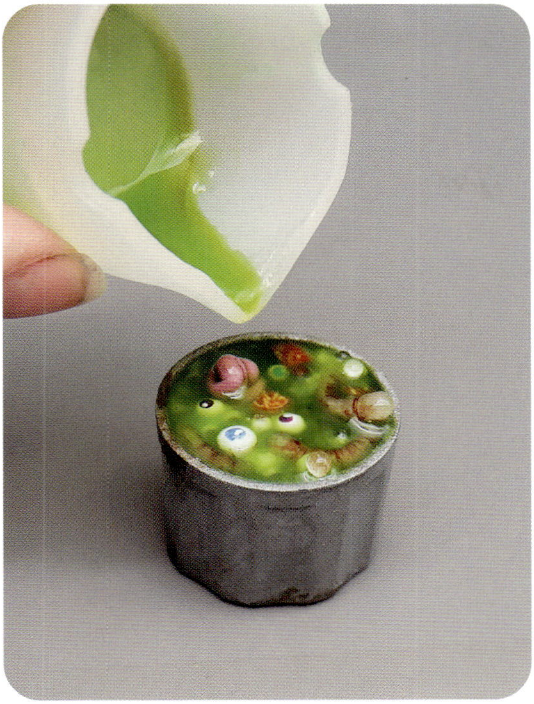

Using green epoxy dye (or with glow powder), color a small amount of epoxy resin green and fill your pot with the yummy goo.

Sprinkle a few silica gel beads on top. This makes it look like your pot is bubbling and boiling. Then cure your resin according to the package instructions.

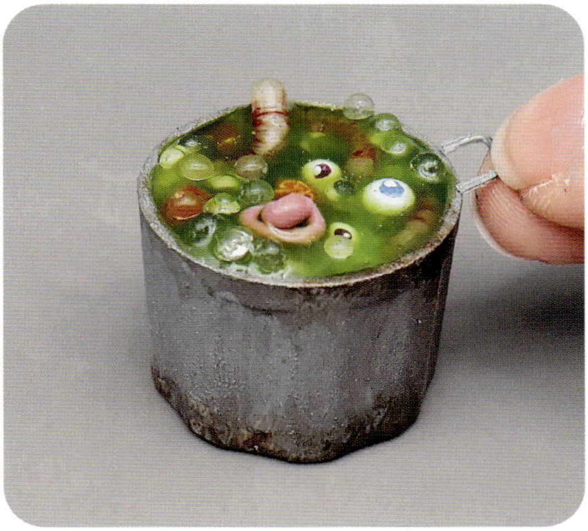

Note: *If you're using UV resin, you can make a little drip down the side with silica beads and resin.*

Bend and cut a paper clip or wire into two small [shapes and glue one to either side of the pot for handles.

Use a shank button for a lid. Set it next to your pot just in case you need to quickly capture something that's trying to get out.

Put your delicious delicacy on the table from page 144.

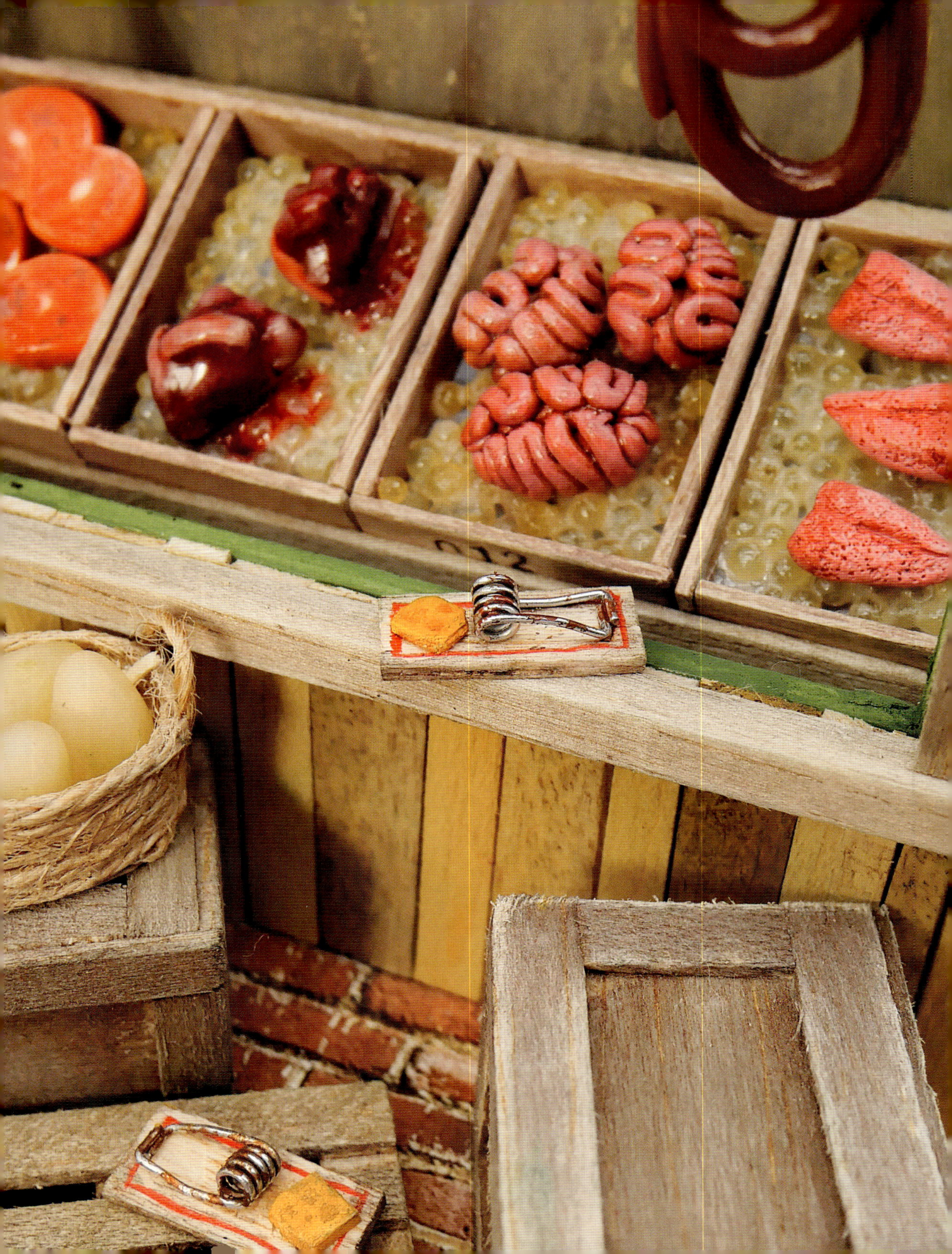

Mouse Trap

If you have to ask why I dedicated an entire project to a single rodent execution device, you're obviously not a rodent. Poor little Nibbles couldn't ask because he just wanted the cheese. SNAP!

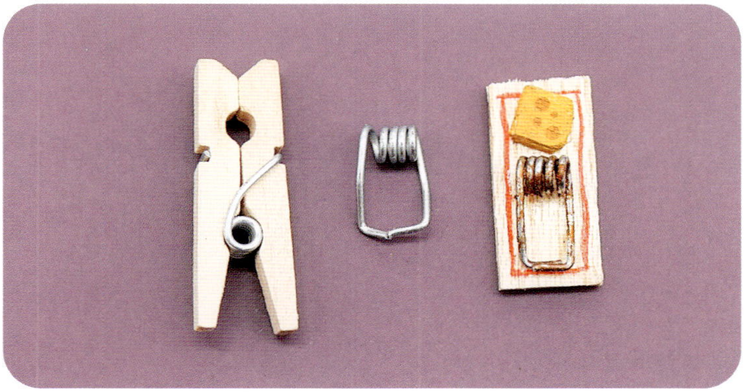

Tools

- pencil
- exacto knife, ruler, & cutting mat
- paint or paint pens
- glue

Materials

- miniature clothespin
- balsa wood

Pull the spring off of your miniature clothespin. (Save the wood pieces for another project.)

The size of your clothespin will determine how large you need to make the base. Put your spring on a scrap of balsa wood and sketch a rectangle around it. Keep in mind the cheese you'll need to add to entice your mice.

Cut out this rectangle and, with acrylic paint or a red paint pen, trace around your rectangle to leave a tiny border.

Using a scrap of balsa wood, cut a small square for the cheese. Paint this yellow with orange spots.

Glue your cheese on one side and the spring on the other side with the spring part in the middle. Now you're ready to trap those tiny mice for your mystery stew.

Tip: *Make your trap rusty by splotching your spring with brown paint.*

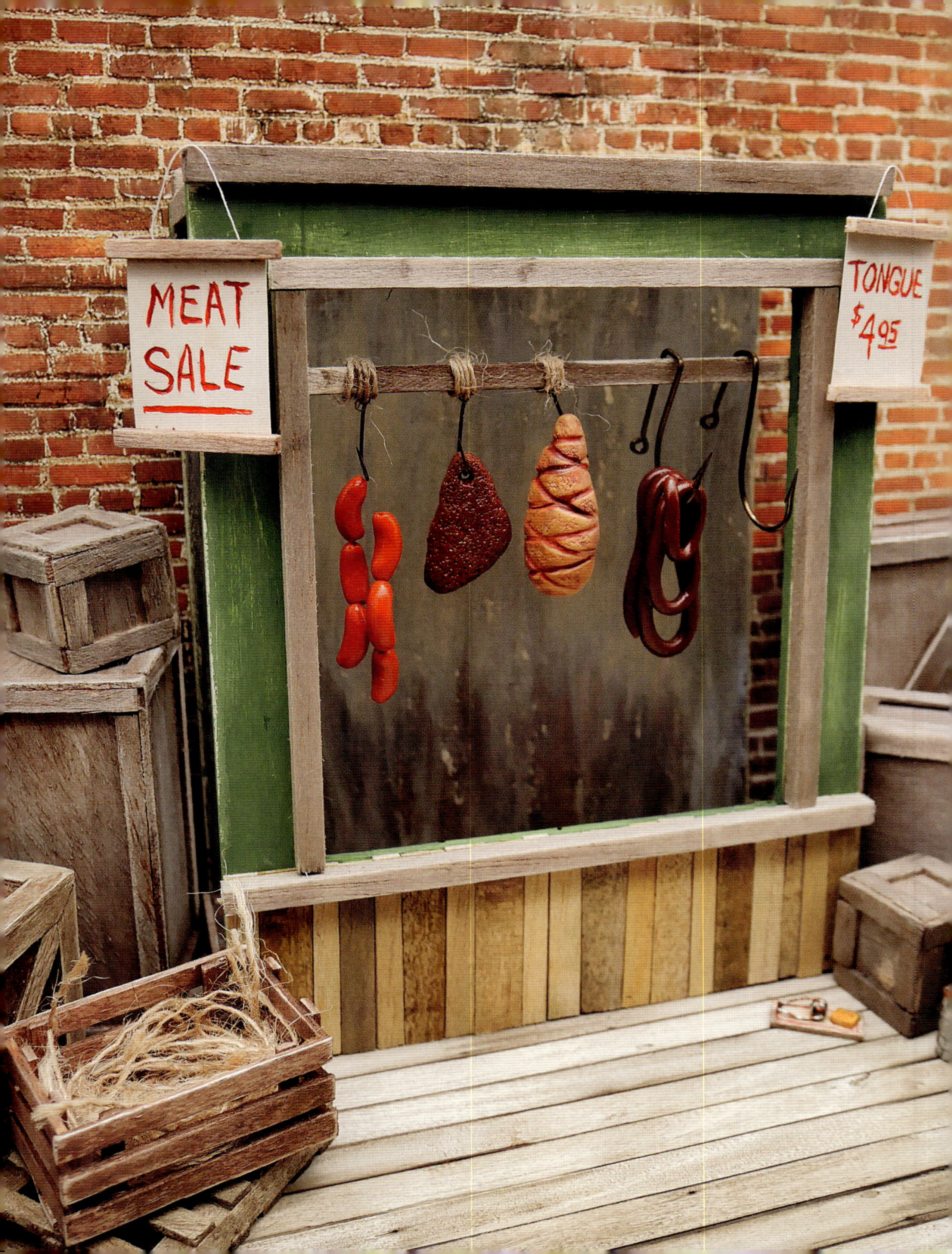
MEAT SALE
TONGUE $4.95

Butcher Shop Window

It's a window for people to gather around and look at various meats. "Look, there's Sally's spleen." "Hey, I think that's Philip's heart." You know, totally normal things you'd say while gathered around a butcher's window!

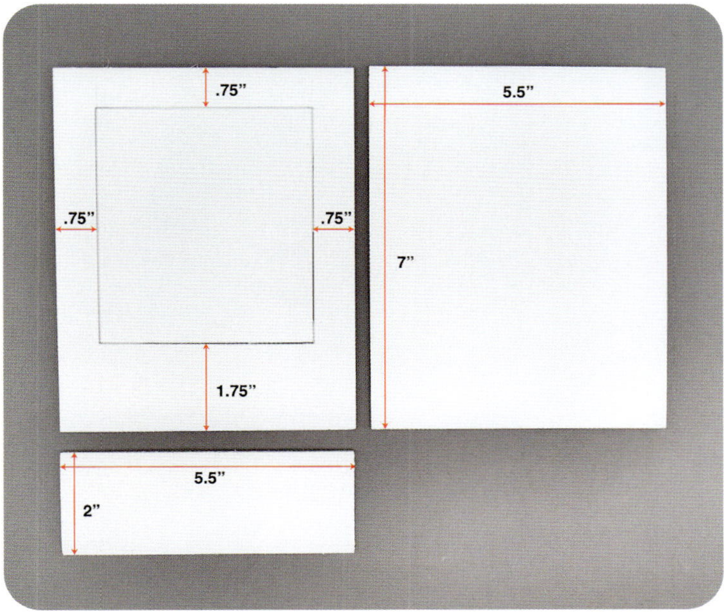

Window

Cut the following out of foam core. There are templates on pages 221, 222, and 223 if needed.

- **Qty: 2**— 5½ x 7 inches (14 x 17.8 cm) ***fronts***
- **Qty: 1**— 5½ x 2 inches (14 x 5 cm) ***bottom***

On one of the ***fronts***, let's cut a window out. Laying it down in "portrait mode," draw a line ¾ inch (1.9 cm) from the top, 1¾ inches (4.5 cm) from the bottom, and ¾ inch (1.9 cm) from either side. Using an exacto knife and ruler, cut this rectangle out.

Tools

- exacto knife, ruler, & cutting mat
- pencil
- paint
- sandpaper
- glue
- pointy object (like a needle)
- clear gloss
- wire brush (or toothbrush)

Window & Meats Materials

- foam core
- balsa wood
- ¼" (6-mm) or 3/16" (5-mm) square dowels
- polymer clay
- fishing line (or string)
- twine/hemp
- 3 small fishhooks (or wire)
- 1–2 medium fishhooks (or wire)

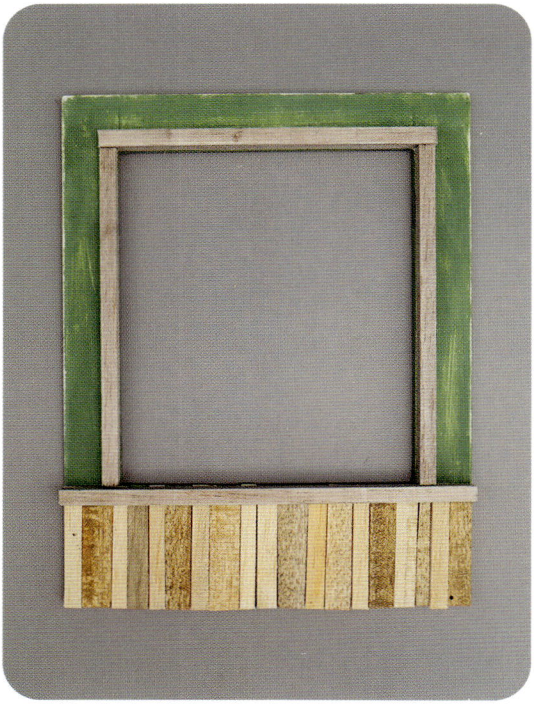

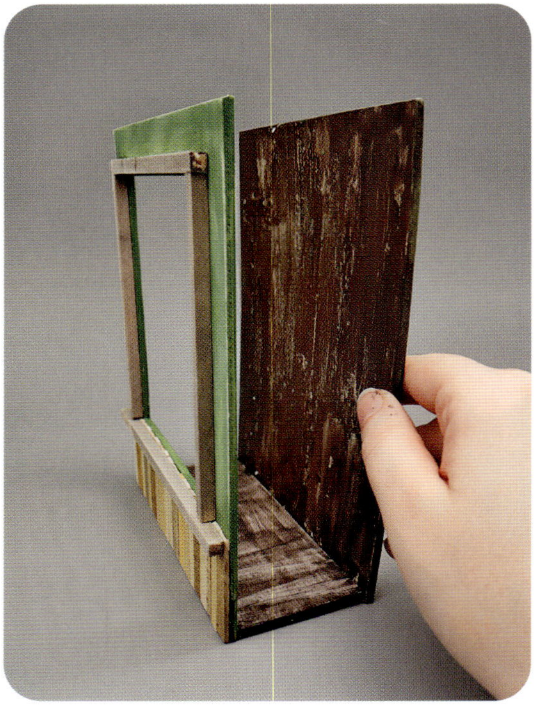

Paint it green and paint the other ***front*** and ***bottom*** brown. Once dry, sand the edges to give the paint a tired, worn-out look. Set them aside.

Stain and cut 20-ish strips of balsa wood that are roughly ¼ inch (6 mm) wide and 1¾ inches (4.5 cm) long. This will be the wood paneling under the window. If you want a more realistic look, cut a few strips wider and a few skinnier and vary them as you glue them down.

Glue your strips vertically below your window. Then glue a 5½-inch (14-cm) square dowel on top of your paneling. Then frame the rest of your window with additional square dowels.

Glue your ***fronts*** onto the edges of your bottom.

Cut two square dowels to 5½ inches (14 cm). Glue on the top edge of both fronts as headers.

Cut five square dowels to 2 inches (5 cm). Glue each dowel evenly-ish spaced between the front and back under the two header dowels.

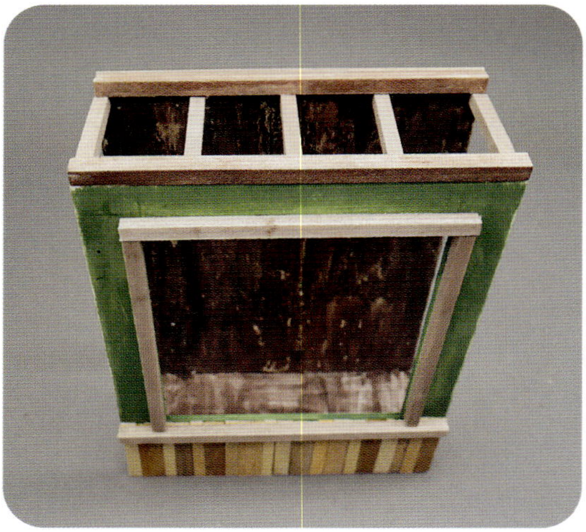

Tip: *A trick to keep the dowels even without having to measure (because measuring sucks) is to start with the two outside dowels then the middle one. This makes placing the last two easier to judge spacing.*

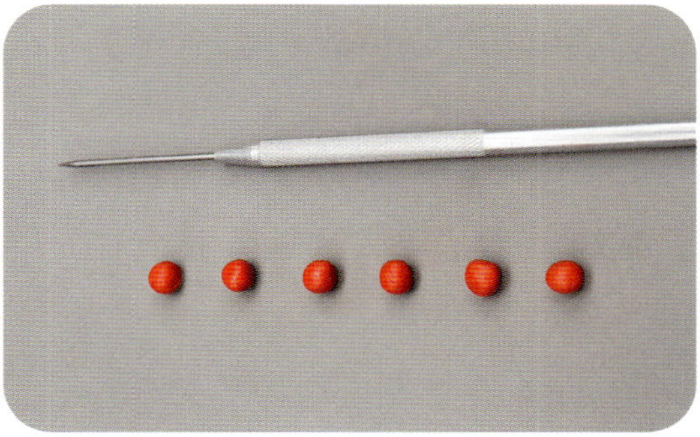

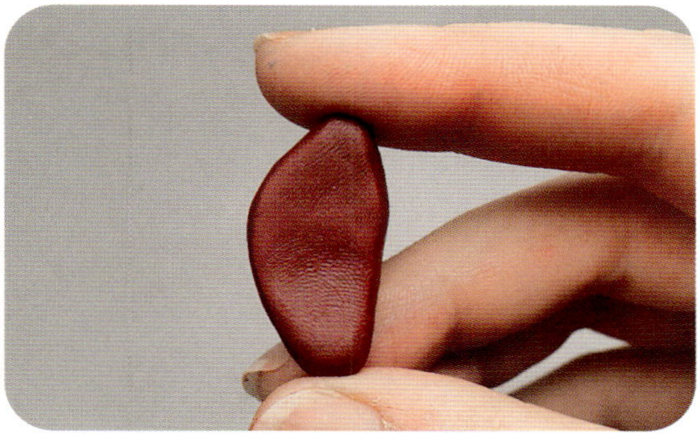

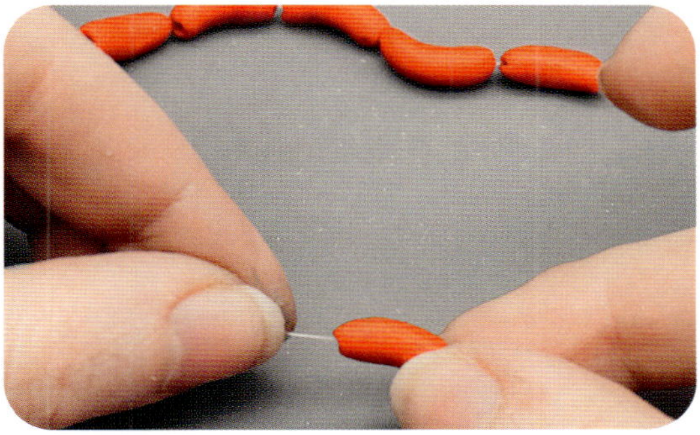

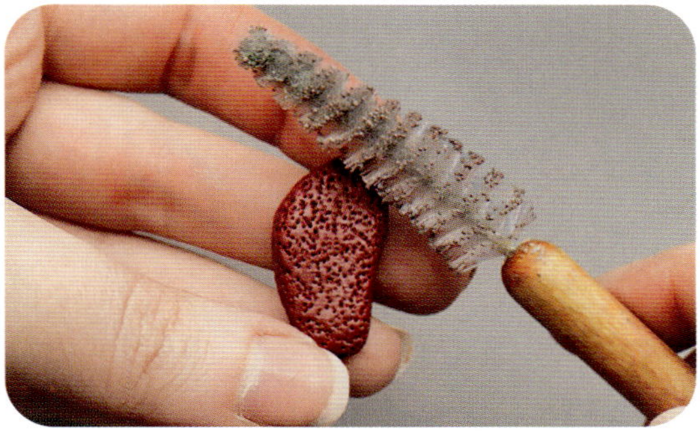

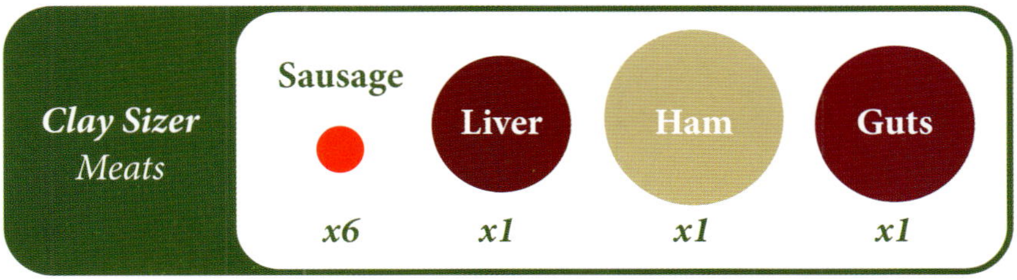

Sausage

Roll six balls of clay to match the diagram. Roll each ball into a sausage and poke a pointy object through the length of each. Slightly curve each one and bake them according to the package instructions.

Thread each sausage onto a string (preferably fishing line) and knot both ends. Because we don't want rogue sausages. Glue the knot inside the sausage.

Paint with clear gloss.

Liver

Roll your clay to match the diagram. Flatten your ball into a liver shape.

Texture your liver with a wire brush or toothbrush.

Poke a hole at the top of your liver for hanging, then harden it according to the package instructions.

Paint with clear gloss for a freshly harvested look.

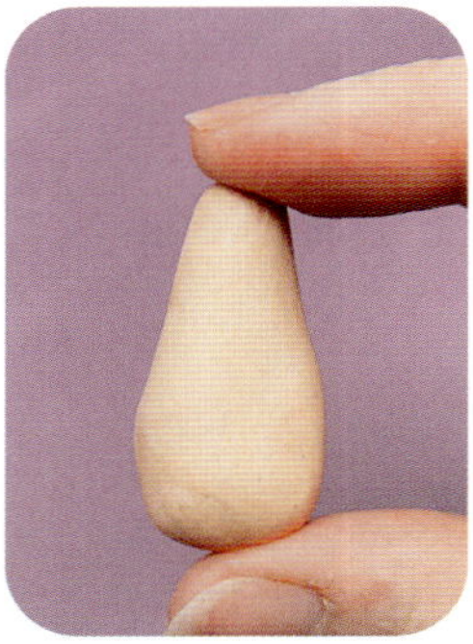

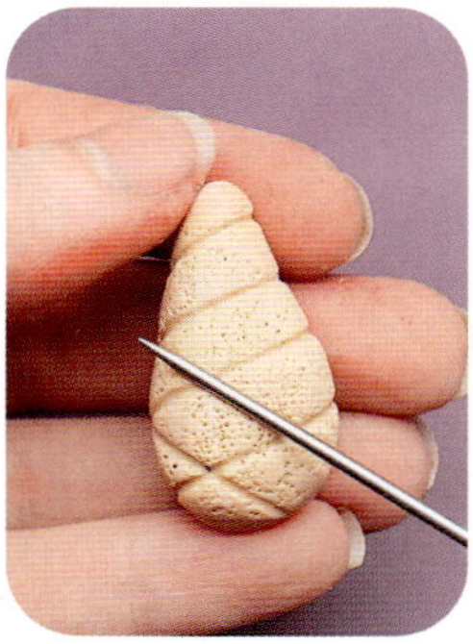

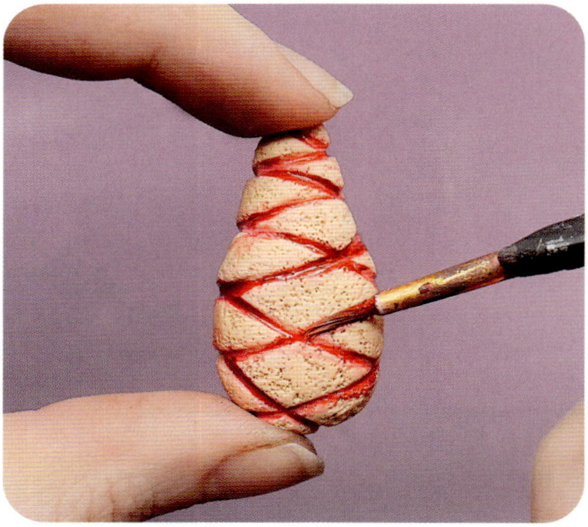

Ham

Roll your clay to match the diagram. Form your ball into a fat cylinder, then pinch the top and roll it between your fingers to make the top slightly skinnier. It should look like a ham shank (or perhaps a human shank . . .).

Texture your ham/human shank with a wire brush or toothbrush.

Take your pointy object and press on the outside of your ham in a diamond pattern. Make a small hole in the top for hanging. Harden it according to the package instructions.

Paint the crevices of the diamond pattern with a watered-down red or pink paint.

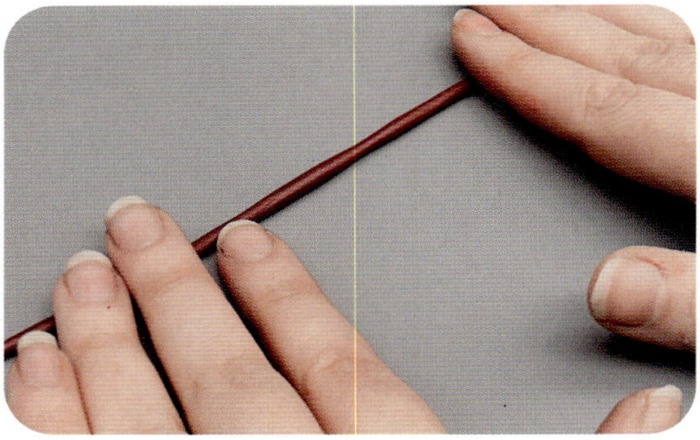

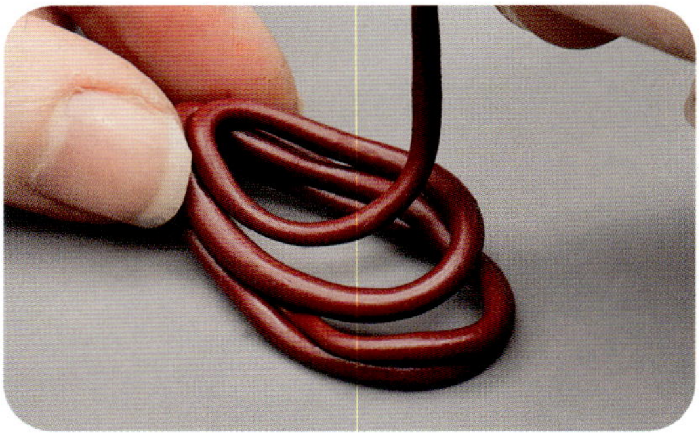

Guts

Roll your clay to match the diagram and roll it out into a long thin cord and loosely coil it into an oval shape. Don't make all the loops the same size. Make them slightly smaller as you layer them. Bake it according to the package instructions.

Paint with clear gloss to make them look moist.

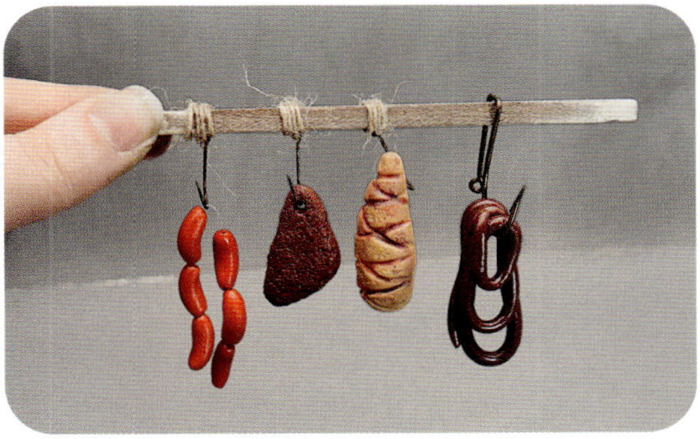

Take a 5-inch (12.7-cm) long square dowel (this will be the beam we hang the meat on).

Wrap twine around the beam and "fish" on a small fishing hook. (Careful, don't skewer your finger!) Do this three times and hang each piece of meat (minus the guts).

For the guts, bend a medium hook directly over the beam and hang the guts on this.

Tip: *Alternatively, if you don't have fishhooks, you can just bend wire into a hook shape.*

Glue your beam on the back of your window. Now the fun part: Make up the story to go with your shop!

Want to jazz up your butcher shop even more? You can let people know you're running a sale on questionable meats with tiny signs! Just glue two wooden sticks on the top and bottom of a scrap of paper and add a string to the back and BLAM-O you got signage!

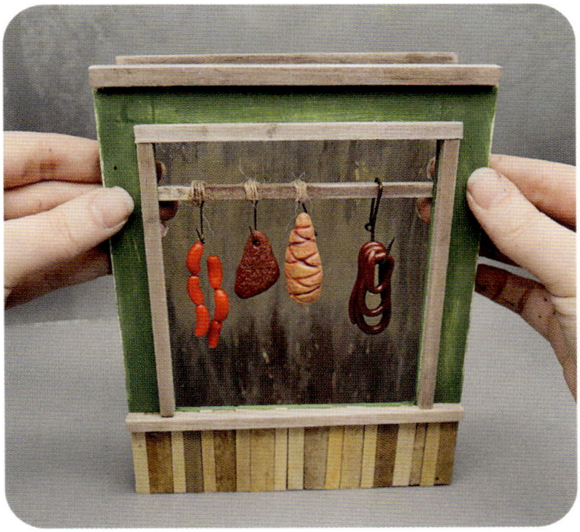

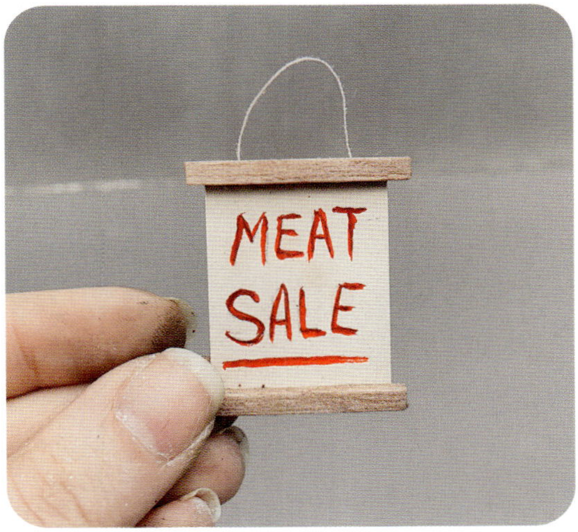

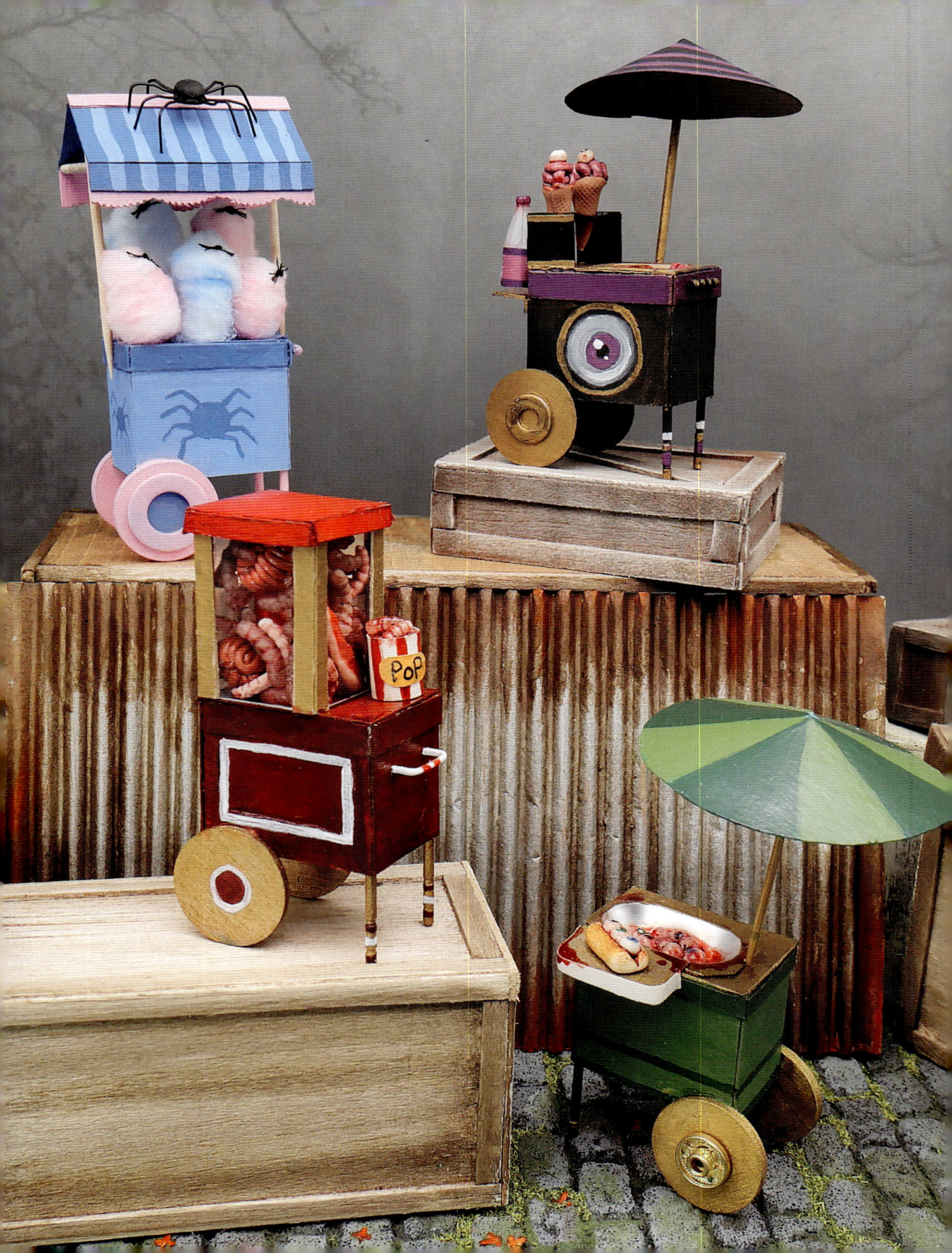
POP

Street Food

Ahh, street food . . . Nothing gets your blood pumping quite like grabbing a hot dog from a cart and wondering, "Will this give me uncontrollable diarrhea?" It's the gamble that makes it exciting!

But here on Lonely Lane, the stakes are much higher. Because here, the food is to die for! Quite literally.

Craving a salty snack? How about a bag of buttered maggots, freshly popped sometime last year? Got more of a sweet tooth? We've got spider candy, spun straight from a spider's . . . butt? Need protein? Don't worry, we got you! With the meatiest eyeball sandwiches around. And for dessert? Nothing beats a refreshing "eye scream" straight from the trolley.

Refunds aren't available, but we rarely get complaints!

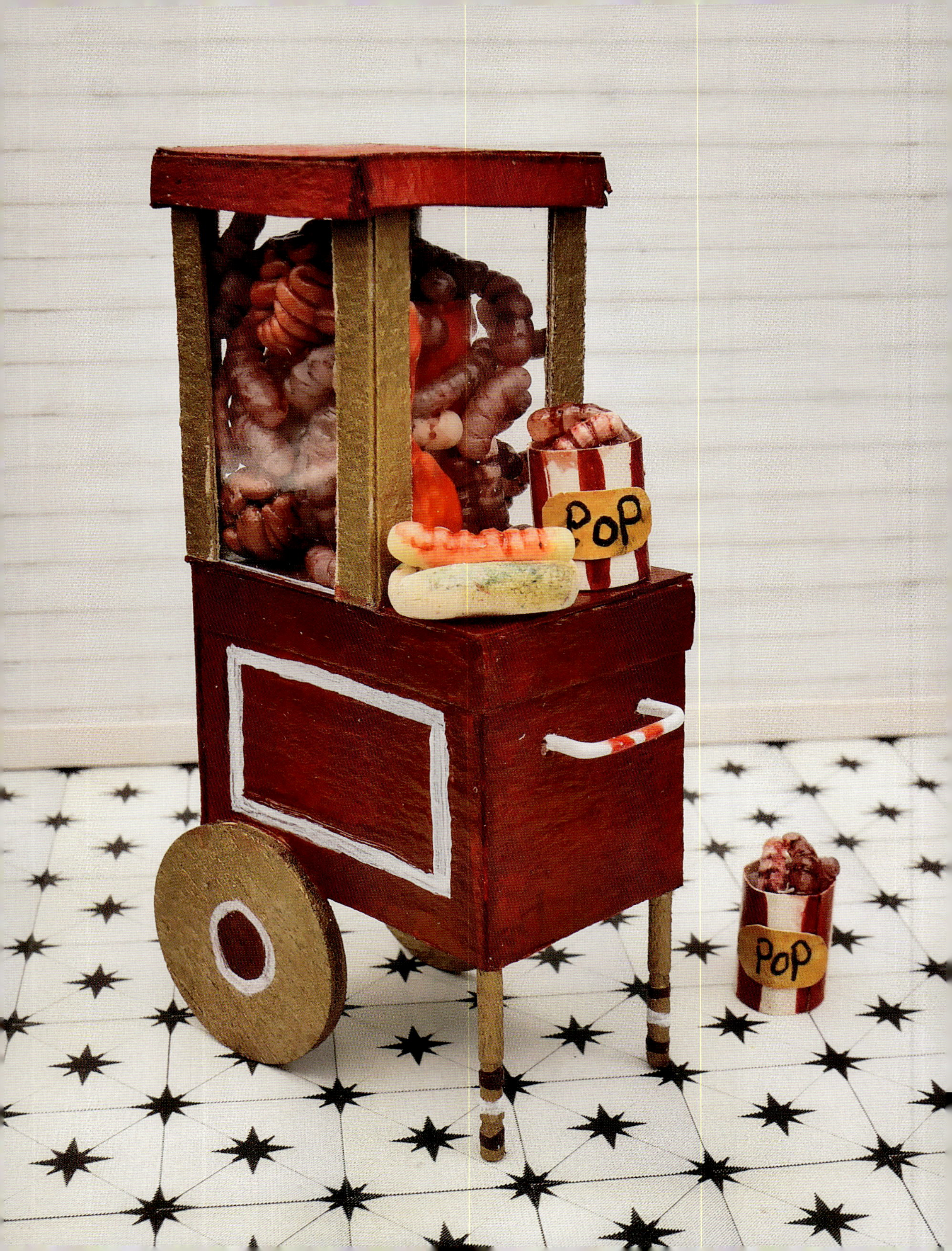
POP
POP

Maggot Popper

Nothing tastes better after losing your soul than a handful of warm popping maggots! They really put the "Mmmmm" in maggots!

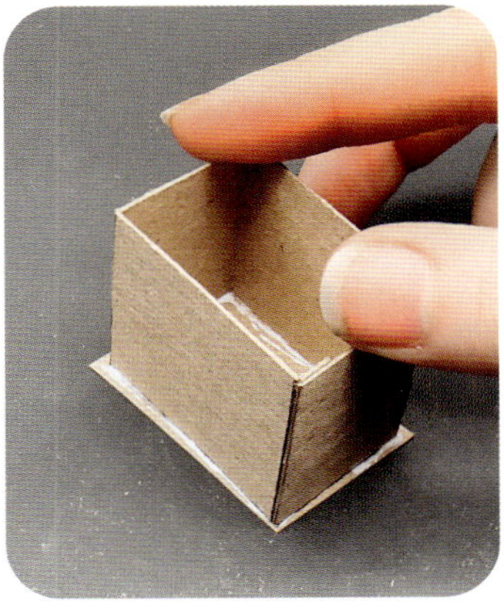

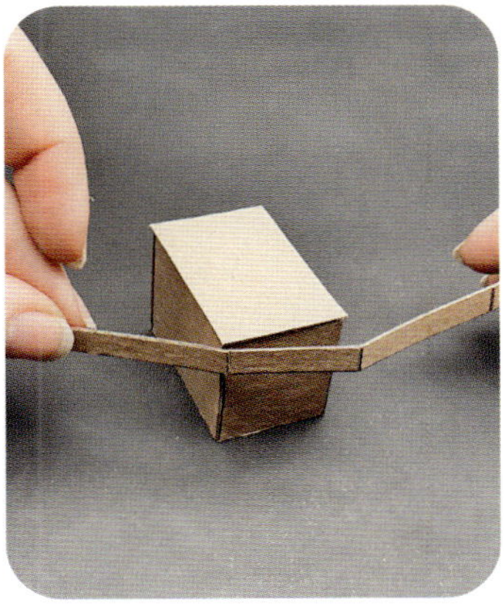

Tools

- exacto knife, ruler, & cutting mat
- glue
- paint
- pliers/wire cutter
- marker cap
- tape

Cart Base & Lid Materials

- chipboard
- 2 toothpicks
- 2 wooden circles (or 2 bottle caps)
- paper clip (or toothpick)

Container Materials

- thin clear plastic
- chipboard
- paper
- paper towel
- 2–3 brains (page 156)

Maggots & Bucket Materials

- 5 toothpicks
- white or translucent polymer clay
- paper
- paper towel
- hot dog bun (page 190)

Cart Base

Cut the following out of chipboard:

- **Qty: 1**—1½ x 5¼ inches (3.8 x 13.3 cm)

Score according to the template on page 224.

Cut ¼ inch (6 mm) off the long edge.

Taking the larger piece, fold at the four scores and glue to make a 3D rectangle. This is your cart.

Glue the opening of your cart to a scrap of chipboard and trim the excess off.

Take your skinnier strip of chipboard and trim off the ¼-inch (6-mm) flap, then tightly wrap it around your cart just below the top. The edges won't meet up on the far side but that's fine.

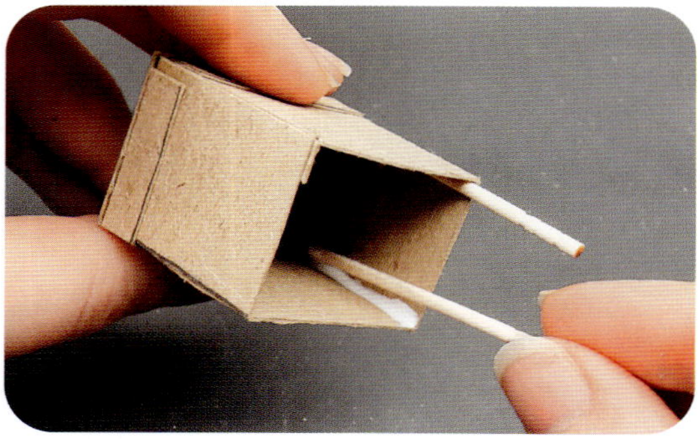

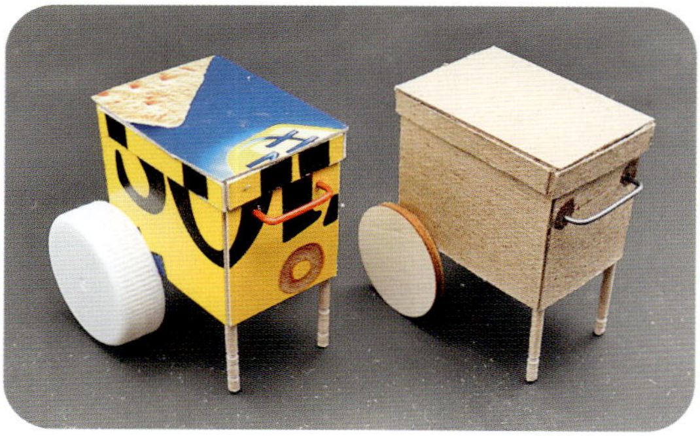

Cut two toothpicks to 2 inches (5 cm) and glue them inside your cart at the corners of one short edge. These will be the legs.

Take your two wooden circles (or bottle caps) and glue them on either side of your cart, opposite the legs, for wheels.

Paint your cart any colors your heart desires.

Add a handle to your cart by gluing a paper clip bent with pliers into a [or the decorative side of a toothpick onto the short end as a pull.

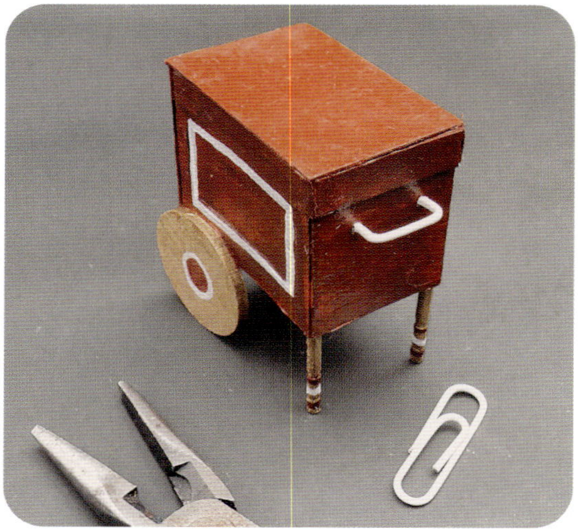

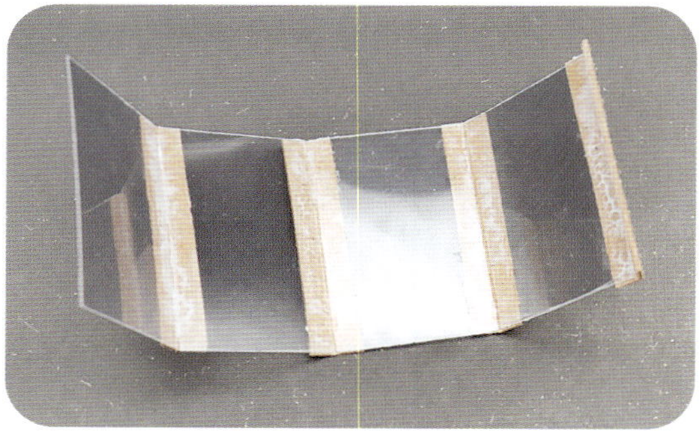

Container

Cut your clear plastic into four rectangles 1 x 2 inches (2.5 x 5 cm).

Cut four strips of chipboard 2 x ½ inch (5 x 1.3 cm) and score down the middle, footlong style.

Fold your strips at right angles and glue them in between each clear rectangle, long edge to long edge.

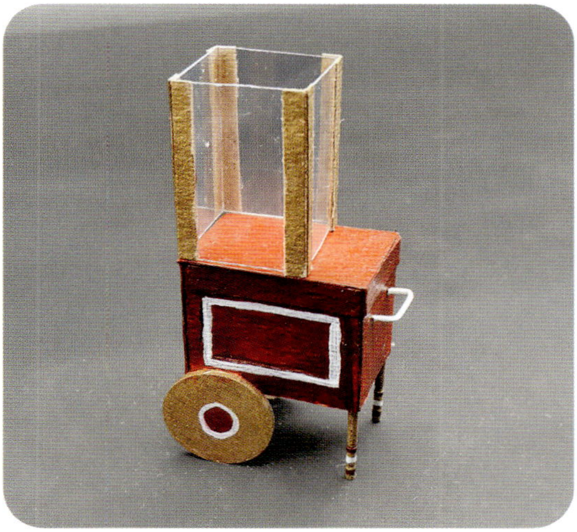

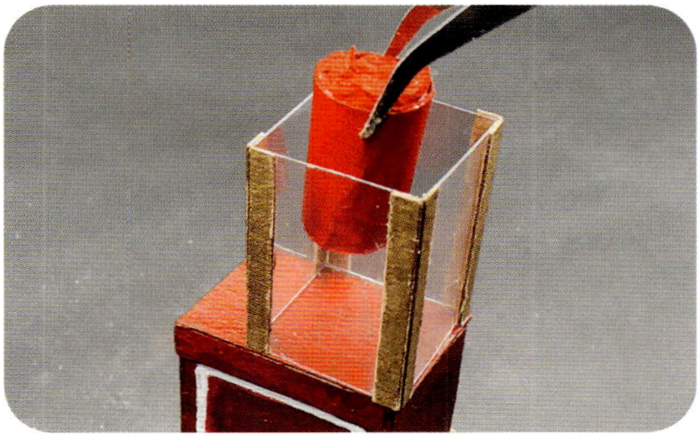

Once the glue is set, fold this into a 3D rectangle and glue it.

Adhere this onto the top of your cart near the edge with the wheels.

Take a strip of 1-inch (2.5-cm) paper and wrap it around a marker cap to make a cylinder roughly ½ inch (1.3 cm) wide. Fill it with a paper towel and paint it red.

Glue it smack dab in the middle of your container. This is just so you don't have to fill your cart with so much meat (because I'm lazy and that's a lot of meat!).

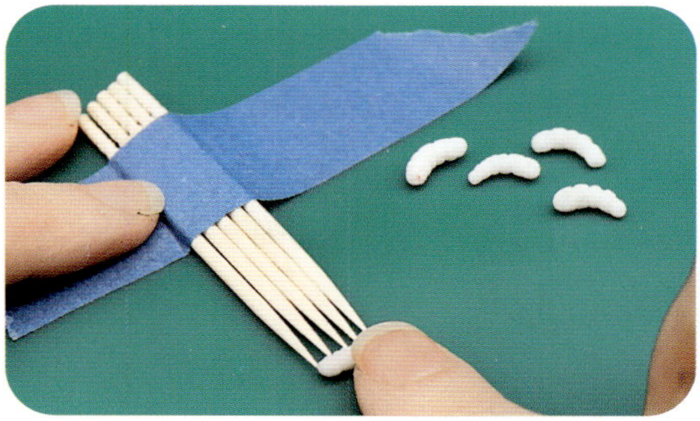

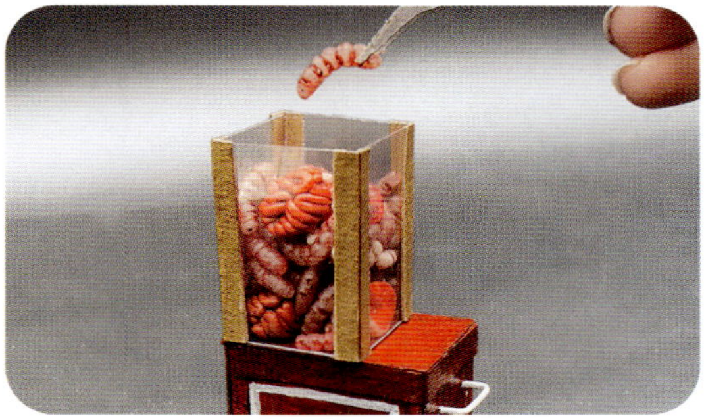

Clay Sizer
Maggots
x30ish

Maggots

Tape five toothpicks flat next to each other to make a comb shape.

Take a pea-sized amount of clay and roll it into a sausage. Gently roll your sausage on top of the toothpicks to give it grooves.

Bend your maggot into a C shape. Repeat this process more than you're comfortable with . . . so probably 30 times. Make more than you need. They tend to wriggle off. Bake them according to the package instructions.

Paint each maggot maroon and gently wipe off any excess paint. This will leave paint in the grooves, giving it more definition.

Fill your glass box from page 180 with *most* of your maggots and brains.

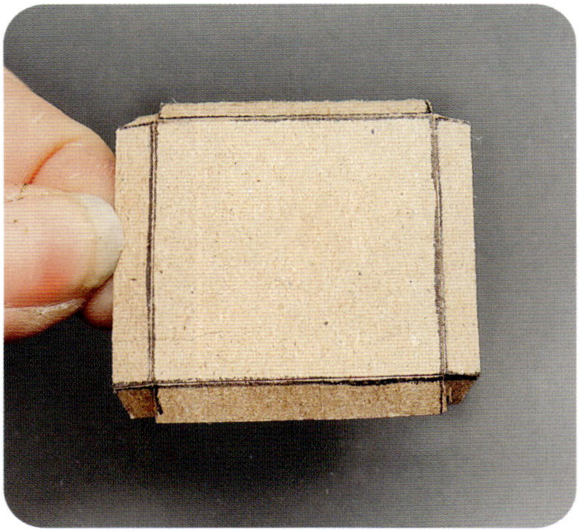

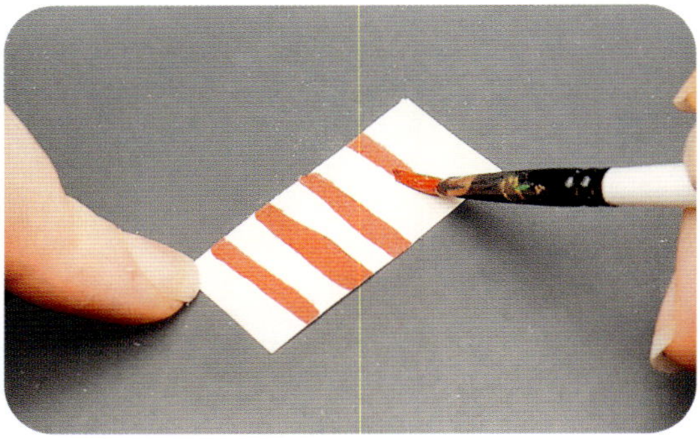

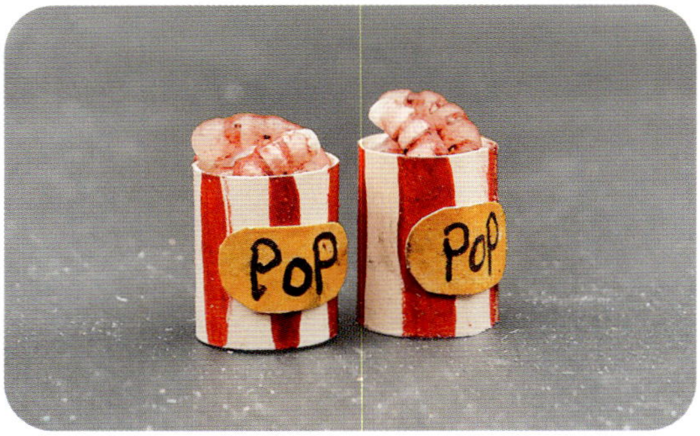

Lid

Let's cap the container so nothing wriggles out! Cut a 1¾-inch (4.5-cm) square from chipboard.

Score the length ¼ inch (6 mm) in on all four sides. Cut one side of each small corner square for tabs. See template on page 224 if needed.

Paint your lid and fold it into a box by gluing the tabs on the inside.

Place your lid on top of your container.

Maggot Bucket

Cut a strip of ¾ x ~2–inch (1.9 x 5–cm) paper, and paint red stripes along the long edge. Glue in a cylinder shape. BUCKET!

Rip off a bit of paper towel and stuff your bucket, leaving a little room at the top and glue it into place. This way you don't have to fill the whole thing with maggots. *Because again . . . I'm lazy.*

Glue two to three maggots to the top of your bucket. Optionally, embellish your bucket with a little POP label so people know what's in them.

Step up your design with a yummy, delicious maggot dog. See page 190 for a hot dog bun. Then just add maggots. Tasty!

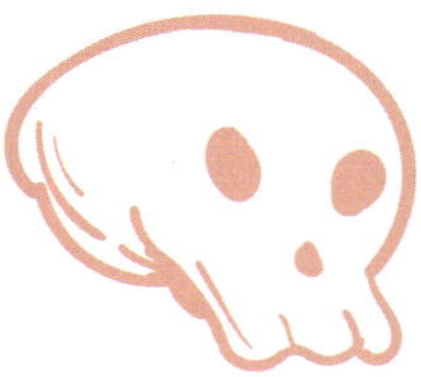

Spider Cotton Candy

Freshly spun by the finest spiders, Spider Cotton Candy is a fan favorite at Carn-EVIL. It comes in two flavors: blue beetle and wiggly worm pink.

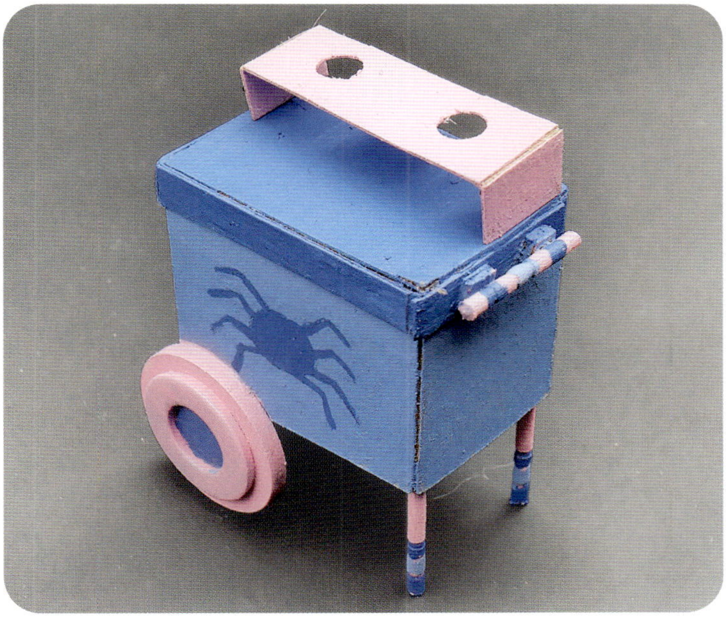

Cart

Take your cart base from page 179 and paint your cart any color you like. I went with pastel blue and pink.

Cut a piece of chipboard 2½ x ½ inch (6.4 x 1.3 cm) and score a ½-inch (1.3-cm) flap on either side.

Hole punch two holes in the middle that are roughly ¾ inch (1.9 cm) apart and paint it.

Glue the edges on the top of one side of your cart so that it will look like a tray for holding cones.

Tools

- paint
- exacto knife, ruler, & cutting mat
- hole punch
- glue
- craft glue
- scissors
- needle (or pokey object)
- "fun" scissors (optional)
- pliers/wire cutter
- silicone mat
- hot glue

Cart & Spider Materials

- 1 cart base (page 179)
- chipboard
- floral wire (preferably black)

Spider Candy Materials

- 3 cotton balls
- 3–5 toothpicks
- paper
- colored chalk (pink & blue)
- black thread

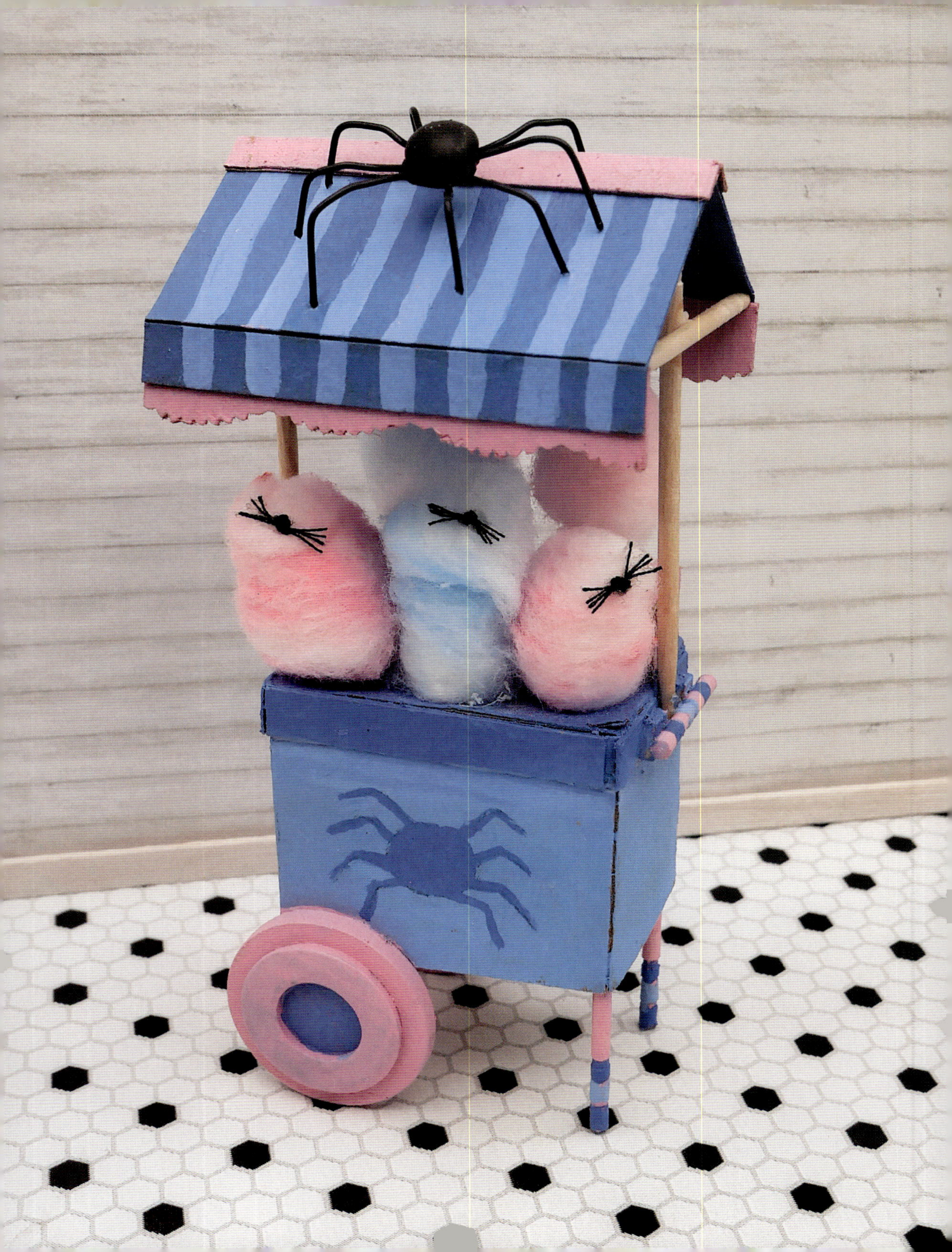

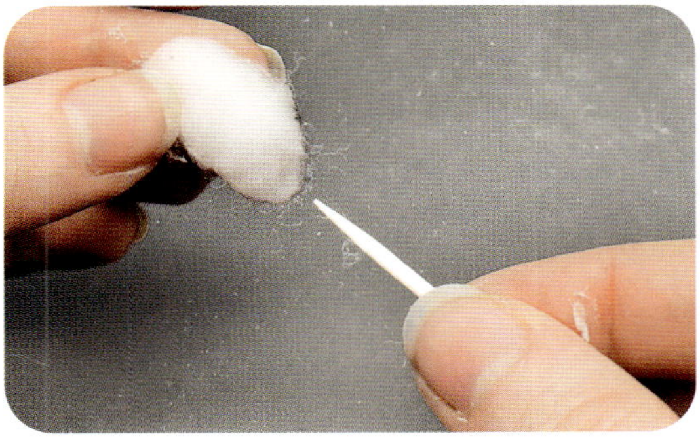

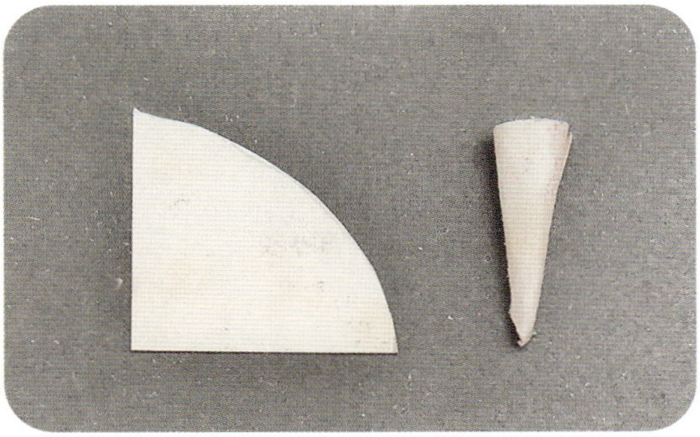

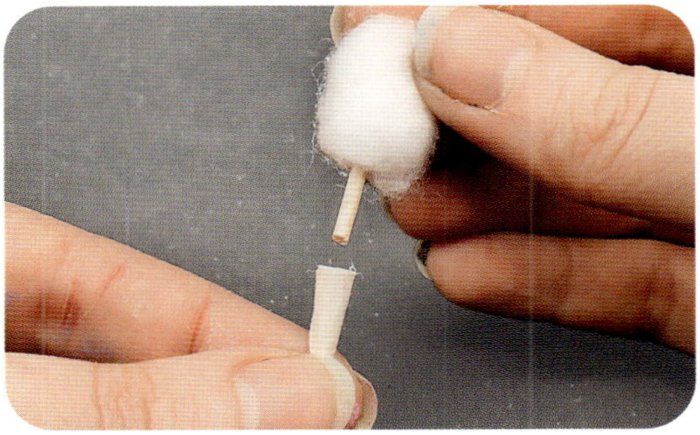

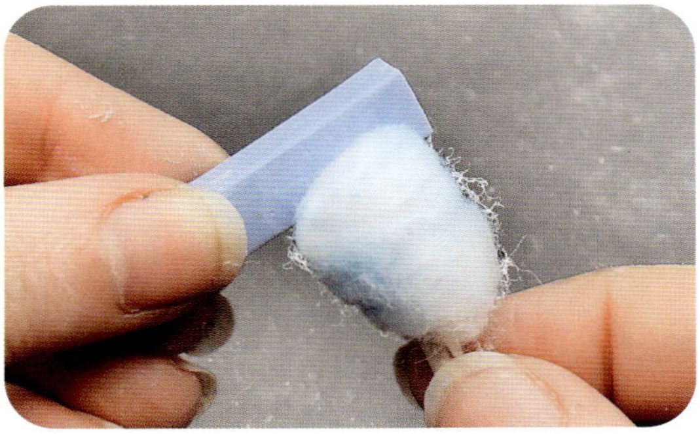

Spider Candy

Unroll a cotton ball and cut it in half. Tightly reroll the halves into two smaller cotton balls and secure them with craft glue.

Repeat until you have five. Half a cotton ball won't be used. *Hoard it away like a good craft gremlin until you forget where it came from.*

Cut five toothpicks down to about ¾ inch (1.9 cm) so that you have five tiny little javelins and jam one pointy end into each cotton ball. Glue them into place and set them aside.

Cut two ¾-inch (1.9-cm) squares from paper. Then cut an arch from one corner to the other so that you have a triangle with a curved edge. Roll them and glue them into two cones.

Jam two of the toothpicked cotton balls into the two cones. Glue them into place. You should now have two cotton balls with cones and three with toothpicks.

Rub colored chalk on all five of your cotton balls. I picked blue and pink, but like I said, "You do you, boo." If you're having trouble getting the chalk to stick, you can shave some off with an exacto knife and rub your cotton ball in the dust instead. Set them aside.

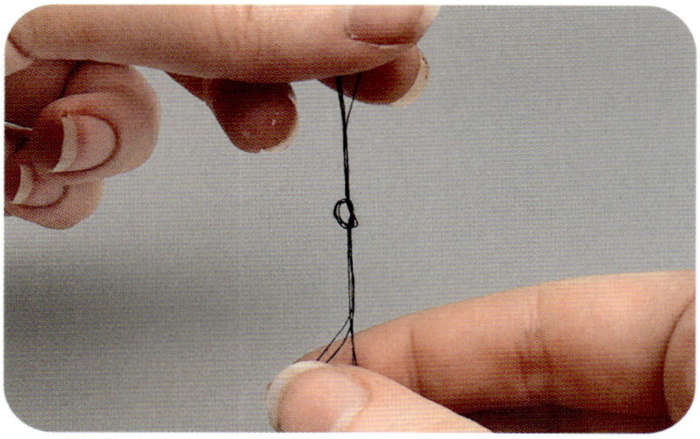

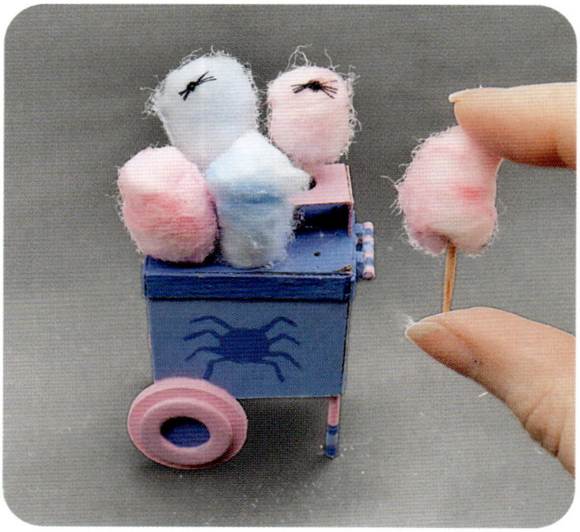

Let's make tiny spiders! Loop black thread four times back and forth until you have four strings roughly 3 inches (7.6 cm) long, then tie a double knot in the middle. Trim the strings on both sides of the knot to make tiny string spiders.

Glue a string spider on the top of each cotton ball.

Set your two cotton balls with cones in the tray on your cart. Glue them in or leave them unglued if you want to act out buying spider candy.

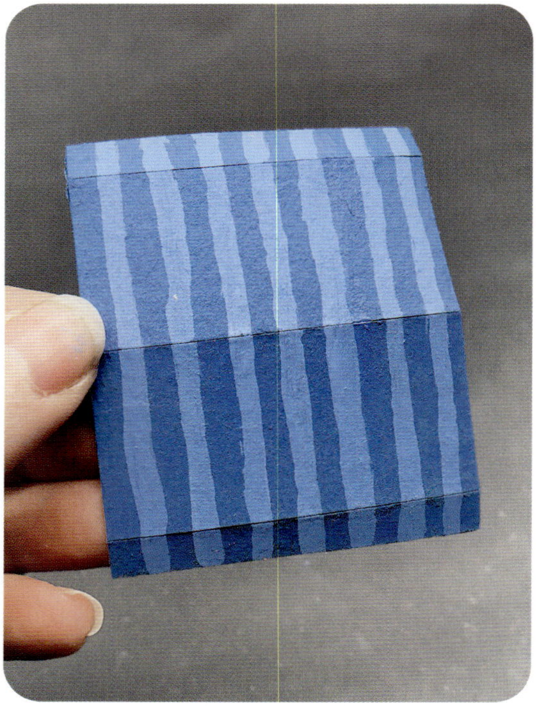

Take a needle and poke three roughly evenly spaced holes in the front of your tray (just eyeball them; it's not that serious), then shove the three toothpicked treats into the three holes.

You could TOTALLY stop here! OR, continue to trick out your spider cotton candy cart even more by adding an awning.

Using the template on page 225 for reference, cut a 2½ x 2–inch (6.4 x 5–cm) rectangle out of chipboard and score it down the middle "hamburger style." Then score two lines ¼ inch (6 mm) in on either side.

Paint this any color you like. I went with blue with light blue stripes. Then fold it into a triangle with flaps.

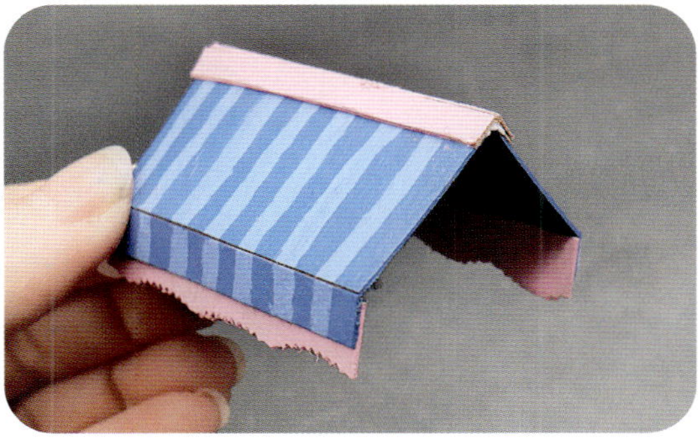

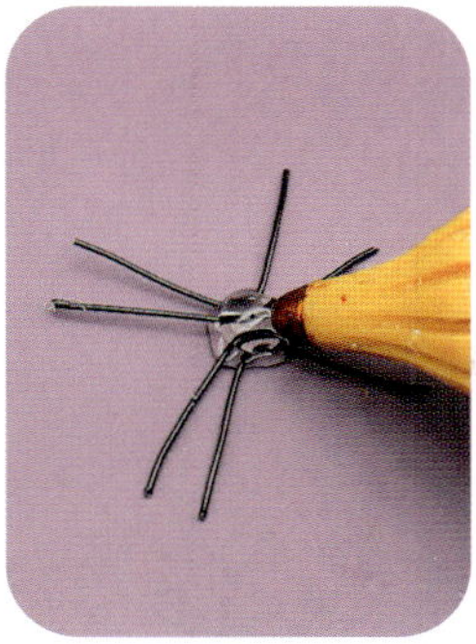

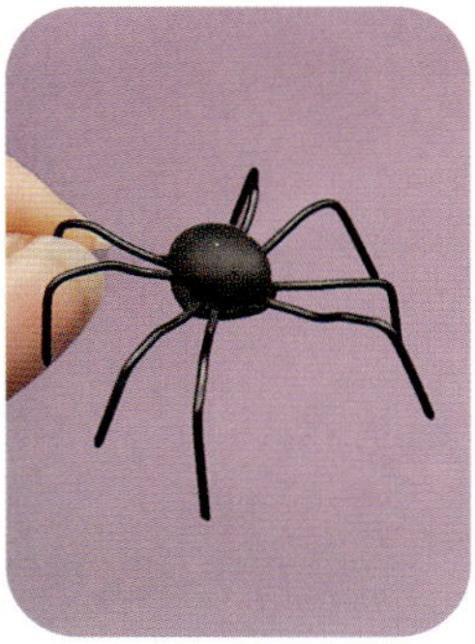

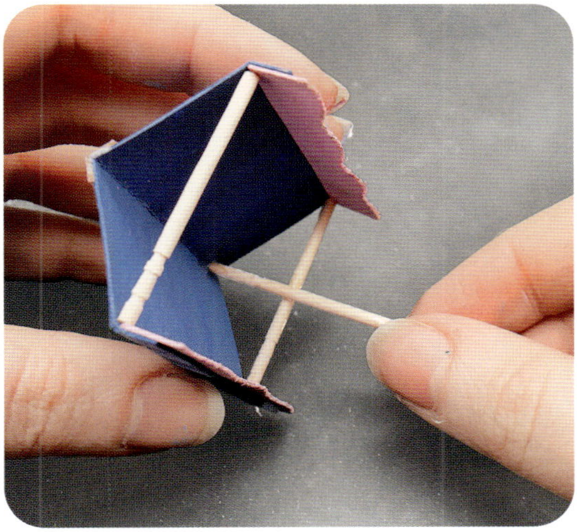

Bust out your "fun" scissors and chipboard to add details to the edges and top of your awning. Have fun with it! Use your imagination!

Cut a toothpick to 2 inches (5 cm) and glue it in the opening of your awning. This will help it hold its shape. Glue a whole toothpick from the peak of the awning down across the toothpick you just glued in to make a lowercase t. Repeat this on the other side.

Spider

Adding a spider to the top will help with advertising! With a wire cutter, cut floral wire into four 2-inch (5-cm) pieces. Bend the wires slightly in the middle and put the middles together to make a starburst shape.

On your silicone mat, squeeze a drop of hot glue about ¼ inch (6 mm) wide and very quickly place your bent wires in the hot glue so that they look like a spider. Add another slightly larger drop of hot glue on top.

Once the glue has cooled, peel it off the mat and bend the wires down into legs. Paint the spider black and glue it onto the top of your awning.

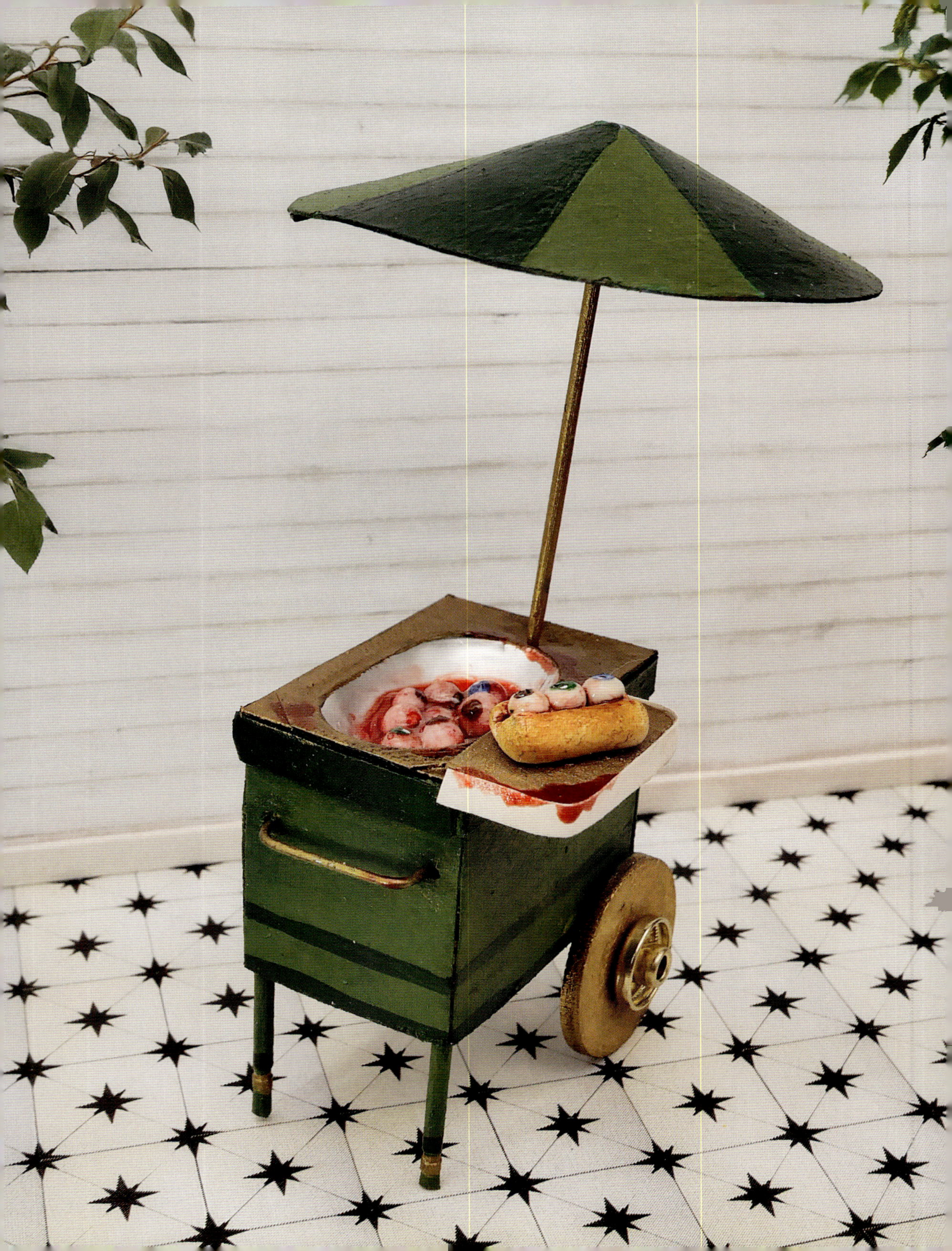

Meaty Eyeball Cart

Get your eyeballs here! Tasty, yummy, *always staring at you*, meaty eyeballs!

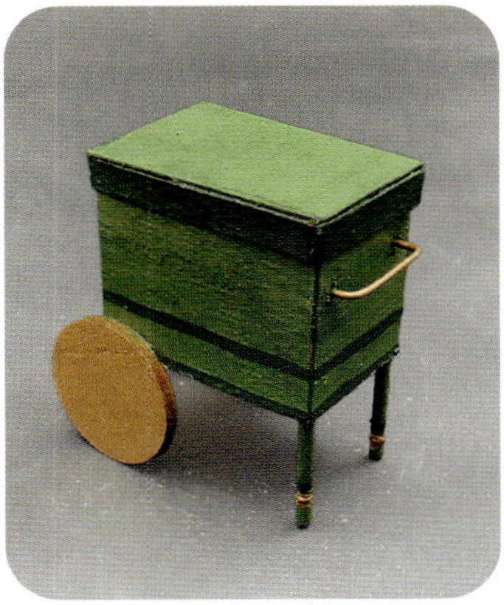

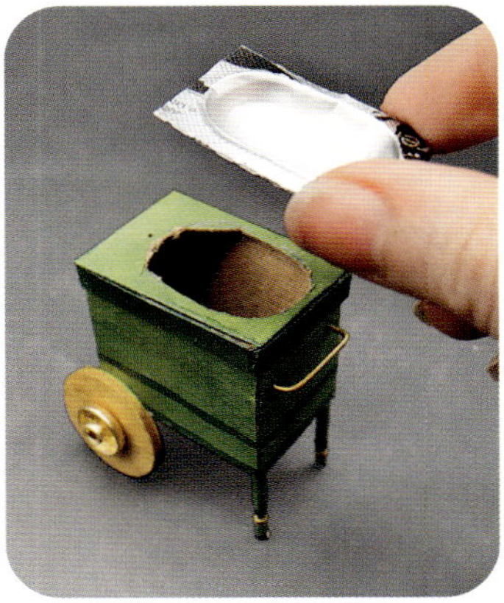

Tools

- exacto knife, ruler, & cutting mat
- glue
- sandpaper or file
- paint
- clear gloss
- pencil

Cart & Umbrella Materials

- 1 cart base (page 179)
- medicine blister pack
- chipboard
- paper
- 1 toothpick

Buns Materials

- 8–10 eyeballs (page 121)
- polymer clay
- colorful chalk (tan or orange)

Cart

Start with your cart base and, using an exacto knife, carefully cut a hole in the top, nearest the handle, just large enough for your medicine blister pack to sit in and glue. This is your "meat bath."

Tip: *Use two medicine blister packs. Cut around the bubble of one and use it as a template for your hole and use the other to glue in your hole.*

Cut 1 x ½ inch (2.5 x 1.3 cm) from chipboard and glue it hanging off the edge of your cart next to your "meat bath" as a little shelf.

Round the corners of your shelf farthest from your cart and paint it.

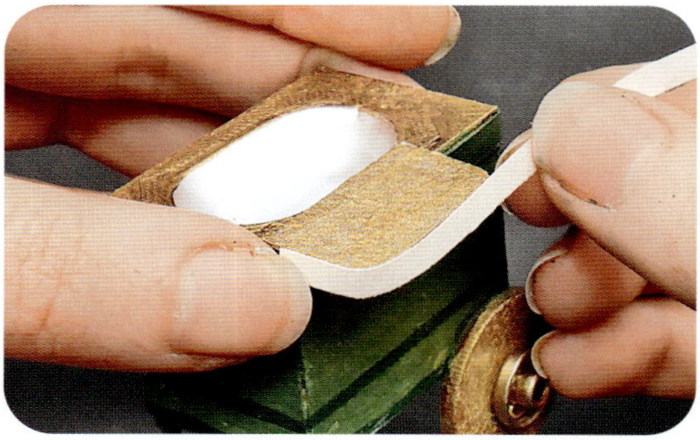

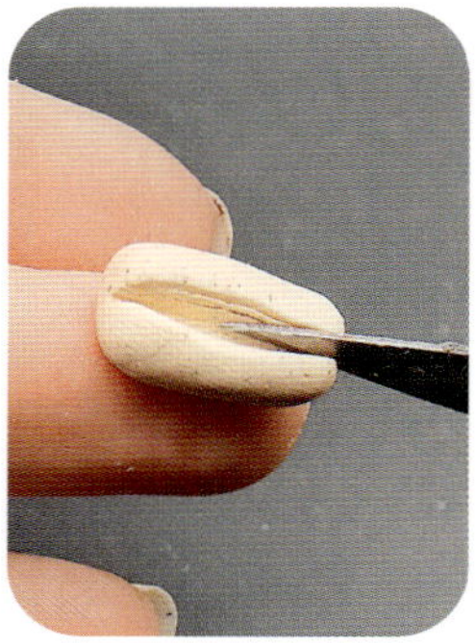

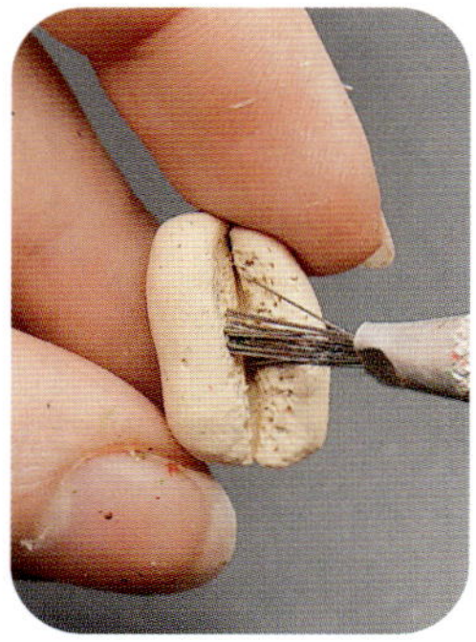

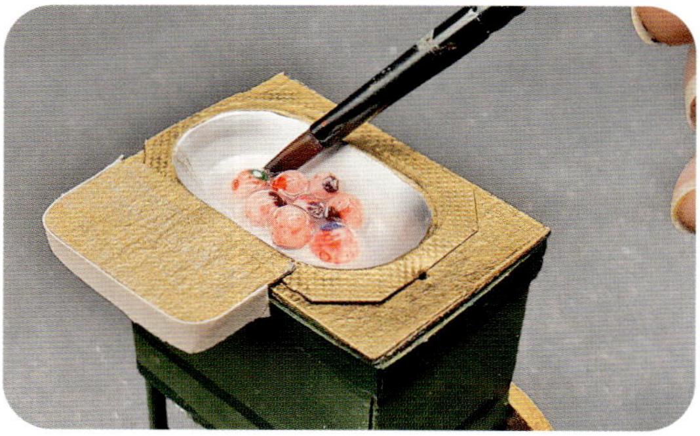

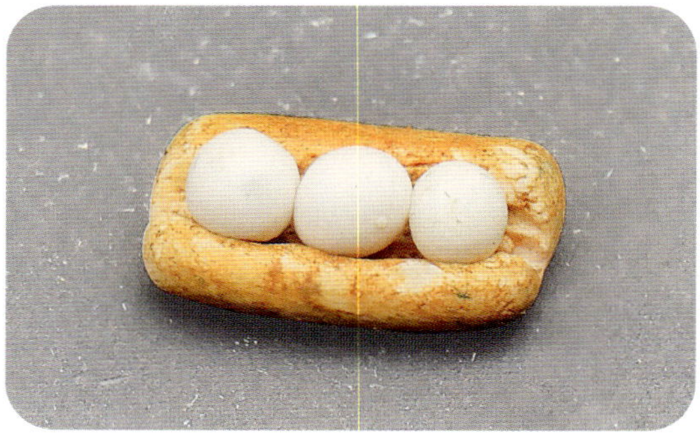

Cut a strip of paper about ¼ inch (6 mm) wide and wrap it around the edge of your shelf, gluing it in place. This just helps finish it off.

Make eight to ten eyeballs from page 121 and glue them in your "meat bath." Since we don't want the FDA called on us, we'll want the eyeballs to look fresh. Cover them with a clear gloss. Don't be shy, glob the stuff on. The more you glob, the juicier it looks!

Buns

Using the bun sizer, roll out a ball of clay and shape it into a sausage.

Using an exacto knife, carefully slice your sausage down the middle, like a hot dog bun. Only for eyeballs, so I guess like an eyeball bun.

Clay Sizer *Sandwich*	**Bun**	**Eyes** ○
	x1	*x8-10*

Take a pokey object and poke the inside of your eyeball bun to make it look more bread-like.

Rub your eyeball bun with tan or orange chalk. This will make your bun look cooked and less like raw dough.

Using the eyeball sizer, roll three eyes and place them in your open bun. Bake them according to the package instructions.

Paint an iris and pupil onto your eyes in your bun. Coat your eyes in a tinted red clear gloss. Glue your eyeball bun onto your shelf.

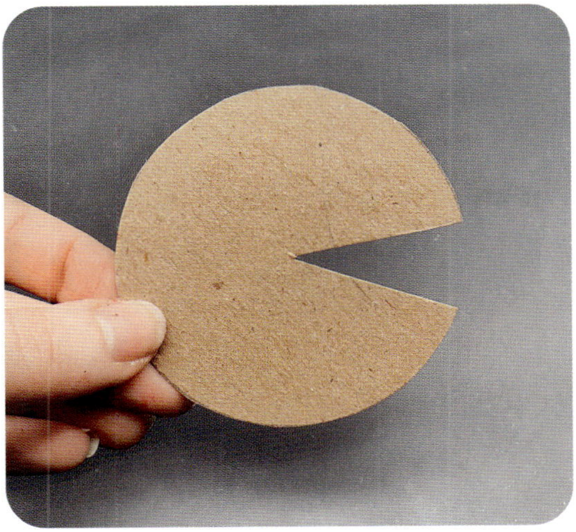

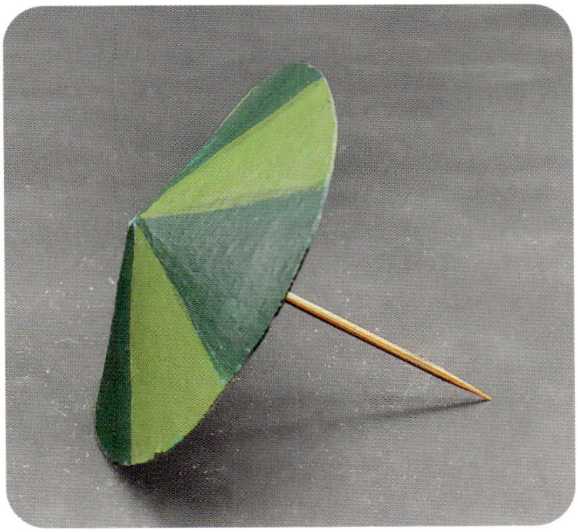

Umbrella

You could just use one of those cocktail umbrellas but if you have a child like mine, you know all spare cocktail umbrellas go to Barbie™ dolls. So, let's make one. Cut a 2¾-inch (7-cm) circle out of chipboard and slice a triangle out Pac-Man® style. Glue the two cut edges together, overlapping them a bit.

Draw eight lines radiating out from the center and paint each section two different alternating colors. Glue a toothpick into the underside with the pointy end facing down.

Lastly, poke a small hole in the top of your cart to stick your umbrella in.

Voilà, you're done!

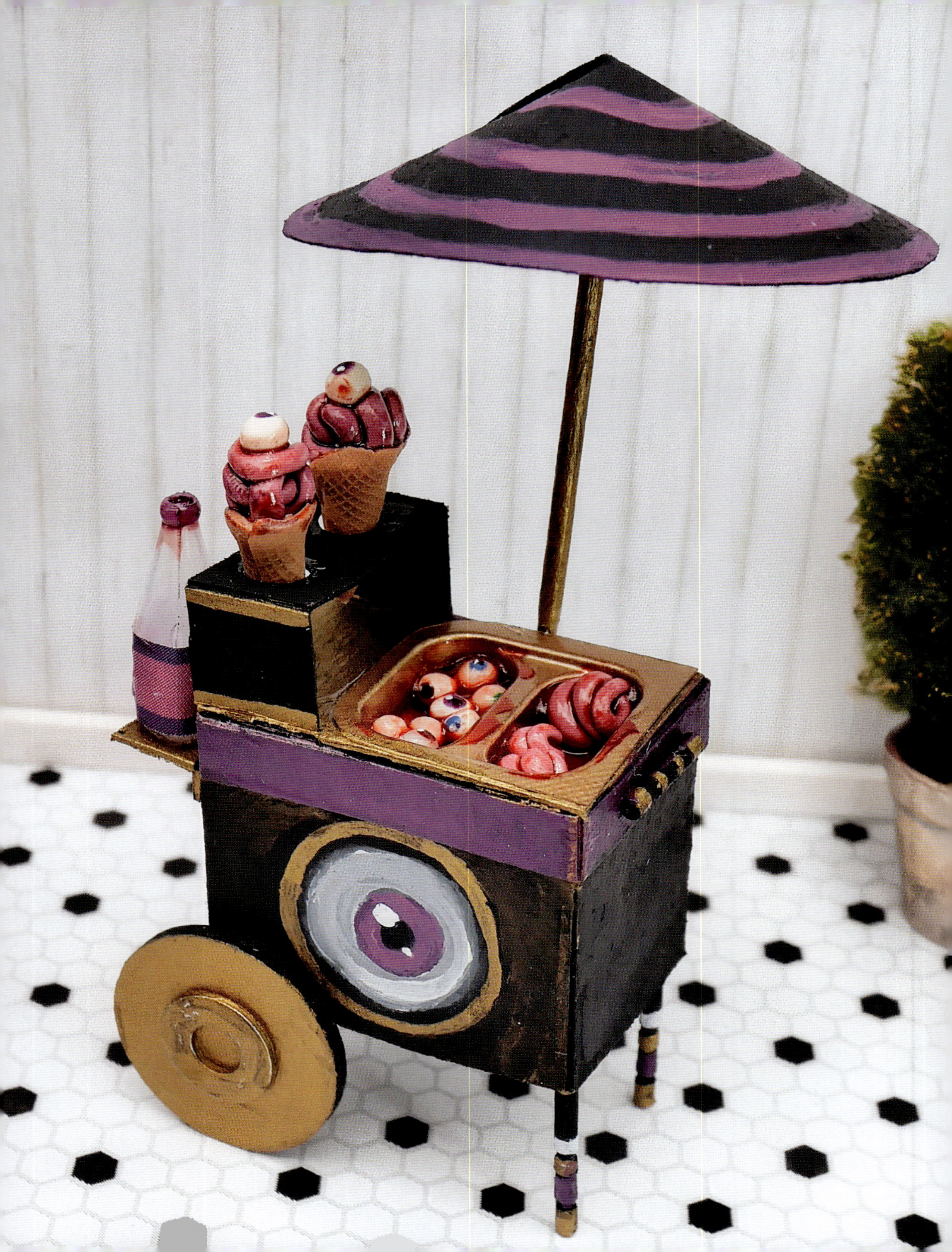

Eye Scream Trolley

Where do we get our eyes for our eye scream? Good question.

Eye scream . . . wait, eyes can't scream!

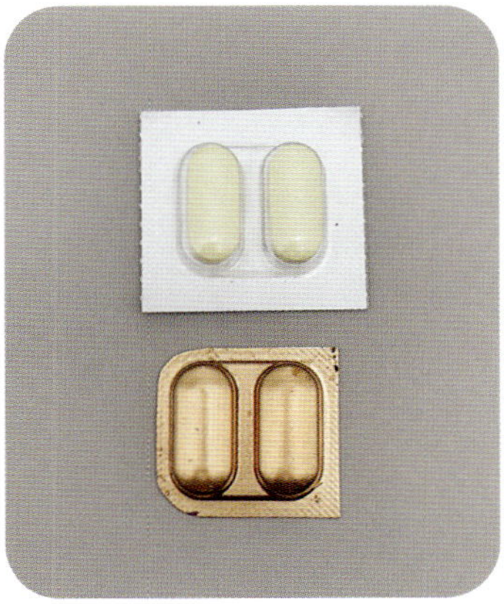

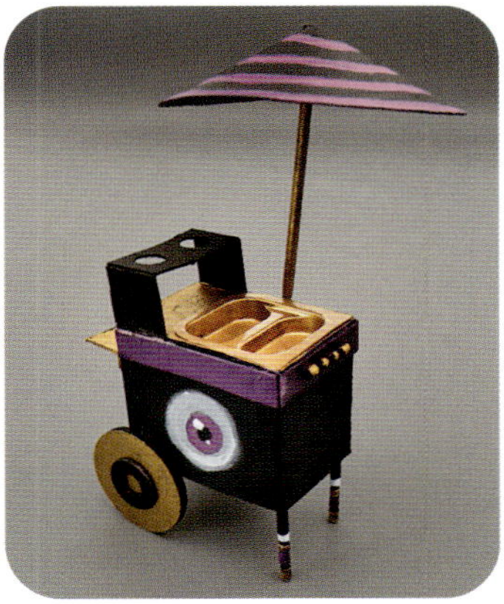

Tools

- paint
- scissors
- gold spray paint
- exacto knife, ruler, & cutting mat
- glue
- hole punch
- superglue
- masking tape
- toothpick
- pencil
- clear gloss

Cart Materials

- 1 cart base (page 179)
- medicine blister pack
- chipboard
- 1 umbrella (page 191)
- disposable eye-drop container

Eyeballs & Cone Materials

- polymer clay

Cart

Paint your cart base from page 179.

Take your empty medicine blister pack and trim it with scissors so that it'll fit on the top of your cart. Spray paint it gold.

Like we did for the meatball cart, cut a hole on the top of your cart closest to the side with legs. It should be just big enough for your blister pack to sit in without falling through. Glue it in place.

Cut a 2 x ½–inch (5 x 1.3–cm) rectangle from chipboard and score each side ½ inch (1.3 cm) in. See the template on page 225 if needed. Hole punch two holes in the center. Paint and bend it into a little tray and glue it onto the opposite side of your "sink."

Add a little shelf by cutting out a 1 x 7⁄10–inch (2.5 x 1.8–cm) rectangle from chipboard and score a narrow strip along the long end (just wide enough to adhere it to your cart). A reference template is on page 225.

Paint and glue it on the side of your cart, below the tray.

Lastly, superglue your umbrella to the back edge of your cart.

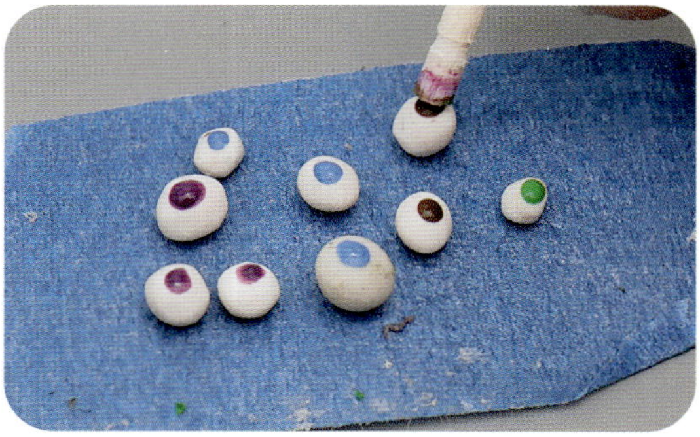

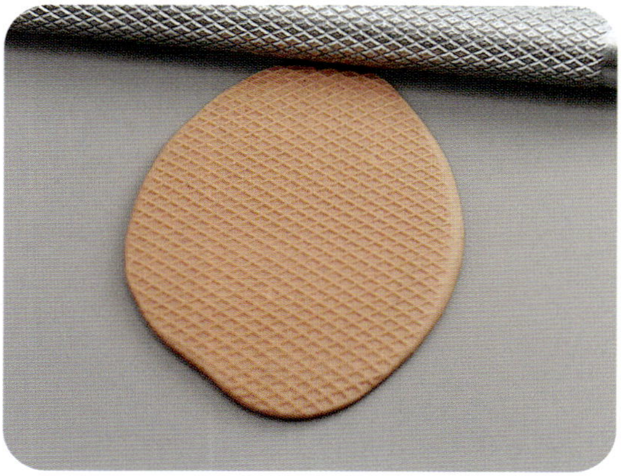

Eyeballs

Let's make some eyes! Using the eyeball sizer and clay, roll 10+ eyes (you always lose one) and bake them according to the package instructions.

Stick your rollie eyes onto a piece of masking tape so that they stay put while you paint.

Using the blunt end of a toothpick, dip it in an eye color and dab your ball to make a dot.

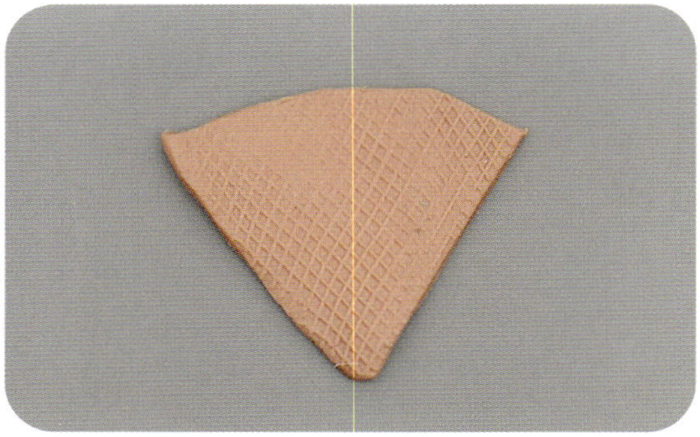

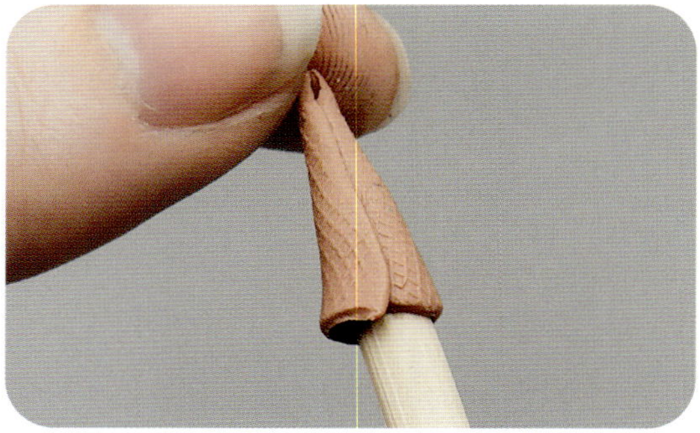

Let this dry, then dip the pointy end of a toothpick in black paint and dab on a pupil in the middle. If you want to get real fancy, add a little white spot on the edge of your pupil.

Cone

Squish your cone-colored ball into a flat disk that's roughly ¾ inch (1.9 cm) wide.

Roll the grip from your exacto knife onto your disk. (It doesn't matter if the texture on your knife isn't a waffle-cone texture; any texture will work.)

Using your exacto knife, cut your clay into a triangle with a rounded top.

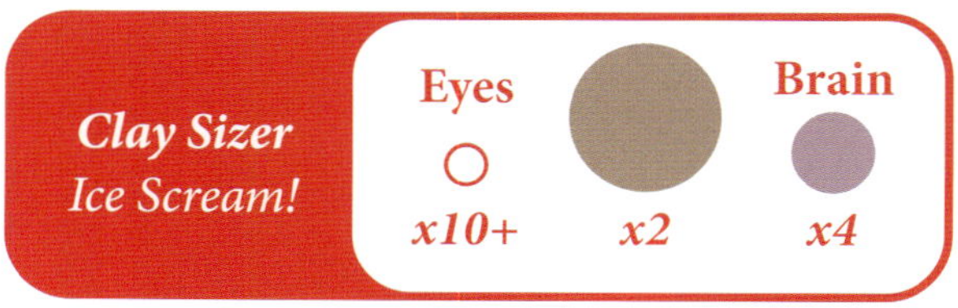

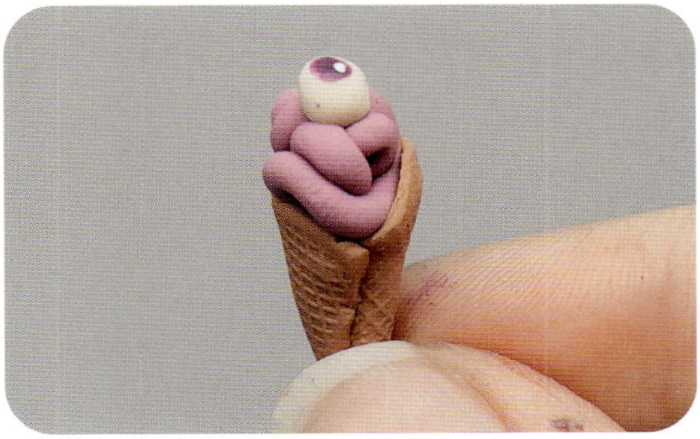

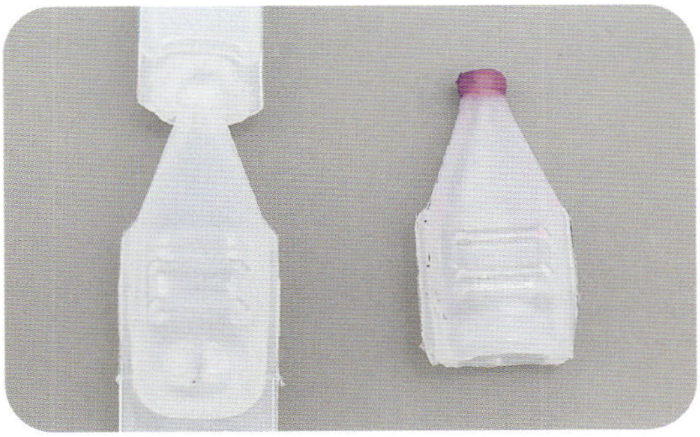

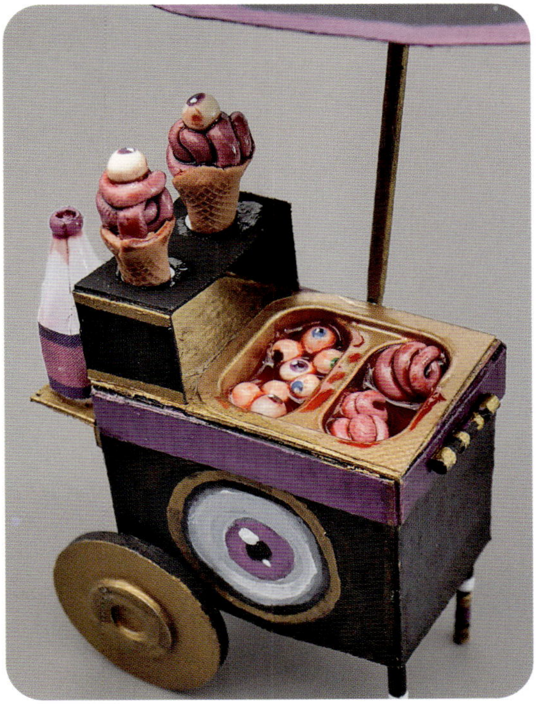

Gently (so as not to ruin the texture) roll your triangle into a cone with the rounded edge at the top. You can wrap it around the pointy part of a pencil if you're having trouble with the shape.

Make two of these and set them aside.

Roll out your four brain balls into long thin snakes and twist each one into a ball so that it looks like a brain. Place one in each cone and leave the other two solo.

Push one of your 10+ eyes on top of each cone and bake them according to the package instructions.

Mix together clear gloss and a tiny amount of red paint. Fill one of your cart food cavities with this mixture and place your two extra brain balls inside. Roll them around the cavity so they get coated.

Do the same with the eyeballs in the other cavity.

Paint the top of your cone with the same paint gloss. Make sure the paint gets in the cracks and folds of the brain.

Glue your cones into the holes of your tray and let it dry.

A disposable eye-drop container makes for a great "syrup" bottle. Paint the top like a cap and make a label with a bit of paper or tape. What kind of syrup do you put on eye scream anyways?

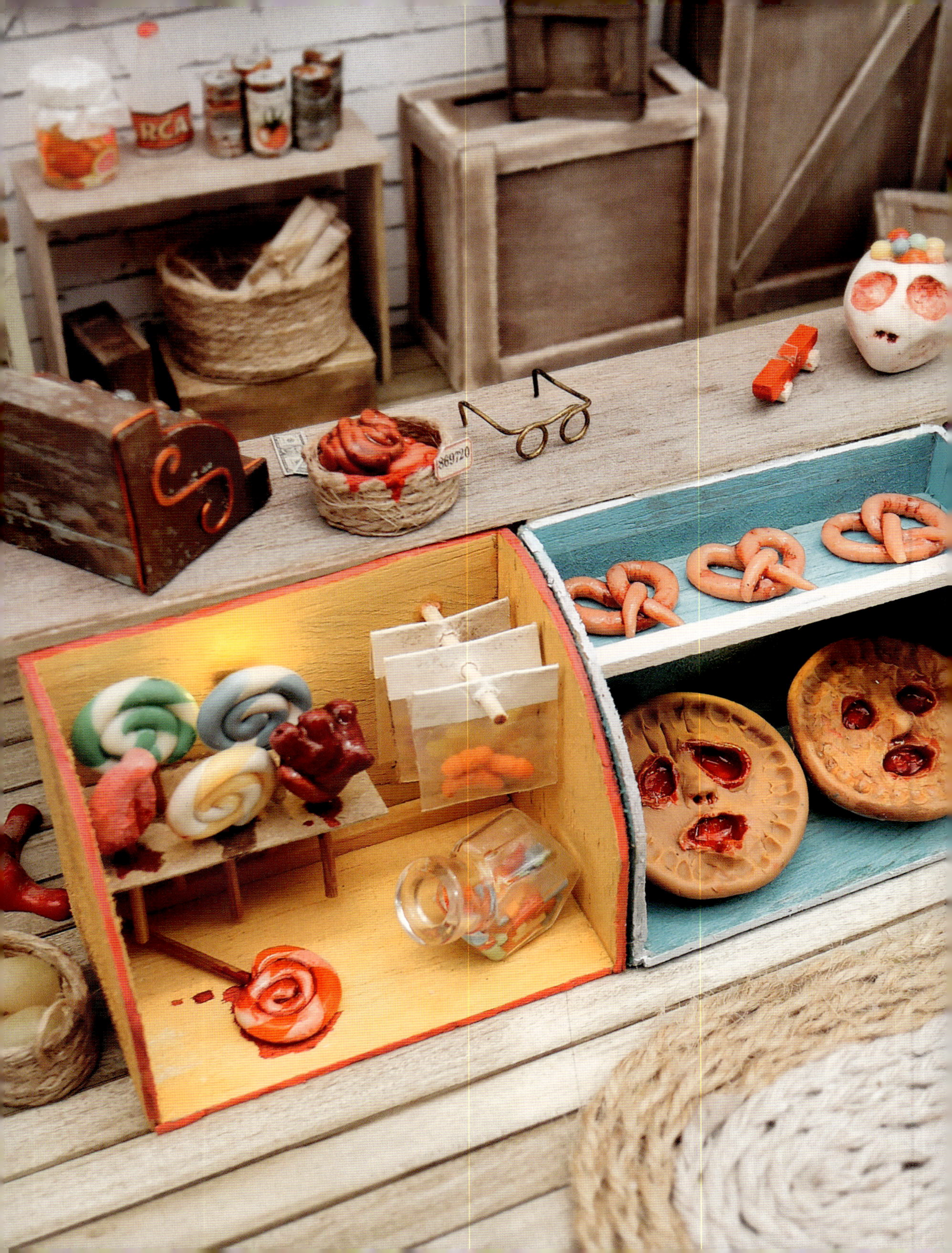
RCA
869720

Unethical Shops

While Kevin was flipping through channels late one night, a commercial caught his eye.

COME ON DOWN to Midnight Mall. Where tonight ONLY, you can sign up for our SUPER SAVERS Loyalty Program! This program will literally save you THOUSANDS! It's to die for!

(Promotion ends at 2 a.m. Not responsible for any loss of life, limbs, organs, or children.)

Kevin, being a super savvy shopper, was at the mall by 1:45 a.m. with a shiny new loyalty card in his hand.

First stop, the pie counter. Kevin bought a yummy looking pie, only to notice the crust looked very face-like. "How odd," Kevin thought, shaking it off. Next, he went on to the candy station where he bought himself a ginormous lollipop. Kevin excitedly licked the lollipop, but strangely it tasted like tears. "Gross," thought Kevin, "Maybe I'll have better luck at the toy store." But as he walked in, a creepy jack-in-the-box turned its head and whispered, "Welcome to the Loyalty Program."

The lights in the mall flickered and a voice rang out over the loudspeaker: "SUPER SAVERS LOYALTY PROGRAM! ONE NIGHT ONLY! MEMBERSHIP FOREVERRRR!"

And Kevin did save thousands of dollars that night because Kevin never needed to spend another penny for the rest of his life.

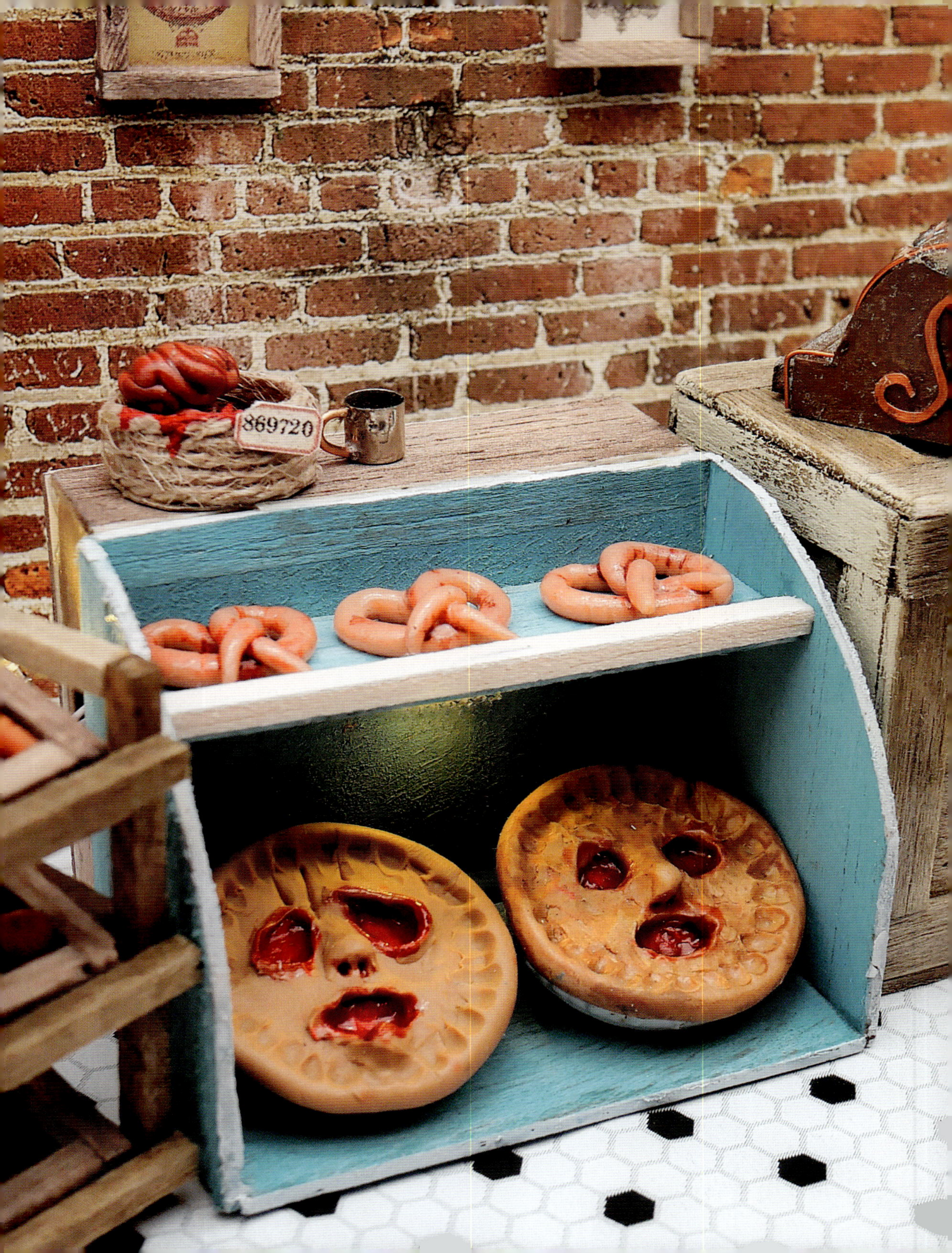
869720

Pie Counter

"Should pie scream like that? Why is it looking at me? Can I speak to a manager!?" These were the final words of Pie #2 . . . now delightfully served in pancreas flavor.

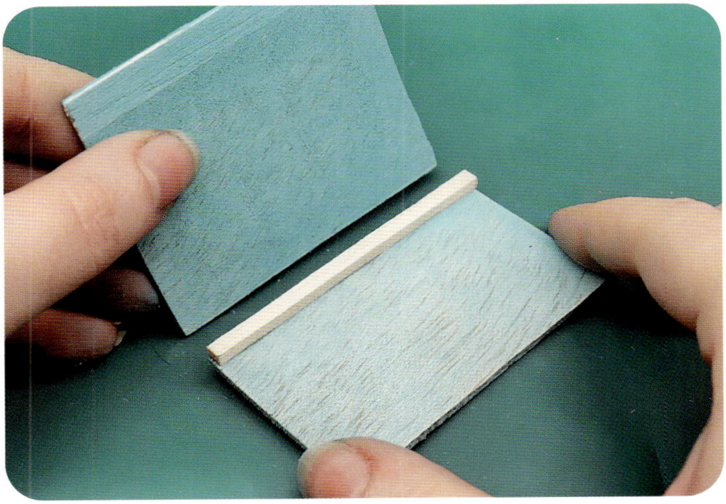

Counter

Cut and paint the following balsa wood according to the template on page 226:

- **Qty: 1**—2½ x 1½ inches (6.4 x 3.8 cm) ***bottom***
- **Qty: 1**—2½ x 2 inches (6.4 x 5 cm) ***back***
- **Qty: 2**—2 x 1½ inches (5 x 3.8 cm) ***sides***
- **Qty: 1**—2½ x ¾ inch (6.4 x 1.9 cm) ***shelf *pie counter only***

Cut the following from ⅛-inch (3-mm) square wooden dowel:

- **Qty: 2**—2½ inches (6.4 cm) ***trim***

Glue one ***trim*** onto the long edge of the ***bottom*** piece.

Glue the long edges of the ***back*** piece and the ***bottom*** piece (***trim*** side) to make an L.

Tools

- exacto knife, ruler, & cutting mat
- paint
- glue
- pointy object
- ball sculpting tool
- clear gloss
- tape

Counter Materials

- balsa wood
- ⅛" (3-mm) square dowels
- thin clear plastic

Pie & Pretzel Materials

- polymer clay
- 2 metal bottle caps
- toothpicks

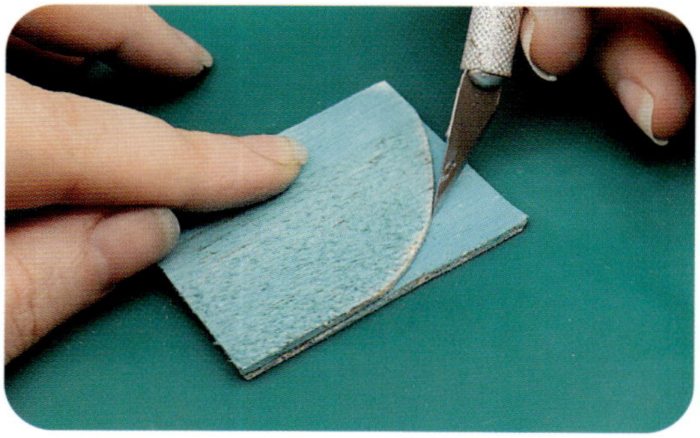

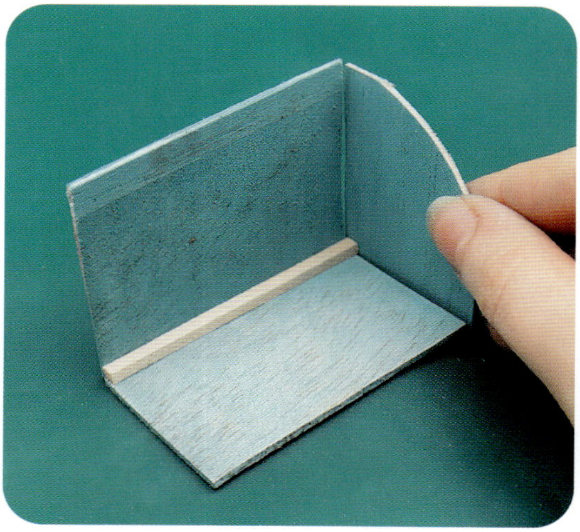

On the short edge of a ***side*** piece, cut a rounded corner. (Think of how a rounded deli counter might look.) The roundedness of the corners doesn't really matter as long as both ***sides*** are equal. You can ensure they are equal by using one as a template for the other.

Glue each ***side*** onto each side of your L shape to make a rounded box.

Pie counter only:** Glue your ***shelf inside your box at roughly ½ inch (1.3 cm) down from the top. Glue your other ***trim*** to the edge of your ***shelf***. (Make sure it doesn't stick out from your rounded corner.)

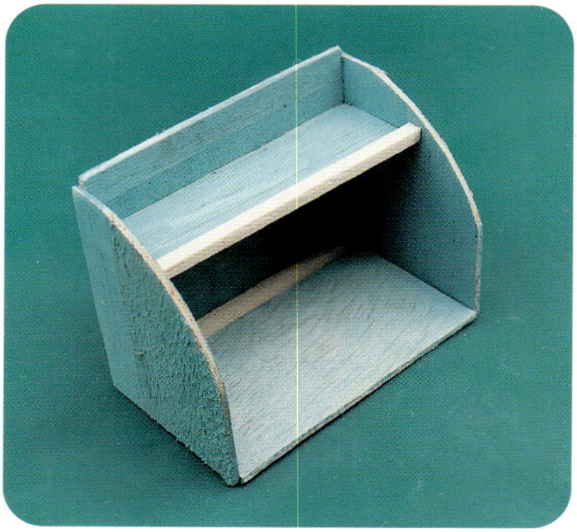

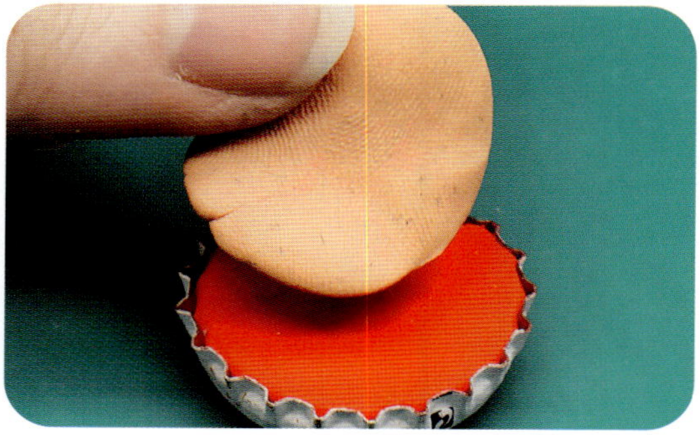

Clay Sizer *Pie*

Nose · Rim · Top · Inside

Pie

Roll out the clay balls for your pie.

Smash your ***inside*** ball into a bottle cap and even it out.

Flatten your ***top*** clay ball into a disk that's roughly the diameter of your bottle cap and place it on top of the ***inside***.

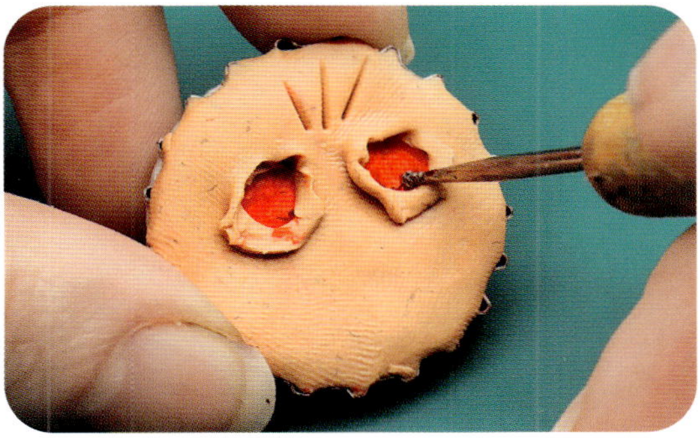
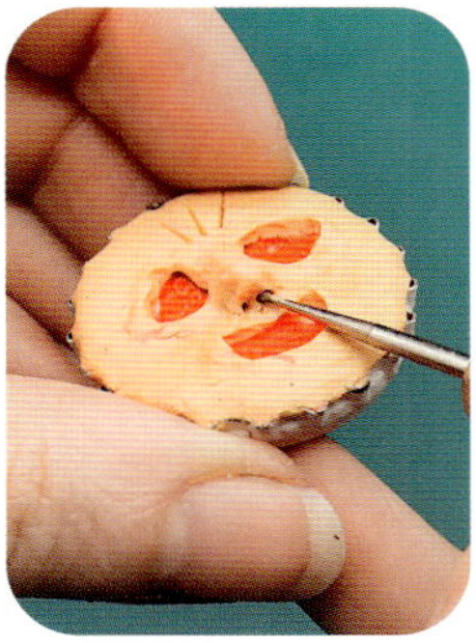
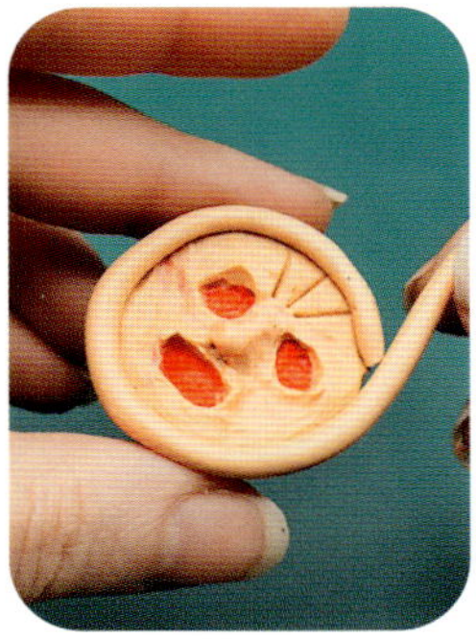
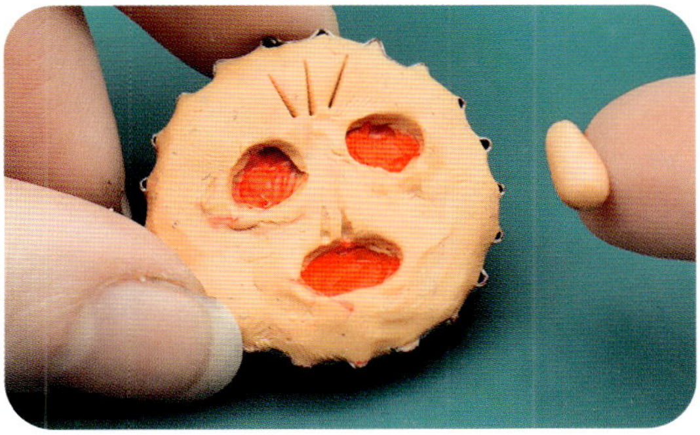
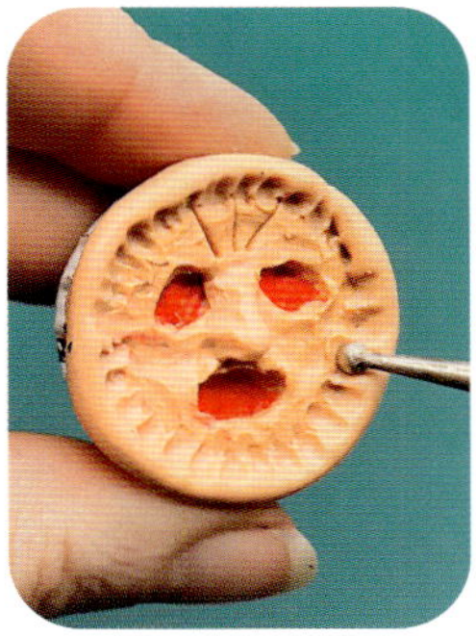
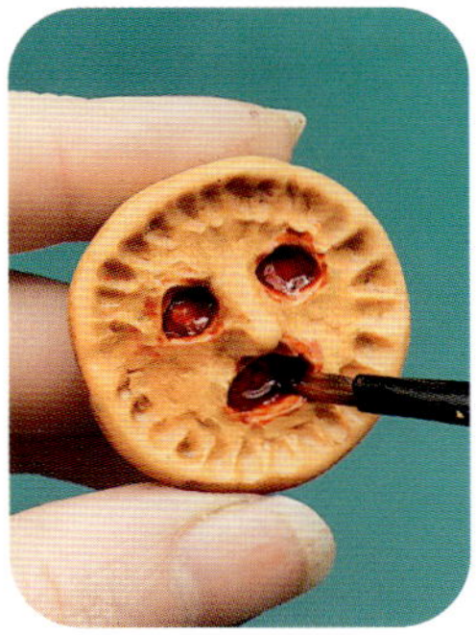

With a pointy object, dig through the ***top*** so that the red ***inside*** peeks through in the shape of two big eye holes. Using a toothpick, make three vent marks between the eyes in more of the forehead region.

Make a hole like you did for the eyes but in a silent scream shape for the mouth. It hurts to be cooked, I imagine.

Elongate your ***nose*** clay to make a fat cylinder and press it into the nose spot. Using a ball sculpting tool, smooth out the top seam and down the two long edge seams. Add nostrils with a toothpick.

Roll your ***rim*** clay into a long thin snake about as thick as a phone cord. (Present day, not one from 1982.) Wrap this around the edge of your pie and trim to size. This is the crust.

All the way around the inside seam of your ***rim***, squish down with a ball sculpting tool and push toward the face.

Make two pies in total and bake them according to the package instructions.

Mixing dark red paint and clear gloss, make a bloody mixture and sloppily paint it inside the eye holes and mouth holes of your pies. *That's not blood, it's pie filling! I swear!*

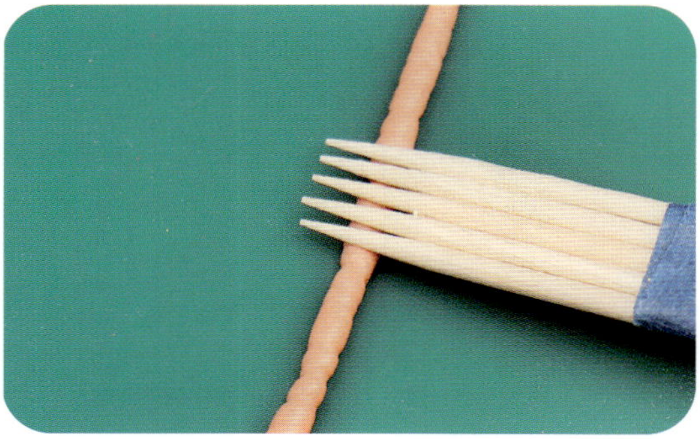

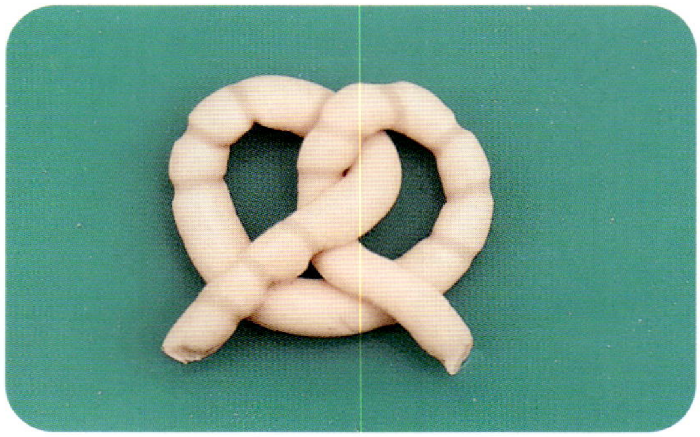

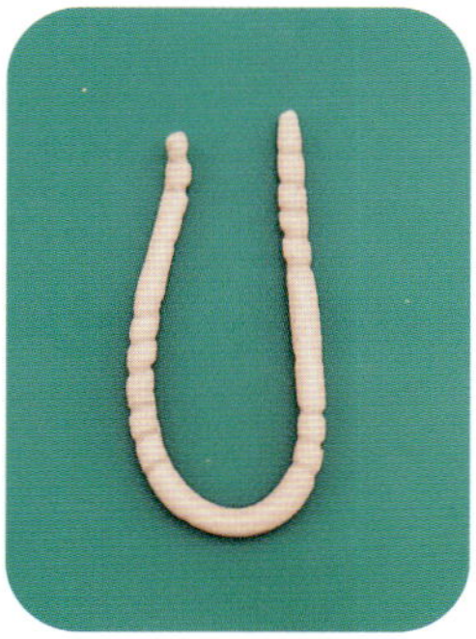

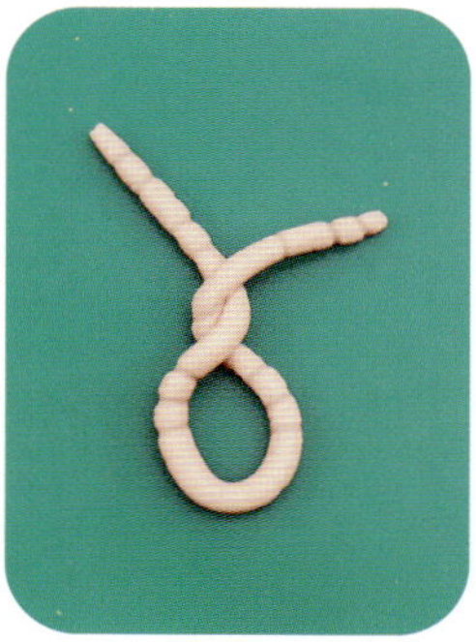

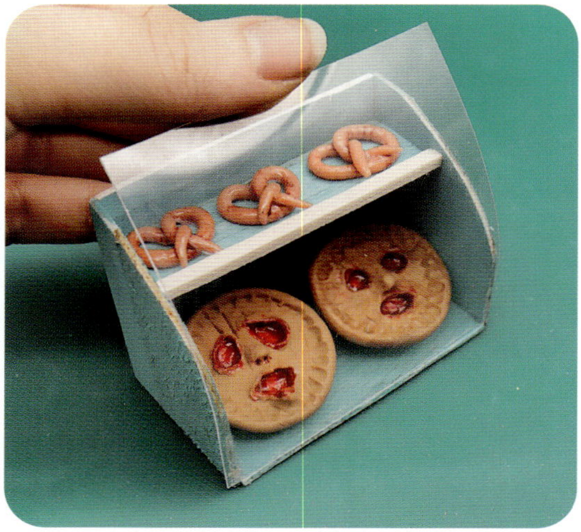

Clay Sizer
Pretzel

Worm Pretzel

Roll out your pretzel ball into a long skinny rope, roughly 3 inches (7.6 cm) long.

Tape together five toothpicks lying flat side by side and roll the pointy ends of the toothpicks on top of your snake to make rings around your clay, like the texture on a worm. (Don't waste time on this. We're just looking for vague worminess.)

Bend your worm into a U and cross the ends over twice.

Fold the twisted ends down over the bottom of the U to make a pretzel.

Make three pretzels and bake them according to the package instructions.

Mix dark red paint and clear gloss, then paint the crevices of your pretzel.

Now that you have all of your baked goods, glue them into your box. Put your pretzels on the top shelf and the pies on the bottom shelf.

Lastly, cover your countertop by bending and gluing a sheet of thin clear plastic onto the front. It helps muffle the pie screams.

Candy Station

Made for children, out of children! Sound gross? Don't worry, children are already like 72% sugar, which makes our candy the sweetest!

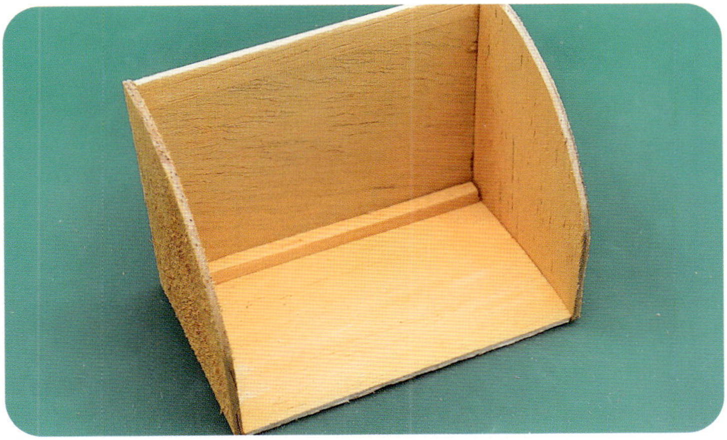

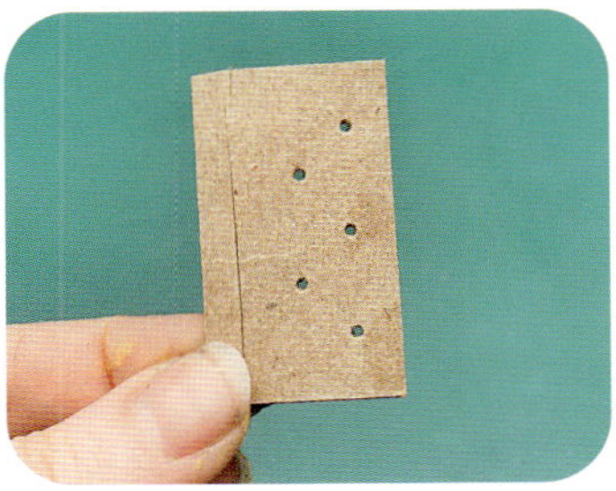

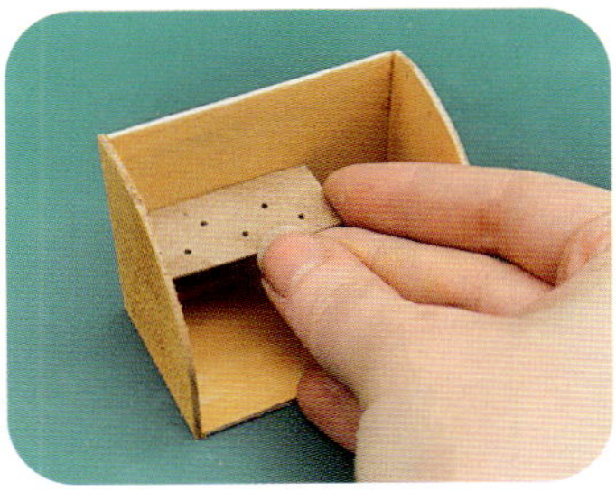

Tools

- paint
- exacto knife, ruler, & cutting mat
- needle (or thumbtack)
- glue
- clear gloss
- candle
- superglue

Counter Materials

- counter (page 199)
- chipboard
- toothpick
- thin clear plastic (optional)

Lollipop, Maggots, & Sprinkles Materials

- polymer clay
- 5 toothpicks
- 1 heart (page 157)
- 1 tongue (page 156)
- sandwich bag
- 9 maggots (3 different colors; page 181)
- paper
- tiny glass bottle (preferably hexagonal)

Counter

Paint the counter from page 199.

Cut a 1½ x ¾–inch (3.8 x 1.9–cm) rectangle out of chipboard using the template on page 225. Score and fold the long edge about ¼ inch (6 mm) in.

Using a needle or thumbtack, poke five holes in the larger side of your chipboard in a zigzag pattern.

Glue the flap of your shelf to the back of your counter. Position this in the middle left. Set it aside.

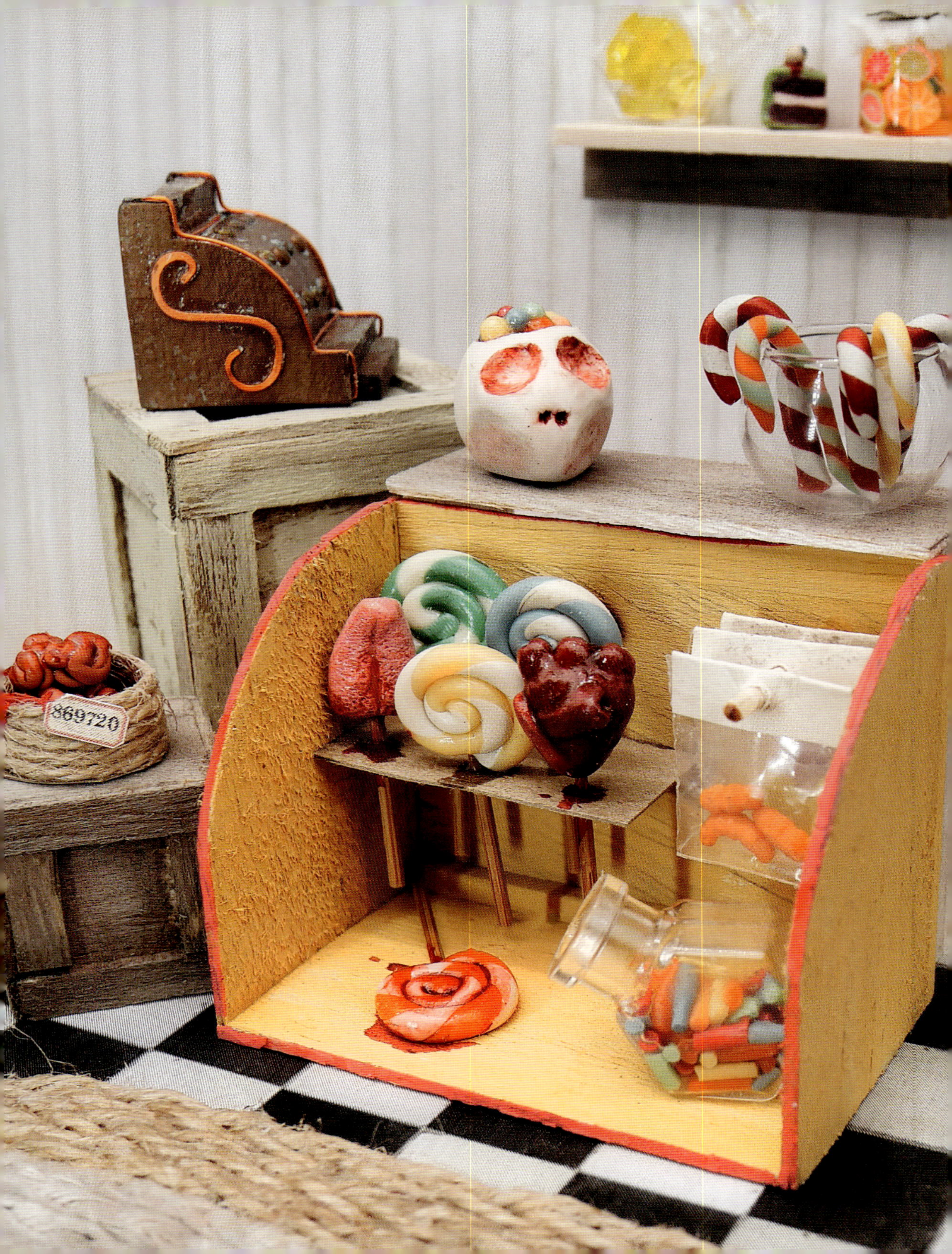
869720

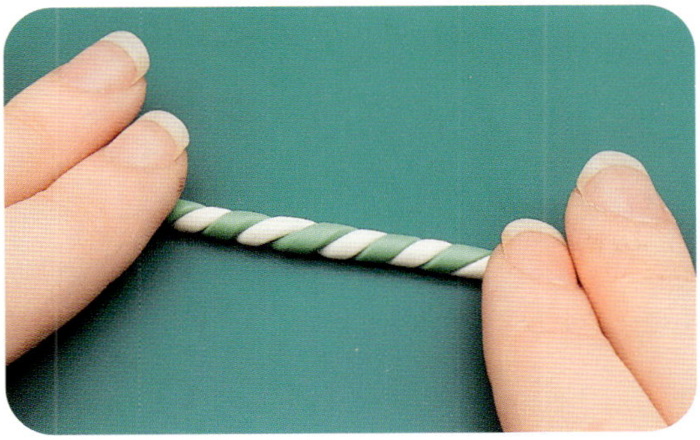

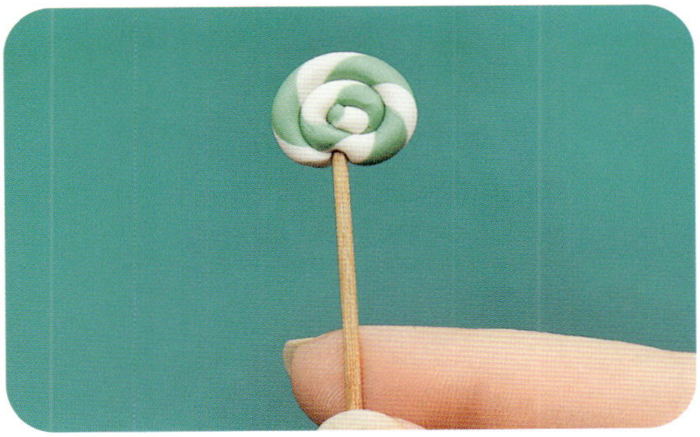

Clay Sizer
Lollipop

x4 x4

Lollipop

Take your two lollipop clay balls and roll them into long ropes.

Twist the two colored ropes together. Roll your twisted ropes into one rope.

Side Note: *You can use this method to make candy canes too.*

Side, Side Note: *If you use a sickly green color, it makes gross candy cane worms!*

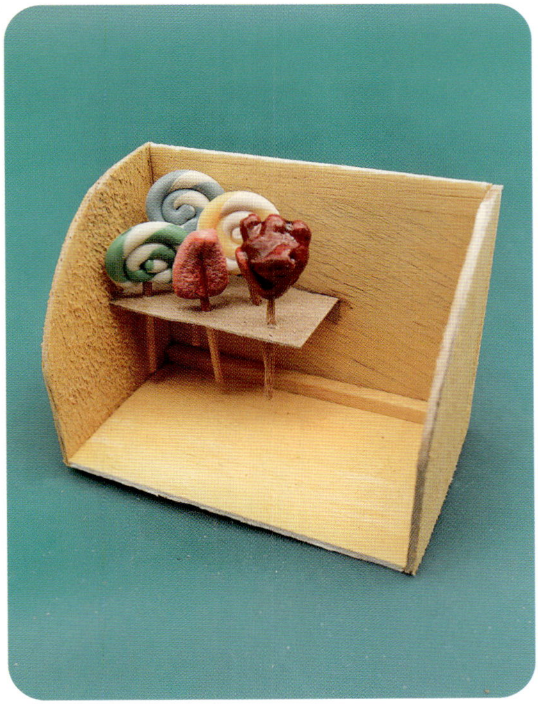

Coil your rope into a spiral until it's as big as you want it to be and trim off the excess.

Stab the bottom with the pointy end of a toothpick. Do this until you have at least four lollipops and harden them according to the package instructions.

Take your heart and tongue and stab the bottoms with a toothpick if they aren't baked yet. If they are, take your needle or thumbtack and make a small hole in the bottom to place the pointy end of your toothpick in.

Paint them with clear gloss and trim the toothpicks to the same length, roughly 1 inch (2.5 cm).

Place them in the holes of your shelf. Glue one under the shelf and add some glossy red paint around the outside. (I'm SURE it's just lollipop juice.)

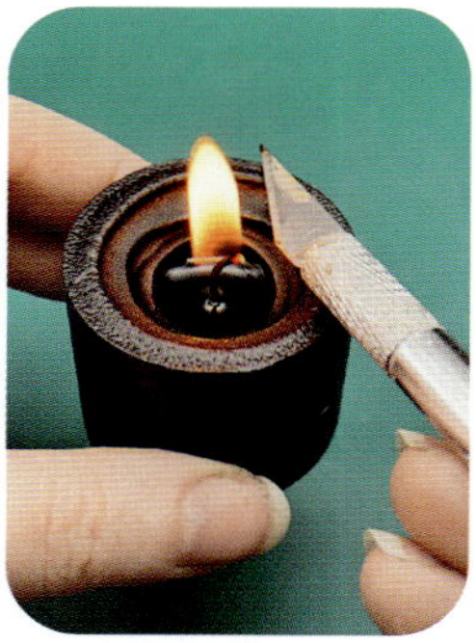
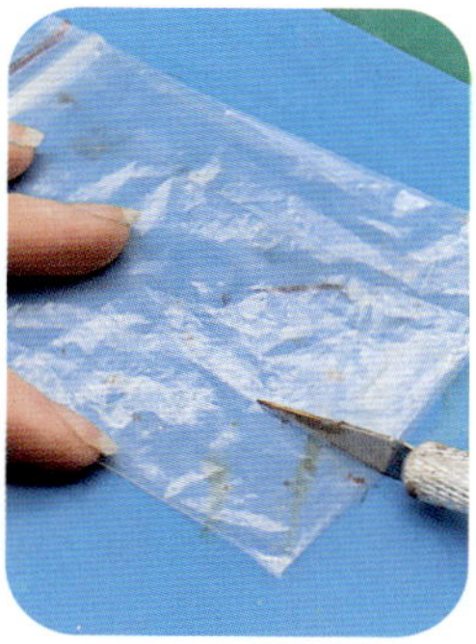
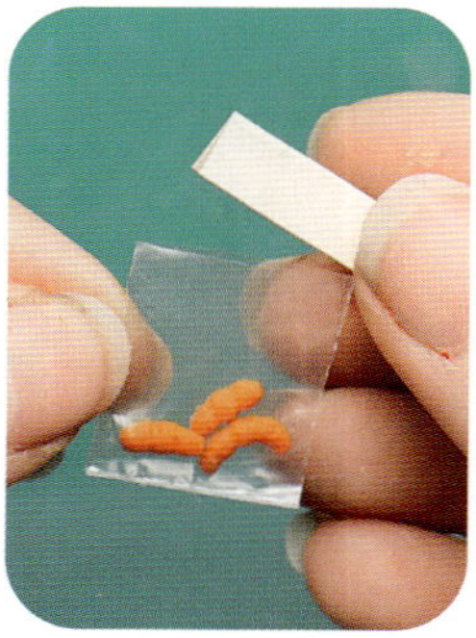
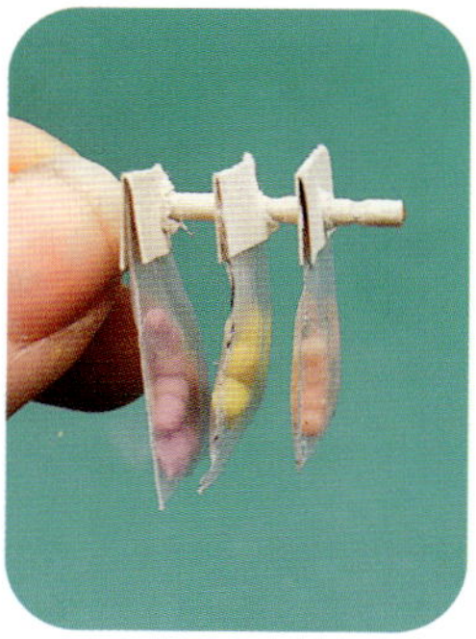
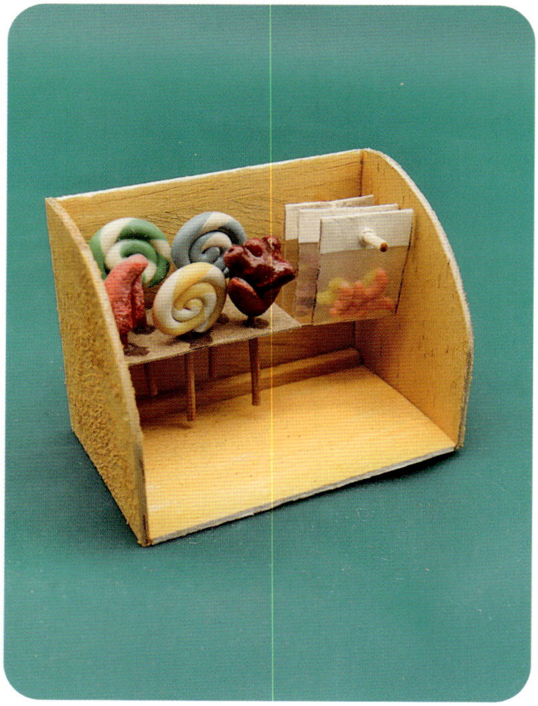

Bagged Maggots

BE VERY CAREFUL WITH THIS PART!!!

Take your sandwich bag and lay it flat on a cutting mat.

Light a candle and hold your exacto knife to the side of the flame for 8 to 10 seconds. Not on top of the flame, not inside the flame, but to the side of the flame. This keeps black stuff from getting on your blade.

Then quickly, before your knife cools off, hold the blade roughly ¾ inch (1.9 cm) from the bottom corner of your sandwich bag. This should seal it and make it a tiny square.

Cut your tiny baggie off and fill it with three maggots of the same color from page 181.

Take a small piece of paper that's ¾ x ½ inch (1.9 x 1.3 cm) and fold it ice-cream-sandwich style and glue it to the top of your tiny baggie.

Do this until you have three little bags of maggots. Push a needle through the tops of your bags, then push a toothpick through the holes. Trim your toothpick to roughly ¾ inch (1.9 cm) and superglue it to the back of your counter.

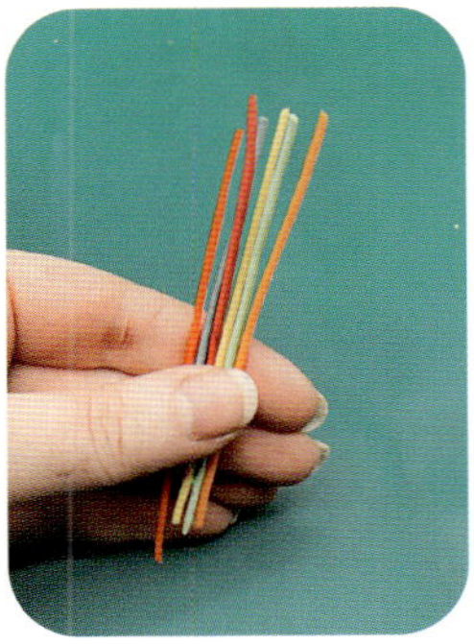

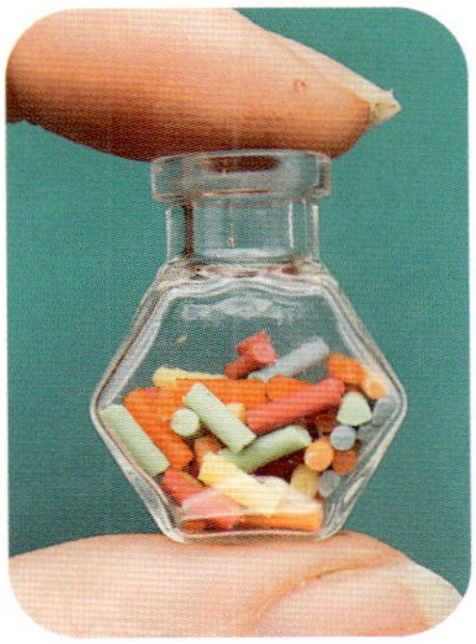

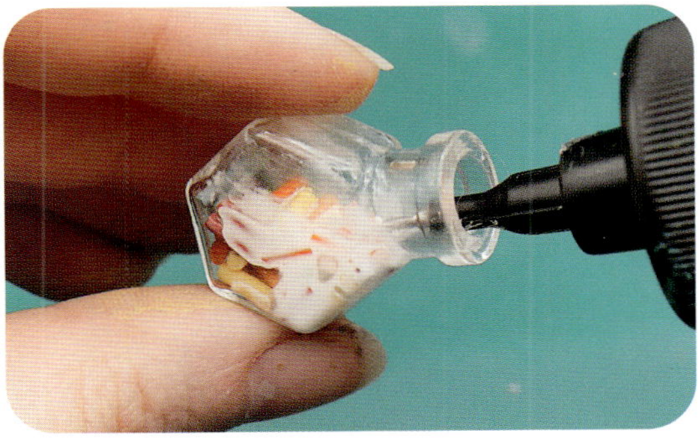

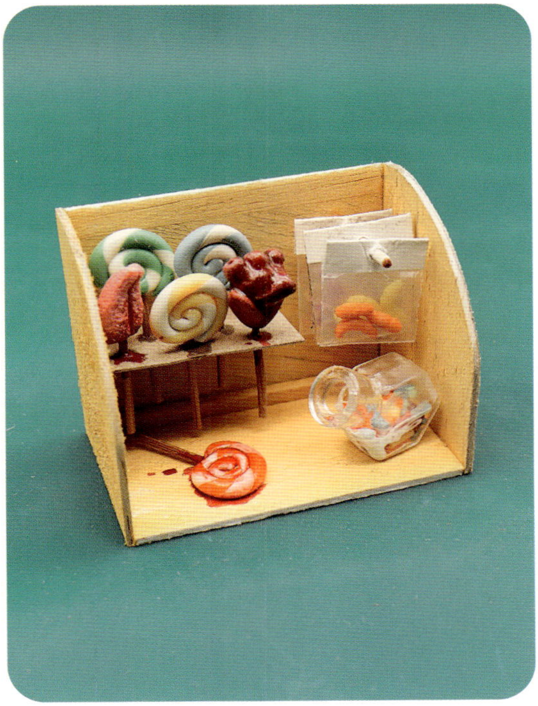

Sprinkles

Using polymer clay, make four to six differently colored long sticks about the thickness of a toothpick and harden them according to the package instructions. (This is actually a great way to use up old clay that is getting gross or weird.)

Break or cut your colorful sticks into sprinkle-sized pieces.

Fill your tiny glass bottle about a quarter of the way with glue and place a small handful of sprinkles into the glass container. It will take a few days for this glue to dry, but once it does, it'll dry clear. Glue this under your maggots.

Optionally, if you want to keep gross yucky dust off your candy, you can finish off your station by gluing a sheet of thin clear plastic to the front. Because we'd hate to have dusty maggots . . . that'd be gross . . .

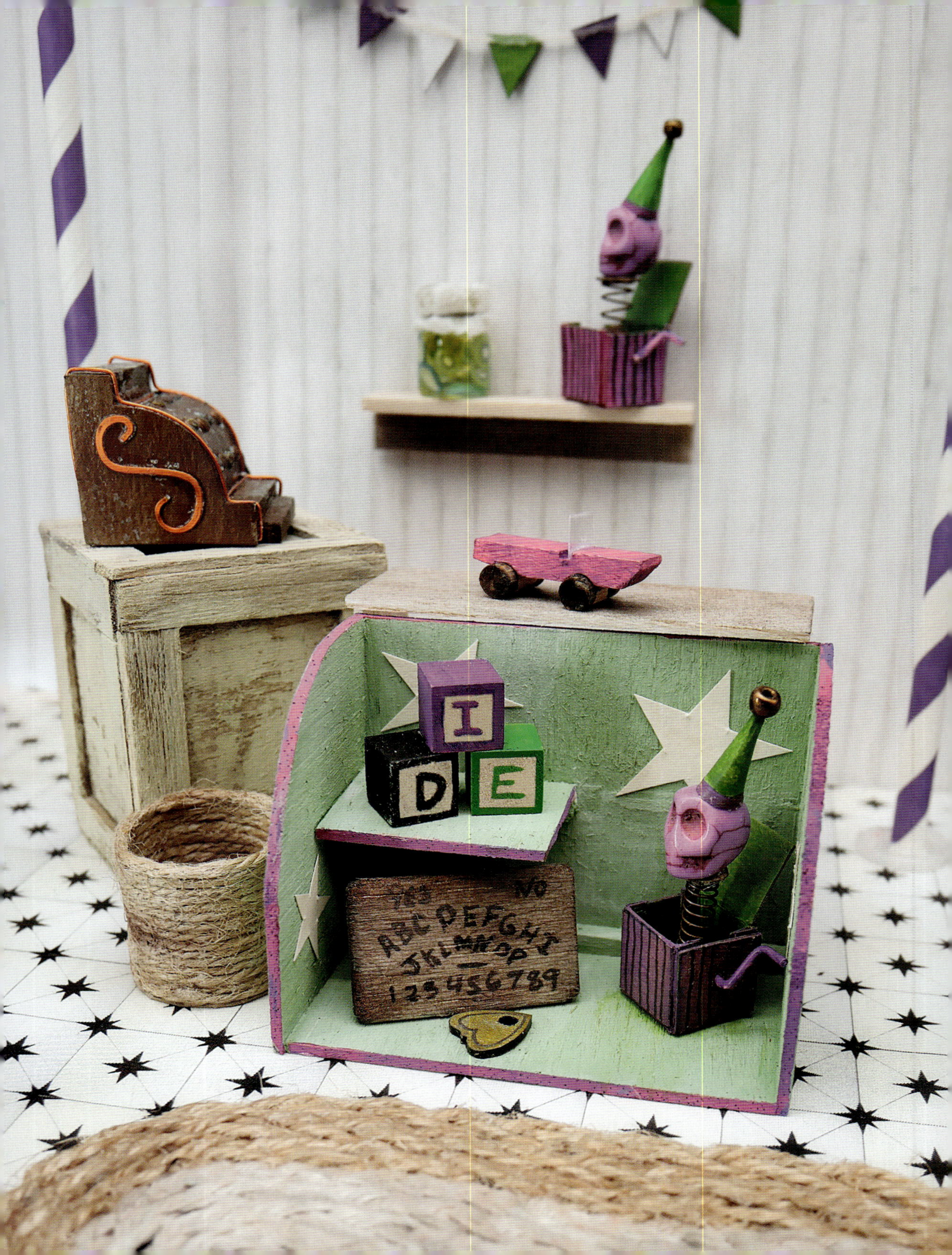
I
D
E
YES
NO
ABCDEFGHI
JKLMNOP
123456789

Toy Store

Ahhh yes, the toy store, every child's dream! Unless that dream is actually a nightmare, and the toys are trying to murder you!

Tools

- paint
- exacto knife, ruler, & cutting mat
- glue
- fine-tip markers
- needle or thumbtack
- pliers/wire cutter
- hole punch
- sandpaper
- scissors

Counter Materials

- counter (page 199)
- balsa wood
- paper
- thin clear plastic (optional)

Jack-in-the-Box Materials

- chipboard
- paper clip
- spring from clicky pen
- paper
- small bead
- skull bead (~¼" [6 mm])

Ouija® Board Materials

- balsa wood
- chipboard
- shrink plastic

Blocks Materials

- 3 wooden cubes (~⅖" [1 cm])

Counter

Paint the counter from page 199. Cut and paint a 1¼ x ½–inch (3.2 x 1.3–cm) rectangle of balsa wood. Glue this on to the back of your counter. Position it middle left.

Decorate the counter with paper stars if you like. If you don't like, that's fine . . . fun killer!

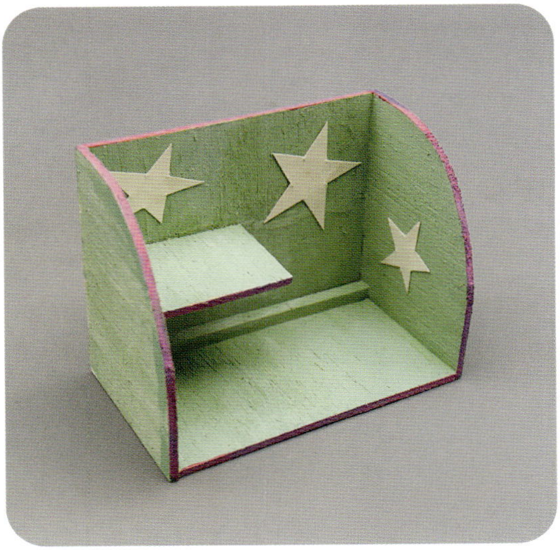

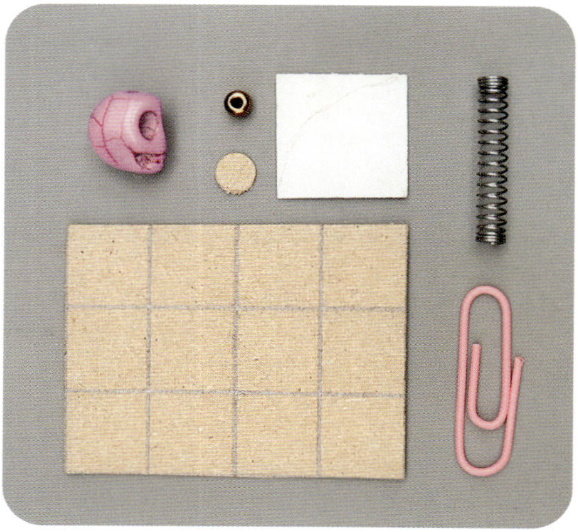

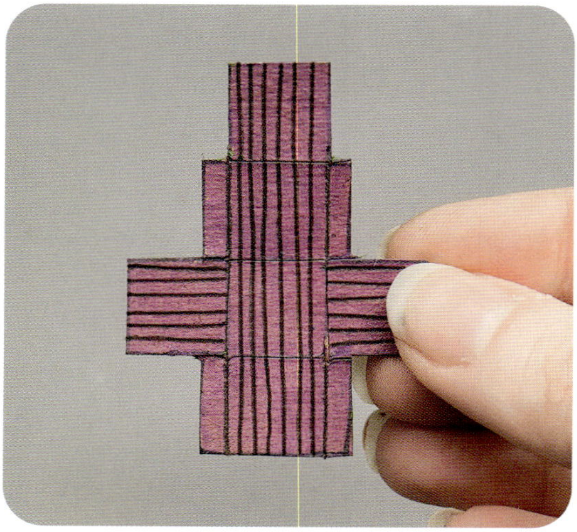

Jack-in-the-Box

Cut out a 2 x 1½–inch (5 x 3.8–cm) rectangle from chipboard. With a fine-tip marker, draw a grid with lines every ½ inch (1.3 cm). (This is easier if you have a cutting mat that has ½-inch [1.3-cm] squares.)

Take your chipboard rectangle and cut it according to the template on page 226. Score on the dashed lines.

Paint one side purple and the other side green. Use a black fine-tip marker to add stripes to the purple.

Fold it into a cube and glue the flaps on the inside of the box.

Poke a hole in the side with a needle or thumbtack.

With pliers, bend the end of a paper clip into a zigzag handle shape and glue it inside the hole.

Hole punch a piece of chipboard and glue one hole punch circle on either end of your spring. Set it aside to dry.

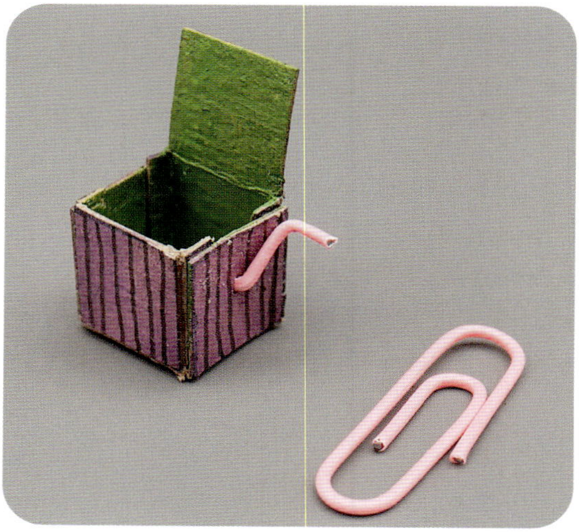

Take a small scrap of paper (roughly ½ x ½ inch [1.3 x 1.3 cm]) and roll it into a cone, gluing the edges. This will be the hat of the jack. Glue a small bead to the top for the pom-pom and paint it.

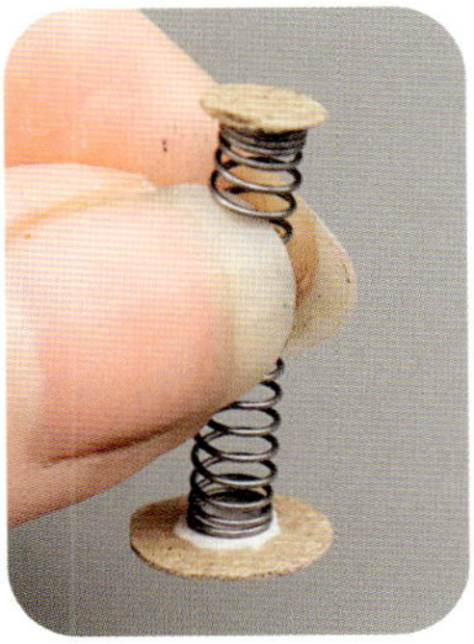

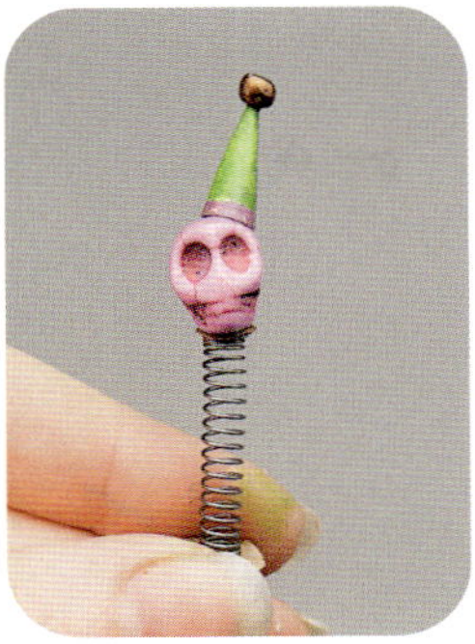

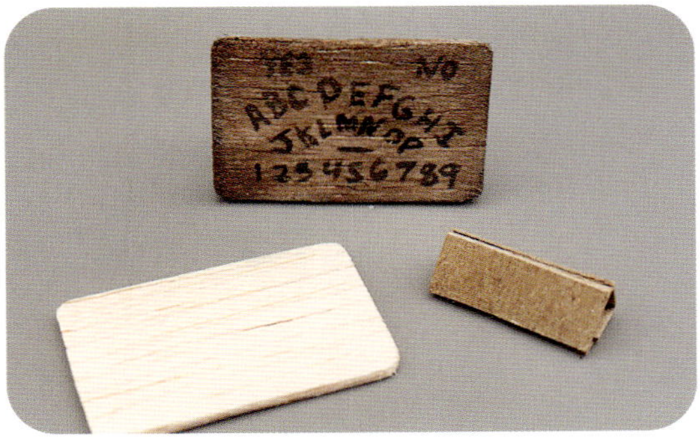

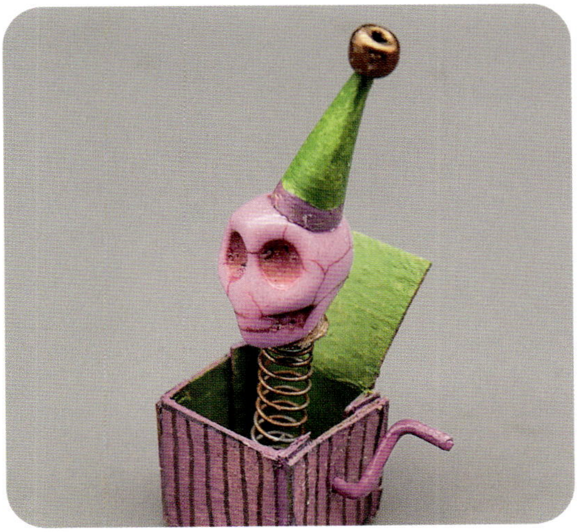

Glue your hat to the top of your skull bead at a slight angle, then glue the skull bead to the end of the spring. Glue the other end of the spring into the box, the box which we'll glue to the right of the shelf inside your counter. *Yes! That was a lot of gluing!*

Ouija Board

Cut a 1¼ x ½–inch (3.2 x 1.3–cm) piece of balsa wood and round the corners with sandpaper.

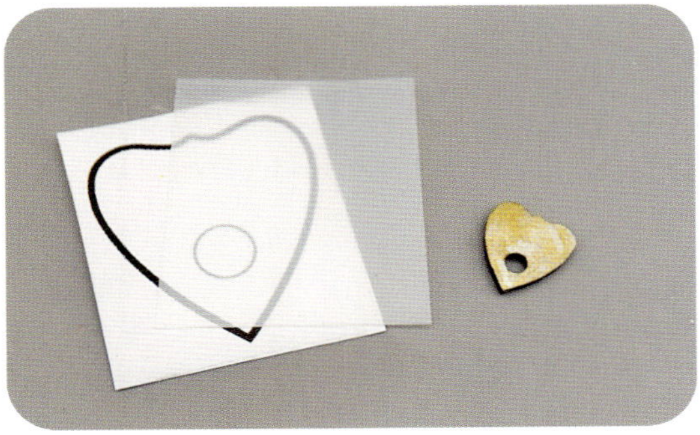

Paint your board brown and, with a fine-tip marker, draw on your Ouija board. (It doesn't have to be perfect! No one's going to notice if you're missing a few letters or numbers.)

Take a scrap piece of chipboard that's shorter than your Ouija board and fold it into a triangle. You won't see this; it's meant to keep your board from falling over. Glue it to the bottom back of your board.

Trace then cut out the Ouija board pointer (Did you know it's called a *planchette?*) onto shrink plastic using the template on page 225. Use a hole punch for the hole and shrink the *planchette*.

Paint your *planchette* gold with black edges.

Glue the Ouija board and *planchette* under your shelf in your countertop.

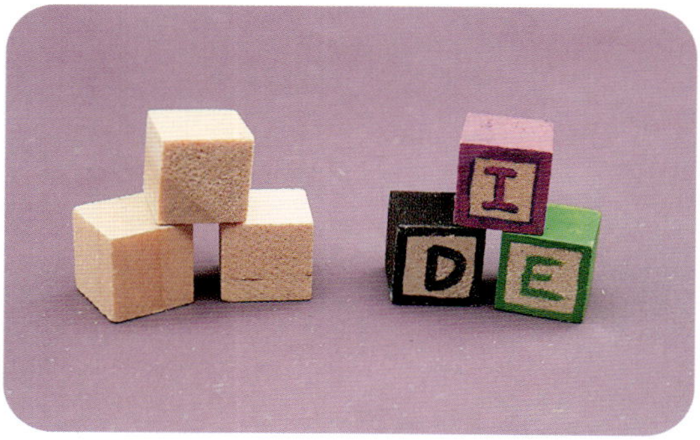

Blocks

Paint four sides all the way around a ⅖-inch (1-cm) wooden cube a solid color. Repeat for the other two cubes, with each cube painted a different color.

Paint D, I, and E on each block in the corresponding colors. Glue the blocks stacked in a pyramid on the shelf to read DIE.

Tip: *Can't paint straight lines? Try using markers instead.*

Optionally, you can finish up your toy store by bending and gluing a sheet of thin clear plastic onto the front. It keeps the haunted souls in the toys!

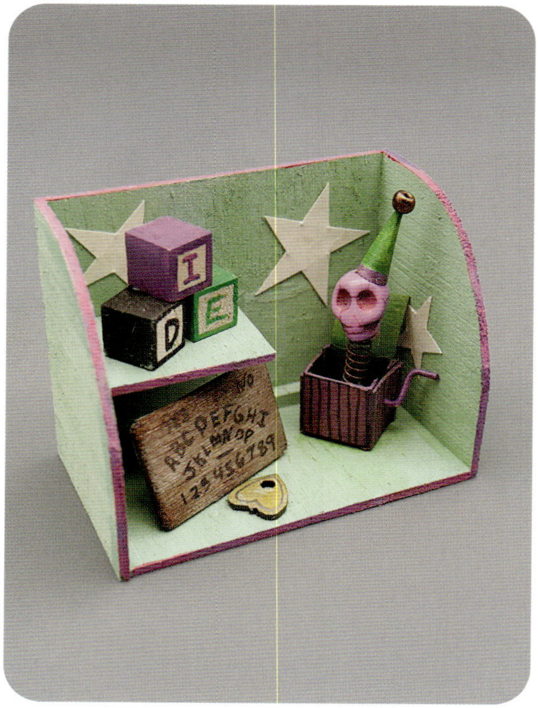

Templates

Chest of Secrets (page 17) x2

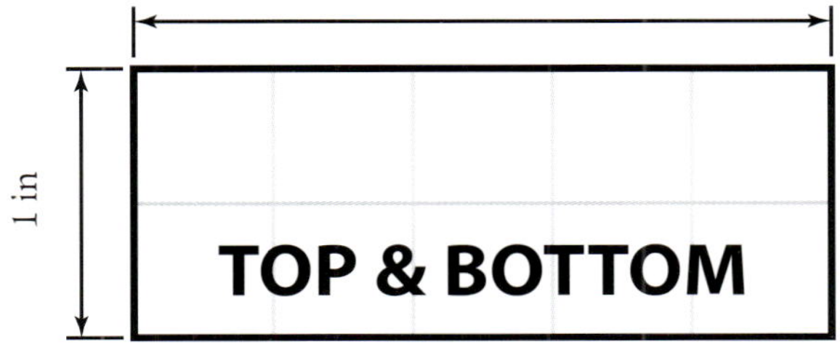

"Prize" Counter Axe (page 85)

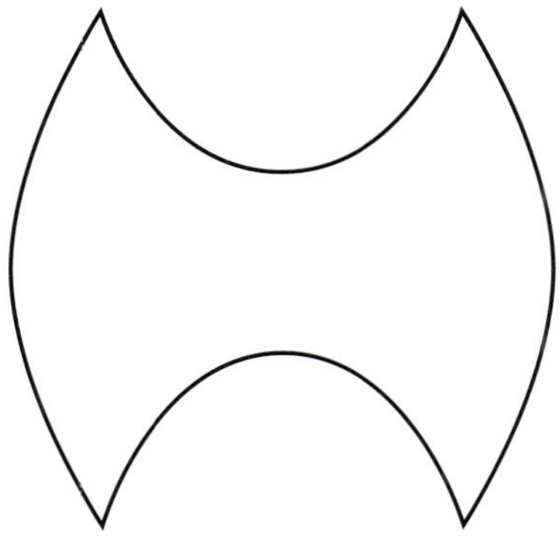

Wand Storage Backer (page 113)

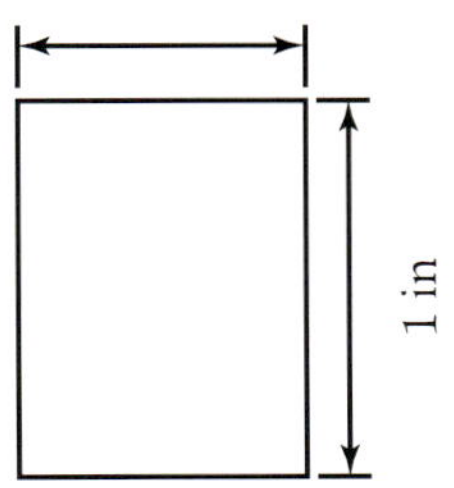

The Midnight Clock (page 21)

CLOCK TRUNK

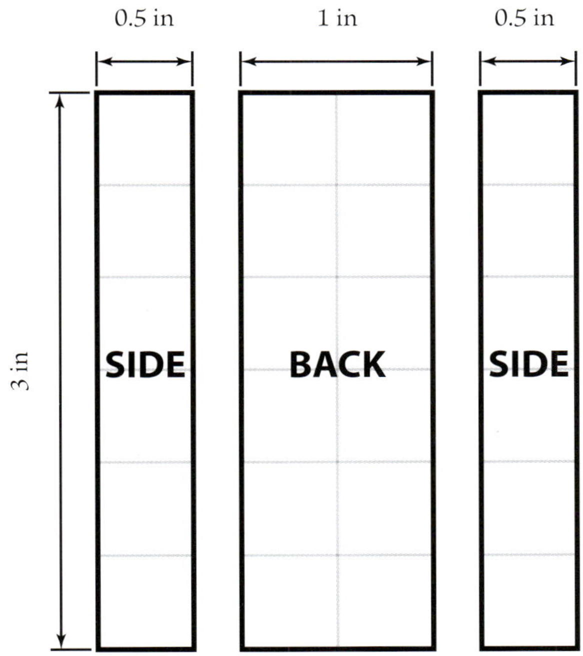

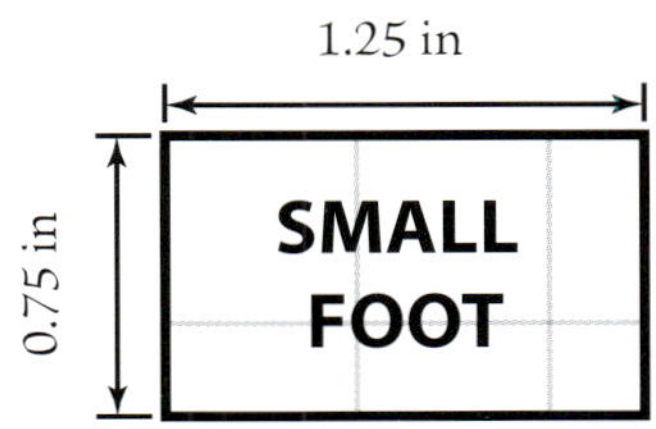

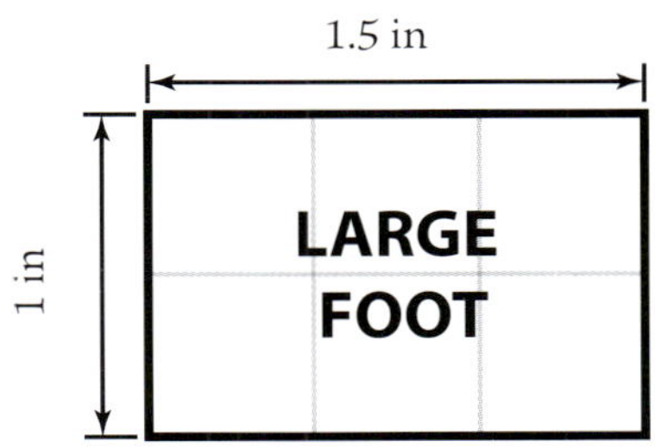

Sinister Stairs (page 25)

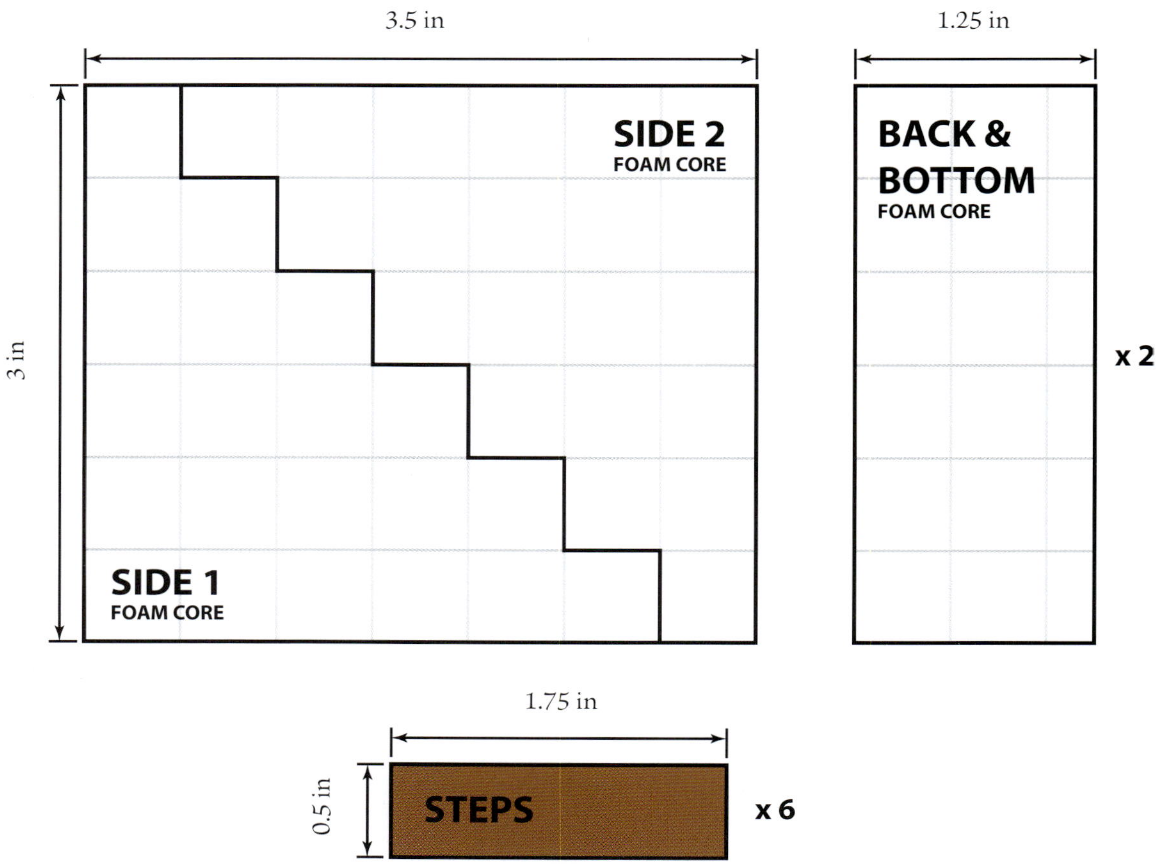

Fortune Teller (page 69)

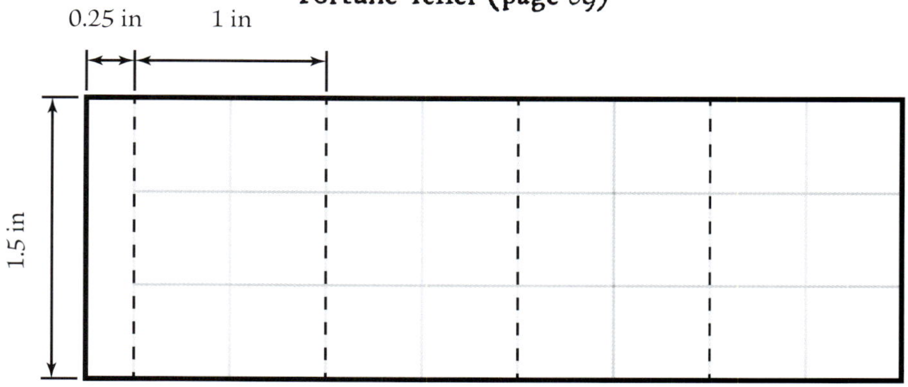

Apothecary Drawers (page 33)

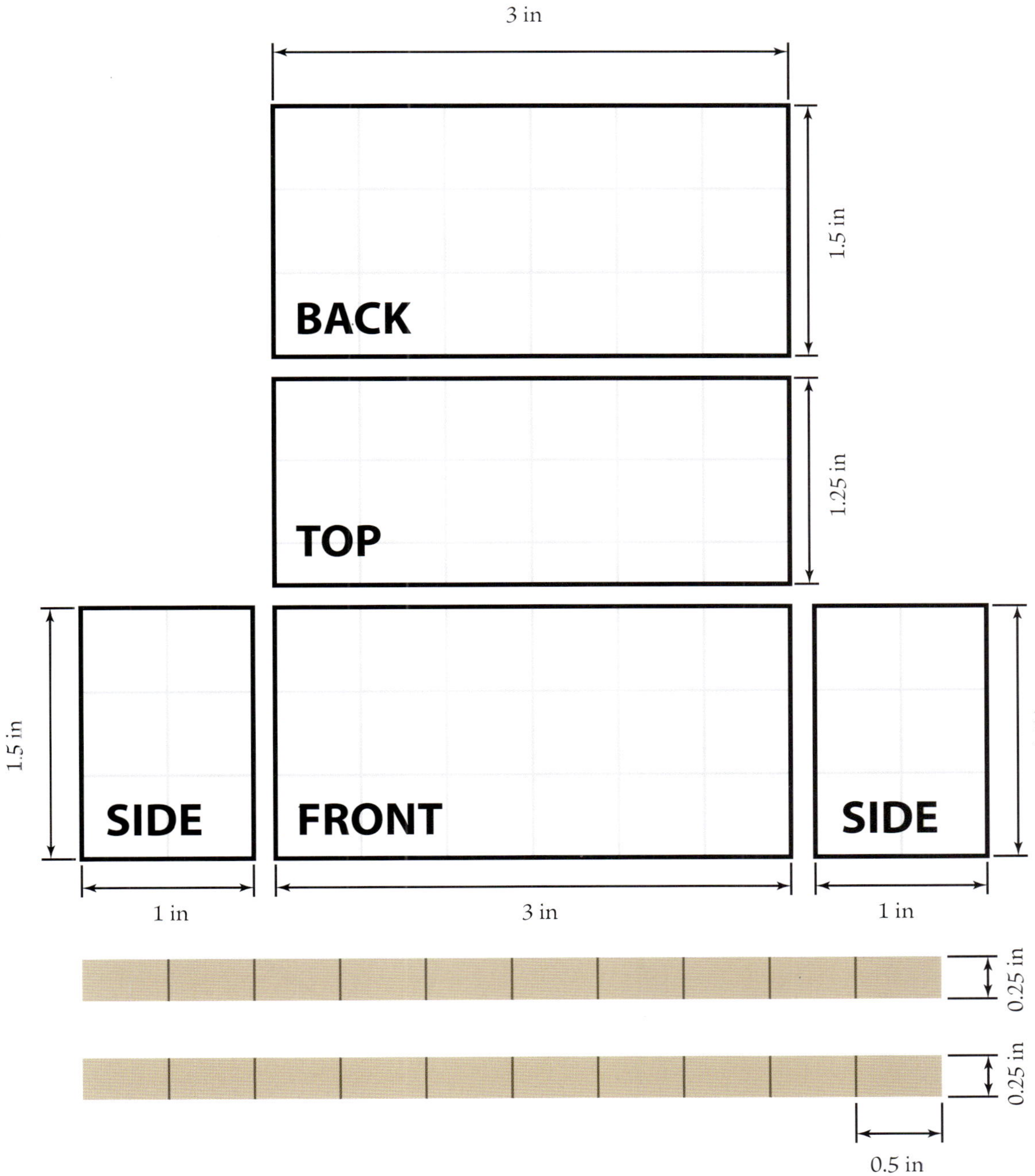

Circle Window (page 99)

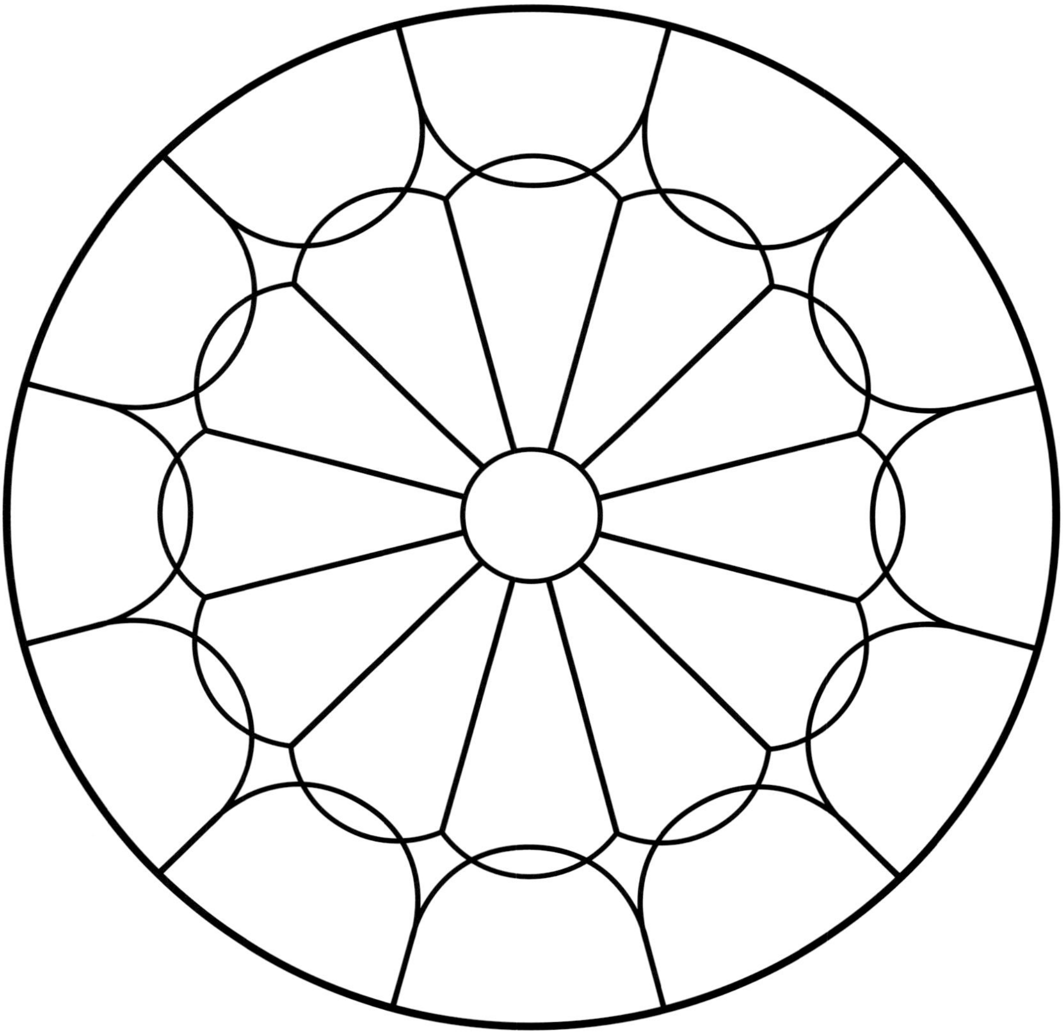

Ticket Booth (page 73)

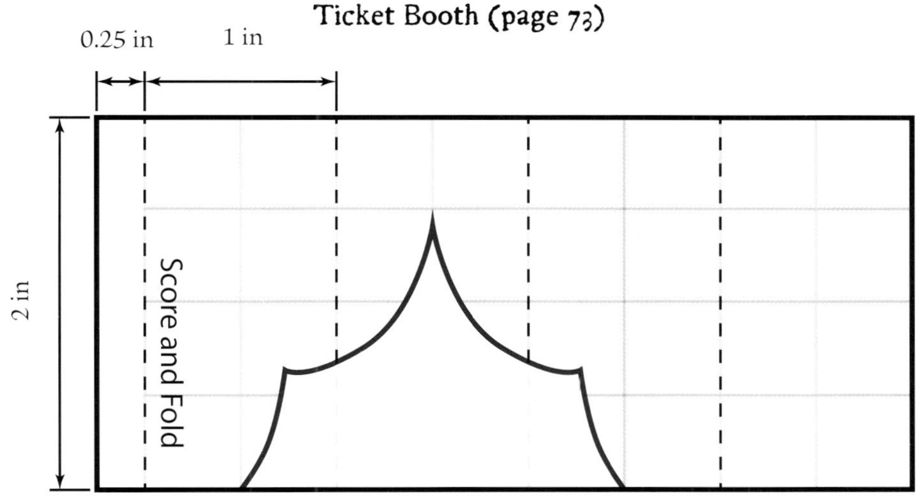

Throwing Knives Sign (page 79)

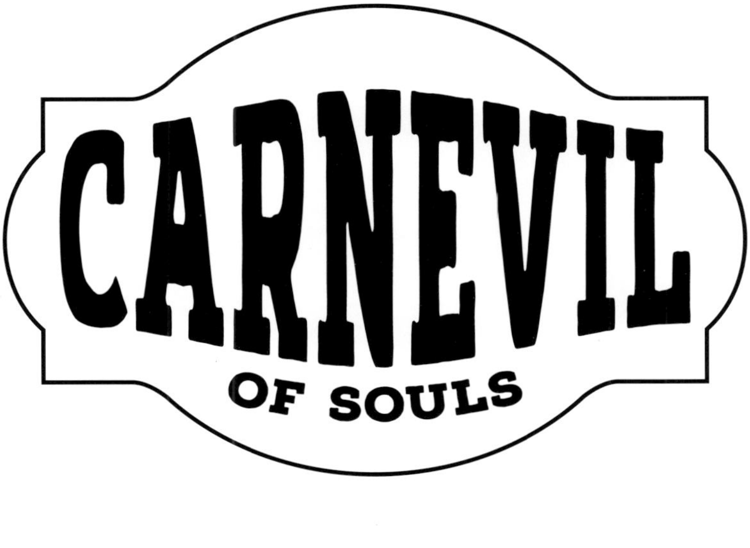

My Specimens (page 119)
Crate & Cash Register (page 161)

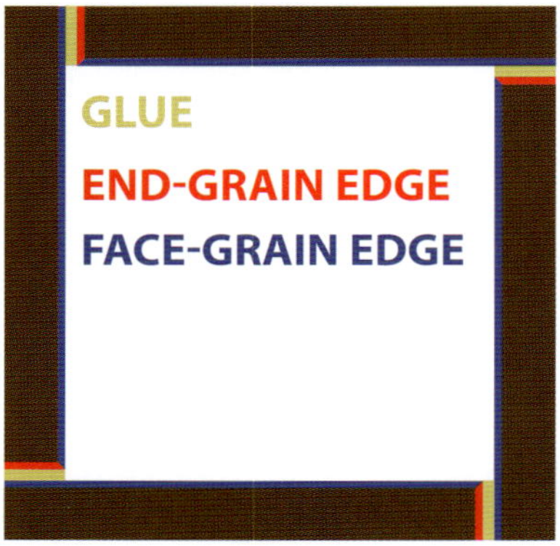

Haunted Toy House (page 135)

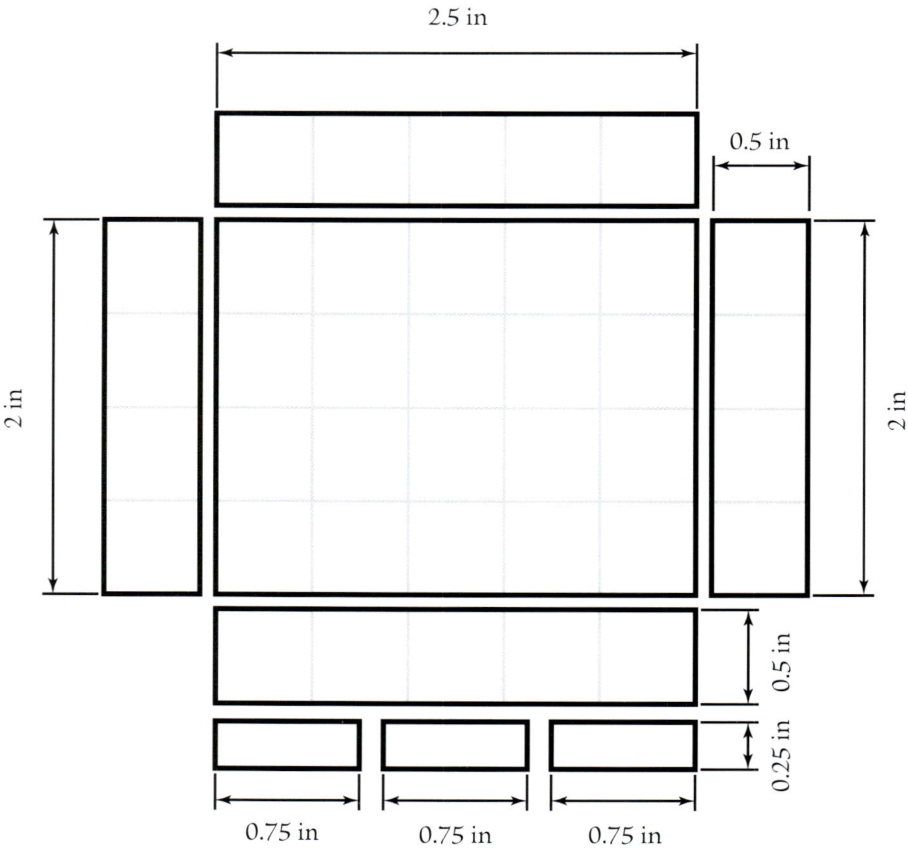

A Monster's Under My Bed! (page 145)

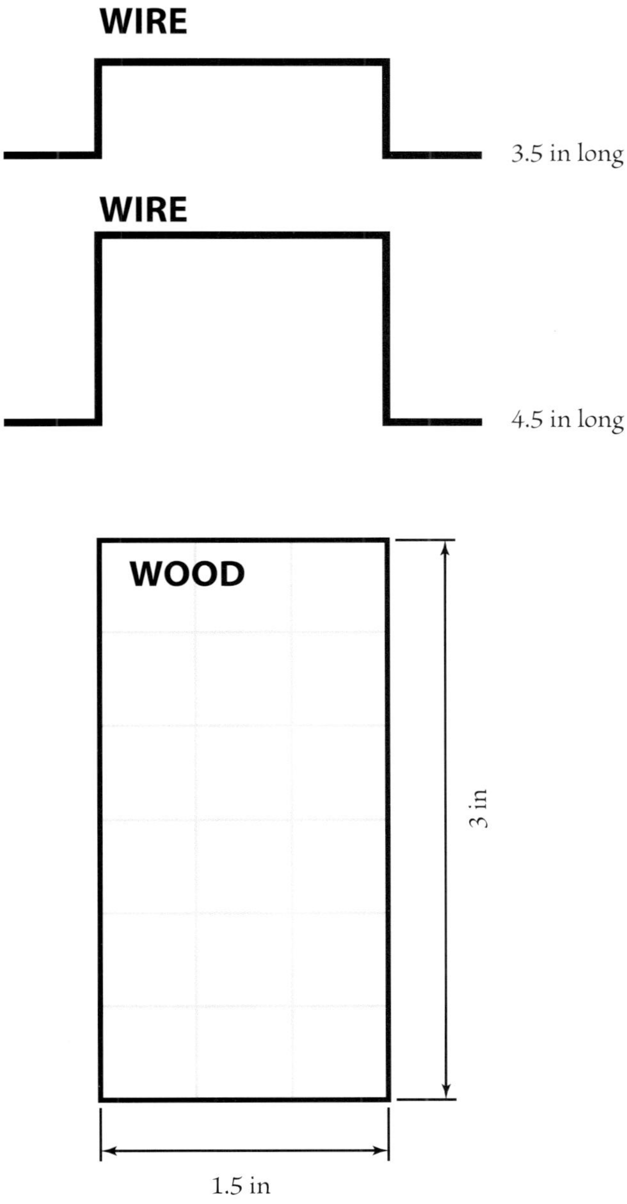

Chopping Block Knives (page 159)

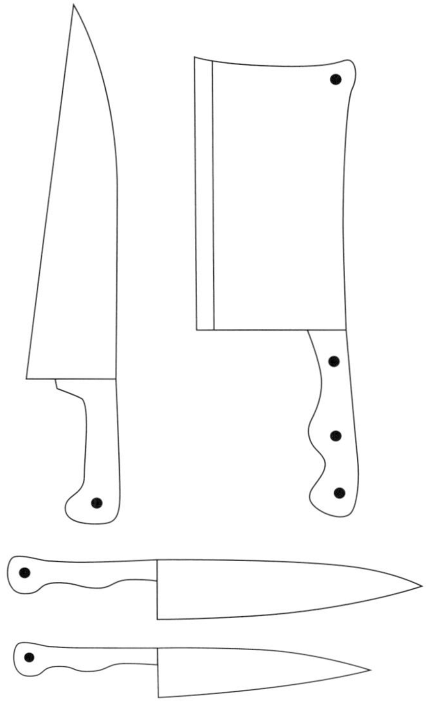

Ice Boxes Angle (page 153)

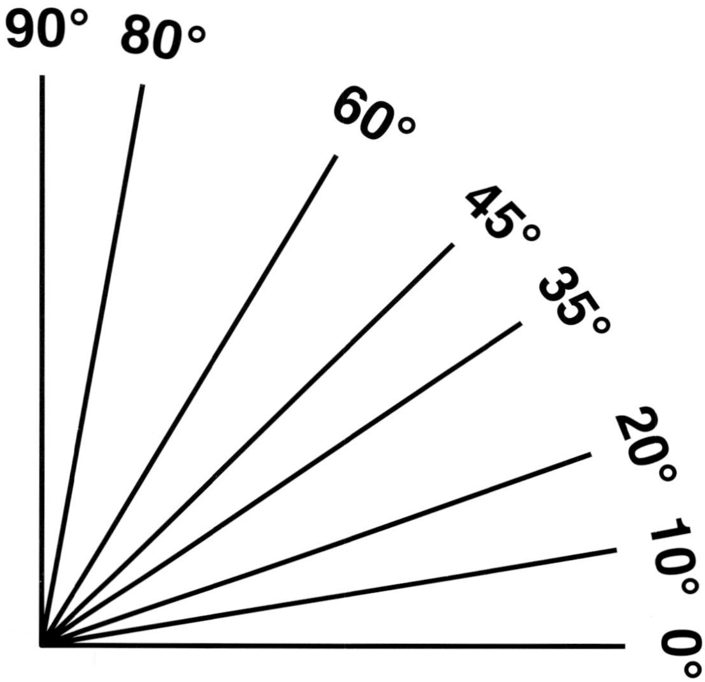

Ice Boxes Tray (page 153)

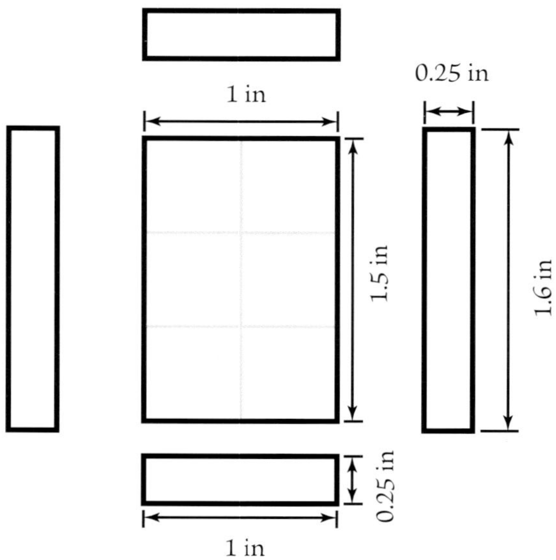

Ice Boxes Rack (page 153)

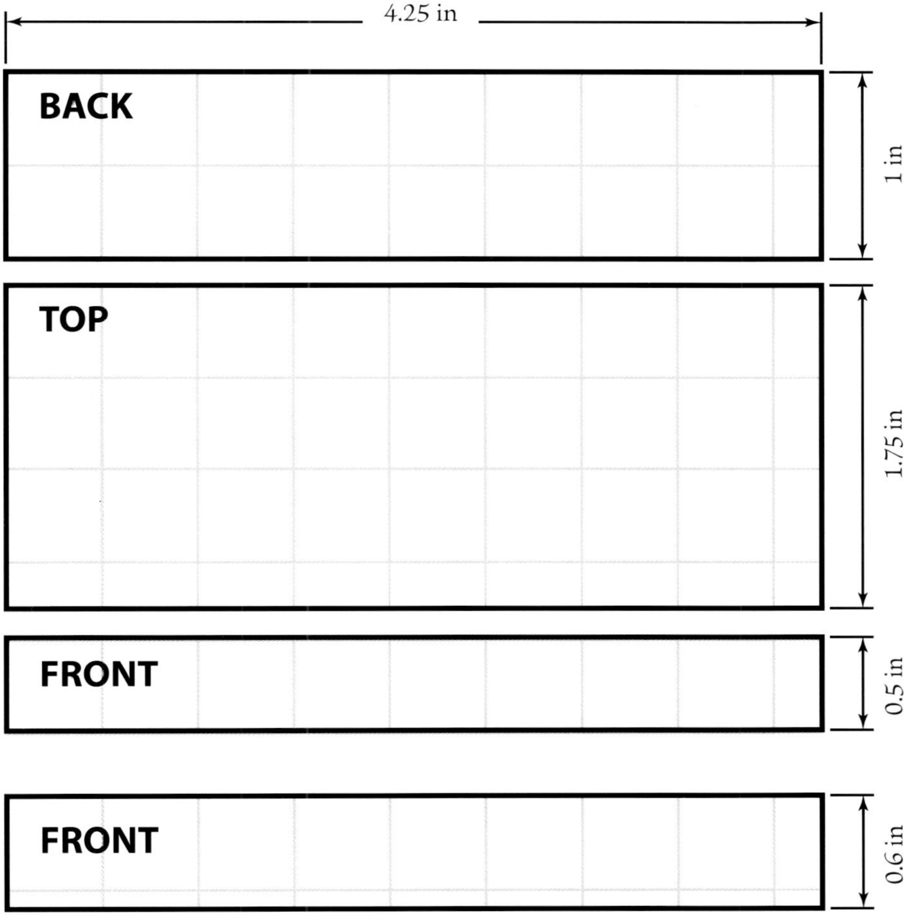

Butcher Shop Window (page 171)

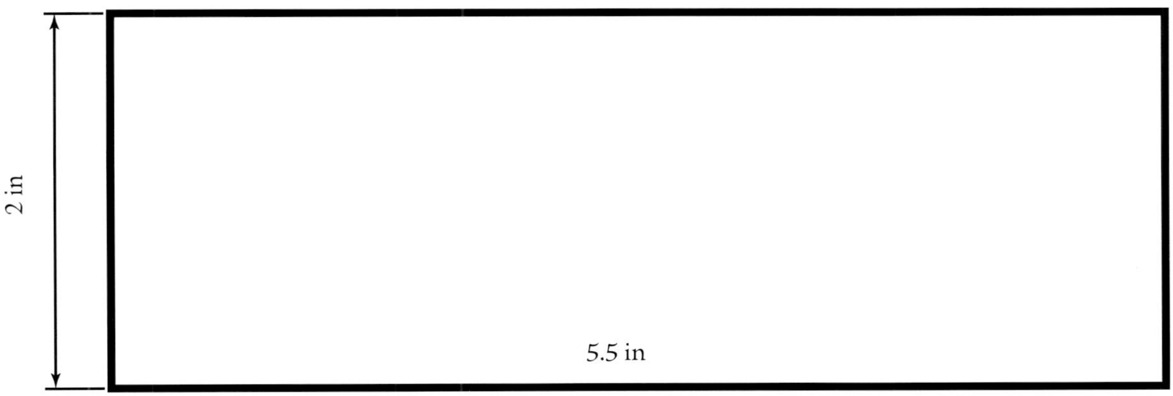

Butcher Shop Window (page 171)

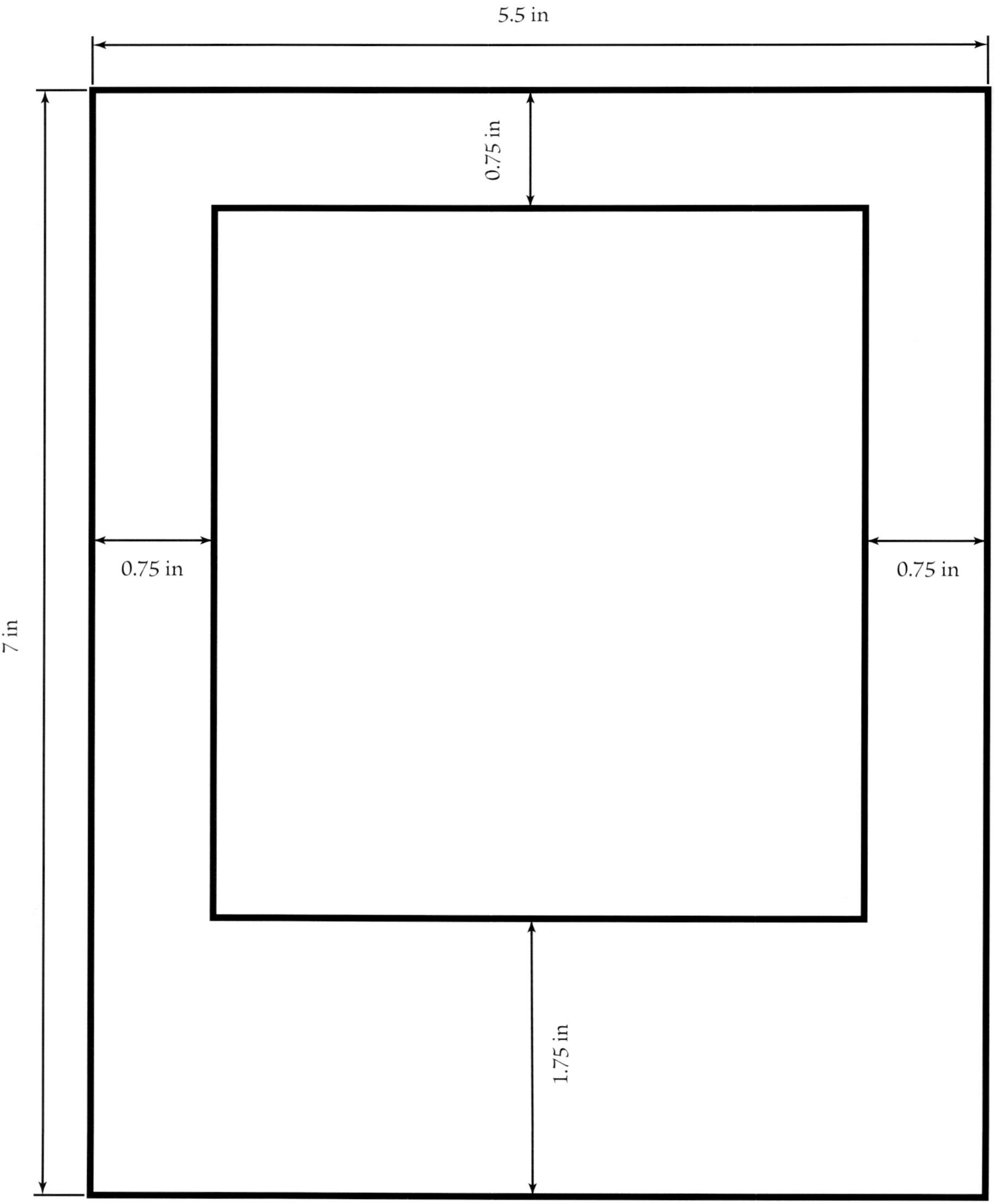

Butcher Shop Window (page 171)

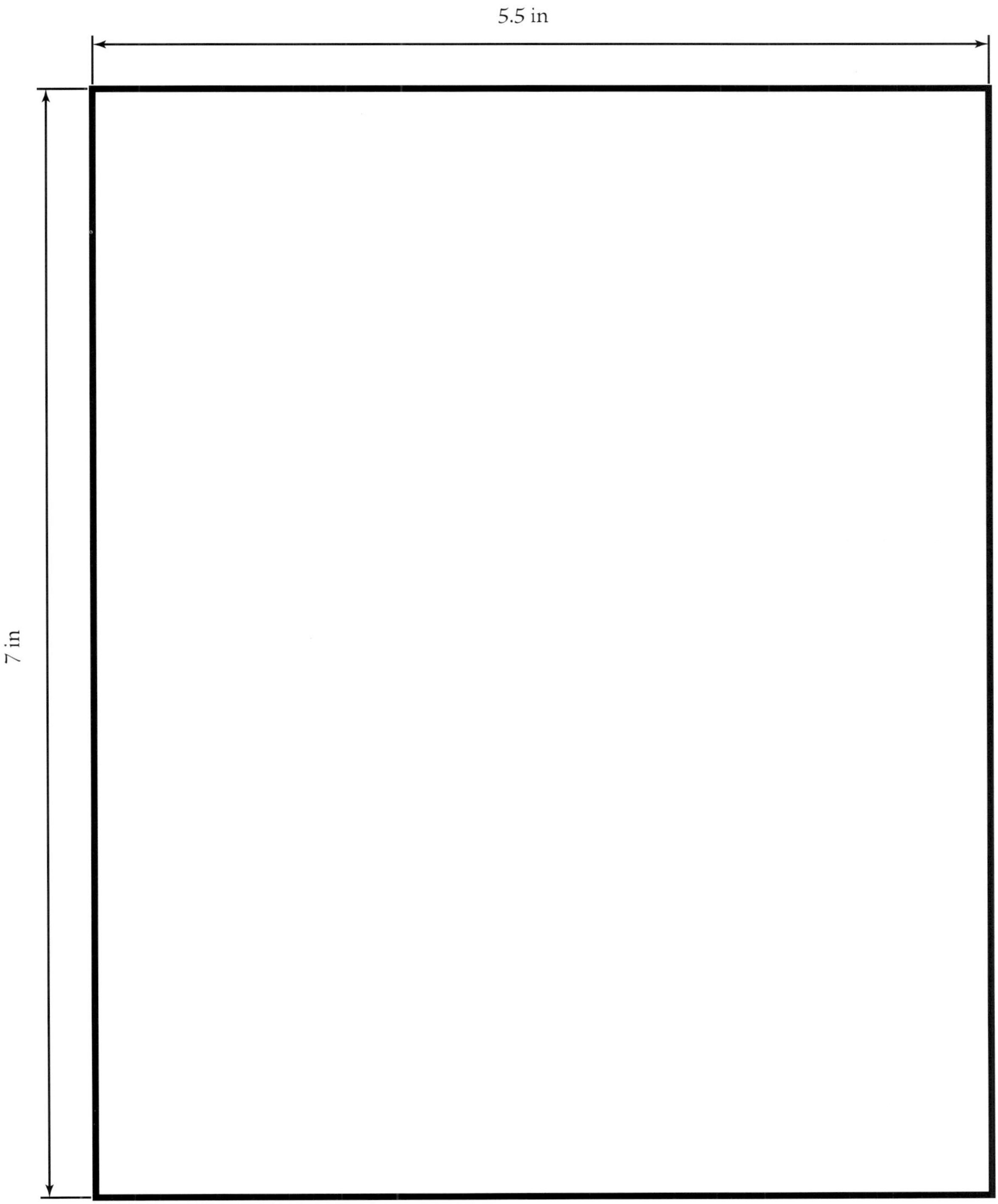

Maggot Popper (page 179)

(page 179)

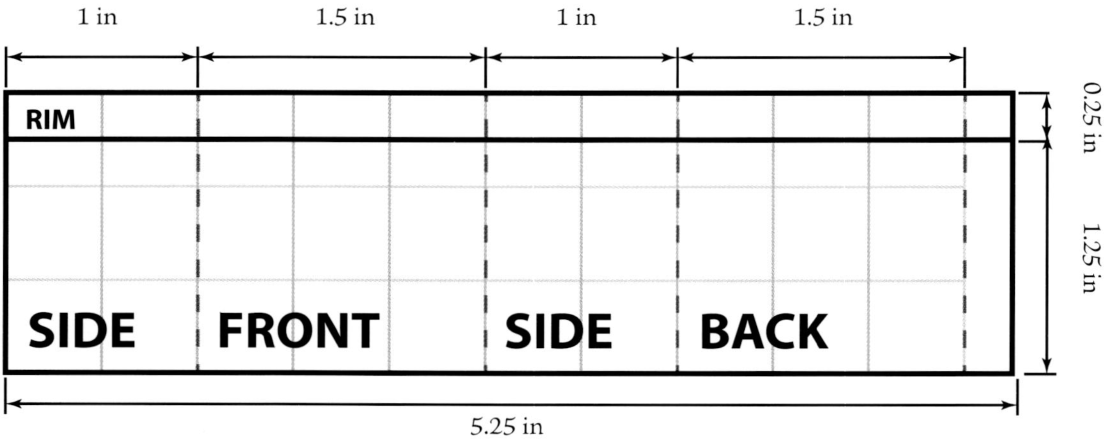

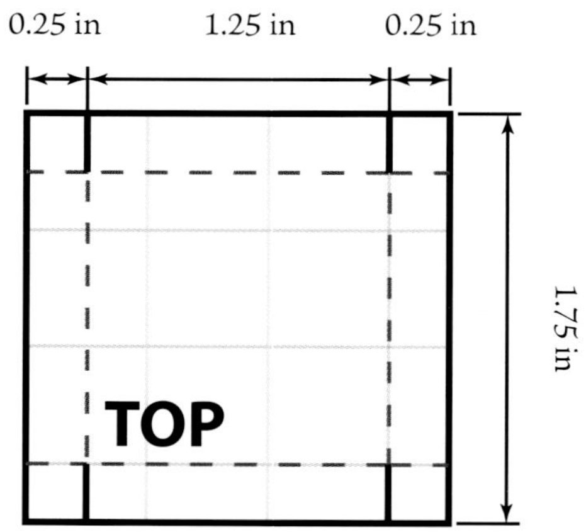

Spider Cotton Candy (page 183)

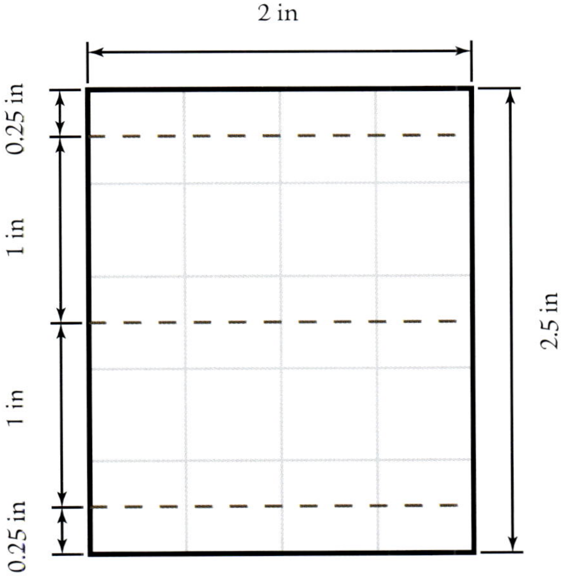

Eye Scream Trolley (page 193)

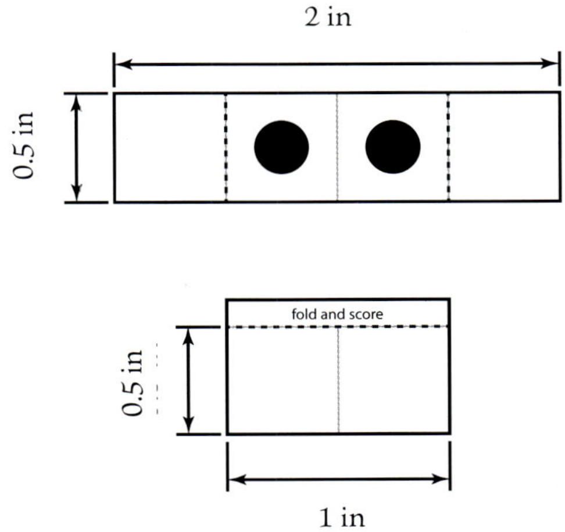

Candy Station (page 203)

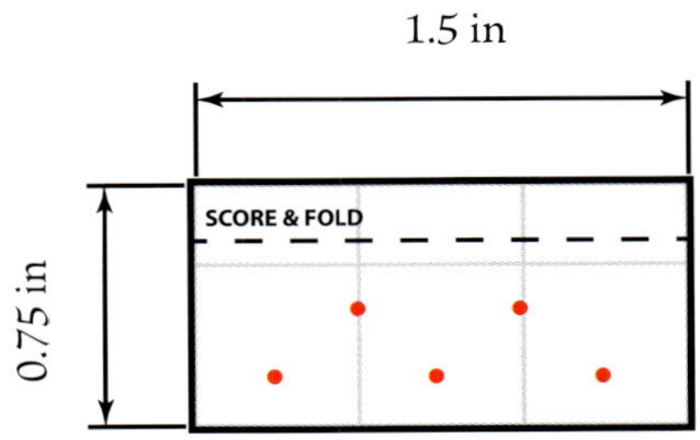

Toy Store Ouija (page 209)

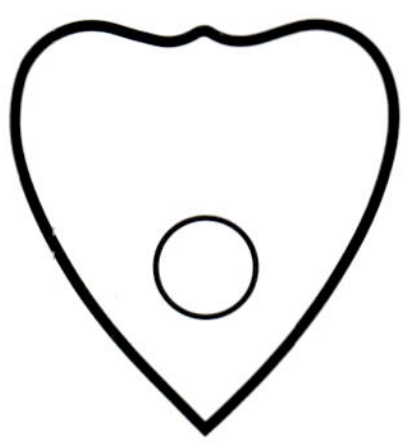

Pie Counter (page 199)

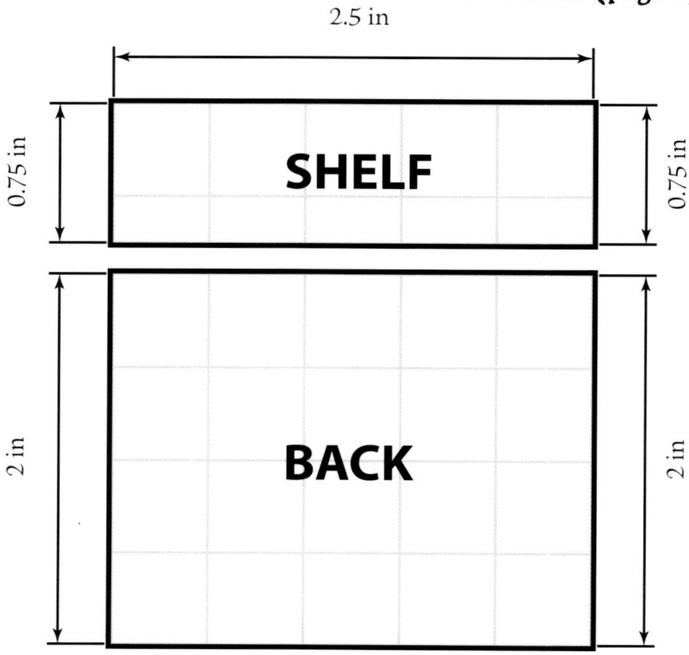

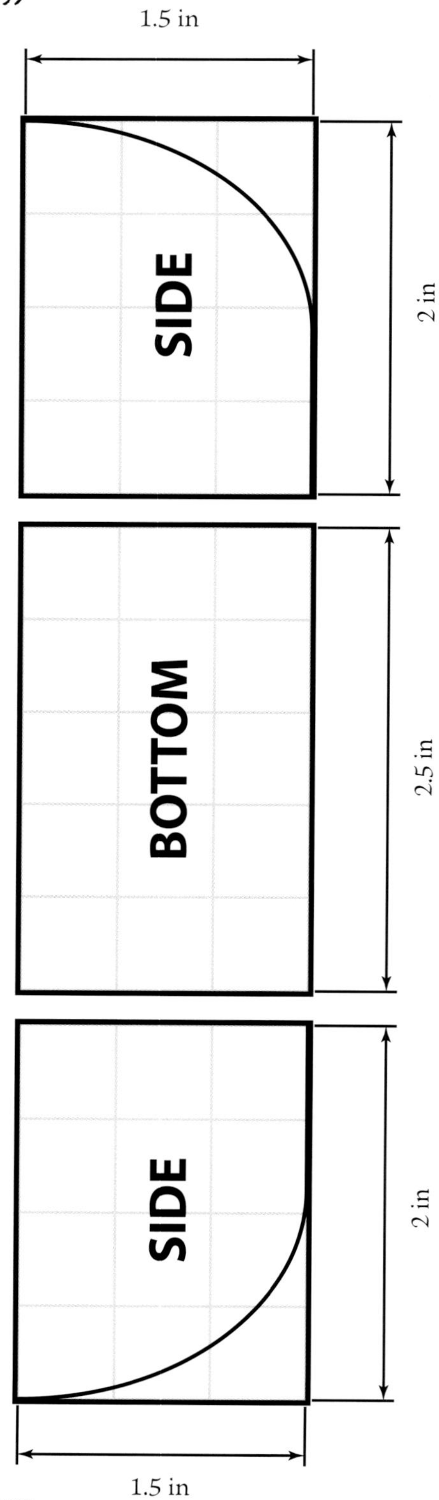

Toy Store Jack-in-the-Box (page 209)

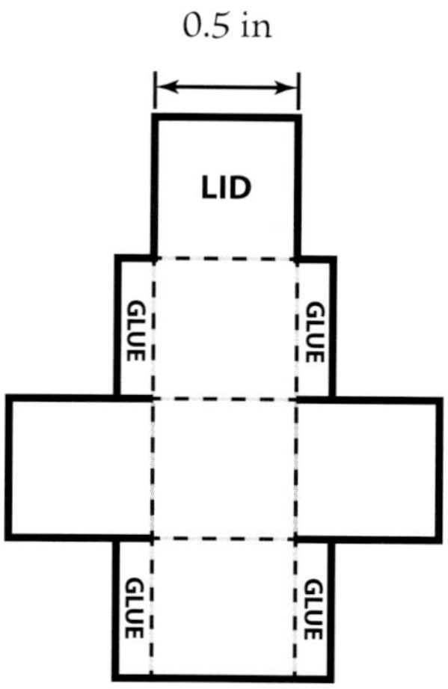

Acknowledgments

I would like to express my sincerest thanks to everyone at Page Street Publishing! I'm sure I was annoying as hell, so thank you for guiding me without so much as an eyeroll!

Also, my husband, Jake, for all the emotional and physical support! You cooked nearly every meal and told me it will be okay when I was tearing out my hair. So, for the sake of my stomach and hair, thank you!

A HUGE thanks to my parents for sending me their tiny trash and to my mother-in-law for the bags and bags of creamer tabs. Your creamer intake is slightly concerning, but I appreciated every single one of them!

Most importantly, thanks to all my readers and crafters out there following my shenanigans! Without you, I would be nowhere, and I truly owe everything to you all!

About the Author

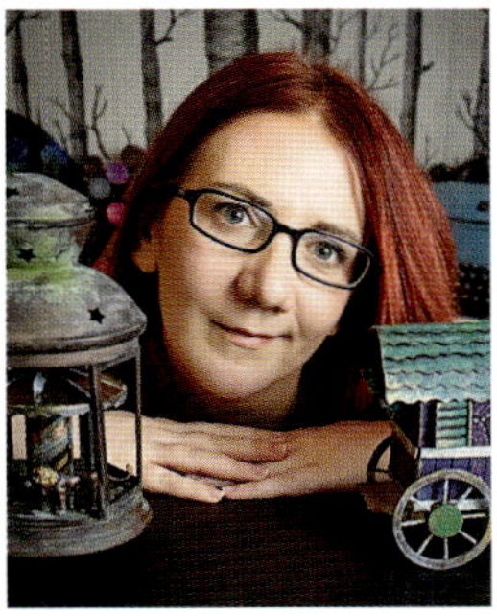

Hi, I'm Ashley Voortman but most people know me online as "Peculiarly Ashley". I've been making art for . . . honestly, I lost count! Thirty years or something?

I've dabbled in all kinds of stuff over the years (painting, sculpting, sewing, felting, jewelry making, wood burning, crocheting . . . the list keeps going), but these days I stick to what I love most: creepy art and miniatures! I started out making weird, creepy art videos online, but it was when I made my first haunted hidey hole inside a teapot that I knew I would fall down the miniature rabbit hole, and I became obsessed!

This is my second book. My first is called *Creepy Crafts* and is about (you guessed it) creepy crafts. This time I wanted to narrow it down to just "haunted miniatures!" (Because little things are adorable, and I love them!)

Index

D

E

F

R

S

T

U

V

W

X